D1546282

LETTERS

of

HANS VON BÜLOW

Letters of
HANS von BÜLOW

to

RICHARD WAGNER	COSIMA WAGNER
HIS DAUGHTER DANIELA	LUISE von BÜLOW
KARL KLINDWORTH	CARL BECHSTEIN

Edited, with an introduction, by
RICHARD COUNT DU MOULIN ECKART

Translated from the German by Hannah Waller

The translation edited with a preface and notes by
SCOTT GODDARD

NEW YORK
VIENNA HOUSE
1972

*T*HERE disengages itself from the pages that follow a quantity of vital facts, comments, inferences, and conclusions which will be found, on ending the book, to have formed itself into a reasonable reflection of the character of Hans von Bülow (1830–94). The letters in this collection, retrieved, as can be read in Count Eckart's introduction, in circumstances of a peculiarly romantic nature, and brought together more by the working of hazard than by the set purpose of a biographer, provide, for all their assemblage was a matter of sheer chance, a just and relatively complete picture of Bülow the man. They begin with his early married life — here seen from a detached view-point, through his correspondence with two friends, Klindworth and Bechstein. They include the tragic period of his separation from his wife, Cosima — here the picture is closer, and the letters to Cosima, in their alternation between intensity of feeling, on the one hand, and, on the other, a business-like discussion of detail which has much the semblance of indifference, are the contortions of a soul defending itself with words and phrases from the gaze of the curious. Lastly, in his letters to his step-mother, Luise von Bülow, and to his daughter Daniela, there is the spectacle of a passionate memory being relegated to the background, and existence taken up again.

Thus in the three phases to which these letters give prominence — pleasure in life, distaste, and again pleasure (with a difference) — a sufficiently clear conception may be formed of the man who lived that life, and some idea of his manner of living, thinking, and acting can be obtained. The attentive perusal of this fortuitous handful of letters will bring to light a fully proportioned figure of a man, and, more than that, of a man of passion in action, one under the stress of events that moved him to the furthest strongholds of an already impressionable being, a man torn between loyalty and pride.

Naturally it is the man that we find here; or rather it is the man, and that only, that we must expect to find. It must, in the nature of things, be so. Of Bülow the executant and interpretative artist nothing remains, unless it be sparse and insignificant memories of past concerts, handed down to us, a material altogether too evanescent for the biographer, as it is too vague for the historian. That is the fate of the great virtuoso — he leaves behind him a fame that owes its continuance to the fleeting memories of minds themselves long since dust.

The remembrance of the first performance of Tristan und Isolde, *which Bülow conducted in 1865, or of the first performance of Tschaikovsky's B flat Pianoforte Concerto by Bülow in 1880, will have lived as a memorable experience in the minds of those who heard these impressive events. Those people — in our estimation, how fortunate — will have begun by recalling actual details of Bülow's playing, or of his management of the vocal and orchestral ensemble, and they will end by recalling only the fact of having been present at the performances. Gradually the clear impression of Bülow's interpretation of the concerto and the opera will have become hidden under an effacing deposit of other, later experiences which the mind has tried to store up as memories, and nothing will remain of the pristine emotional experience. The labour that Bülow spent in preparing the performance of* Tristan *has left no measurable permanence, and no one can tell precisely what it was that he brought to his playing of the Tschaikovsky concerto that made it what it intrinsically was. And thus that most precious possession of the great interpretative artist, that ineffable personality which he so keenly strives to keep intact, whose presence makes his interpretations live, whose absence robs him of any claim to be called an artist — this essential quality leaves no impression behind it on any substance more permanent than the mental process called memory, which is at once the key to a storehouse and to a lumber-room. The creative artist does at least bequeath a bundle of scrawled sheets which, bad or good, bear witness to his achievement. The interpretative artist, who must live for, and on, other men's work, leaves only rumours. His activities have practically complete impermanence.*

It has been taken as an axiom of life, and a standard for

*behaviour, that " a man dies, his work remains." In the case
before us the opposite appears to be the more true. Bülow's
work is dead, but in these letters the man flushes with life again.
Inevitably a mist, which must always dim, although it need never
distort, comes between us and Bülow. The years which have
withdrawn him in time have also made mental contact with his
period a hazardous and arduous task for us. Furthermore, the
written word — treacherous as a means of communication between the living and the living, but doubly so when a third participant is enlisted and entrusted with the dangerous post of
watching the workings of two minds — the writer's and the
recipient's, which latter, known to the writer, will colour his
every expression — even the written word, our most exact ve-
hicle for conveying thoughts, does much to hinder Bülow the
man from being clearly apprehended by us.*

*Yet it cannot be denied that with care it can be made to help
in the quest. The reader who will be at some pains to get a clear
background to the happenings commented on here will find
the letters yield, as has been suggested, a fully rounded portrait.
Bülow is a shadowy figure, now, in the history of nineteenth-
century music, only taking concrete shape when brought into
contact with the notable persons and events among which he
moved. And yet, when placed in the forefront of the stage, as in
his letters, he is fully capable of holding the attention and of
withstanding the glare of such extreme publicity. Some slight
knowledge of the main facts and aspects of the Wagnerian
circle is necessary if the reader is to get the full significance of
Bülow's life. Once those facts are in our possession, Bülow is
found to have taken his place among these great figures on a
footing of equality both of personality and of character.*

A book such as Ernest Newman's Wagner as Man and Artist
*is invaluable in this connexion and contains everything a reader
could want for forming a properly proportioned background of
the period. Count Eckart's biographical study of Cosima Wagner is the latest reputable account of those happenings, viewed
from the kindest standpoint. These, with the eight volumes of
Bülow's own correspondence and writings to refer to, will make
plain the events among which his life was guided. I have used
them in compiling the notes to the present volume, together with*

*the usual dictionaries, in particular Grove (third edition) and
Riemann.*

*Many famous names are to be met with in these pages. Three
of them especially rise up with an impressive insistence: the
King, Bülow's wife, Wagner.*

*Ludwig II of Bavaria has been greatly mocked and much
vilified. It has not been forgiven him that instead of taking the
opportunity of a nineteen-year-old accession to the throne to become a hard-living young captain of his army, and thence to
decline into the regulation disciplinarian and military martinet,
he immediately grasped the full implications of his extraordinary position and unhesitatingly decided on a life of high,
impossible romance. He would bring Wagner to Munich, he
would build Neuschwanstein, his life should be wholly contained
in immense operas and superb castles. Ludwig had all the German fondness for romance, and all the Wittelsbach inability to
keep a dream outside the bounds of his waking hours. Like all
visionaries he was continually at odds with the petty details
of his own existence (which was a galling enough state to be
forced into) and other people's (which was intolerable). The
only woman who really understood him (Cosima, who flattered
and wheedled and urged him, never did that; she only knew, or
thought she knew, how to humour him) was his cousin Elisabeth
of Austria. The similarity between them is striking. She too was
a Wittelsbach and a visionary, and like Ludwig was placed in a
position of ridiculous restraint and preposterous publicity from
which she, as he, was for ever endeavouring to escape. Both
Elisabeth and Ludwig were surrounded by people who must
have seemed to them to be alternately doltish and spiteful. She
fought against her fate until, merely for want of any other handy
royalty, a nihilist stabbed her to death. Ludwig, driven to desperation, strangled his last oppressor.*

*Cosima Liszt followed the example set her by her parents
and remained throughout her life loyal to her instincts. Her first
marriage cannot have been altogether of her own making, and
certainly proved to be not wholly to her own liking. Her second
marriage was very definitely both. There she found all the happiness that Bülow, a man of keen temper and as wayward as a
child, had been incapable of giving her. There too she found*

*greatness of mind and a courageousness of spirit in her partner
such as she must have often dreamed of, and which, when it
came into her life, she was unable to withstand. Her remarkable
character was a blend of Liszt's Hungarian impetuosity and
Marie d'Agoult's French astuteness. If ever there was a woman
fashioned to satisfy and be a worthy companion to Wagner, it
was Cosima Liszt. It is unfortunate that she had first to become
Cosima von Bülow.*

*Wagner as man we have learned to separate, in a benevolent
spirit of discernment, from Wagner the artist. Cosima alone was
able to work the two into a consecutive pattern — visible to her
eyes. Bülow, on the other hand, refused until the end (of his life
with Cosima) to entertain his father-in-law Liszt's judgments on
the discrepancy that had already become noticeable to those
who had had dealings with Wagner. What Bülow eventually
came to realize, what his thoughts were when he was forced to
take notice of how too closely connected Wagner's life had become with his own and to take steps which entailed unmistakable
acknowledgment of the Master's defections, words evidently
failed to express. The letters say little.*

*Undoubtedly Bülow was a much wronged man. When all
has been said on Cosima's behalf — that Bülow became progressively dull and wearisome for her whose imagination was
increasingly filled with the looming vastness of Wagner's purpose and the blinding fire of his intense personality, that Bülow's
temper was uncertain and his temperament liable to distressing
alternations of passion — even then by no canons of decent
human relationship could Cosima be held to have won for
herself the right to act as an eager, growing child does who
leaves her doll out in the rain when her attention has been led
away by the gift of a real live animal. With magnificent assurance she persuaded herself that she had been expressly chosen
by fate to be Wagner's companion and guide. Unquestioningly
she accepted the position and by so doing wounded Bülow mercilessly. Later she was to write (it was on the day of her marriage
to Wagner): " My thoughts are intent on two things: Richard's
well-being, that I may always be able to forward it, Hansen's
happiness, that it may be granted him to lead a calm life, far
from me."*

Bülow reached that calm. First he threw himself into the work of raking together money enough to educate his children. He travelled widely on large concert tours, becoming one of the first great " Reisekünstler." Later he married again, and safely.

In preparing this edition of the Bülow letters which were fetched from Italy I have had in mind the making of a manageable volume and have made sundry cuts where I felt the matter of a relatively small interest and of a kind whose disappearance would do nothing to hinder — would, in fact, help — the reader in getting a fair view of the writer, of the characters of the drama, of the main events of the tale. All these cuts have been marked by dots, and thus the student can, if so disposed, immediately find his way to the omitted passages in the original. As further aid the letters are here numbered according to Count Eckart's plan in the German volume.

I should like to take this opportunity of placing on record my gratitude to the translator, Mrs. Atkinson, for the sympathy and understanding she has shown in lightening my part of the work of this volume.

SCOTT GODDARD

CONTENTS OF

LETTERS
of
HANS VON BÜLOW

THERE are a number of poets, artists, and other great men whose significance can never be fully realized without a knowledge of their letters. In many cases we find in these a stronger proof of the writer's creative impulse than his works are able to reveal. This has been so in all ages. We cannot understand a giant such as Michelangelo without his letters, for they alone give us real insight into his inner life, his discontent, his musings, and his aims. It is to them, too, that we owe Heinrich Thode's picture of the mighty creator of *David*. Similarly the letters of Goethe and Schiller and, one might say, of all our poets are to be regarded, not merely as literary and historical material, but as poetical experience. Wagner's various written communications constitute as it were a collective work which supplements his powerful compositions, and one is surprised to find evidence of such immense productivity side by side with the many business worries in his correspondence. It is indeed precisely in his letters that he frequently appears as a prophet, and the same may be said of many of our outstanding men. Bismarck is a case in point. It would be hard to find a more moving book than the volume of letters to his wife; his long correspondence with Gerlach, too, in the Frankfurt days and indeed all his letters, short as these became towards the end, show us the old man in his Saxon forest home as a giant, indeed, but a human, tender one. Letter-writing is said to be the province of women, and up to a point this is true. A woman's mind vibrates exquisitely when she has the gift of expressing herself in letters, and she often attains a degree of greatness through this medium. But there are others who struggle all their lives to produce the great and even greatest things which they carry in mind and heart, serving their art in word and deed and thus achieving immortality, but in whom a profound yearning is the nearest approach to a complete fulfilment of the creative impulse. For these unfortunate beings, hard-pushed by fate and unloved of the Norns, letters are to some extent the only artistic outlet: they think, and it is as if they sang. Among these martyrs to art, as I like to call them, Hans von Bülow has undoubtedly a place. There exists an admirable collection of his letters in seven volumes, which in itself forms a picture: not a picture of his whole life, but a picture on its own merits. It does not, however, reveal in its entirety the world which he built up for himself in his letters, a world directly inspired by the moods of the moment. There is a whole series of emotional and intellectual processes, still withheld from us, which can only become accessible through letters written to those personalities with whom he stood on a quite special footing.

By the help of a friend, supplemented by my own efforts, I have been able to obtain several of these sets of correspondence, which I now offer to the public. I did not secure them without certain adventures: for the greater part of them were hidden in the Villa Cargnacco, the home of my esteemed friend Heinrich Thode and his beautiful first wife, Daniela, Bülow's eldest daughter. This lady was obviously the proper guardian of her father's correspondence and she carried out her trust in the finest, most touching way. A true daughter of her mother, Frau Cosima, she is an original and talented woman, intellectual and finely strung; but although she might well assume her treasure to be safe in Gardone di Sopra, fate was stronger than she. The war came, and the villa was seized and handed over to Gabriele d'Annunzio, who was put in charge of this fine German property by the enemy government in Rome.

When, finding myself in possession of a wealth of material, I set about writing Bülow's life, I naturally felt it incumbent on me to secure the correspondence that was still in Italy. Accordingly, in the beginning of 1921, I made my way, with Frau Daniela's sanction, to Gardone to try the effect of personal persuasion on the poet. It was an extraordinary journey. On the Brenner Pass our engine gave out, after several hours' delay we were towed back to Innsbruck, and only at midnight did I reach Mori, where the line branches off to Riva. The simple *trattoria* which, before the war, had stood there, affording a modest shelter, still lay in ruins. I had no choice, therefore, but to spend the night in the waiting-room, stoking the fire with wood which I collected from around the station building in the bitter cold. Eventually I reached Maderno by the same boat as originally planned. The journey was an extremely painful one, for it was the first time I had travelled through any of Germany's territory which had been taken from her by the war and was doomed to remain alienated. I choked back the many beautiful memories of Lake Garda and shut my eyes to its beauties.

At Maderno a faithful maid and friend of Frau Daniela put me in touch with d'Annunzio. I will not dwell here upon the legal side of the question, or upon the controversial side, which has been published in a pamphlet by Karin Michaelis. I regarded my mission to d'Annunzio as a diplomatic one. On the day of my arrival I left a card on the new master of Cargnacco and on the following day was informed that he would see me. Arriving at the beautiful villa, I was ushered straight into the presence of the hero of Fiume — for even his opponents cannot grudge him this title. The extremely interesting negotiations, which were conducted in French, lasted several hours. I acquitted myself of my mission in diplomatic fashion and found d'Annunzio definitely inclined to meet Frau Geheimrat Daniela Thode's wishes. A vivid memory of the master of Bayreuth and his family evidently carried great weight with the commandant and I may say that, during our exchange of ideas on the subject, his expression took on a certain cordiality. At all events I carried my point and was promised access to the letters on the following day. Thus I succeeded in finding and taking back to Germany a large portion of the present correspondence.

As I have stated, I kept strictly, at this interview, to the immediate object of my diplomatic mission. That further discussions should follow was only natural, but I prefer not to deal with these here. This memorable meeting, which was interesting from more than one point of view, will be fully described in my memoirs, for it bears not only on my Bülow studies, but on other matters. I must admit, however, that d'Annunzio treated me most considerately throughout and that it is to that journey that I owe this mass of valuable material. There was no tarrying at Lake Garda on that occasion. On January 6 I was allowed to select and take away the letters, and on the 7th I took the first boat back, passing Malcesine *en route*, where for so many years I had stayed for my health. From the deck of the little steamer I could see the hotel, formerly in German hands and now completely decayed, with its windows broken, and I longed to be at home again. It is only fair to say that in my hotel the general feeling about us Germans and especially about Frau Daniela had been infinitely touching and impressive, and I discovered that she was remembered by the population as the good genius of Gardone di Sopra. I shall never forget how a girl of sixteen or so, who had entered d'Annunzio's service, came into the room where I was sorting the letters and asked after the noble Signora Daniela. I asked the child if she knew her and she replied almost indignantly: "Didn't you know I came from Gardone di Sopra?" The old gardener at Cargnacco also spoke with tears in his eyes of this noble and beautiful lady. What a joy it was to find that no war, no governmental measures, had been able to kill the memory of this true German woman! My journey in the interests of research therefore left me feeling proud and hopeful if also a little sad.

The most important section of this book is undoubtedly that containing Bülow's letters to Wagner. Alas, they are but a torso. Much interest and curiosity has been felt about them. My luck in finally obtaining this remnant of the correspondence is due to a fortunate chance. In any case it would be wrong to regard the withholding of them until now as intentional on the part of Bülow's daughter. The letters had drifted to Riga and were only returned to me through friendly intervention. I do not think the remainder will ever be found; it is to be feared that, together with much other precious material, they were burned by Frau Cosima's own hands in the Triebschen days; for this marvellous woman was possessed of a strong determination to give the world no access to anything that was absolutely her own. Only by her daughter's action were certain items saved from destruction. As a historian I am bound to deplore this; as a man, a friend of the family, and an admirer of this incomparable woman I understand it only too well. Living as she did in the centre of so great a world, a spectator of such an overwhelming output of genius, it must have seemed to her that everything else was secondary and worthy only of the flames.

I fancy, then, that I can see Frau Cosima throwing all she possessed in the way of letters into the fire-grate even as she wrote down her recollections of Wagner. She herself told me that she had burned Nietzsche's letters to her, together with many others. Only by putting oneself in her place can one understand her actions. But these letters from Bülow to Wagner bear upon a period which was the most difficult, inwardly and outwardly, for the composer; above all, it was the period of collaboration between himself and his pupil, the time when Bülow was preparing the pianoforte score of *Tristan and Isolde*. So that the history of this period in the lives of both these great artists is probably of more importance even than the Munich period, when Bülow sat at the conductor's desk and so completely absorbed Wagner's intentions that he became progressively more able to interpret them with intense musical power and feeling. That Bülow found it extremely difficult to live himself into the score of *Tristan* is evident both from his letters and, where these fail to show it, from his whole development. No one was so well able to grasp the astoundingly new in music, yet his reaction to the score of *Tristan* was that of an artist of the preceding epoch. All the more admirable is it that he should have made the effort to grasp it, emerging from the limitations of his own productivity to throw his whole weight into the establishment of the new order. He had nothing of that feeling of the rich man in the parable who was unable to follow the call of Christ because he could not bear to leave his many possessions. In spite of his own inner treasures he became a pupil and disciple of the Master. There was infinite nobility in Bülow's attitude, and it would be wrong not to recognize this point of junction as the most important in his life. *Tristan* is his life-tragedy, because he saw gleaming from it a new music-world, the light of which, though it dazzled him, compelled his allegiance.

With regard to other aspects of Bülow's relation to his master, there are three main points to consider: that Bülow went from his own powerful musical sphere into Wagner's, feeling himself to be a creative artist; that side by side with the Wagner connexion he had the benefit of Liszt's teaching, and that this brought him into a different world, to which he became more definitely attached by his marriage with the brilliant daughter of that brilliant father. Yet it was at Weimar that he first realized where his special strength as an artist lay. It was not for him to create large new compositions, but he was unsurpassed in his gift for conveying a knowledge of the great composers to the world. It was in some respects a sorrowful pilgrimage. Franz Liszt, his master and fatherly friend, had begun as a pianist, and nothing could better characterize him than the melancholy and painful remark made about him by Wagner in Paris, when young. Yet the path of outward fame was to Liszt only the steep road of an artistic and human martyrdom. The period which he called his *Années de pèlerinage*, the artistic output of which still has power to move and delight us, was his purgatory in the fullest sense. And through the almost indescribable human and artistic experience thus gained, he reached the solitary heights of creative work. There he met Wagner, and from that time on was inseparably linked with him in his art, notwithstanding the undeniable contrasts in their two natures which could only be smoothed over by the affection of the one and the affection combined with noble-mindedness of the other. Bülow began at the other end. He first felt the urge to compose and then followed the career, forced on him by outward circumstances, of a reproductive artist. Both as pianist and as conductor he was in the front rank. As a pianist he did not carry on the Liszt tradition, as his master hoped, but struggled through to a conception of his own, which first became clearly defined through his third activity: that of teaching and editing. His fine editions, particularly those of Beethoven, are indeed unique. It was given to him, not only to hear the voice in the wilderness, but to recognize instantly all that was great and render it with all the clearness and authority of a classical interpretation. This applies equally to his work as conductor, pianist, and, above all, editor. As an interpreter of classical music he deserves a place among the classics themselves. By his devotion to them he forced so much of his own rich life into the background as to earn for himself both the laurels and the martyr's crown.

I have deliberately put the correspondence with Carl Bechstein, his " *Beflügler*," [1] in this series. It is perhaps one of the most touching and impressive in literature. For Bülow reveals

[1] *The man who lent him wings. (From* Flügel — *wing, also grand pianoforte.)*

himself here as the friend of a man who had been a simple crafts-man and at first worked for him as such, but on whom his influ-ence was so great that he rose to important achievements and became a pioneer among German pianoforte-manufacturers. Frau Cosima has told me how she remembered seeing Carl Bech-stein in a blue blouse among his workmen, and how he would often lend a hand himself. This was after Bülow had begun to coax such wonderful tone out of his instruments. The centenary of Carl Bechstein's birth was very rightly made the occasion for celebrations. He was born on January 1, 1826 at Gotha. His father, a court official, died suddenly while young, leaving the family in poverty. A year after his death his wife felt it her duty to marry the schoolmaster and cantor of Altdietendorf, named Agthe. The boy went to school in that place and later was apprenticed to his sister's husband, a pianoforte-manufacturer at Erfurt. He was an excellent and skilled maker, and the boy received a thorough training. The domestic conditions in which he lived were, however, sufficiently deplorable. His brother-in-law was addicted to drink and treated the boy very harshly. He finished his apprenticeship, however, and then made his way — on foot, as was the custom for apprentices — to Dresden, pay-ing his way as he went, to the best of his ability. In Dresden he entered the firm of Pleyel, where he stayed until about the year 1846. He then went to Berlin and became foreman to Perau, who presently put him in charge of the factory, which employed only a few men. But Bechstein's ambition led him in 1849 to Paris, where he worked for Kriegelstein, making so good an impression that later, after he had returned home, he was called back to superintend the work there. In 1853 he definitely took over the control of Perau's firm and within the year had set up an independent business in the face of many financial difficul-ties. He had, however, good friends, who realized his worth. He married in 1856 and at once enlarged his own factory, while continuing to superintend Perau's. But the very first of his own instruments that he was able to show to his friends were such outstanding specimens as to arouse keen interest in the musical world.

After Theodor Kullak, the pianist, it was Hans von Bülow who was the principal supporter of this clever master of his craft.

Bechstein was able through his help to perfect himself more and more. The first grand pianofortes were soon finished and it was Bülow who, so to say, advertised these new instruments, which soon became famous beyond the German frontiers. The factory grew rapidly and the instruments improved from year to year. Serious rivalry soon set in, but Bülow proved an exceptionally fine champion. When he devoted himself more and more to concert performances it was Bechstein's turn to be helpful, and he was ever at hand to assist with concert preparations. It was natural that there should be conflicts, but the relation between the two had with time become one of such loyalty and intimacy that it could survive even these storms and disputes. Bülow put his friend in close touch with Liszt and — particularly in the Munich period — with Wagner. He was also able to introduce his instruments into the solitary apartments of Ludwig II of Bavaria, who expressed his great satisfaction with them.

The letters which passed between these two, particularly those from Bülow's pen, have therefore a special significance. In all business matters, even those concerning capital — Bülow had at a difficult moment invested a small sum in the Bechstein firm — Carl was the intimate adviser of the eccentric and magnanimous artist, who wrote to him on matters of which he spoke to no one else. Thus we have here probably one of the most comprehensive pictures of Bülow's life, since he never failed, in his best days, to keep his friend informed on all matters of business, while at the same time he touched on everything that life brought him, from the profound, secret things down to such details as jewellery, cigarettes, linen, and tailoring. The peak of the correspondence was reached while Bülow was in Munich and, after the great catastrophes, in Florence. The part which Bechstein played in Bülow's relations with Karl Tausig (also an intimate of the Bechstein firm) seems to have been particularly touching.

Bülow's life was full of quarrels and opposing factors which not only interrupted his relations with the Master, whom he loved more than anything in the world, but estranged many others. But it would be a mistake to regard this correspondence as the unsophisticated visitor regards individual pictures at an exhibition. It is not the material alone that is interesting, not the *what,* but the *how,* which allows us to look more closely into Bülow's mind. A certain amount of judgment is required too, as with the letters of all ages, if we are to read them aright. Nothing would be worse than to treat every fact in the good old historical fashion and look upon the letters purely as a source. For these facts are in a way only supplementary and never of primary importance. What is important is the mood, the momentary feeling, the pressure under which the letters were written, in particular the artistic moment which they reveal. Nowhere else do we see this ever-present agitation of Bülow's over his failure to produce, or rather over the grief and pain caused by that failure; for he underestimated for a long time his great qualities as conductor and pianist. Therein lies a tragedy and, to be frank, a cause of the disagreement between him and Liszt; for Liszt had, from far back in the Zürich days, tried to steer him into the practical side of musical activity and had even shown him, in the municipal theatre there, the first tricks of conducting. At a later stage, too, it was he who best understood Bülow's inner struggle and tried to put him on the right road, although he repeatedly inspired him to fresh attempts at composition. But there were clashes which had no bearing on the one great, tragic question of their two lives, and it is in his letters that we find more allusion to these than anywhere else. On musical problems he wrote much of importance to Richard Pohl, Karl Klindworth, Karl Tausig, and many others. But it is only when we come to read his letters to so simple a person and yet so strong a character as his friend Carl Bechstein that we really understand these communications. That hardly anyone had so much influence over him as his *" Beflügler "* is evident from these fighting days. When he broke away from Munich and retired to Wiesbaden to seek consolation from Raff, it was to his old Berlin friend that he unburdened himself; and when he paid his fateful visits to Berlin in connexion with the dissolution of his first marriage, it was to the Bechsteins that he went for rest and solace. This simple man had a wonderfully balanced mind and was able to calm his nervous, passionate friend as no one else could. It was a lasting service that the house of Bechstein rendered and we feel that this worthy, loyal man might well have figured as a special type in the ranks of the Mastersingers' school. A serious breach in their friendship occurred on the occasion of Bülow's first American tour, but, stranded entirely amongst strangers and suffering from a dangerous illness, the traveller forgot his grievances and held out the hand of reconciliation across the water. Bechstein was not the man to refuse it. He could forget and forgive; for not only did he possess the abiding quality of true German gratitude, but he instinctively understood Bülow the man. There was hardly a house in which the man and artist were so thoroughly appreciated as in that hospitable house in the Johannisstrasse.

On Bülow's return, his old friend Hans von Bronsart bestirred himself on his behalf and obtained for him the musical directorship of the court theatre at Hanover. There followed a period of uninterrupted happiness and success for Bülow. This ended abruptly, however, in a bitter misunderstanding with his friend, which led to the most serious quarrel in his career. It was then that Bechstein came to the rescue, warned by a tragic letter from his friend of his intolerable state of depression. Arriving at Hanover, he was just in time to prevent Bülow from shooting himself in the garden and was able, by skilful handling, both to soothe him and eventually to bring him back to his work. Bechstein remained his good and loyal adviser as long as their intercourse lasted. The gradual estrangement and coolness which appeared to creep in towards the end was purely external. Inwardly Bülow's feeling for his friend remained, while Bechstein cherished his friendship until his last breath.

Their correspondence is therefore not only intensely interesting but throws a pleasing light on both writers and, indirectly, on the whole firm of Bechstein, whose feeling for Bülow was one of truly German — one might say, Prussian — warmth and sincerity. In addition, Bülow's relations with this house provided links with many other friends and led to innumerable connexions which proved important in his career as a virtuoso. The growth and retention of such connexions were facilitated by the development of this firm, which by its enterprise initiated the popularity of the German pianoforte abroad. Much was indeed owing to Bülow's periodical championship, but the firm also succeeded through its own quite different methods. For the Bechstein pianofortes may be said to be their own best ad-

vertisement. Apart, however, from every musical or biographical consideration, it is peculiarly interesting to follow the life-
long association between an artist and a man who raised a small
and simple undertaking from its mechanically limited begin-
nings to such a height that the instruments produced were in a
sense works of art, exercising a decisive influence on German
pianoforte compositions. Long indeed is the list of great and
outstanding pianists who are intimately bound up with the house
of Bechstein and its activities. But the beauty of it is that, behind
the actual tone, there was a heart-beat, and thus do Bülow's letters stand, in a way, for the history of a German firm.

We possess all Wagner's letters to Bülow, from the very first
down to the Master's last outpourings, when he writes: " We
are all of us unhappy." I have already alluded to the letters and
to Bülow's utterances relating to the Master, but I also wish to
say something about the correspondence itself as it is reproduced
here. Bülow's side of the correspondence, as given here, will at
first appear disappointing; for without Frau Cosima's letters to
Wagner we have only half the story. During this period particularly, Bülow frequently communicated with Wagner through
his wife. As far as I know, these letters do not exist. They were
probably consigned to the flames in the Triebschen *auto-da-fé.*
But Bülow's attitude to the score of *Tristan* is of great importance, and the marks which he inserted in the original can be
read by the light of his letters. The writing of this pianoforte
score at a time of such exaltation and receptivity was a harassing
task for Bülow; for he was dealing with something incredibly
new and it was imperative to find a new form of pianoforte score
to express it adequately. The whole psychological process re-
vealed in these letters gives us a glimpse also of a new sphere of
artistic activity, which has been passed over practically un-
noticed; for in music, as in all else, technique, so-called, has
progressed so far as to become the ruler of the age and, in
a sense, of music. The " cerebral " has gained a new and wide
significance in the new music, demanding a degree of technique
beside which the score of *Tristan* and Bülow's pianoforte adaptation appear simple in the extreme. Yet *Tristan* did represent
a new world, and Bülow was able so to live himself into it that,

aided by his powerful and finished technique, he could follow
closely in the steps of the composer. One thing emerges clearly,
therefore: that Bülow, through the process of making the pianoforte score, came to accept the work itself. A similar case was
that of Hans Richter, who, when working as Wagner's collabo-
rator at Triebschen, watched the *Meistersinger* grow under his
eyes and was able to live himself into it in the same way. But
Bülow's insight into the mysteries of the *Tristan* score and the
whole nature of the music was incomparably deeper. It is
hardly possible to compare the two instances, however, for
Bülow was not in touch with the composer, whereas Richter was
able to take the fresh sheets of the score every morning and
copy them out. Also the *Meistersinger* score is very different
from that of *Tristan;* the psychological interpretation and com-
prehension of the latter was a far more difficult task, and one
to which Bülow devoted all his power. Amongst other points
which will strike the reader in these letters, it will be plain that
there was creative force behind this pianoforte score. It was
an epoch-making work, and the doubts which Bülow expressed
on all sides may be taken to mark the turning-point of an age
in which the Master himself trod new paths, creating for himself a fresh technique with every composition and ever pushing
forward. The exquisite *Siegfried Idyll,* for instance, written at
Triebschen, carries us into a vast new sphere of symphonic
writing.

But the tragedy of Bülow's life undoubtedly began with
Tristan, although the problem of that tragedy can never be
fully gauged. It was here, where he was most loyal, that he was
most deeply wounded, as we see from the letter of separation
which he wrote straight from his heart to his wife after long
inner struggles. It is the most valuable document in this collection and I am glad I was able to find the letter at Gardone. To
waste a single word over it would be a mistake; to withhold it
from the world, an injustice. It clears up the whole of the natural
and yet inevitable development — for as such it is to be taken
— which, as we shall see, was doomed to bring unspeakable
suffering to himself, his wife, and not least the Master.

It was one of fate's amazing necessities, a law against which
there could be no appeal; for any appeal would have had tragic

results, and Wagner's great life-work would have been left
unfinished.

Next come the letters which Bülow subsequently wrote to
Frau Cosima. These are eloquent of the writer's chivalry no
less than of his firm sense of duty. They are a testimony both
for him and his wife, if indeed any such testimony were needed.
It is evident that, over and above all worldly envy and hatred
and all clashes of temperament, he did homage, as he was bound
to do, to this great and noble woman who had come into his life
— too great for him, almost, as he realized in his clearer and
even in his despairing moments. But a man who can write such
letters is indeed truly great of soul. Nothing can be more affecting than the one in which he expresses his gratitude for having
been allowed to see his daughter Daniela after she was grown
up: he " would like to build a chapel to mark the spot " where
her grandfather Liszt had brought her to him. We see from this
that throughout his solitary life he regarded his relation to Liszt
and to this marvellous woman as sacred. For, apart from many
other outstanding qualities, he had a strong feeling for family
ties. His correspondence with his stepmother, daughter of the
victor of Dennewitz, and particularly his relations with his sister
and stepbrothers, whom he dearly loved, are sufficient evidence
of this. But the figure who linked him most closely with his
wife and father-in-law was Liszt's son, Daniel. The story of
their friendship is well known. The memory of it affected Bülow
strongly at all the critical moments of his life. He once threw
himself weeping on the grave of this wonderful youth who died
so young, more angel than human being owing to his long sufferings, and whom he and Frau Cosima nursed devotedly in Berlin
until the end. Later, when Frau Cosima, on hearing of the Master's death, declared that she must die too, he wired to her:
" Sister, you must live," feeling himself in that moment to be
in truth the brother of both brother and sister, and drawing
from this feeling a truly noble and sacred emotion. It was under
the shadow of those impressions that he wrote these letters and
also those to his daughters Daniela and Blandine. The touching
and really fatherly letters to the latter must unfortunately remain unpublished, by her own wish. But the letters to Daniela
form a complete unit and are all the more moving on account

of the relation in which this daughter stood to both her parents, filling her difficult position with infinite tact and affection. To these daughters, of whom he was justifiably proud, Bülow showed himself peculiarly magnanimous and affectionate. They were indeed rare beings. Both of them — Countess Blandine Gravina as well as Daniela Thode — had inherited from him, from their mother, and from their grandparents a certain quality which placed them on a lofty plane. Bülow loved them both equally and delighted in the difference of their characters. For through this very contrast the individuality of the sisters became more delightfully apparent. His own youth had been an unhappy one. It was not the fault of his father, an exceedingly kind-hearted man who, particularly in his last years, after he had divorced his first wife and was living peacefully with the daughter of the victor of Dennewitz in his quiet Swiss château, showed much affection for his son, whose first great successes he lived to see. But Bülow's own mother was a hard woman who stood, musically, between Liszt and Wagner and the old régime so steadfastly upheld by Mendelssohn and Schumann in the house of her friends the Freges. She could not reconcile herself to the new world, and, being of a passionately tyrannical nature, she domineered over her son until she had reached a ripe old age, and even in her blindness still tried to influence his course. It was, therefore, fortunate for the children that they were entrusted to Frau Cosima, who brought them up in an individual way. Both girls had artistic talent and both were eminently worthy of their parents. From the correspondence with Daniela, in which there is evidence of an intimate understanding on both sides, we realize how fluctuating were Bülow's feelings during this period.

I have limited myself to this sequence of letters, discarding all isolated ones. Neither have I included Bülow's letters to my father (who had been introduced to him by Wagner), for I wish the book to form a whole, not an ordinary collection of letters, forming a source of biographical material. For a biography it would be necessary to go further and gather in the many sets of letters which are not generally known to be in existence. But this, from my point of view, would be a mistake. It has been my endeavour here to show Bülow from three sides: in his relations

with his own people (who always remained his own people),
with Bechstein, and with one of his most faithful musical friends,
Karl Klindworth, to whom he expressed himself in so special
a manner on musical matters in his letters that it is, as it were,
a point of honour to publish them. The relation between these
thorough-going musicians is infinitely moving. Their correspondence opens up for us a totally new world, which shows us both
of them labouring to enlarge their horizon. These letters speak
for themselves. It would be wrong to add anything to them in
explanation.

Other letters which should undoubtedly have a place here
are the few which are left of those written to Countess Moucha-
noff-Calergis, a marvellous woman who had a great and touching
influence on Bülow's life, one whose last hours he transfigured
by his playing. For while she was fighting her death-agony on a
bed of sickness, he played her favourite pieces in the adjoining
room. But as the whole collection was not to be found, these
letters formed only a torso and did not therefore come within
the scope of this book, which it is my desire to publish in completed form.

I naturally assume full responsibility for the editing and
for occasional omissions. It is not for the historian to set down
everything as he finds it: it behoves him to be as tactful as any
other man of the world. I may say, however, that I have suppressed nothing which might prove essential to a comprehen-
sion of Bülow himself, the personalities connected with him, or
the musical developments of the period. I have worked quite
independently, guided solely by what I felt and what I knew.
One often hears it said that Bülow still stands under a shadow.
This is untrue. His own greatness and everything great that he
achieved were directly bound up with Liszt and Wagner and
with that whole world in which he figured as a great man in spite
of all subsequent opposition and in spite of all his devotion to
Brahms — for which he by no means got the thanks he deserved.
Here he ministered to great men and had necessarily to raise
himself to their level. As regards the others whom he took under
his wing, his genius as performer and conductor lifted him far
above them and often above himself. In the case of some of
the works — to name no names — which he produced, one is

reminded of the fairy-tale of the boy who went into the wood and found the fallen leaves looking like pure gold; he collected a sackful and took them home, only to find them in truth withered leaves, once the spell was removed. Just so did many things which Bülow performed in his incomparable manner seem golden to us; yet when we found them and heard them again, the spell had been broken and we were left with withered leaves.

RICHARD COUNT DU MOULIN ECKART

October 6, 1926
Bad Wörishofen,

Hans von Bülow
to
Karl Klindworth

6]

Biebrich am Rhein
August 5, 1862

Herr Biel had the bright idea of sending your letter to my summer habitation, where, since the end of June, I have had to be an idle fellow, living in a state of complete pianolessness and only making the most chary use of pen and ink. To regale you with a description of my nervous break-down would be but a poor way of thanking you for your letter, however. I will only say that my condition is made worse by my wife's poor state of health. Be thankful that you have only your own troubles to worry you; anxiety about a beloved wife is far more paralysing.

My choice of Biebrich you will rightly have ascribed to Wagner's presence here. He has found a charming house where, but for the usual disturbing elements of every description, he would have the leisure and the amenities necessary for his work. You know that he has been enjoying his solitude here as a grass widower since February. His wife [1] has settled in Dresden and has now been for some weeks at Reichenhall in the Tyrol [*sic*], where she is taking an expensive cure. In *one* respect, therefore, your wish for him is fulfilled: he is separated from Madame. In the other respect the strain is as great as ever: advances from Mainz do not suffice for present needs.

Prospects there are, it is true. His *Meistersinger* is such an inspiration, so poetically conceived in a popular vein, that the Master's outward circumstances are bound to improve from the moment when the work is finished and produced. The opera must and will be an unheard-of success for him, compared with which the success of *Tannhäuser* can only be called a *lamento*. You will be immensely impressed with the text, which will probably be published as a literary production in the autumn, and should arouse in the public that lively curiosity which the *Tristan* poem failed to inspire. Half of the first act is sketched out, and the overture is already orchestrated. And what an overture! C

[1] *Wagner's first wife, Minna, who died in 1866.*

major, in $\frac{4}{4}$ time, bright and joyous, with a marvellous swing, fiendishly polyphonic, yet always clear and fertile, with an extraordinary, broadly treated combination, at the close, of three (at one point, four) motifs! Weissheimer,[1] who is in the next hotel to us, has been deafening us with his arrangement of it for the last week. He really does it quite well, only, in spite of the best intentions and experience gained from a critical survey of his predecessors' work, makes it far too difficult for any possible consumers and purchasers.

I need not tell you that Wagner's style, as developed in his recent works, shows no falling-off in this, his latest. There is the same fairy-like shimmer in the orchestral texture, the same autocratic management of the parts. Melodically it is naturally nearer akin to *Young Siegfried* than to *Tristan*.

Ad vocem Tristan. The outlook is not, after all, as bad as we all imagined. In Vienna the order went forth from on high to Salvi recently that rehearsals were to be started in the beginning of September at latest. Ander [2] will come round in the end and do his part. (Wagner has sacrificed various paragraphs in the third act.) Frau Dustmann,[3] who took advantage of an engagement at Wiesbaden to call on Wagner, confirmed the contents of Salvi's document. Provided that the beautiful house is not sold meanwhile (you know how he hates these perpetual provisos), Wagner will look on quietly from here, shaking his head incredulously until all the rehearsals are fixed. Apart from Vienna a similar prospect has now opened up in Dresden. If anything, this offers more security, in so far as the pair of lovers is concerned, for the tenor Schnorr [4] sings Tristan (and Brangäne in between whiles) by heart, and his wife is fairly well up in Isolde. Last month these two, who are as keen as they are competent, spent a number of days at Biebrich, and Wagner put them through the whole thing thoroughly, to my accompaniment. As soon as the season begins in Dresden, the Schnorrs will enlist

[1] WENDELIN WEISSHEIMER, *composer, conductor, Wagner enthusiast.*

[2] ALOYS ANDER (1817–64), *lyric tenor, Vienna Hofoper.*

[3] MARIE LUISE MEYER-DUSTMANN (1831–99), *dramatic soprano, Vienna Hofoper.*

[4] LUDWIG SCHNORR VON CAROLSFELD (1836–65), Heldentenor, *the first Tristan, one of the great Wagnerian figures. His wife, Malwina Garrigues (1825–1904), was the first Isolde. After her husband's death she became a troublesome anti-Wagner intriguer.*

suitable colleagues (Mitterwurzer [1] as Mark, and so on) and rehearse with them privately at home until they are able to announce to the intendant that they have a new opera ready to produce, complete except for orchestral rehearsals. There is, of course, the question of Wagner's conducting it himself. He will not give that up, and artistically, no doubt, he is right. But will the court agree to that? It might, for, after all, the court theatre would do brilliantly over it, and that is the main consideration in all-highest places.

I am telling you all this, and you only, because I take you at your word when you say you would be glad to hear how things are going; and you will certainly wish to be *au courant* about Wagner, at least.

He is really much better in health than he was. For ten days he has had a poisoned thumb — the right one, unfortunately — as the result of a dog-bite. (You know his kindness to animals; he brought it on himself by trying to wash the house-dog, a bull-dog who is not used to such attentions.) It is not dangerous, but he has been quite put off his work by it, and will probably be incapacitated for another week or fortnight. True, he has set himself to write the last note of the *Meistersinger* on his fiftieth birthday; I do not see, however, how he will find it physically possible to write out so voluminous a score as the many ensembles promise to make it by May 22, 1863. For one thing, the *Tristan* performance in Vienna will upset his calculations considerably. Moreover, his thirst for self-expression, for contact with the public — in short, for performance of his opera — is so great that, despite all the unfavourable and depressing experiences he has had (in Karlsruhe and recently in Wiesbaden and elsewhere) and his firm resolve " not to be caught again," he will undoubtedly fall into every new trap of the sort, and this *ad majorem gloriam* of Schopenhauer's theory of free will with which he is so familiar. . . .

[1] ANTON MITTERWURZER (1818–76), *Wagnerian singer, Dresden.*

7]

Munich
Luitpoldstrasse 15
July 13, 1865

. . . Positively not a day has passed, especially no Tristan-day, without Wagner's making inquiries about you and your unlucky star. Impossible to shine more brightly than you do by your absence. At the last performance — the unexpected fourth on July 1, which was perhaps the most successful and certainly the most applauded — we reproached you violently, though really without justification, for there had been much wavering over the date. Wagner believed, all the same, that you might have managed the journey by that time. Also it would, of course, have had to be made good to you by your noble creditor here (of last autumn). He was inconsolable over his failure to invite you. And now the season is ended. . . .

Finally last night came the bouquet: a big private concert in the Residenztheater with the house brilliantly illuminated, and no audience except His Majesty and between thirty and forty special Wagnerites. Wagner conducted.

1. Pilgrims' March from *Tannhäuser*, with a surprise: on the final E flat of the 'cellos, eighty military-band players struck up the *Huldigungs March* behind the scenes. (You will know it by this time in my arrangement for pianoforte.) The effect was magnificent, the point of it all being the special relationship between the composer and the King.

2. Prelude to *Lohengrin*.

3. Introduction and close of *Tristan*.

4. First finale of *Rheingold*, beginning with "*Schwüles Gedünst schwebt in der Luft*" — Zottmayer, Schnorr, and the Rhine Maidens (Förster, Diez, Seehofer) excellent. This was repeated by the King's request at the end of the second part.

5. *Walküre:* The Ride, Siegmund's Love-song, Wotan's Farewell, and the Fire-music (Simons good).

6. *Siegfried:* the Forging-song sung *marvellously, brilliantly,* by Schnorr.

7. *Meistersinger:* (a) Overture, (b) the big scene between the Masters and Walther (first finale) as far as " *das hehre Liebeslied.* "

You can have no conception, until you hear this, of its incomparable freshness, its euphony, its electrifying effect as regards both lyrical feeling and humorous expressiveness.

The orchestra was beside itself at rehearsals — their enthusiasm knew no bounds. Zottmayer as Kothner, and Simons as Beckmesser were very plucky; Schnorr surpassed himself as Walther. In the interval the King gave him an audience of forty minutes. This made him blissfully happy, of course, and his voice pealed out as never before.

This morning the Schnorrs went back to Dresden; Wagner is at the castle, seeing the King; my wife has gone to a women's luncheon, and I am taking advantage of the general dispersion to pay off old debts of correspondence, working backwards, as you see. . . .

To return to June 10. Congratulations on your concert, which will, I hope, have proved worth the trouble. As far as my incomplete knowledge of the circumstances goes, I should say that your local arrangements had been most practical. The list of patronesses proves it; there is absolutely no possibility of doing without such things on the other side of the Channel. I liked your program, too. If the choice of the G major, op. 31, surprised me somewhat, my surprise was tempered by the conviction that your rendering would justify it. Can you not send me a notice of it so that I may insert it in Brendel? And why not get Karl Biel to do the same for you in Bock's paper? It would surely be a good thing for Germany to hear of and read about you again. After all, one of these days you will be able and willing to flee from that London purgatory (not a suitable term for that filthy fog, I admit) and we shall then, I hope, be in a position to employ you in the ranks of the Wagner family. Hurry up and pay your debts, man, and save something into the bargain. Push on, push on, push on!

Wagner is greatly delighted with the success of the *Tannhäuser* march. How one gradually becomes possible! He no longer counts on any London royalties, but thanks you very much for your renewed elaborate efforts in that direction.

Schott's have at last returned the original score of *Walküre*. What a foul crew they are, printing abusive articles on *Tristan* in their paper! Härtel's seem to have no further desire to take their revenge, for they are running an even worse anti-*Tristan* campaign. Where is the sense of it, anyhow? They announce the score and selections in big letters in the very number that contains the vilest abuse of the work from Munich. Well, " Good night, Jews," as they say in Berlin. When all of a sudden the court theatres of Karlsruhe, Hanover, Darmstadt, Dresden (Hamburg is after it, too) approach him with offers to buy *Tristan*, the composer will tell them quite calmly that H. M. Ludwig III [*sic!*] has become possessor of the performing rights, and wishes that this " opera " shall be played only in his own capital and residence! That will make these contemptible curs sit up!

Finally I come to a topic which I should find it difficult to discuss with anyone but you. R. W. wishes me — as I happen to be close at hand — to get ahead quickly with the pianoforte edition of *Siegfried*. As a preliminary, however, I am to — spoil the first act by a popular arrangement. I am reluctant to do it, but it must be. Your paraphrases are impossible for me to play in Wagner's *tempi* (he has become steadily more " sanguine " in this respect, as I realized when *Tristan* was under way) and, I assume, for the majority of pianoforte-thumpers, even though my small stretch is not normal. I am therefore obliged to eliminate and simplify. You will allow me, I suppose, to consider Act I as still your work, in spite of my vandalism, and say — as you would, were the situation reversed — that it was a fair division of labour. Tell me, how did Schott pay you for the first two " dramas," by the sheet, or as a whole? If possible, I mean to get Benjamin's portion raised a bit.

The delay in publishing *Walküre* (we have had four sets of proofs) is growing wearisome even to Wagner. But he has had the inspiration to print his poem to the King in the front of the book, and the whole world will thus be informed of the exquisite relationship that exists between him and the King. Do you know the poem? A similar one is to preface each drama, so that the whole book " belongs," you may say, to the King.

Dear friend and comrade-in-arms, write soon and *soothe*

me. You know why and in what connexion. Send me your program at least as a token that you understand my situation. . . .

13]

Munich
June 10, 1869

Many thanks for your letter and for all the signs of friendly
feeling contained therein. Do not, however, insist upon a written
reply from me, for I am incapable of it. I am morally and
physically at the last gasp. Yesterday I handed in my definite
resignation.

To you before all — for it is with you among all my fellow-
artists that I feel myself most in sympathy, and from you that
I hope for the greatest understanding — I should so much like
to unburden myself, and I therefore propose that you should
*leave Moscow at once and come to Munich to stay with me for as
long as you will.* It will not inconvenience me or my mother
in the slightest. (My wife and children are in Switzerland.) We
have any amount of room, and until the middle of September
(practically until the end) the place is still mine. Why at once,
you will ask. To repair the ill fortune of four years ago, is the
reply. *On Saturday, June 19, there is a full rehearsal* of *Tristan
and Isolde* with Herr and Frau Vogl (they sing the notes and
nothing more) and some very unimportant cuts — by the *All-
Highest order* — to the supreme wrath of the composer, who is
angry with me for lending myself to the " profanation " (which
he greatly exaggerates). Probably the public performance will
be on June 22. On the 27th is *Meistersinger.* Richter conducts
this, however, as I have to devote the whole of my nervous
energy to *Tristan,* after which I shall be " done."

On August 25 *Rheingold* is to be given, by royal command.
The cast is complete but for Alberich.

I have proposed to R. W. that he should put you in my place.
You have vigour, whereas I ought to devote a year at least to recovering my nerve. Perhaps he will agree, in which case I would
gladly go to Moscow instead of you, if fit. From the beginning
of July the theatre will be closed for the necessary rebuilding,

reopening on August 25. My hasty scribble today will seem to
you decidedly crazy. Explanations when we meet. If you have
the desire, the time, and the journey-money (this last I regret
not being able to lend you, for the moment), pack up quickly
and come to your collapsed friend. . . .

14]

Munich
July 29, 1869
In great haste

. . . *R*HEINGOLD is still announced for August 25. The
rebuilding of the stage and orchestra will soon be finished, scenic
preparations also. Richter is in charge of the music. I hear from
other people that Liszt is coming for the performance. It is quite
impossible for me to stay and listen to it. My health is ruined,
physically and morally. I can hardly pull myself together to
carry on with my official duties until the holidays. My career as
conductor came to an end with the newly-rehearsed *Tristan* on
June 22. You will wonder why, but there will soon be plenty of
people to solve the mystery for you. Spare me the necessity, I
beg.

How glad I should have been to arrange for you to succeed
me here! Alas, I have now no say in the matter. I no longer
have any communication with Switzerland.[1]

If you want to hear any more about Munich, write to Cornelius.[2]

I am afraid I shall soon go to pieces, but am trying the last
radical remedy, that of absolute personal resignation.

[1] *By this time Cosima von Bülow had definitely taken up her residence at Triebschen with Wagner.*
[2] PETER CORNELIUS (1824–74), *the composer.*

26]

Munich
July 12, 1875

Please kiss your wife's gracious and helping hand for me and thank her warmly. I hope you are both in rather better health than I, and also that the weather is kinder towards you.

Gye [1] wrote to Ullmann [2] on July 9:

" We have not got the music of *Benvenuto Cellini*. Either Berlioz had it back or it was burnt in the fire. The opera was a fiasco and, if I remember rightly, was only played two nights."

I am very sorry to have pursued you in this way with letters and telegrams. If not for *your own* sake, please refuse for *mine* to have any more of these forwardings. Simply say: " Addressee gone away, destination unknown." Then leave the post-office to decide what next. This is their affair, do you see?

The matter of the will cannot be settled as quickly as I hoped, as my attorney Gotthelf, whom I have also nominated as executor, has cases today and tomorrow away. . . .

27]

Boston
October 31, 1875

. . . First of all I must tell you how inconceivably glad I am to have crossed the ocean. The New World is to be preferred to the Old in every respect. New Englanders are a great improvement on their forbears in the old country — more receptive, warm-hearted, and amiable in social intercourse than the " Nibelheimer." As regards material comforts, too, life is far pleasanter. If it were not for my beloved (!) countrymen, who have got on my nerves in Paris, Petersburg, and London in turn, everything would be too heavenly.

One man at least has fallen a victim to the Tschaikovsky

[1] Frederick Gye, *impresario and manager at Covent Garden.*
[2] *Concert impresario.*

concerto — namely, Bergmann.[1] He will not be the last. . . .
Have already had three rehearsals — proper ones, too — of the
Tschaikovsky. Tell him that I had already corrected the ⌒ ⌒ ⌒ in
the parts of the Finale, off my own bat, before his letter arrived;
that is, inserted them in place of the *staccato*. The performance,
conducted by Lang, an American, improvised, and promptly
made famous, by me, was very decent, and yesterday, when we
did it again, it was most spirited. . . .

28]

New York
November 24, 1875

Do not exclaim impatiently: " Once more, once more I am
to act as postilion — of friendship — between America and
Russia " (to my mind, the only two parts of the world that are
not played out).

I admit (for I am no fonder of leaving things half-done than
are you) that it is again a matter of Tschaikovsky: I want you to
give him a little pleasure by showing him the enclosed cuttings.

You see, it was through you that I first knew him and learned
to appreciate him, so it is a case of *les amis de nos amis,* etc.

The concerto went much better here under Damrosch [2] than
in Boston. It was a distinct success and is to be repeated next
Saturday. In fact, Tschaikovsky has become popular in the New
World; and if Jürgenson were not such a damned jackass, but
would send over a reasonable quantity of Tschaikovsky's music,
he could do a lot of business. Yesterday a woman actually
bought the score of Tschaikovsky's symphony, op. 23, at Schuberth's, simply because there was nothing else of his to buy.

How are you, old friend? And your charming wife? Much
proof-correcting? How about those Chopin recitals? I am 66⅔%
better than in the Old World, and I grow more enchanted every

[1] KARL BERGMANN (1821–76), *violoncellist and conductor. From 1855 onwards
conducted the New York Philharmonic, also the Männergesangverein Arion.*

[2] LEOPOLD DAMROSCH (1832–85) *came to the United States from Germany
(where he had filled various important musical posts, chiefly in Breslau) in 1871.
Conductor of the Männergesangverein Arion, the Oratorio Society (1873), the New
York Symphony Society (1878). Friend of Liszt, who dedicated the* Triomphe
funèbre de Tasse *to him.*

day with this glorious country, which is almost half a century (minimum) ahead of nearly every part of Europe. I notice the most extraordinary transformation in myself. Whereas, before, I frequently played like a pig, I now occasionally play like a god. Chickering's[1] gorgeous pianofortes — undeniably the best in both worlds — have made me into a first-rate pianist. Certainly I practise as I never did before: four hours a day, on an average. *Enfin,* I enjoy myself and my music.

Mason is growing rather fat. A nice fellow, but unfortunately, it appears, wholly in the hands of Steinway. Has he written to you? He wanted to recommend an agent for his brother's much played, but not particularly beautiful, parlour organs. . . .

[1] JONAS CHICKERING *of Boston, a great name in the annals of pianoforte-manufacture.*

Hans von Bülow
to
Carl Bechstein

106]

Berlin
December 20, 1859

I NEITHER know Herr Becker's address nor feel I ought to go out in my present exhausted state. Would you therefore very kindly ask Herr Becker if he would do me the pleasure of calling here tomorrow between ten and eleven. If he is agreeable, I am prepared to hand over to him four lessons a week at the conservatorium during my absence (from January 13). Stern [1] has given his consent. I must, however, have a good long talk with my part-deputy in which I can discuss the characters of individual pupils as well as the course of instruction I have laid down. These details are important, and I should like to have the main points settled before the holidays. I shall be at home, and at leisure, this afternoon also.

For my third recital, on January 6 (Friday evening), I naturally want a Bechstein. This time I am having a Blüthner from Leipzig (from Friedländer's shop) to replace the Erard. Would you be so kind as to get me yesterday's *Berlin*? My best thanks for the recent cuttings. I was hardly prepared for all this animosity and lying. Still, these people enjoy it, and it does not hurt either me or my cause. Could I, by the way, have the pianoforte overhauled and tuned on Thursday or Friday?

PS. Let us hope that Kossak's [2] report will not do us any harm. It could only damage our interests on both sides. I need hardly say that I dissociate you from it entirely. The labelling was my own carefully considered idea.

[1] JULIUS STERN (1820–83), *violinist and conductor. Founded the Stern Gesangverein (1847) and, with Kullak and A. B. Marx, the Stern Conservatoire (1856), both in Berlin.*

[2] ERNST KOSSAK (1814–80), *writer on music, founder and editor of the* Neue berliner Musikzeitung.

107]

Paris
March 6, 1860

Many thanks for your communications, particularly for the pleasing news that the great Dreyschock [1] has taken to playing your pianofortes exclusively and that these are at last qualified for court, without, I assume, having deteriorated in value. But I must not waste time in scribbling, as I want to draw your attention specially to Vienna.

When I made the proposal, through my wife, that you should send me one of your fine concert grands for my appearance at the Philharmonic concert in Vienna on March 25, this was less from the selfish motive of hoping to make a more brilliant effect on a Bechstein than on a Bösendorfer or Streicher than from my ambition (as yet unauthorized by you) that you should gradually make for yourself the name and reputation abroad to which your excellent instruments entitle you.

Let me be quite frank. I am far from denying that a grand pianoforte from your workshop is more favourable to the display of my modest talent than any other German instrument of whatever make; on the other hand, you will not fail to realize that, in addition to the sufficiently numerous enemies I already possess in Vienna, I should be letting loose on myself the whole pack of Austrian Imperial pianoforte-manufacturers. Such considerations will not, however, prevent me from carrying out an idea the realization of which really appeals to me. My idea is to assist you to gain such a reputation *throughout Germany* as the firm of Streicher possessed some decades back, or the firm of Erard throughout the world. My scheme is to establish the undisputed supremacy of Prussia in one thing at least; namely, in the manufacture of pianofortes.

The pecuniary disadvantages which you would *certainly* incur through entering upon my scheme (you have enumerated them in your letter) appear to outweigh by far the advantage of the reputation your firm stands to gain by it. Of this I am incom-

---

[1] Alexander Dreyschock (1818–69), *pianist and composer.*

petent to judge. I can only say that I would gladly pay the costs of carriage and duty, did my means permit. But these very limited means at my disposal are devoted to other purposes: for instance, the performance of various works by detested composers, for whom I feel it my duty and my mission to take up the cudgels until, finally, these snails and donkeys are no longer in the majority and that lousy regiment of Berlin pressmen, for instance, has been wiped out — and the sooner the better! From the way I write, you will probably think me discouraged. I am far too honest to deny it. I admit, I am greatly harassed by the obstacles that are put in the way of my plan. But this does not in the least alter my firm and loyal appreciation of your achievements. On this point I am no Berliner, even when dealing with other Berliners!

108]

Berlin
September 20, 1860

Do come in some time this afternoon. My father-in-law [1] is here for a few days and would be very pleased to see you, though he wishes to go out as little as possible lest he should be obliged to pay a quantity of calls. I too am tied to the house by this bad weather and my bad health. . . .

109]

Berlin
October 3, 1860

You have just done me a great favour in sending a grand to Herr Lassalle,[2] who is in raptures over it, and now I immediately set about asking you another. To come to the point: could you dispatch a concert grand to Danzig straight away? You may be assured the instrument will not have to make a return journey.

[1] LISZT.
[2] FERDINAND LASSALLE, *writer and socialist agitator. One of the founders of socialism in Germany.*

Fräulein Ingeborg Stark — my friend Bronsart's [1] *fiancée,* a
pupil of Liszt and a grand pianist, whom we shall hear in Berlin in the coming season — proposes to embark on a cycle of
concerts next week in Danzig, where she is staying with her
future father-in-law, General von Bronsart, commandant of the
city. She is in despair at having " nothing fit to play on " and
has written me a four-page lament on the worthlessness of the
Visznievski productions, with a view to my enlisting your sympathy — if I have not drawn too heavily on it already. Naturally, she will undertake the cost of carriage, and the sale of the
pianoforte seems to her, as to me (knowing as I do the general
dissatisfaction which prevails with regard to the Danzig instruments), a foregone conclusion. I hope your kindness will not
damage you, but rather certain other gentlemen in the neighbourhood — for instance, at Königsberg. Fräulein Stark's concert is on the 13th of this month. Please try to give this young
artist the chance she wants; she will do your pianofortes credit.
If it really cannot be done, I shall not be offended, but please let
me have a word of assent or dissent as soon as possible, as I
must reply. . . .

110]

Berlin
January 4, 1861

I HAVE just heard from Paris that the first *Tannhäuser*
performance cannot take place before February 15. I shall
therefore stay in Berlin until the beginning of that month and
shall be able to give my third recital at the end of this, about
January 25. This removes any obstacles in the way of the Stettin
concert, which might take place any time from the 18th. . . .

[1] HANS BRONSART VON SCHELLENDORF (1830–1913), *pianist (pupil of Liszt),*
succeeded Bülow as conductor of the Gesellschaft für Musikfreunde in 1865.

111]

Berlin
October 19, 1862

My fear was not groundless. You never sold my pianoforte for all that money! I shall have to put you on your oath. You wanted to make it a round sum. I hope you will accept my protest, and consent to take back the extra and use it to release some poor pianist who has got himself planted at a Berlin hotel. Such things do happen, and I know you:

Robert the Devil, Act II, sc. i.[1]

The house of Erard is not a charity concern, neither does the firm of Bock-Falk [Buck-falcon] occupy free lodgings at the zoo.

This sale is a myth, and you know it. Seriously, I implore you, let us straighten it out. Don't treat me like a child and do cultivate a better opinion of the ordinary man's intelligence.

112]

Berlin, Enkeplatz 5
October 18, 1863

I am sending you with this the proposed document, of which you are at liberty to have a number of copies made for me to sign. Is it clear, and have I kept my word? I think so — to an extent, possibly, which might lead you, were you a Jew, to circulate an advertisement for Steinweg (or Bechstein) so that my declaration could be turned to good account. As far as I am concerned, you have *carte blanche*.

A pleasant journey, then, and would you bring back from Dresden a program of my first recital? I have mislaid my

---

[1] *This quotation, of an instrumental cadence before a recitative, in Meyerbeer's opera, seems to have been used here by Bülow to express finality.*

copy and cannot remember what fare I promised my native place.

Many thanks for allowing me the use of your premises for my rehearsals.

A Defence

The use by the undersigned of an in many respects admirable concert grand by the firm of Steinway and Son (Brunswick, New York) at the first concert of the Gesellschaft der Musikfreunde on October 31 has given the all too ardent friends of this firm an excuse to issue various advertisements which are calculated to mislead the public as to my real judgment. To avoid being confronted with this sort of thing in the future, I feel constrained to make the following announcement:

My preference for instruments made by the Royal Prussian Court manufacturer Carl Bechstein in Berlin is, I believe, well known. It rests upon the conviction — obtained after many tests and comparisons — that the said firm has brought pianoforte-construction to a level which can only be described by the French technical expression " *hors de concours,*" and, having captured the *Prussian* market, is bound before long to receive *world recognition*. Whenever I give a solo pianoforte recital, I am as dependent upon the Bechstein " colour pianoforte " — if I may use so unliteral a term — for the interpretation of my artistic intentions as upon my ten fingers; and the more trouble I have taken to acquaint myself *instantly* with all the products of foreign industry bearing on my profession, the less am I inclined to waver in my preference for the Bechstein manufactures. Nevertheless I feel it my duty as a " working pianist " to sacrifice my personal taste when it is desirable to encourage some other praiseworthy and thorough industrial effort (Herr Steinway's achievements are a case in point) and the device " *suum cuique* " may be appropriate. To this principle of equity and justice I shall continue to subscribe as far as is reasonable and practicable; I do not, however, wish conclusions as to my general tendency to be drawn from such well-meaning attempts at patronage. For the rest, all such comparative decisions may well be left to an unprejudiced audience (" *de gustibus,*" etc.), and just as I shall certainly refrain from influencing public opinion

by any prejudicial theories, so shall I treat any misinterpreta-
tions of my opinions, once stated, with complete indifference.

HANS VON BÜLOW
Court pianist to H. M. the King

Berlin, November 1863

113]

Munich
Hotel Marienbad
November 23, 1864

I PROMISED to let you know the date of the first performance
of *The Flying Dutchman*. It is December 4. Try to come yourself,
W[agner] would be very pleased too.

Although still in the thick of moving, I am longing for pianofortes. I do not suppose I shall be able to leave my furnished
rooms until next Monday, but my flat at 15 Luitpoldstrasse (first
floor) is ready to receive the grand.

Will you send me a line as soon as possible to say when I
may expect it, and whether you yourself are able to carry out
your promise? You might let me know at the same time how the
first concert conducted by Herr von Bronsart came off. I can
think of nothing which is of anything like the same interest to
me at the moment as my successor's activities in Berlin and
their results.

Wagner's health is tolerably good and my own not so bad.
This climate seems to me no worse than that of Berlin so far, in
spite of the perpetual downpour. . . .

PS. The King is coming at the beginning of next month. The
first thing that Wagner and I intend to make him import is of
course a Bechstein.

114]

Munich
December 2, 1864

YOUR letter has consoled me, though very partially, for the
failure to send the pianoforte. Many thanks for your informa-

tion with regard to Bronsart's concerts. It is the only thread
which still binds me to Berlin. If I could but do anything to
set that enterprise of mine on a firm basis! For the rest — open
Goethe's *Werther* and read the first line.[1] It is my constant
refrain.

One minor injustice you do me: in criticizing my deputy
you have at him rather pettily, with the idea of flattering my
vanity. It is my most earnest wish to be missed by neither friend
nor foe and to have Herr von Bronsart really fill my place. It
will give me undivided pleasure to hear that this has been
achieved. As regards your extravagantly favourable opinion of
me, I shall ask of you the one thing that lies in your power: to
make things easy for my successor and so further the good
work in which we are both implicated.

So you are going to present the King with a grand pianoforte? That is a bold idea, original and new, and as such has
my entire approval. I will speak to Herr von Pfistermeister about
it at once — that is, simply give him your letter to read, and
sound him as to the possibility of realizing that idea of
the *Pelzversatzzettelseinlösegebührenanpumper* [2] (you understand?). How I should rejoice over it!

The King arrived the day before yesterday. First of all, he
has to deal with the ministers, the musicians will have to wait
awhile. The rehearsals for *The Flying Dutchman* are fixed for
today and tomorrow, however, and the launching is definitely
fixed for Sunday. It will be a gala performance. The most elaborate preparations; singers, comparatively speaking, not too brilliant, but a wonderfully good and true orchestra. They are all
inspired by the best of feelings, which places them on an excep-
tional level. Wagner is confident of success in spite of his illness.
What a pity you are so unenterprising! This first performance
would have particularly impressed and delighted you. And who
can say whether Wagner will conduct the other performances?
Then on the 11th there is the big concert (*Faust Overture*, Ride
of the Valkyries, the Forging-songs, the *Meistersinger* — in
short, the most exquisite of the exquisite). It will be a tremendous triumph for Wagner to set against the general jealousy
which has ruled ever since Oscar von Redwitz was made a

---

[1] "Wie froh bin ich, dass ich weg bin (*How happy I am to be quit*)!"

[2] *Meaning deliberately veiled in the German. Literally: "Cadger for the amount
needed to redeem a pawned fur." —* Tr.

knight of the Order of Maximilian in Wagner's place, and is now, fortunately, on the wane. Why will you not permit yourself the little treat of witnessing such rare spectacles? You are wrong; remember our Dutch tour: at first you were unwilling to undertake that.

Well, eloquence and persuasion are not my strong point. Especially as you are so obstinate that I am always forced to give in. I warn you, however, that a ticket was reserved for you — weeks ago — for the whole theatre (seating 2,500) was sold out, weeks ago, for the first three performances.

At least keep your promise for New Year! And between now and then be so good as to write to me. Perhaps after Bronsart's second concert? You can then tickle my sympathies and antipathies a little, for instance, by telling me nice things about Tausig [1] and indulging in a few insults to his majesty of trills! Don't forget. And abuse a few of those flashy Jew musicians a bit, too!

Once one has a bad habit, one must stick to it, else it is no longer a habit. Therefore, do me the kindness to forward the enclosed.

My piano-thirsty wife joins me in kindest regards to you and yours. Should you see Kroll,[2] Weitzmann,[3] or any of that brand, remember me kindly to them. I don't feel like writing to them. Only you and Bronsart will get letters from me — otherwise I write to Berlin on business only. . . .

115]

Munich
December 20, 1864

THEY are here! The little one arrived nearly a fortnight ago and the big beauty this very afternoon. My warmest thanks. It is not the fault of the grand ("wings") if I cannot fly. But I have had to spend some perspiring days in bed and am still

[1] KARL TAUSIG (1841–71), *one of the greatest of contemporary pianists, pupil of his father, Aloys; editor of Clementi's* Gradus ad Parnassum, *among other things. One of Bülow's most intimate friends.*

[2] FRANZ KROLL (1820–77), *pianist (pupil of Liszt), teacher at the Stern Conservatoire.*

[3] KARL FRIEDRICH WEITZMANN (1808–80), *violinist, choral conductor, writer on music, one of the Liszt circle.*

in the clutches of that ghastly influenza. Heaven knows how and
whether I shall be able to acclimatize myself here. I will not
abuse the weather, though. A dull sky, but a dry, windless cold.
I probably got my chill in these cold rooms. I would give one
of your grand pianofortes for a good Berlin stove! But that is
all swagger, I must not blaspheme.

I gave Counsellor von Pfistermeister a scrap of your letter
to taste the other day. He was greatly touched, but deprecated the
suggestion vigorously. Took down your name and address. I
hope it may lead to an order before long.

Our handsome young King has been out of sorts for several
days. Takes the pleasure of ruling too seriously and vigorously,
exerts himself and gets irritable. God keep him — but not in the
sense of receiving him!

Wagner is also ill, but has been able to force himself to
work. His concert on last Sunday but one was an even greater
triumph than *The Flying Dutchman*. A pity you were not there.
It will be a long time before it comes again.

The animosity, or silent opposition, is still in full swing. It
rains prejudices, it snows absurd rumours. The only point about
this place is that one can look on quietly and wait. *Tristan and
Isolde* is to be played at the little Residenztheater before an
audience of picked listeners from far and near. The public are
to be left out entirely for the present, the blockheads! Not that
the musicians are much better. Orchestra slightly more decent
than in Berlin, but contains many bad elements. Naturally, it is to
be radically reformed, but very — *poco a poco*. For my part, I
am lying low altogether this year, restricting myself to the court
concerts — that is, the King's concerts. Am beginning to select
a few of the best strings from the orchestra and train them for
chamber-music evenings at the palace.

These pianoforte-tuners! Your grand in the oak case arrived
in perfect tune, but I practised with such ravenous fury the first
few days that I had to send for a man, who duly came and put
the whole thing wretchedly out of tune. In defiance of strict
orders he actually tuned it up: as you know, Munich is the worst
sinner with regard to high pitch. Our A in Berlin is A flat here.
The fellow didn't go quite so far as that, but quite far enough,
as you see. When are you coming over? Are you coming at all?

I assume you will accompany the King's grand when it comes; let us hope the occasion will not be long postponed. But here I am gossiping. That is only because I want you to gossip in return. Do tell me things — I get no news from Berlin. Is Bronsart ill? I am afraid he must be, as there is no concert advertised this side of Christmas. What is Kroll doing? And Weitzmann? And the unmarried Fischer? It's true I don't know her, but I feel a certain tenderness for her as being wrongly accused. Was she set free at the appeal? I hope so.

Dr. Nohl, a writer on music (formerly a Mozartite, now a Wagnerite — in which there is no apostasy), spoke of you to me last week as if he knew you. Is that just swank? . . .

Nothing but interrogation-marks. Yet I have so much to exclaim about. Your two pianofortes give me great joy. Heaven knows that if I don't give up tinkling altogether, it is you who are to blame, for you drive me back to playing over and over again. You spoil me for and shut me out from every other career. What is it but this fatal habit which restrains me from snatching Herr von der Pfordten's [1] portfolio and, in my detestation of the Berlin critics, abusing Prussia from the Munich point of view?

It's queer, but the whole of the musical squabbling centres in two Franz L.'s and two Richard W.'s:

Lachner [2]	Würst [3]
Liszt	Wagner.

. . .

---

[1] BARON VON DER PFORDTEN, *Bavarian statesman, head of the Cabinet, remembered for his anti-Wagnerian machinations, which had as result Wagner's departure from Munich in 1865, and eventually led to the dismissal of Pfordten's own Cabinet by the King in the following year. It was at the time of this letter that he and Pfistermeister (q.v.) tried to get Wagner imprisoned for debt, reckoning without Ludwig, who paid the bill. It must be said in part extenuation of the behaviour of the Bavarian Cabinet between 1864 and 1866 that they were brought into contact with circumstances which could hardly have seemed, in their eyes, favourable to the good governance of the State: a youthful King (Ludwig II came to the throne in 1864, at the age of nineteen), insistent on playing a decisive part in matters to do with his realm, when those matters seemed likely to forward, or conversely to threaten, his passionate plans for music or architecture — for Wagner, or for the building of fresh palaces; then, Cosima von Bülow, enthusiastic worker in the Wagnerian cause, go-between for Wagner and Ludwig after the former had been turned out of Munich, viewed with increasing suspicion by Bavarian statesmen, who naturally could not easily forget Lola Montez; lastly, Wagner himself, who with his strange new music, his gigantic schemes, his unquestioned sway over the King, must have appeared a menace, not only to the State exchequer, but to political peace as well.*

[2] FRANZ LACHNER (1803–90), *composer, Hofkapellmeister, Munich, 1852–65. Friend of Schubert.*

[3] RICHARD WÜRST (1824–81), *composer and teacher, pupil of Mendelssohn.*

116]

[Munich]
Sunday, December 25 [1864], 10 p.m.

THE enclosed concert notice speaks for itself. I wanted just to let you know, before you hear it from elsewhere, that our association has again proved its merits. We both had an enormous and unqualified success. Lachner conducted quite passably, and the orchestra was furiously enthusiastic. I was rather afraid of so big a hall — though very fine to look at, it is acoustically anything but favourable — but your pianoforte sounded splendid, ringing, clear, and full. Everyone agrees that no such pianofortes have been heard in Munich. I hope the *Augsburger* will say something about it too. . . . You will ask how all this fits in with my last letter. The answer is: the King's wish = a command. Baron von Perfall, the court intendant, came to see me the very day after I had written to you to say I did not propose to appear again here this winter. But the King had either not been able or not wanted to attend any of the Odeon concerts this year and the public had taken offence. He had therefore decided to make an official appearance at this one and wished to have an extra inducement in my performance. So I had to go. It was not easy, as I have been suffering for a fortnight from a hideous cold in the head, combined with rheumatic twitches in the neck. It has been outlandishly cold, too, and I could not nurse myself, what with buying Christmas presents and all kinds of domestic and other agitations.

But I forced myself to do it and am glad I did. The musicians now have the respect for me which I need to support me in future undertakings. These concerts are for the benefit of the court musicians (Academy), so I have earned the gratitude of the corporation into the bargain.

The unrelievedly classical tone of the program was obligatory for various reasons. The weeping and wailing over futuristic music in certain circles was beginning to be intolerable; on Wagner's account, the King's account, and finally my own insignificant account, therefore, it seemed desirable. Next time I can go my way calmly. During the coming months, up to March, there will be no concerts (with the exception of the Patti mania, which begins on January 6), for these Müncheners spend this period dancing like mad creatures, masked and unmasked. Later there are four orchestral concerts, one of which I shall no doubt honour with my presence.

On March 13 I am playing at Utrecht by invitation, with the guarantee of four other engagements. How would it be, friend Bechstein, if you were to repeat the Dutch duo-excursion? Haven't you the wish, the time, the pluck? Take the plunge. No one will see you, no one hear you; you can safely do it.

Wagner is ill again — not seriously, but enough to be uncomfortable. He sends kindest regards, my wife also. Let me hear something or, still better, see something of you soon. You must admit that it is moving of me to write to you tonight. Then move me in return — by moving yourself.

Best wishes for Christmas and the burial of the year. A villainous one, this 1864!

PS. Oh this tuning! At first I did not know which of the two grands to have tuned, so had them both·done and finally decided to play on the big new one, although it is a little soft for me, if only because it was higher in pitch. Did you have that done to suit Munich's conditions? Even so, it was not enough. Can you imagine it! Exactly a semitone higher than in Berlin. Well, all that is going to be altered. What a blessing, from every point of view, that we have some power! Send me news of everything I am interested in. Don't be so lazy with your pen. You will not be let off under two sheets any more.

117]

Munich
February 17, 1865

For a week I have been suffering from that painful rheumatism in the joints which pestered me during the latter half of last year. Writing is difficult, for every dip of the pen makes me twitch. Your anxiety and kind sympathy make it imperative for me to send two lines of reassurance, but it is *only for you* that I do it.

Do not believe a word of the newspaper lies. Wagner is still in the King's good graces and I am less than ever inclined to persuade the Master to give up Munich. This very morning he was with the King, who gave him definite instructions about Semper's [1] appointment. A little patience! Very soon the irrefutable facts to be proclaimed from on high will shatter all the infamies of the press without our having to soil our hands with that filth.

I admit there have been the most impudent intrigues on foot for weeks in the *antechambers,* less in those of the King than in — well, you know the complications of this court (look it up in Gotha). Then, too, in connexion with a Bavarian-Saxon union, all possible attempts have been made by a certain high-placed translator of Dante to bring about Wagner's fall. These calumnies and perfidies will all rebound from our serious, strong-minded monarch, but, believe me, they will ricochet against their originators; it is only a question of time.

Do not discuss it with anyone. At the most, smile diplomatically when they tell you these idiotic things, whether from malice or sympathy. We can wait and we intend to put the enemies completely to shame, but in *his* good time. I implore you, not a word in reply. Say at most that I have written to you and that you know where you stand and are under no obligation to orientate other people, but rather to spare yourself this human kindness.

What has affected me terribly — you need not regret having told me, for I am sincerely grateful — is the information about this impostor. One of these days I propose to send in my resignation to the Gesellschaft der Musikfreunde (possibly through you) and I authorize or rather beg of you to set me a good example by handing in yours first.

I am greatly distressed by the whole affair and the person in question. I do not easily shed salt water, but today I could not help weeping. The fact is, my nerves are now totally ruined.

I had announced the soirées for the benefit of the Platen

[1] GOTTFRIED SEMPER, *architect, drew the plans for the Festival Theatre at Bayreuth.*

memorial, but my wretched health made it necessary to post-pone the first till March 3. I hope I may be better by then. You shall hear from me how the first one goes off.

Thanks for the balm you administered. Satter! Splendid idea, the insertion of those press notices! How long will the fellow hold out?

Kindest regards from Wagner, Cornelius, and my wife, who is well, as are the children. . . .

Was the Thuringian enterprise satisfactory? Let me hear from you soon.

PS. If you have to tell the tale in Berlin, tell about my visit to Pfistermeister, the private concert in the Residenztheater, and so on. That can do no harm, quite the contrary. As regards news-paper gossip, however, preserve a diplomatic silence. And — on Wagner's account and mine — and unruffled imperturbability and indifference. You know how excitable I am? Well, now I am fabulously calm; you should see me! Only I should like to strike off my namesakes from my memory, or to alter my own Chris-tian name!

If you will do a real good deed, call on my mother. For heaven's sake, keep her from being uneasy or listening to what people say. She must not insist either, for the time being, on hearing from my wife, who writes three or four sheets to her regularly every week when there is really anything to say. . . .

118]

Munich
March 4, 1865

You will have received my letter which arrived on the same day as the disturbing telegram. The latter I will deal with orally — it was inspired by certain extraordinarily complicated circumstances which my possibly unjust suspicions (not of you!) led me to connect with the idiotic Truhn [1] affair. Mean-while many thanks for your prompt reply. We have led a ter-rible life here, but I hope all this disgusting business is at last

---

[1] HIERONYMUS TRUHN (1811–86), *critic and composer, pupil of Mendelssohn, toured with Bülow in 1884 as conductor.*

at an end — certainly I am at the end of my tether. You see from the enclosure that my first recital came off last night, though under unspeakable difficulties. Hall half empty, but still it was enough of a success to guarantee the two others. Your pianoforte sounded heavenly and stood the test magnificently. Wagner and my wife were quite charmed with it. My wife insists that it is the best of your instruments that she has ever heard. The whole thing gave me renewed strength and vigour. I wore myself out with a week's practising and got rid of a fair amount of gall at the same time. . . .

What do you think about a concert in Berlin? It would have to be all done with by the end of March, for I am obliged to be back here in the beginning of April (soirée on the 3rd, then *Tristan* rehearsals). For one thing I expect my wife's confinement about that time. I should of course spend only two or three days in Berlin. Whether I play or not depends on the Patti mania.

What sort of a pianoforte of yours is it that Director Hol has at Utrecht? It has been offered me for my concert on the 14th, together with an Erard — about which I have misgivings, as you know. Please tell me what you think.

The King's pianoforte might be sent at any convenient time now, as I hear from all sides this morning that the two of us made a tremendous sensation yesterday and that the next soirée is to be packed. His Majesty had gone to see *Antigone,* which was put on that evening purely to spoil my show. It had been postponed several times and I was so foolish as to let myself be bullied into postponing my recital also.

They are a crew! You can have no idea of such insolence and baseness. They say, however, that the Cabinet is *tottering,* and Pfistermeister [1] is hanging on with all his might to Wagner, who is standing firm, though nearly worn out.

PS. Liszt's Psalm [2] — how did it go, how did they like it?

[1] *It was Pfistermeister who bore Ludwig's ring to Wagner in Paris in 1864. The journey appears to have left a deposit of bitter feeling, for Pfistermeister became a pronounced anti-Wagnerian and supporter of Pfordten's faction (see page 27, note 1).*

[2] Liszt's Thirteenth Psalm (*1865*).

119]

Amsterdam
March 21, 1865

How aggravating you are! To this hour I do not know whether I have reason to rejoice over something or not. Have you got it, have you, have you? Surely you have not swallowed so much Dutch phlegm as not to have taken the trouble to find out?

Your pianoforte, on the other hand, was anything but aggravating last night. It sounded great. A small hall and small audience — two hundred and fifty at most — but all picked people and amazingly cordial. A triple recall after the Schubert trio — they refused to go away — and so I sat down again with Koenen (who is, by the way, a more refined and intellectual violinist than any we have in Berlin or Munich) and we gave them Beethoven's G major Sonata, op. 96, obtaining a better ensemble than I have ever heard. Roothaan was beside himself. It seems to me there's a sluice opened for your instruments now.

How are you arranging the Berlin affair? It will be a worrying day for you. I've been thinking it over — we can hardly leave out the Earthworm (as you call Tausig) or the Pearl. But to keep the Jew pack within bounds we must have a contrast, a damper. What say you to my proposal to invite a " friend," Baron Korff (Oranienstrasse 101, 102) to the Hotel Royal with us?

In that way the whole show would gain an air and — you will guess, perhaps, why I should like Herr von Korff to be your guest.

It is now twelve. I have had four visitors. How many more will come? Your assumption with regard to yesterday evening appears to have gone wrong. I am in a position which obliges me to be very well-behaved and allows me to have no pretensions.

Next season I may very well receive several invitations to Holland, in which case I shall arrange matters more comfortably. How I hope you will have sown grand pianofortes over the country by then!

Siegel [1] in Leipzig? I suppose you had no time. Well, it was a luxury. Please give no warning of my Berlin visit until a day or two before to those concerned (Weitzmann, Kroll, Mützelburg [2] — Schönberger, etc.).

PS. Knighted yet?

120]

Munich
April 3, 1865

Back yesterday. Since our parting at Görlitz, dear friend and *caballero,* terrific exertions, obstacles, toothache, and what not. Musically all is well. Löwenberg [3] was magnificent. Thursday *and Friday,* played for two hours at Jena. Such enthusiastic, appreciative, charming people!

Counsellor Seebeck, curator of the university, is now about to order a grand pianoforte from you, thank God. You wish to be generous to Jena and I argued against it the other day; now I should like to argue for it, first because I have been generous myself, but also for a *new* reason. There is a movement on foot to bestow an honorary doctorate on a certain *Herr* in Munich shortly. It will be difficult, particularly as the philosophers are at loggerheads just now and it takes great cunning to secure unanimity. The greatest secrecy about all this, please.

To my amusement, I found a nice letter from our nice Schubert on my arrival. Prepare for the worst. Ha ha! Shrill barkers have not a sharp bite.

Wagner is in form, my wife and children are as well as can be expected under the circumstances.

The day after tomorrow we expect Schnorrs and Mitterwurzer. Also Zottmayer from Hanover for the part of King Mark. First performance fixed provisionally for May 10.

A letter in bad taste from Truhn, and a shameless crawler from his Bêthge daughter, *who asks for an engagement here* (!!!).

What a pack of parasites!

[1] C. F. W. SIEGEL, *Leipzig publisher.*
[2] ADOLF MÜTZELBURG, *novelist, wrote sometimes under the name of Justus Severini or Karl Weber*
[3] *Seat of the Hohenzollern family.*

Also a Munich press notice (from the official paper, Grandauer). That is the kind of criticism I like. You need not abuse him for making such short work of me. In his first notice he let fly any amount of janizary invective.

I am interrupted by Herr Deprosse,[1] who is sighing for pianofortes and requests me to — kick you into answering his letter with all possible speed.

Now to the main point, old man. On all important problems I consult my wife, whose mind and instinct are always right. And my wife, who sends kindest regards, *advises you most decidedly not to carry out your proposal.*

Pf[ordten] has only sons, by the way, who are being educated abroad. And his wife does not play the pianoforte. So you may drop this story! It simply has no " apropos." On the other hand, do send as quickly as possible a warm, detailed, informal letter of thanks to H. M.

I am longing to see the promised copy. I am sure you will do it splendidly. . . .

Au revoir, then, until May, though I expect we shall communicate by letter before that. Has the All-Highest signified his approval by that ribbon yet? Do tell me what impression it makes on the good Berliners.

PS. You will have to collect a photograph of my wife and children when you come in May. These are all disposed of.

Once more, not a word to Pf[ordten]!

121]

Munich
April 14, 1865

MANY thanks for your communications, Knight Bechstein. The letter in question falls short on a few points. These are — at least in this case — relatively unimportant. I note them down, not to depress you, but so that you may profit by them for any future occasions.

1. The opening should read:
" Most Serene and Magnanimous King! "

[1] ANTON DEPROSSE (1838–78), *composer and pianoforte-teacher, Munich.*

2. The customary ending would be:

" I remain, with profoundest respect, Your Majesty's most humble and obedient —."

But these are bagatelles. The body of the letter is quite happily expressed.

I must now begin my letters with official bulletins, so here goes:

On Monday, April 10, my wife was delivered of a third daughter (Isolde) after a quick and, as far as one can tell, satisfactory confinement. Neither mother nor daughter gives cause for anxiety. Excellent nursing, glorious spring weather — *all right.*[1] As regards myself, I have my *eighth* pianoforte rehearsal today, not counting smaller private practices with individual singers. It will be a model performance.

TRISTAN	—	Schnorr (admirable)
ISOLDE	—	Frau Schnorr (ditto)
BRANGÄNE	—	Fräulein Deinet (extremely musical and hardworking)
KURWENAL	—	Mitterwurzer (magnificent)
MARK	—	Zottmayer (fine voice, but very imperfectly trained)
SEAMAN	—	Simons (good high baritone)
SHEPHERD	—	
MELOT	—	Heinrich (quite good enough for his few bars)

On Monday, Tuesday, and Wednesday there were orchestral rehearsals, one act conducted by me at each. The orchestra was docile and willing — winds especially were excellent — and the basses realized at once that I knew the ropes, and treated me with due respect. It made quite a sensation.

In the midst of this uninterrupted activity I feel as paradisically fit as never before.

And that idiot Truhn calls this sort of thing page's work. Quite apart from the honourable nature of the task — a real service to art — what a contrast it forms to my slavery for the Berlin Jews! The first performance is still announced for May 10, but it is possible that it will be postponed a day or two.

[1] *English in the original.* — TR.

You will hear, of course. If you see Dr. Hofmann, tell him that he, as *Tristan* enthusiast, will not be forgotten: that is, that he shall have a seat reserved if he has money, time, and the desire to hear it.

Have my busts arrived? Hautmann thinks they should have been there some time ago. But as neither you nor my mother has made any acknowledgment, I feel doubtful. . . .

Have had a glance at Michel's songs. A decided talent for dramatic expression. Here and there superficial amateurishness in the accompaniment. I will look into them more closely as soon as I have a spare quarter of an hour. What possesses you to think I should reject the first song? As a *song* it is the best; naïve and not trivial — that is high praise.

Tuesday the 18th is my third Platen recital.

The Saturday after, Schnorr will sing Beethoven and Liszt songs at my concert, I accompanying him. I can tell you, we are going gradually to clear things up here and thoroughly reorganize everything. . . .

122]

Munich
May 22, 1865
R. W[agner]'s birthday

You have a good nose. Singers' throats and so on led to a tragic postponement. The first performance is now on Wednesday the 24th, the second on Saturday, and the third on the Tuesday or Wednesday following.

After your last telegram I was bound to expect you here. I wanted to hand you my father-in-law's letter in person. Since you preferred the delights of Stettin, however, I am forwarding the precious document.

I no longer expect you, but have given you the dates so that you can still come if you like.

The newspaper screed was interesting, though nauseating. I hope you withheld your explanation, for I should consider it worthy of neither your reputation, your merits, nor your character. . . .

PS. I am not franking this, because of the enclosure. In some cases it is safer not. You will hear nothing more of *me* in *writing*. If you are anxious to do so you must come here!

123]

Munich
July 2, 1865

Your letter was forwarded to me at Baden-Baden, which place I was obliged to visit for a much needed change of air; also for the purpose of laying my farewell respects at the feet of Her Majesty, my so-called patron, and finally in order to pass Madame Viardot's [1] pupils in review. The very day after my audience, I heard through you of the Berlin rumours, of which I had been entirely ignorant.

It is not nice of you to have so little faith in my reliance on you as to suppose I should fail to inform you first of all of anything essential concerning my future or what not. I did not inform you of the immense *Tristan* success simply because I supposed you would never have doubted it. At least the Jewish critics have not been able to suppress or distort the event.

Yesterday's was the last performance, being the fourth — or fifth, counting the general rehearsal. Except for the first- and second-tier boxes — except for the real rabble, that is — the house was full in spite of raised subscription prices. The Schnorrs were recalled twice after each act, and the composer three times at the close. How's that, eh?

And so Wagner's most difficult and eccentric opera has received the best performance and the richest success. And that in Munich! Yes, but Munich has become the centre also of every artistic movement as of many another (time will show); yet I am expected to go back to the place where Jews abound and Offenbach and Meyerbeer have their principal altars — absurd!

Were I so unfortunate as to survive Wagner or King Ludwig II, I should go with my wife and children to Persia. Until then I shall sit tight here; though it will not prevent me from ruining

[1] PAULINE VIARDOT (1821–1910), *daughter and pupil of Manuel Garcia; sister of Malibran.*

a few Bechsteins in Holland, Belgium, and possibly north Germany next winter.

Schmidt the trombonist had to return to Berlin today. He did his job excellently. Wagner inquired particularly about him and I shall agree to having him engaged. I asked Schmidt to call on you and tell you all the details of the *Tristan* performances. If he does not come, please send for him.

Shall I, or shall I not, voice an idea that has just occurred to me? I should be glad if the various Berlin rumours of which you tell me could be made public in the popular press. It would do the *worse* part of the population of Munich no harm to discover that I was not entirely without value or interest, that Berlin did not exactly throw me out, but, on the contrary, would not be displeased if I went back. Can you do anything in that direction?

You know, though, that I do not like to commandeer my friends for *such* purposes when it is after all only a question of my own egoistical person. Therefore, if there is any difficulty about it, do not for heaven's sake trouble yourself.

What is Weitzmann doing? Silly fellow, we were so nice to him! I met him at the station and took him to R. W., would have invited him to the dinner the day after *Tristan*, had he stayed; but without a word he went off into the mountains with Seifriz [1] and Köhler,[2] stayed there two or three days, then without taking leave hurried back into the arms of his wife. And really I had no time to run after him.

What about Mützelburg? Kroll? Korff?

Goldstein [3] really is and always will be a brute. Do you really think him trustworthy as a banker? He has some small savings of mine, about 3,600 marks, which I should like to withdraw so that I need have no more dealings with the fellow. But as it is a case of the Austrian national loan, I hardly know whether it would be wise. Would you allow me to appoint you my chargé d'affaires with regard to him? You could then handle him at any time in the manner suited to the occasion.

[1] MAX SEIFRIZ (1827–85), Hofkapellmeister *at Löwenberg.*

[2] CH. LOUIS HEINRICH KÖHLER (1820–86), Theaterkapellmeister *at Königsberg, writer on music.*

[3] ED. JULIANITSCH GOLDSTEIN, *conductor, gave first performance of Mussorgsky's* Kovantschina *in Petrograd.*

How are you all? And the factory? And what of your brother's health?

Do send me the current gossip. I don't expect long proper letters from such a busy person, but should like frequent signs of life.

My wife sends kind messages and regrets, as I do, that you could not be present at the triumph of *Tristan*.

Thursday we shall probably have the *Flying Dutchman* (conducted by myself); Sunday, a grand official concert in the Residenztheater for H. M., conducted by Wagner: selections from *Rheingold*, *Meistersinger*, and so on. The newly-copied parts have still to be corrected. God bless our King!

PS. Liszt goes to Budapest in the middle of August for a music festival from the 20th to the 26th. How would it be if — ? N.B. He is not going there to read *masses!* Newspaper lies again. I *may* be playing at Wiesbaden on the 18th to raise money for the journey. How about — a pianoforte?

124]

Munich
August 4, 1865

THESE past few weeks have been very sad ones. We shall never recover from our terrible loss.[1] No worse blow could have befallen us. Yet life goes on — and we with it. There is no time for mourning. . . .

For the moment we are giving ourselves the relaxation of a visit to Pest (on the 8th), where we shall sun ourselves in Liszt's presence. You know there is a festival there to celebrate the twenty-fifth anniversary of the Pest-Ofen Music Society and Conservatorium.

They are doing the *Legend of St. Elisabeth*, conducted by the composer, on the 15th and 18th; there is a *Künstlerkonzert* on the 16th, and on the 20th a popular concert in the park. Now, could you not manage to come over for it? I write to insist on your coming, for I have not the eloquence to persuade you. Be

---

[1] *The death of the singer Schnorr (see page 4, note 4), who caught cold after the first performance of* Tristan *and died within a month.*

sensible and nice and charming about it. You know you belong to us. It is bad enough that you do not live in Munich. I want to see you and talk over things. It can't be done by letter, and, anyway, you are so sparing of your replies that our correspondence never really gets going. . . .

125]

Luitpoldstrasse 15
Munich
September 21, 1865

. . . THE latest is that I have decided to spend a month in Berlin and in the neighbourhood (Breslau, Hanover, etc.) and to give two, or possibly three, evening concerts. What do you say to it? Are you against it? I think not.

May I count upon your friendly services? The first would be to find me a convenient and not too expensive flat (two rooms, furnished bedroom) in a private hotel not far from the Bechstein establishment in the Behrenstrasse. I shall be writing to Bote and Bock next month about the announcements. I shall make the tickets dearer this time, if only because of the higher price of the Singakademie.

I am fairly free during the winter quarter of this year, but not so from the beginning of January on. Therefore I want to make use of my time in November. It might run to seven concerts in a week.

May I be frank about Hanover? Steinweg once offered to arrange everything for me there if (naturally) I would play his pianofortes. The first part of the proposal would suit me well, the second only if you did not object. Or, on the other hand, if you have a " Wolkenhauer " in Hanover who would act as my " *homme d'affaires*," I shall of course not trouble to write to Herr Steinweg.

Hanover has got to come, I have felt it in my bones for some time. I feel sure it is worth while.

What are you doing and how is your family? My wife has taken the liberty of asking yours to help her in a domestic matter, as my mother and sister are away from Berlin and " some clothes *had to be* dyed." Foolish, but true! Wagner is very well and is working as diligently as if the Holy Ghost were dictating to him. Well, and He does dictate to him. Ah, if He would but dictate to me! But enough, now it is your turn. This time I have so arranged matters that you cannot remain wrapped in your silence, haven't I?

I am quite looking forward to Berlin. I shall do all the sights, the museums, and perhaps the theatres. We live hermit-wise here.

Good-bye for today. Write soon, old man, in time to keep me from undertaking the wrong things, and support me in the right ones.

PS. Beautiful pianofortes! And I play more beautifully now too. You don't believe it? You will see. Since hearing Liszt again, I have got my paws into marvellous condition and shall send all your shanks and hammers flying for you! (I learned to bray like this in Pest.)

126]

Munich
September 29, 1865

Your kind letter just received. I must try not to abuse your friendly offers of help. . . .

To think that you were not in Pest when Liszt played! There will hardly be such a chance again anywhere. Although it is possible he may visit us in Munich this winter if, as we hope, the King should command a performance of *St. Elisabeth*. Then you would come over?

For consolation here is a photograph of Liszt, the latest from Pest. As you see, the clerical garb is not unbecoming to him. Imagine Taubert, Dorn, or Würst in it, though!

My wife thanks Frau Bechstein warmly for undertaking her little commission. As you only mention the "brown" of the children's clothes, she assumes that it was possible to dye her costume violet, as she wished, not being fond of brown for her own wear.

An influx of pupils has made me busy with teaching again.

A very talented American has run away from the Leipzig Conservatorium to come to me. Fräulein Heintz, being restored to favour, has turned up again, and similarly a very pretty girl from Brunswick.

Yesterday Marpurg [1] wrote to me from Sondershausen, asking me to recommend him a court pianist, able to play solos with and without accompaniment, but also to play second violin or viola at the so-called Loh concerts. There is a fixed salary of 400 talers, and ample opportunity to earn extra money by teaching. Comparatively little to do and long holidays. I can think of no suitable individual, particularly as regards the second condition (fiddling). Do you know anyone? Would Werkenthin [2] care for it (he plays the fiddle) or Rötscher, [3] about whom I cannot say? I mentioned both the names to Marpurg. If you can suggest anyone who would like the post, I will willingly try to arrange it.

Here all is peace at present, but soon, soon, we may expect decisive events.

So that is all that the backing of Berlin's foremost critics could do for our good Willmers? H'm! And Julius Stern has turned courtier, Stern the progressive! Shade of Bismarck!

What about the Gesellschaft der Musikfreunde? Bronsart? Nothing decided or projected? . . .

127]

Munich
October, 1865

Best thanks for yours. Have written Bachmann and explained how things stand. On the 18th and 25th — whatever happens — I am in Hanover; on the 7th and 11th, in Breslau; on the 5th, in Berlin. It just occurs to me that you may as well save yourself the trouble of flat-hunting, for I shall be travelling most of the time. So that a hotel or furnished flat (not a furnished room)

[1] FRIEDRICH MARPURG (1825–84), *violinist, pianist, composer (pupil of Mendelssohn),* Hofkapellmeister *at Sondershausen.*
[2] ALBERT WERKENTHIN (1842–1914), *pupil of Bülow at the Stern Conservatoire. later teacher there. Composer, critic, author of a book on pianoforte-playing.*
[3] RÖTSCHER (1853–71), *dramatic artist and critic, Berlin.*

by the day may come to the same thing? . . . I want there to
be no misunderstandings on any point and should not like you
to think — you, of all people — that I am given to pettiness and
incapable of forgetting injuries, that I bear malice and so on;
in a word, that I am not the conductor of *Tristan*.

If I do not intend to send out press tickets in Berlin, it is
not a question of rancour. I know them, the rotters. Did my absence cause them to stop their villainies? Think how they lied
about Munich. They neither can nor ever will do me any good.
To do me harm, on the contrary, is in their power: that is, the
power of the press (with all due respect) enables them to do
so. They would spoil my prospects for Berlin, for Hanover,
and even for Munich. Or do you doubt that wherever I have
enemies and enviers — which is everywhere — every unfavourable line in a Berlin paper would be joyfully pounced upon,
reprinted, and circulated. "There, you see, in Berlin they think
nothing of him — he could not stay there — and we Munichites
are to have a Berlin failure dumped on us as an authority." Yes,
yes, my friend. I have had my experiences, and every one of
them invariably teaches me that it is impossible to see black
enough. The German music world is a Sodom. Berlin was hell
to me; Munich, if I stay, is purgatory at least.

Can you give me any positive proof that I am mistaken in
the case of Berlin? If so, I should certainly follow your kind
advice.

Now this — (*see* parliamentary dictionary) of a railway
management has taken off the noon express, and I do not know
whether I shall leave here on Wednesday morning or evening.
You know how I hate day travelling. I will let you know, however. . . .

Meanwhile my best thanks. Take care you don't get ill, so
that we may have some pleasant hours together.

PS. For your amusement I enclose a caricature. Wagner is
in Vienna until the end of the week. Bülow is for the present
" director " of nothing but " his own affairs."

Motto as ever: *All* or *nothing*, chances being in favour of
the former. But it takes time. If it comes off, you will see something.

128]

Breslau
November 10, 1865

BEST thanks for yours. It is ghastly here. But the press was so unanimously (all five papers) and fabulously kind that it nearly put me in a good temper. I didn't realize that my recent success had been so considerable. It is even possible that my concert tomorrow will be relatively fuller than the first Berlin one. Bock sent a letter; meanwhile the correspondence with the Old Testament patriarch was rather more lively than my nerves could stand. But people seem to be growing more reasonable. The letters are less and less objectionable, so that there is some possibility of a peaceful settlement. At least I do not despair of it yet. . . .

Has Wickede [1] left, and Moritz? The Damrosches return warmest greetings. I took your omission to say good-bye on my own head, so do not worry. Kindest regards to your wife, and put on something nice for us at the theatre.

129]

Munich
January 13, 1866

I WAS, to begin with, rather reluctant to start on my journey — it is an awkward one to Amsterdam — and on the top of it I developed a violent cold. I therefore cancelled it by wire and am still in Munich. Your recent telegram, for which many thanks, I have just made use of by writing to Herr Schmitz to ask him to let me know whether the Barmen concert can take place between the 18th and 22nd of January. I shall then arrange to play at Duisburg the day before or after, acting on the advice of Professor Nohl, [2] who has many friends and acquaintances there. Should the museum hall (or whatever there is) at Barmen not be available, I can fall back on the room you recommended to me at Elberfeld. . . .

[1] FRIEDRICH VON WICKEDE (1834–1904), *Civil Servant and composer.*
[2] LUDWIG NOHL (1831–85), *the Beethoven writer.*

N.B. Wagner is in Geneva, not Paris; so there you see again how the papers lie and invent for the mere fun of the thing.

Yours sincerely,

BÜLOW,

enemy of the freedom of the press (except when it's a matter of very pretty ladies), admirer of Bismarck the Great, etc.

PS. Why doesn't Tausig go to Perl and so make the concerts of the Gesellschaft der Musikfreunde play into his hands? If only my friends would have a little sense!

Shall I find one of *your pianofortes* at Duisburg?

130]

Munich
February 14, 1866

As you have not thought good to tell me of your " attachment," I really ought not to congratulate you. But I can't play the innocent, so here goes: Bravo!

Meanwhile you have a bone to pick with me; or, rather, I with you.

That pianoforte of yours on which I played at Barmen (Elberfeld) was very good, but I endured tortures at the concert through its heavy inelastic touch and its bad repetition (in *forte*, satisfactory in *piano* and *pp*). In short, I had to make superhuman efforts. You are growing very selfish — in making it sound soft and more pleasing to the audience you allow the individuality of the music and the player to go by the board. I was obliged suddenly to reject the interpretation of years and conform to the mood of the pianoforte action. Having made oneself master of the composition, one is to become the slave of the instrument! Much obliged!

But now comes an opportunity to atone for what you have done. On the 15th and 22nd of March I am playing in Düsseldorf, in between those dates at Barmen again and at Cologne. I am prepared, if you behave nicely, utterly to smash your rivals (the Klemens and the Parisians), but — you must send me pianofortes to my taste. Believe me, it is better worth your while to work for *me* than for a Gustav Schumann and his like!

It would be nice if you would take a little exercise (it always does you good when I suggest it) and meet on the Rhine.

For I suppose you would not care to come here?

There is my first evening recital on the 17th, the second on the 26th, and a possible third on March 8 (for the benefit of the Bavarian victims of the fire).

On the 24th there is the grand performance of *St. Elisabeth* at the Royal Court Theatre. I conduct it, of course, and am already having daily rehearsals, now for soloists, now for chorus or orchestra. It will go well. We shall probably repeat it on the 28th. Later there is a private performance of Liszt's symphonic poems for His Majesty, who has also deigned to command me to prepare *model performances* of *Tannhäuser* and *Lohengrin*. The rehearsals begin in April, the performances are in May. Then, in the middle of June, I conduct the Coburg festival.

So you see I am in full swing. In spite of Schiedmayer I was received with colossal enthusiasm at Stuttgart. Shall probably be there for the 31st. Should love to play a Bechstein there some time. So would Pruckner,[1] *also* because Schiedmayer is such an impossibly conceited and disagreeable fellow. Ratzenberger longs to do the same at Würzburg; he is a decent sort and quite a good pianist. In Würzburg there are plenty of moneyed visitors (Russian, English, and so on, attracted by the famous doctors) who might well buy pianofortes. Why do you leave such a preserve to Blüthner? How I have cursed those wooden boxes of his! Particularly for their poor tone, their plebeian character. All the same, their action was *far* easier than that of your Barmen (*Erbarmen*) grand.

Well, I suppose you think I've been abusive long enough. Herr Franz Schmitz will have told you the gist of the Elberfeld newspaper war. Very entertaining. It is my fate to cause scandal and rouse temper by even my most peaceful attitudes. . . .

Raff wants a pianist for Wiesbaden who can also teach at the conservatorium that is being founded there. Have recommended Werckenthin and Barth.

The meaning of the black seal? Liszt's excellent mother died, after a short illness, on the 6th of this month. Seventy-eight. I wish she could have had the joy of seeing her son this

---

[1] DIONYS PRUCKNER (1834–96), *pupil of Liszt.*

year and of witnessing his triumph as a composer (performance of his great mass in Saint-Eustache on March 15, followed by a concert with the symphonic poems). But in this lousy world everything goes wrong — nothing happens at the right time.

Would you have the enclosed pitched into a letter-box for me? *Better still if it can be delivered direct.*

PS. Nothing fixed for end of March in Holland yet. Have you any influence in Cologne? I want someone to recommend me a concert-arranger there (music-shopkeeper or something of the sort), as I propose to launch an attack on Hiller [1] and his clique very shortly.

131]

Munich
February 25, 1866

THIS is merely a telegram to announce the enormous and completely unopposed success of *St. Elisabeth,* which was repeated at the Court Theatre on March 1. Everything went beautifully. It was impressive in every respect, important as art and effective for the public. I am rather tired today and have still to give a small festival dinner at the Bayrischer Hof at three. In March we are to give three public concerts by royal command with instrumental works by Beethoven (*Coriolan, Eroica,* the *Ninth*) and Liszt's *Faust Symphony, Tasso, Hungaria,* etc. My second soirée next Tuesday. A great improvement on last winter. . . .

Pruckner was here yesterday. Believe me, he's a thoroughly good-hearted, decent fellow with a craving for grand pianofortes; he was inconsolable at having missed you. A pupil was playing in his room in his absence when you left your card. Asks me to thank you for calling and express his regret at not seeing you. . . . You shall have more communications of sorts presently, when the Rhenish concerts begin to define themselves. Meanwhile kindest regards, also from my wife, to you and Frau Bechstein.

[1] FERDINAND VON HILLER (1811–85), *composer, pianist, conductor, and teacher, pupil of Mendelssohn. Not to be confused with the composer Adam Hiller.*

Have given up Paris on the plea of pressure of business. The Dutch tour will probably fall through too.

PS. In the *Augsburger Allgemeine* there will shortly be a notice by Cornelius of yesterday's performance.

132]

Munich
March 6, 1866

. . . I AM very much upset to hear that you cannot meet me on the Rhine yourself. Had counted on it. Confound your philistine festivities. If you see so little of my society, you will become a philistine yourself. It makes me almost sorry to be no longer in " Bismarckopel." For the last soirée tonight there has not been a ticket to be had since yesterday morning. I am becoming tremendously the fashion and even popular.

How the gallery roared at the repetition of *St. Elisabeth* the other day! You should have heard them! And these are the very people who were ready to stone me less than a year ago!

The Thirty-three Variations *electrified* everyone here the other day. Certainly my bright idea for the program was chiefly responsible. I ought to have done it before in Breslau and Berlin. But one lives and learns how to awaken people's interest.

Tomorrow my wife is going to Wagner in Geneva for about a fortnight. Our poor lonely great man is in need of a little consolation and friendship. . . .

133]

Munich
April 5, 1866

I AM just as hoarse as I was on the 25th. All the same, I held four big orchestral rehearsals and last night achieved a quite excellent performance. Audience small, but very enthusiastic. It tasted " fine," as we used to say in that æsthetic Jew-ridden Berlin. How it thundered from the gallery at the close! The King quite enraptured; ditto the ducal family.

A pity my Berlin friends could not have been present on this compensatory occasion!

Tell me more about your adventures. We parted at such breakneck speed that our usual farewell shots were not fired.

There are various things I want to know for the sake of fitting in future plans.

I am terribly sorry that I was too late in writing to the authorities about your friend Fricke.[1] Dr. Schmidt of Vienna had already accepted. Betz [2] will come, I hope. Unfortunately he is making difficulties over his contract, which is a pity, as he could hardly have been more courteously treated. The contract was sent to him with all the pecuniary conditions left blank for him to fill in at his discretion.

Are you still in the same amiable frame of mind, and will you send me some English fancy biscuits and an instalment of cigarettes? In that case, please give Perl only a hundred talers or thereabouts, and reserve the other fifteen to pay for these. . . .

With regard to Wagner's return, things have begun to shape favourably.

Do you hear anything of Death and the Devil, Truhn and Tausig, from the Danish towns? I'm very curious to know how *that* came off.

134]

Munich
April 11, 1866

As you see from this mode of address, dear Friend *and* Bechstein, it's again a question of pianofortes.

I had really given up the Amsterdam excursion when my father-in-law suddenly asked me to meet him there. They offer me five hundred florins for the two concerts, so I can now afford to take my wife with me.

Liszt arrives on the 23rd and I shall also be there on that

---

[1] RICHARD FRICKE, *bassist at the Berlin Royal Opera, later in Dresden.*
[2] FRANZ BETZ (1835–1900), *baritone at the Berlin Royal Opera, the first Hans Sachs.*

day if possible. Rehearsal on the evening of the 24th, concert on the 25th, and for me again on the 27th *chez* Stumpff.

On the 27th the *Graner Mass* is to be given in Liszt's honour — the *eighth* performance in Amsterdam; on the 25th, Liszt's *Psalm XIII* and the Second Pianoforte Concerto with myself as soloist.

The point is, my dear Bechstein, there is at present no pianoforte of yours in the place — so Roothaan tells me — so let me know if you can send me one and bring yourself with it? It is so much easier a journey from Berlin than from here. The weather is charming, and who knows whether we shall ever hear the Master in Germany again! They say he is going to withdraw still further from the world on his return to Rome.

So you will give a fine instrument, won't you, as I shall be playing to Liszt!

Wagner has moved to Lucerne.

Today week there will be the second concert in the theatre: Liszt's *Hungaria*, the *Eroica*, and in between several pieces for pianoforte.

Herr von der Tann made his début at the Odeon the day before yesterday with Schumann's pianoforte concerto. He played excellently and was enormously liked. His Bechstein grand still sounds splendid. Young Bärmann is saving up, his father tells me, to buy one of your instruments in due course.

Do get yourself cured. I was so sorry to hear of your going back to Berlin in such a state. Now perhaps your wife will not allow you to take any more long journeys! . . .

135]

Triebschen, near Lucerne
July 15, 1866

ALL *this for yourself alone!*

I have received your — too gushing — letter. Did I not grow soberer every day, I might think myself a devil of a fine fellow when you praise me as your " rescuer." Seriously, I am delighted to have been able to do you that small service — a pity it could not have been five times as great! For the present

let the insignificance of the object prevent you from feeling yourself under any obligation. Time enough for that. And, by the
way, is it not incredible how much time we all have? Up to the
present I have really come to no positive decision about my
future. I wait in hope that things will change in Munich —
though without there being the least probability of it — and
content myself with the negative certainties of my position. To
remain in Munich is pretty well impossible; to return to Berlin,
absolutely impossible, if only from material motives. Living is
too dear there for me — I have no prospect of any *fixum* —
lessons bring in nothing, and the concert season is sure to be
a rotten one this winter, when, I suppose, music will be made
for the benefit of the killed and wounded exclusively. So what
then?

Paris or London impossible for the like reasons. Especially
as the Music of the Future is anathema there. There remains
Florence or Milan. I shall see how the land lies there as soon as
is feasible. America? That would be the most sensible perhaps.
But — you know the law of supply and demand — the sum
which Strakosch [1] offered me through Röder, eighteen months
ago, was exceedingly small. Today, if I were to propose myself,
I should probably have to be content with less. All the same, I
feel inclined to do so in default of anything better. The question
is, how to contrive that Strakosch or Ullmann should hear indirectly of my inclination. Do advise me if you have any idea.
Could you find out diplomatically from the theatrical agent
Röder where Strakosch is at present and insinuate to the latter
(through a third party) that I was now prepared to consider *reasonable* proposals? Or I may still throw my false or real modesty
to the winds and write to Strakosch direct. Only I must first have
his address. Can you get me it?

One more request today: *please take out a subscription in my
name* for the *Norddeutsche Allgemeine* in Berlin for the current
quarter and let me have the copies sent here *daily, post-free.*
Here we read mostly south German papers, all more or less anti-
Prussian, and I am longing to revel in my triumph as an " intolerant Bismarck-supporter." Austria, Bösendorfer, Schweighofer are all going to pieces. Are you not glad? To me, Bismarck

---

[1] MORITZ STRAKOSCH, *pianist and impresario.*

represents revolution in its most uncompromisingly energetic aspect — at least today, and you know that, as a revolutionary, I am notoriously " anti-progressive."

Presently it will be my turn to ask you a great favour. When the time comes and I can *without risk* clear up and *pack*, I hope you will not refuse your aid. I am terribly unpractical and have no intimate friends in the place. So would you come over for a week and help me to put my house in order? Can you, will you? And I should be so glad if you would store everything I should do better not to take to Florence with me: my library, works of art, pictures, busts, and so on. Tell me if I may rely on you, and in any case write soon.

PS. Let me tell you something that will help you to understand many things: a certain letter which pleased you particularly was literally dictated by Richard (Würst).

Cigarettes not yet arrived. Let us hope for a daily increase in the activity of the *Prussian* postal authorities.

Would Stern reconsider the matter? Sound him, just for a joke.

136]

Triebschen, near Lucerne
August 5, 1866

STILL none of the promised cigarettes. Is Pulgian-Hirsch-Budethal dead? Have you yourself departed this life? Did my letter to you of about a month ago go astray? Or has the consignment of tobacco been intercepted by a Bavarian commander-in-chief?

Or has your dislike of writing, which has not so far affected me greatly, risen to such a pitch that you have destroyed all the writing-materials in the house? Be that as it may, we have a truce at last. Not that it pleases me, for Prussia's enemies, among which I count all anti-Bismarckians, have not been at all adequately punished; but I should like to benefit by it to the extent of a letter from you. Bismarck, Mützelburg, Perl have all written to me — you have maintained a placid silence.

I conjure you by the name of Hannibal: answer my last

letter, always supposing that it ever reached you. There is one point in particular about which I am anxious to hear. I asked you to get Strakosch's address out of that theatre-pirate Röder. Before I import or export myself to Italy for good, I wanted to try to get one decent transatlantic engagement; but I do not know what steps I ought now to take about it. It would have to come off as soon as possible.

Break your intriguing silence and let me blot out this bad spell, unless you want me to think you will have no more to do with me.

At the end of this month I am going to Munich for a short time to convince myself that my wife can spend the winter there without danger. For during the first experimental year in Italy (probably Milan) I can only live as a bachelor. It would be rash to move there with the family straight away.

In the name of St. Michael, send me the promised cigarettes!

Would you also do me the kindness of asking Robert Lienau (Schlesinger) when he is going to send me the score of *Euryanthe* which I ordered for Wagner. Perhaps you would pay him in my name temporarily and enter it to my account.

137]

Triebschen
August 5, 1866

THE cigarettes have arrived safely in unexpected profusion. All the better. I shall leave half for the Master. 'Leave'? Yes, in three or four days I am going back to Munich with my wife, whatever the risk. It has to come; why wait any longer? Our personal horizon, far from being clearer, is decidedly more overcast; which makes it all the more urgent to carry out the inevitable decisions, or at least the essential preliminaries. Once I have done what is most necessary and convinced myself that my wife can spend the winter in Munich without anxiety as to life and property, I shall get ready to start for — Milan, Turin, and Florence I have postponed for various reasons, but if I can wait until October 1, it will come off then. Perhaps some favour-able Berlin or American proposal will come along in between and upset my plans. Last week, Aide-de-camp Prince T. U. T.[1] was here. It was terrible. Both indirectly and directly we learned through him that there is no more hope of justice or recognition for us in Munich, no fulfilment of the royal promises. My dear Bechstein, it is impossible to see things in a black enough light. I thought I did, but —

[Fragment]

Triebschen, near Lucerne
August 13, 1866

Things have turned out far blacker than I foresaw.

What do you say to this proposal, so close upon us, of a war between Prussia and France? As a business man, how does it smile on you? I regard the fatality (for such it will be) as unavoidable. Bavaria and Württemberg will side with the French. Oh, we shall see some pretty things. Bismarck is too noble to surrender the left bank of the Rhine without a struggle, but the war will take it as its spoil, depend upon it. Napoleon can do this one thing more if he will, and that he most emphatically will we can hardly doubt at this stage. Many thanks for the two numbers of the *Norddeutsche Zeitung*. To my amazement, each had a two silver groschen stamp on it. Since when has the wrapper tax been raised so scandalously? Or was it an oversight? As I shall be packed and ready to go when these lines reach you, please stop sending the paper here. I should rather have any sort of news by letter from you than the finest politics.

So will you address your next syllabus to the beautiful address: Munich, Luitpoldstrasse 15. N.B. Do you remember a man called *Nicholson*? He is wandering about Munich, enticed thither perhaps — or probably — by a perfectly infamous rumour that is rife at court. Is it not frightful? How can one stay in such a place? Wouldn't one be bound to get away even if one were nailed to it?

PS. I wonder if you could make inquiries direct of Graf Redern about my affair? You see, I am still thinking of the impossible return to Berlin.

[1] LUDWIG *of Bavaria's aide, Prince Thurn und Taxis.*

138]

Triebschen, near Lucerne
August 6, 1866

As it so often happens, I wrote you a lamentable letter yesterday in which my eloquence ran riot over the sorrow your many weeks' silence had caused me, and the first post this morning brings me *your* letter, which renders my effusion quite superfluous. I am answering by return so that you may know that yours has arrived.

Best thanks for all notices, expert and other opinions. Your offer to write to Steinweg's through a third person is most acceptable.

Perhaps these gentlemen could find me a reputable and yet shrewd agent who would arrange everything for me. Berlin, you ask? I might of course go back and face the derision of those sausages, vultures, angels, and what not if there were anything positive and solid in the background. . . . The court of Queen Augusta is horrified at my ingratitude in exchanging an unsalaried " honorary post " with her so suddenly and unceremoniously for a more salaried prospect in Munich. They would insist on a *Regina, peccavi* from me, and if I were so weak as to give way to them, they would leave me to kick my heels. As to their wretched court concerts, Bronsart on the one hand and Tausig on the other would keep me out of them. It would be the same with other things. I could only go back to Berlin if either Stern or Kullak gave me a decent engagement at the conservatorium and I received supplementary proposals from the court at the same time.

If I am to be reduced to playing in private, then let it be in some Italian town where there are English people and so on, and one is secure from colleagues, in particular German musicians with their beggar-like importunity and jealous intrigues. Munich? I have no more faith in it; Ludwig, the child? Nine hundred years ago a German emperor once bore that name. All the same I shall at the end of the month look into and consider the circumstances once more.

Meanwhile I am corresponding with friends in Italy to collect information about a suitable place in which to settle, but no one so far has been very enlightening. In the beginning of October I shall probably go over myself — grope by the aid of my own eyes and sniff with my own nose.

You see from the above that I am by no means throwing your friendly suggestions to the winds and that I am determined to consider everything most carefully before I make a definite decision.

Many, many thanks for your willingness to give me the assistance I shall probably need in Munich when packing up to go. If it is at all possible, I will spare you; I fear, though, that you will not be released from your promise.

Bavaria is not dangerous, but the Jesuits and the mob which is egged on by them. They have made it impossible for us to stay in Munich, nest of Jesuits that it is. There is just *one* possibility (though even then it would be sufficiently uncomfortable): that the principal *canaille* — that creature of the Jesuits whom Friedrich Wilhelm IV in polite irony called the " chief bourgeois " — may be forced to retire. This is bound to be decided very soon. If one had but access to the great Bismarck and could explain Bavarian conditions to him! He could help us all quite easily. Unfortunately, neither R. W. nor I has any claim on him unless it be that I have " compromised " myself by the public confession of my intolerant devotion to him. It pleases me to think that this was before the world discovered his greatness.

So you think you are to be promoted to " Imperial " purveyor. When? . . .

I am glad you are feeling cheerful and seem to be so well. I wish I could keep my nose in the air a bit.

Tr[uhn] and Ta[usig]. Death and the Devil! That must be a crazy household! Remack wrote to say he had heard from Tausig that Truhn had quietly vanished, leaving his unpaid bills as a pledge behind him. So see that he does not blow in on you one of these days.

139]

Lucerne
August 24, 1866

You are one of the noblest and kindest of men I ever knew, and therefore one of the noblest and kindest in existence; for how incredibly many people have I known and not liked in my life! I am greatly touched by your letter and all the refreshing, practical signs of sympathy that it contains.

Now listen. Time brings wisdom. I have to tell you of a new turn in my affairs which arose out of an idea of my own and is about to be given a practical " shove." I am going for the present to Basel as a bachelor. On September 15. It is near to Wagner and not far from Munich, where I still hope to leave my wife for the winter, as a complete removal would be inadvisable in more ways than one. In Basel I shall find plenty to do, playing (the neighbouring Alsatian towns — Mühlhausen, Thunn, and others — are badly in need of music), earning money, and gradually, by modest plodding, tenacity, and resignation, achieving the little that I can expect after all my more important prospects have been dashed, my health lowered, my nerves wrecked, and my mind strained. *Basel* it is, then. Don't talk of America (I feel too weak), of Italy (too risky, too utterly uncertain), of Berlin, least of all of Munich (why this last is so impossible I can only tell you by word of mouth in strict secrecy).

Nevertheless I am very pleased and grateful for all the steps you have taken in my interest. It was a good idea to talk to St[ern] too. The explanation of his stiffneckedness is simple: he has already engaged Brassin,[1] a good pianist who made his name through the Patti-Ullmann lot. So you see Stern is provided for. I was glad to hear of the American correspondence also. Nothing should be left untried. I can now retire to Basel with all the better conscience, for after all I can be effective, make myself felt there as soon as my own position is to some extent defined. If you have a chance of speaking to Redern I

---

[1] LOUIS BRASSIN (1840–84), *pianist, pupil of Moscheles, teacher at the Stern Conservatoire.*

should be glad. Not that I have the least doubt that nothing whatever will be done for me, but to have this, so to say, officially confirmed would soothe me still more.

Could you talk to Hans von Korff? He is a relative of Count Eulenburg, through whom one might perhaps get our great Bismarck interested in me. After all, the whole trouble in Munich arose from my being a Prussian and a Bismarckian. In all the ultramontane papers inflammatory articles denounced the Prussian agent and spy Hans von Bülow and accused me of the authorship of every anti-Bavarian article in the Berlin *Nationalzeitung*.

Your telegram the other day was a happy thought. It intensified the effect of the warnings I had received from Munich, which I had been inclined rather to discredit. Instead of going to Munich I therefore went straight to Basel, where I saw Dr. Merian and discussed with him the matter of my settling there.

Merian's grand has worn very well except in the treble, which shows severe signs of wear and is shrill. I consoled him by telling him that, when I came to Basel, you may be persuaded to pay me a flying visit and undertake to do a little repairing.

Here is a big request or a small nuisance, as you like to take it.

Merian is my political co-religionist and he yearns to possess a *good bust of Count Bismarck* (plaster or ivory) and I want to make him a present of it. Would you be so very kind as to obtain one and have it well packed and sent to him, as soon as possible? Address: Herrn Dr. Emil Merian, Neue Vorstadt, opposite the Hospital.

And pay it out for me for the moment, my dear creditor and debtor. I don't want my two thousand just now. For heaven's sake keep this sum and use it as and when you want it — until I am on my beam ends again. But I shall not be in that state again just yet; that is the point of Basel.

On the first of the month I return to Munich with my wife to arrange things, pack, and so on. If things go badly there, I shall repeat my great request of some weeks back: that you will come and help me in the disposal of my possessions and the like. In Munich I have no Bechstein, no half-, no quarter-

Bechstein available for such friendly services. Should it be at all possible, I will spare you the agonizing cry, the appeal to your friendship to undertake this tiresome task.

I am really hugely anxious to see you; everything that I have been and still am unable to explain to you in writing will be quite easy to tell you by word of mouth, when I need not weigh my words and am able to put right any misunderstandings on the spot.

I am sure you are glad it is Basel, and not Milan or Florence? I am saving up my Florence for ten years hence.

Reading your letter again for something like the fifth time, I feel, my dear fellow, that Berlin is really impossible. What connexions should I have there on which to build? The Gesellschaft der Musikfreunde? Wrecked by Bronsart. Stern, who pays for my lodging? You know how it stands there. The court? No serious interest, no stability. The public? Remember our experience in the beginning of last winter: without your generous assistance I should have been bankrupt.

Above all, you see, Basel secures me *nearness to Wagner*. You did not understand about the *Norddeutsche*. I am very glad to have it and they charge me nothing for it. I was only surprised to see such an expensive stamp as the *two* silver groschen on each wrapper. To amuse you I enclose a letter from Satter, which of course I shall not answer. If it should be necessary, I authorize you to *show* it, but please keep it for me eventually. An even more grotesque epistle from this swine arrived simultaneously for the Master, who equally of course has not replied.

140]

Basel
St. Johann Vorstadt, No. 31
October 26, 1866

How are you, my dear friend?

This time it is I who owe you a letter for a change. First of all, my belated thanks for the American notices and suggestions. Strakosch unacceptable; Steinweg, on the other hand, has written direct and I shall consider his offer for next year. One

Koch of Brunswick, public prosecutor (do you know anything about him?), forwarded me his letter.

For the present I stick to Basel. See enclosure.

I played on your pianoforte the other day (Raff quintet), and my pupil Levin of Hamburg used it shortly after for the Schumann quartet, which he played quite respectably. The pianoforte created a furore, as a result of which you will soon receive an order (with a card of recommendation from me) for (unfortunately) only a *semi*-grand from Frau Burkhardt-Stefanie. According to my pupil Holcamp, everybody is asking about Bechsteins. How are you doing elsewhere? Annexed many towns? Congratulations in case!

Have found no house for the family here yet. My wife and children are therefore still in Lucerne. Return to Munich very, very doubtful. True, the chief scoun . . . (you know, the one you loved so dearly that all my blandishments could not induce you to part with a pianoforte to him!) has been sent about his business, though decorated of course with a broad ribbon back and front, but this would only be the preliminary of preliminaries towards cleaning up the place in such a manner as to make it fit for me again. And I have small reason to hope that the needful will be done.

Just one query. At Mühlhausen we also intend to give trio evenings with solos interspersed. But there is a lack of good pianofortes. Would it be possible to place an instrument there for a month or two, say four to six weeks? Mühlhausen is an enormously wealthy town and there is no doubt that your pianoforte would be sold there in a very short time. It might indeed be a very good beginning in French territory. What do you think? If it causes any difficulties, I must do what I can with a Pleyel (which the firm will probably send me). To drag the pianoforte I have about with me would be an anxious and expensive business. Think it over and send me word.

How are Tausig and his enterprise? I hope you can send me good news of them.

Bismarck arrived safely. Many thanks. Write another nice long letter soon (miss a performance of *L'Africaine* to do it!) and enliven my solitude. Really I'm almost ready to hang myself. Health not so terribly good either. I have fever nearly every

evening about six and am taking quinine for it. But in these circumstances the remoteness of Basel suits me better than any
other place to stay in. When I read the fourth page of the
Kreuzzeitung (the mass of concerts and so on), I feel as jubilant
as a Red Indian (see *L'Africaine*) that I did not return to the
Jews' capital. I couldn't stand it with my nerves as they are.

Next year, though, I shall take a proper cure at St. Moritz
and then go to America early in the autumn. . . .

142]

Basel
November 22, 1866

. . . Do send the enclosed program with my best greetings to Kiel [1] and tell him his trio was most carefully rehearsed
and had an unusually good reception. It is the first time anything
by Kiel has been heard in Switzerland. If we give a third cycle,
we shall play either a violin sonata or another trio by him. May
that console him for the Satter affair. How it did make me laugh!
All the same, that beast Satter was a profound judge of men!

First soirée at Mühlhausen the day after tomorrow.

Last Sunday Jaell [2] was the soloist at the subscription concerts. He played a horrible concerto by Hiller very well indeed, then some Chopin, Rheinberger, etc., coarsely and in the
worst taste. He is going off as a pianist, our good fat Jaell, and
really he will have to have a grand " cut out " for him next to
give him room to sit. His Erard was not up to much and was
considerably inferior to my Bechstein in every respect.

You will perhaps be interested to hear that I went to Mühlhausen for the Joachim concert a fortnight ago, when I renewed
my friendly relation with that unique (really unique) artist after
an interval of ten years. It was an impressive moment for me.
But it had to take place on French soil, our meeting; German soil
is too infamous in my eyes.

Heavens, man! Are you still thinking of my return to Berlin?
Never — never, said the stone statue on the Leipziger Platz.

[1] FRIEDRICH KIEL (1821–85), *composer and teacher.*
[2] ALFRED JAELL (1832–82), *violinist and pianist.*

Rather Munich, in spite of everything. There it was only the human side of me that suffered; in Berlin it was the artist, and unspeakably, incurably. Can you tell me of a single real friend in Berlin except yourself? Leaving out Tausig — I wish him all success. " Good night, Jews," says Remack. . . .

I shall certainly accept the Steinweg offer for next autumn (1867). . . .

143]

Basel
31 Vorstadt St. Johann
December 1, 1866

You are a splendid fellow. The letter to Merian came very promptly. He wrote at once to thank you and has dispatched the keyboard.

The point of my writing is to ask you particularly to hurry on the repairs and return it as soon as possible. Why?

Because by the 16th at latest I *must* arrange a matinee at Merian's for my admirable pupil Götz [1] of Königsberg, at present organist at Winterthur. He has a couple of charming manuscripts — a pianoforte trio for me — with which he is to make his début before the connoisseurs and amateurs here. The poor fellow has been under the thumb of the Schumann clique in Switzerland and we want to help him to break loose and gain the recognition he deserves.

There is a nice concert the same day. I am playing Beethoven's E flat Concerto and the Hungarian Fantasia (with orchestral cheese) by Liszt. Almost the whole of the Berloiz *Romeo and Juliet* symphony is to be played too. (N.B. I am not conducting it, but am superintending rehearsals.) . . .

Today is the day on which the Great Knave of Munich [2] enters the ranks of the hereditary nobility and is kicked out of the royal Cabinet with all his dirty crowd. . . .

[1] HERMANN GÖTZ (1840–76), *composer, pupil of Bülow at the Stern Conservatoire, composed the opera* Der widerspänstigen Zähmung, *based on* The Taming of the Shrew.

[2] PFORDTEN (*see page 27, note 1*), *who had been relieved of his duties by the King on December 1, 1866. Hohenlohe succeeded him, and Pfistermeister's post went to the more sympathetic Neumayr.*

If you see Kiel, tell him that his trio went down very well in Zürich too and that the Swiss will now begin to take notice of him. Perhaps Rieter-Biedermann will make him a proposal one of these days. (Peters does little for his firm, is too Jewish, stingy over advertising and so on.)

144]

Basel
December 17, 1866

No miracles, please! The hundred and twenty-five reichstalers left over from Düsseldorf must have gone long ago in cigarettes, Bismarck busts, and the like. But Schmidt has already sent the clothes, to my great satisfaction, so I will only thank you for so promptly carrying out my wishes and for all your news. Bravo, Tausig! He knows how to do it. Just the right one for the Berliners. How I laughed over " Madam "! But then you tell it all so humorously.

As regards *your* request to become the possessor of a bust of Liszt, my wife wishes to give herself the pleasure of sending you the latest executed by the Russian sculptor Lax in Munich, as a Christmas present.

Yesterday I played the Beethoven E flat here with unprecedented success. A pity you were not here — I should have been unusually inspired by my jealousy of Tausig's success, still singing in your ears. There was a very fair performance of Berlioz's *Romeo and Juliet* at the same concert. . . .

I give more private lessons now than I did in Berlin or Munich, and do not mind it. They are more appreciative here. One talented young lady from Alsace makes a fifty-mile journey twice a week on my account. . . .

PS. By the way, what is Perl up to? I have heard nothing for so long! Surely not gone bankrupt? Do send me a nice photograph of yourself some time (*with* your order!).

145]

Basel
February 1, 1867

IT is rude of me not to have thanked you yet for the beautiful grand you sent to Baden. I as nearly as possible did not get it. It was a job to transport it back from Freiburg in time. I gave it a good dose of playing there and managed to get rid of the cold and stiffness by rubbing the keys and applying warm cloths, after which it responded splendidly.

Unfortunately I heard from Pohl that he had sent it back before your orders came to dispatch it to Cologne. A pity! But you see how zealous we were about returning it. Here is Pohl's notice of the concert, which may amuse you.

Some of the great were present, the Hesses (she is Prince Karl's daughter), Augustenburg, and others. . . . Tomorrow we are playing at Schaffhausen, and a week hence I have a concert at Lausanne (Pleyel).

So you see I am in full swing. A great many lessons — more than I ever had in Berlin — and more discreet people to deal with, who do not steal two hours where I only owe them one. How wise I was not to succumb to the enticements of you and my Berlin friends! Soon there will be news perhaps. Negotiations are in progress. Meanwhile we stand on our hind legs, and our motto is: *Aut Cæsar aut nihil.* The *nihil* — that is, Basel — is not at all bad. They want to found a music school here and offer me the directorship. How's that?

How are you and yours? And the business? Why do you never write me a single word about anything? By the way, we three (the trio) nearly succumbed to coal-gas poisoning the other day. The 'cellist and the violinist fell fainting on to the floor. I was terribly stunned. The others were quite jolly next day, but I had the most atrocious head- and stomach-ache for a day and a half. Moral: Always take a good look into the mouth of the stove before closing the flap. This is the sort of thing one calls valuable experience (or invaluable, if you prefer it). . . .

146]

Basel
February 16, 1867

I AM taking a half-sheet only: otherwise I might grow absorbed in my scribble and I have no time for that. Tomorrow morning (it is now eleven p.m.) I go to Lucerne to see my wife. I am rather anxious about her: she is on the eve of her confinement and is in bed with a temperature. A nice situation all round: here I have been a bachelor for six months, without house or home and with all my belongings still in Munich, where I pay rent until the end of April. Long live King Ludwig II of Bavaria, the source of all this misery!

First let me offer congratulations on the recent Gewandhaus concert. I am becoming so impersonal in my dear Basel that Herr Tausig's apparently stupendous success gives no more pleasure than if I had had it myself. And Bernsdorff praises your pianofortes too in the *Signale*. Excellent! Let him continue. I am particularly glad on Brendel's account, whose disgusting enthusiasm — or rather that of his Zöpffe and Co. — for the Blüthner goods has been irritating me for a long time.

Did my last telegram annoy you? I confess I was feeling very bitter over your undoubtedly well-meant and loyal letter. Why, you ask? That is just the worst of it: we have not seen each other for so long and I have become such a stranger to you that you can ask why!

I was angry about another thing too. How can you suppose that I had any intention of taking interest on the two thousand talers I once lent you? Please simply give the amount back to Perl as soon as you are able. Perl will invest it well, I am convinced, although his long, long silence has made me uneasy. If you see him, please give him my kind regards and ask him not to forget me altogether. The national loan has been going up quite respectably in the last few weeks; I should be glad if I could retrieve my losses of '66. Have just had to pay a tax of forty-eight talers to the Fatherland. Never mind, once I am settled here, I shall snap my fingers at the Berlin Landtag and Reichstag, leave the royal Prussian State union, and pay my money and become a Swiss citizen. Yes, my dear Bechstein, that is how I feel and this vulgar tosh is what I have descended to. . . .

147]

Munich
Arcostrasse 11
May 9, 1867

I HAVE run you to earth after all by a roundabout way, you see. But why such a short stay? Was it a prize? Or what? Do say.

I did not receive the Basel letter. It must have been lost. Have been in Munich since Maundy Thursday. Behold me a royal Bavarian court conductor in ordinary (far too ordinary) and a colleague of the royal Prussian court manufacturer in the capacity of Knight of St. Michael (first class). Congratulations, please, to me and yourself.

And now, see that you *return by way of Munich or* you earn my eternal enmity.

Tomorrow I enter on my functions: fourth performance of Liszt's *St. Elisabeth* in the big theatre; June 10, first (" model ") performance of *Lohengrin; July 10, Tannhäuser.* Stall for you?

The music school of which I am to be director is still somewhat shadowy. It will certainly materialize though. I am going to Switzerland for my health in the middle of July (cure at St. Moritz, Graubünden, indispensable, say the doctors). Then rehearsals for the *Meistersinger.* First performance October 12 for the All-Highest's wedding festivities.[1] Do you still like me a little or has Tausig quite quite crowded me out? If he has not, do come and see me here. Everything is most charming. All the *cochonneries* have ceased, now that the Pf's[2] (not " pianofortes ") have been banished. N.B. The Wagner pianoforte (we

---

[1] *On October 10 Ludwig of Bavaria broke off his engagement to his cousin Sophie, sister of the Empress Elisabeth of Austria. Sophie later married the Duc d'Alençon, thus becoming the Duchesse d'Alençon. She perished in the charity-bazaar fire in Paris in 1897.*

[2] PFORDTEN *and* PFISTERMEISTER (*see page 63, note 2*).

are so glad it is ready) is an official All-Highest order for May 22, but it was all my wife's doing.

Heavens, here I am breaking my vow not to overrun the first sheet. Here are greetings from my wife, then, and thanks for the six letters received only today by way of Switzerland. How I should like to make a trip to Paris! Impossible. Duty! His Majesty is pressing for performances of *Tannhäuser* and *Lohengrin.* Which reminds me, Betz is coming, but the intendant does not want Fricke, as Bausewein can do it, and native forces are to be employed as far as possible. . . .

148]

Munich
May or June 1867

I AM quite prostrated by your kindness. I had made myself sufficiently familiar with the two Bieber and Irmler boxes in Aibl's [1] shop to be able to use them next Tuesday. Indeed, I quite enjoyed it; one ought to be able to play without a grand, to play with leaden weights. After all, my reputation generally plays for me nowadays! So if your grand does not arrive from Nuremberg in time, it doesn't matter. On the other hand, do you think I could have it here at a second concert on the same Saturday, the 19th? . . .

149]

Munich
July 9, 1867

IT was not nice of you not to come through Munich and see me in my glory. I conduct everything now — *Trovatore, Wilhelm Tell, Hans Heiling,* [2] music to *Egmont* — and we have nothing but model performances and the house sold out. Betz is having a tremendous success. I am more delighted than I can say, for he is so splendid and such a good sort both as man and as

---

[1] JOSEF AIBL, *name of a Munich publishing firm, founded in 1824 by Eduard Spitzweg. The firm was later incorporated into the Universal Verlag, Vienna.*
[2] *An opera by Marschner.*

artist. He is incredibly popular with the management and the public. If the funds will run to it, we are going to deprive the Berliners of him. About me there is only one opinion — in *Lohengrin* (first and second performances) I was called out after each act.

Yesterday I was honoured by a new commission. The Bavarian consul in Paris wrote to the Minister for War here and asked to have me as Bavarian commissioner on the jury for the prizes competition on the 21st (Austrian, Prussian, Belgian, French, Spanish, and *Bavarian* military bands). I leave on the 19th and return on the 23rd. Dress rehearsal on the 24th, first performance of *Tannhäuser* on the 25th, second and third of *Lohengrin* on the 28th and 31st. First of August, to Switzerland for my cure (St. Moritz). Now for two requests. *Pro primo,* would you have the announcement of my mission put in the Berlin papers? It would never have happened to me in Berlin. Think of it, the ministers for War and Commerce are sending me to Paris as an authority! Wieprecht had better look out — " our " Bavarian band acquits itself admirably and is to the Prussian as the Munich court theatre is to the Berliner. Well, I must not boast. But just ask our Betz, when he comes back, how things look when *I* am on the job. . . .

. . . I have rehearsals daily from ten to two, and three to six, and sometimes conduct the same evening. So you can imagine the rush in which I live. But it amuses me to see how everything fits to the minute when the *maestro di cappella* is on the spot. You should see what respect my method of holding rehearsals and my general alertness of eye and ear everywhere inspire. Again, what a pity that you cannot see me in my glorious popularity (I shall take care that it lasts!). You would revel in it. Your pianoforte has given great, great pleasure to the revered Master. Have you received the return present of his bust? And has the court secretariate rewarded you for your work of art? Please tell me *positively* how it stands. If they have not, write and tell me at once; because I shall then remind them — to good effect. . . .

PS. Your fine concert grand is, in spite of the journey to and from Switzerland, so well preserved that I shall be able to use it for my three soirées in the autumn.

No news of Kroll, Mützelburg, Remack, Perl?

On October 15 the new conservatorium comes into being! Definitely. We are progressive here, nothing of the kind could *ever* have happened in Berlin.

150]

10 Arcostrasse
Munich
July 31, 1867

PARIS was heavenly. Made me quite home-sick — I want to live there. The exhibition is, after all, a more glorious achievement than the " German " campaign of last year. Unfortunately I saw hardly anything! The people were too interesting: Berlioz, Rossini, Rubinstein, Lassen,[1] etc. The Americans — Remack and Steinway — took up much of my time too, but I must not complain, for they were very nice. I only saw the extremely interesting cases of their pianos!

I hope to make another trip there in the late autumn. To-morrow we are at last giving *Tannhäuser*. It will be unimaginably brilliant. Sunday, the second performance; Monday or Tuesday I leave for my cure at St. Moritz. Back on September 15. Still in a wild rush.

But to answer your questions:

1. Liszt is already at Weimar. He will certainly be present at the Weimar conference. Your humble servant, on the other hand, will be conspicuous by his absence (at St. Moritz, as I told you).

2. About sending a grand to Rome? I should think it would suit my father-in-law very well. Why not ask him?

3. Paint me in petroleum if it pleases you. Here is the latest photograph. If you insist upon it, I will send you a life-size portrait (by Albert) in about a week.

I entirely approve of your arrangement. Thank you for all the notices, but I wish you would write oftener. Rubinstein is going to America shortly. Steinweg has made terms with him to the satisfaction of both (this *between ourselves*). . . .

[1] EDUARD LASSEN, (1830–1904), *Danish composer, succeeded Liszt at Weimar in 1858.*

In any case, do go to Meiningen. My father-in-law will be
delighted to see you. N.B. Prussia has nothing to thank *me* for.
I was not enormously impressed with Wieprecht. The Austrians
were far better artistically. Still better was the Garde de Paris.
In the main I subscribe to Hanslick's report in the *Neue freie
Presse*. The Berlin papers exaggerated the Prussians' victory.
Bavaria made a brave show. *Professionally* I have to regret
that you were so un-American in Paris, but personally I am
glad.

What are all our Berlin acquaintances doing? I never hear
a word. Perl's absolute silence rather alarms me. It goes without saying that your credit with me is still on the same basis:
that is, I authorize you to draw on Perl whenever you need it.
I talk as though I stood for goodness knows what! Always the
way. The least consciousness of capital flatters one's vanity
unspeakably. Fare thee well and ever weller in every respect. . . .

151]

Kuranstalt St. Moritz
Engadine
August 11, 1867

Are you surprised to have another letter so soon? It is only
just to tell you, for your satisfaction, that His Eminence Bülow
called upon His Eminence Tausig at Ragatz on the 8th of this
month, and that the two dignitaries visited Bad Pfäffers together,
dined and tea'd together, played skittles, aired their grievances
and witticisms, consoled each other about their rheumatic and
other pains, were equally pleased to see each other, and to some
extent renewed their old friendly relations as fellow-artists.
Wasn't that nice? Both Their Eminences referred frequently to
their *Beflügler* in terms which he would have found incredibly
touching. Do your ears burn?

As you can have nothing to do now, knight of distinguished
orders, you will please write amusing letters to us at St. Moritz
as well as at Ragatz. It is true we are supposed to devote ourselves earnestly to being bored, doing nothing, hearing nothing;

but — a nice amusing humorous epistle from you could do neither of us any harm.

On the day of my arrival I did a thrilling climb in a thunderstorm which quieted me for a week. Now I stay politely at home and restrict myself to the plain. Sublime scenery, impressive and yet not gloomy. Not spoilt by humanity, although there are three hundred and eleven visitors in the institution at the moment. From Berlin we have: Dr. Leo, whose child has fallen ill with scarlet fever — as a result of which the whole of the Orleanist crowd (Duc de Nemours, Comte de Paris, etc.) have decamped, to the intense joy of the Bonapartists; then Dr. Hermann Lessing and his wife; and, besides these, only Zürich and Basel acquaintances, thank God, all modest philistines. There is also the Englishman Matthews, a music enthusiast from Florence, whose brother was once a pupil of mine at the Stern conservatorium. He tells me, by the way, that there is a Bechstein concert grand in the establishment; I am careful not to make any inquiries about it, though, as I must keep to a strict diet musically. Two days' rest has sufficed to show me how terribly strained my nerves are and how much I need the cure. I have great faith in the fresh air and water treatment (baths and springs). At ten I go to bed and by half-past six a.m. the boy is at the well. This is our rule — every day.

If only I could be rid of the rheumatic pains! Poor Tausig is in the same plight.

Wagner is working hard at the *Meistersinger* in Lucerne (I was there for a day), but there is no question of a performance at the wedding festivities (October 12), and it is not even desirable, for various reasons. When I go back at the end of September, however, we shall get to work at *Lohnhäuser* and *Tannengrün*. Do come over for them. Why not accompany my father-in-law? That would be charming. You are going to Meiningen, I hope? I should be so much obliged if you would send me an account of it. I particularly want to know how Fräulein Heintz acquits herself and whether my *Nirvana*[1] for orchestra is well played. (It will not " take," in any case — is not intended to.) Will you do me this favour?

How is all your family? It is so long since you have told me

---

[1] *A symphonic poem by Bülow.*

anything, and I should like to know whether you are as satisfied with things at home as with the factory.

My wife is staying in Munich for the present. St. Moritz is too high up and too cold for her. We shall meet at Lucerne, however, in the beginning of September. . . .

I am writing the most idiotic nonsense. Let it move you to write to *us both* (N.B.!) soon. Did you like my photograph? *If* you do, I can send you an almost life-size specimen, or, still better, a knee-length one *à la* Levinthal and Paez which Hanfstengel will soon have ready. But you had better choose for yourself in Munich.

Good-bye for today. Do not forget your private and professional pianists who are condemned to a rest cure in Switzerland after the fatigue you have indirectly caused them!

PS. Will you send me two hundred Pulgian *Entreactes*? The big ones are too heavy for me. It would be most kind of you. A similar gift would be not unwelcome to Tausig, I have reason to believe.

152]

Kuranstalt St. Moritz
Engadine
September 1, 1867

THANK you for writing at last, also for sending the hundred and fifty " pearls " and giving me a statement. But your cigarettes were — I should say, *are*, for I can only use them as fumigators — horrible. Beware of ever procuring paper with tobacco in it from Müller of Petersburg. As you pretend the stuff was a present to you into the bargain, I may safely break the rule, at second hand, of not looking a gift horse in the mouth.

You extraordinary person to feel obliged to assure me that the two thousand which were lent to such good purpose are safe! I solemnly assure you in return that I regard Bechstein as one of the most charming of fire-proof safes. But those cigarettes are really beneath contempt. Wait, though: it was really an inspiration of yours. You see, I am not supposed to smoke. Have had a frightful cold for twelve days, constant fits of coughing, bad nights and so on. As soon as I begin to drink the waters and take baths, I go all to pieces. So throw up your hands in amazement that I am not beside myself and have not lost all sense of humour: for my journey to St. Moritz is a failure and the cure — as the local doctor has just frankly admitted — is dangerous for me; I have to break it off a third of the way through and my health is so bad that I cannot risk any of the delightful excursions by which one can easily undo all the good of the cure.

Did you go to Meiningen and to Weimar? Did you see my father-in-law? He has not written (in reply to mine); can it be that he is angry with me? Do tell me how the unfortunate Heintz played. I stayed two days longer in Munich on her — or her bashful fingers' — account. My orchestral piece *Nirvana* was a failure, as I see from the papers. It is what I expected. My own opinion of the work remains unchanged. What does amuse me is that good friends helped to condemn it.

Yes, my dear Bechstein, I am ill and embittered. The coming winter causes me great anxiety. Yet I have not lost my indestructible humour, even though I do lose at dominoes with Herr von Magnus for two hours a day and at whist with Dr. Leo of Berlin and a government counsellor from Merseburg. . . .

The Mastersingers of Nuremberg will hardly be ready for performance in Munich before the beginning of 1868, whereas H.M.'s wedding takes place as arranged on October 12. When are you going to honour us with that promised but always diplomatically adjourned visit to Munich? .

The sun is so powerful now that, when I cough, I prefer to be roasted rather than to go on scribbling. How is your own corpse? And is your family in good health? Mine has been sent off to Wagner at Lucerne and I shall fetch them home from there in about a week (must be back in Munich by the 16th).

Why did you not send the Lilientals to see me? The people here are not really aggressive, but sufficiently vile. A damned lot of Englishmen. Had I been able to *italiano parlare*, I could have fallen back on the Italians. That can wait, however. Perhaps until 1868, although I am afraid of war now that Prussia has become so impossibly insolent. All the same, I hope to try

St. Moritz another time. Everything needs rehearsing if it is to be a success, even a cure or a health tour.

Have you read the conservatorium prospectus? Just imagine, that little Jew Simmel has written me six quarto sheets to ask me to get him an appointment with the court theatre management in Munich. What do you say to that? *Molto starko.* . . . .

153]

Munich
October 20, 1867

DELIGHTED to hear that Rubinstein played your pianoforte at the Leipzig Gewandhaus last Thursday and that you shared in the great success. That is right, go on in the same way. I should be very glad if *I* could play the pianoforte — that is, play a Bechstein — again, but for the last week, as you know, I have been wretchedly ill. For six weeks now I have had no voice and even now I shall have to brush my throat for some time with lunar caustic. It is doing good, however, and I can at least teach again and attend the teachers' councils, where I expand and enforce my views. . . .

I heard through the Merians that Captain S. had rendered great services. That is your doing again. Would this extraordinary man, who can do everything and knows everything, give me his advice and help in a matter of state-citizenship with which I am greatly concerned? You see, I intend to leave the North German Alliance in order to be perfectly free as regards politics. I am not thinking of exchanging Bavaria for Borussia, I only wish to *de*-Prussianize myself and shall probably become — guess what! — an official republican — namely, a Swiss citizen. You will perhaps remember that at the time (for instance, December 1865) when I was a Bismarckian before any of you, you all abused me. To rave about a thing *after* it has proved a success is not in my line. How did Bratfisch put it? " It is easy to praise a fine day at nightfall." True, Bismarck is a great man (though he was possibly greater when he had to fight above and below) ; but Munich is to be an art centre, and we do not intend to be gobbled up by the Prussians and make over to them the money which can be used for nobler ends for their little military games. Neither do we wish to have the Munich Court Theatre placed under the general control of Sellinger.

That makes you democrats angry, eh?

In brief, will you be so good as to speak to your friend some time (in the course of a gossip) and ask him what steps I ought to take to be released from the Prussian state-union? Naturally, I do not mind about the cost, if only I don't have too much fuss about it. So — don't forget, will you?

One other point. At a café here the other day I saw a Berlin theatrical paper, the *Coulisse,* in which, to my astonishment, I read laudatory stuff about myself. It proved to be one of a series of " armoured letters from Munich." Blushing like a virgin, I put the paper aside lest I should be caught reading it (in which I should be believed to be the author), but took down the necessary. The editor is L. Fränkel — offices, Kronenstrasse 19.

Now, would you do me a favour and obtain at the source all the numbers of this paper (which is only a few months old) and send them to me here? These " armoured Munich " letters give, as I saw, a quite accurate historical sketch of Munich and my doings.

Do you know that the Topp[1] has left us for America? I wish her well, but am heartily glad to be rid of the indelicate, excitable creature. I am going to let Fräulein Heintz give elementary lessons to the solo singers at the music school. Meiningen did her good. What is friend Tausig doing? Tell him his *Gradus* edition has been introduced into the school and that several copies have been ordered. The publisher (Behn) is authorized (that is, *if he wishes;* he is not obliged to) to print on the title-page of new editions:

" Used by the higher pianoforte classes of the Royal Music School, Munich."

If you see Betz, remember me to him, and to anyone else you like.

My mother will probably move over here. You probably know that my brother-in-law and sister have gone to Moscow. What odd tricks of fate! You alone stay in the land and make a respectable living. I no longer believe in that trip of yours to

[1] *A pupil of Bülow.*

Munich. You had the best of opportunities before or after Paris. Perhaps you will come with Betz in the spring?

As a matter of fact, after I have been here a couple of years, or three, I shall perhaps follow Rubinstein's example and take up the career of travelling virtuoso again. Such " fame " is not for me this winter, worse luck. And, on my word, the difficulty of finding Bechsteins to play on in south Germany is one reason why. If only you would extend your sphere southwards — we don't mind that sort of Prussian conquest. By the way, Knaack of Düsseldorf tried to unload a pianoforte on me recently. I sent him about his business. What sort of stuff is his?

154]

Munich
January 4, 1868

. . . WHAT lovely dolls for my little maids! I decided to be prudent and keep them on ice for their birthdays, although naturally that will not prevent " Uncle " Bechstein's receiving his due as Father Christmas. The fine medallion of Franz Liszt which you sent for me is a great joy. It atones for all the bad cigarettes. Is there any civilized way of thanking you? Rescue me from my awkward predicament.

Do you know, I used the Christmas holidays to take a very cold trip to Prague and Dresden for the purpose of inspecting the strength — or weakness — of their respective opera-establishments. In my beautiful native place I met Friedel, who told me that friend Bechstein was flourishing — even without Friedel. I decided that Bachmann the tenor would be useful to us. My work had piled up nicely by the time I got home.

Tomorrow I am conducting the *Merry Wives*, which has been newly mounted. I have had repeated invitations from Lienau [1] to play at the Berlin philharmonic concerts. Once more I refused, which ought to please Tausig, who cannot bear any poaching on his preserves. I am, however, playing at Hanover in the middle of February. . . . I have one painful piece of

[1] ROBERT LIENAU (1838–1920), *founder of the publishing firm of Schlesinger.*

news to break to you. Wagner is coming to Munich to stay until the *Meistersinger* comes on (which is unthinkable before April) and his jolly secretaire-pianoforte is badly out of sorts. The dampers do not act and the resonance is such that it is impossible to play distinctly on it. Deprosse is helpless. What shall we do? . . .

PS. Have I told you that my mother has come to live here and likes it better than in Berlin? How do you come to have business relations with Aibl? Not that I mind, but Deprosse is hurt about it.

155]

Munich
February 1, 1868

I HAVE just been discussing the opera repertoire for this month with the intendant and have so arranged it that I can take a short leave from the 21st to the 24th, which enables me to play in Hanover on the 22nd (Saturday). It is very charming of you to want to provide me with a pianoforte again. Please note that I am playing only Beethoven in this particular subscription concert; so let me have a really responsive instrument. I am delighted that you had a good time in Holland, and also thought of me. Your perpetual praise of my " human " side begins to be tiresome though. My only merit is that I do not treat others basely (simply humanly) merely because they have often treated me so. In the case of T. there is also my warm admiration and personal sympathy to take into account. The Heckmanns [1] are splendid people, don't you think?

Certainly I could make money in Vienna, but as I have enough to live on here, my official conscientiousness obliges me to refrain from amassing non-official wealth. A pity, because I should like to be able to put something by again. However, there is still time for that. I don't think I shall crumple up yet awhile, though the hair may vanish even more alarmingly from my head and " tooth-brush." As regards Aibl, you misunderstood me. I

---

[1] GEORGE JULIUS HECKMANN (1848–91), *violinist; his wife, Marie* (1843–90), *pianist.*

was only surprised. Really, though, Aibl has been paying court to me for such a long time now that I must take him under my wing. (He allows forty per cent discount for the whole music school, and so on.)

I only went to Dresden and Prague for change of air and to sniff round for tenors. How are you going to see about the Wagner pianoforte by telegram? I am curious to know.

156]

Munich
February 9, 1868

. . . RICHARD WAGNER left here yesterday for Lucerne, where he can work with less disturbance. He is to return in the beginning of March, when the *Meistersinger* rehearsals will be going on. By that time I hope your wonder-pianoforte will be in form again. The deputy in question was rather helpless last time he came, and was going to write to you in greater detail and consult you about the damping.

Warmest congratulations on Tausig's triumph in Berlin and yours. I rejoice over each of his successes as if it were my own. Ehrlich's parallels did not appeal to me. So I cannot play Liszt! H'm. Besides, I play coldly and intellectually. Oh, you ox! Berlin's chilling atmosphere and the animosity towards me which it engenders have always dried up my inner warmth, so that I invariably played like an advocate of my own " classical " intelligence.

Here in the south, I am thankful to say, I have been able to expand more freely. The misunderstood " Joachim of pianoforte-playing " (for such M. Malhonnête really considers himself) would have had an opportunity on the occasion of R.'s [1] concert visit here to work out his parallels. . . .

Meanwhile kindest regards, also to Tausig, whose pianoforte edition I am preparing to tackle vigorously. It is excruciatingly difficult, but exquisitely done.

---

[1] ANTON RUBINSTEIN, *who was doing concert tours in Europe between 1867 and 1870.*

157]

Munich
March 1, 1868

IT was really a bitter disappointment to me that you did not come to Hanover — both because I was deprived of the rare pleasure of meeting you and particularly because of the reason for your absence. How are you now? I am most anxious for news, but for good, consoling news.

That you thought well to produce a doctor's certificate in excuse touched us — Bronsart and myself — and amused us. It was — almost necessary. Both the Bronsarts, by the way, have become exclusive Bechsteiners. I spent some charming days with them. Your pianoforte sounded very fine at the concert. Particularly in *piano* was it splendidly equal and pleasing in tone and easy to play. Less so in the *forte* — or am I forgetting how to handle your instruments properly? It is true I am somewhat out of practice, but I shall get into it again. The more often I conduct, the less does it stiffen my hands. An invitation to Nuremberg with the bait of Bechstein concert grands I refused *à la* Tausig: stating that I would either play gratis (for a charity) or on receipt of a sum of twenty-five florins d'or, not twelve louis d'or. The death of Ludwig I means the closing of the theatre until March 15. All the same, there is a devilish lot to do, as we are employing the time in reviving several of the best operas (*Seraglio, Water-carriers, Freischütz, Abu Hassan* by Weber). Naturally we shall go on with the *Meistersinger.*

Tausig had another colossal success at Leipzig. Always glad when I read it. At Elberfeld he spoilt Rubinstein's chances before he appeared on the scene. Had I not been forced to return to Munich with all speed (a theatre rehearsal on Wednesday morning), I should have gone to Leipzig to have a drink with Tausig and Senff.[1]

But, seriously, how are you?

[1] BARTHOLF SENFF, *publisher, started the* Signale für die musikalische Welt *in 1843.*

When you are better, I have a small request. The manufacturers of ribbons for orders and decorations here are entirely uncivilized. Could you therefore ask Godet to send me the various rosettes and other combinations of certain of my orders — say, half a dozen? . . .

158]

Munich
March 15, 1868

ALTHOUGH I have no time, I must dash off a line of thanks for your entertaining letter and the pretty toys, which do you and Godet honour.

This evening, *Armida* (I now conduct all the big and also the decent little operas), and an extra rehearsal in consequence of the chief baritone's indisposition.

Tomorrow, rehearsal of the first subscription concert, which takes place on Wednesday. I am playing a Beethoven concerto on the Knake grand *en attendant mieux*. Thursday, *The Water-carriers;* Sunday, *Freischütz* (both newly rehearsed); Tuesday, Schumann's *Manfred;* Thursday, second concert; Sunday, *Lohengrin;* Tuesday, *Abu Hassan* (Weber); Thursday, Gluck's *Orpheus* (both these operas newly rehearsed by me). In addition fourteen lessons a week in the music school — apart from interviews and conferences — and constant little and big rehearsals for the *Meistersinger,* which does not come until May 3, but requires enormous preparations. A curious coincidence: this very morning I suddenly had a letter from the beautiful Minka (Unter den Linden 19, consulting hours? Do go and see her!). Her sister, the not at all beautiful Amelia, has married a Prince Wittgenstein, what do you say to that? You really must have the whole swindle described to you in detail. So Pratfisch has become Tausig's Belloni. Good. I'm inclined to envy T. rather than pity him. People simply worship him (Mostrich at Leipzig, for instance). Well, he deserves it. He put Rubinstein completely in the shade in Holland, as he did on the Rhine (Elberfeld and so on). Still, if you insist, I'll pity him too and pray that he may soon be released from his worse half. Give

him my most cordial greetings. His *Meistersinger* arrangement
is ruining my fingers and eyes, but it is *great*.

If you were only here, I would pour out all sorts of con-
fidences. As regards my cause, I have nearly achieved what has
always been my ambition: I control the musical life of a city
which, in its art manifestations, is presently to outshine completely Berlin, Vienna, and Leipzig. Yes, that and no less!

So your health is still bad, or at least poor? Do take care of
yourself, you will live to have much pleasure in your pianists
(*Beflügelten*).

We Weimarists are going to win, you'll see; we shall rule
and our opponents will dissolve in gall and be poured away
down the closet of the past! And our art — the true, the noble,
the high — will thrive greatly; and Liszt will be hailed in books
(handsomely bound editions, not newspapers) as the founder
of interpretative art, with all its implications, and the initiator
of a new era.

Fürstner? Oho! Scholz? Aha! Is said to be a capital capi-
talist-artist. Poor Bechstein! . . .

PS. I confess my playing in Hamburg was not brilliant. I
had a bad cold, and my nose was weeping over your absence. It
is really kind of Vulkov to have treated me so considerately.

159]

Wiesbaden
on Goethe's birthday (*Jöthes Jeburtstag*) *'68*
Adr.: Taunusstrasse, care of Herr Hosenstein
(*sounds rather like Lilienstein*)
August 8, 1868

THE essential is on the back of this. Have " played " here in
both senses, but do not intend to leave without having my revenge on the bank, and to that end the hundred on account will
come in useful; I therefore beg they may be sent to me with all
speed. Last year you sent me a hundred to St. Moritz — or was
it more? — and this makes two, reducing what you owe to Perl
and Mayer to eighteen hundred. This is liquidation, eh?

Why did Tausig not come over? Sorry to say I hear all sorts

of things about his wife, who seems to be all things to all men here with a few exceptions. Have you seen Klindworth? He must have been having a high old time; otherwise he would have written — that is, replied. In about a week I must plunge into the fray again. Until then I shall take it easy.

Hasard is the most difficult game in the world, I assure you, far more so than pistol-shooting, which I have learned to do quite nicely here. My wife and children in Switzerland and well. How are you all?

160]

Munich
October 16, 1868

Your letter, which (as has invariably been the case) calls for thanks on my part, finds me in a very depressed mood. My dear wife's health is very uncertain (please let nothing of this reach my mother, who is staying in Berlin) and the doctors recommend a change of climate. Munich is too bleak for her and I shall probably have to be separated from her for some time. She is going either to her stepsister in the south of France or to Italy. It is very hard for me in many ways. Just now, too, I am overloaded with work. The music school reopens with several new pupils; then there are my continual exertions — not all remunerative — to keep the opera going; so that you must not expect my usual long, gossipy letters. . . .

I am very glad you liked Klindworth so much. He is a splendid man and musician, one of our tried friends. He writes rather depressingly from Moscow.

My dear man, how can you want me to be a journalist and write articles for a Berlin Jew-paper! How should I find the time and the wit when I am so dog-tired at night that I go straight to bed and have often to run through orchestral scores after that? Remember, Cornelius is already writing for the *Börsenkurier* on Tausig's account. And that article on Wagner was really only an advertisement for Eckert.[1] Whether Eckert deserved it Betz

[1] KARL ECKERT (1820–79), *infant prodigy, composer, and conductor. In 1867 he lost his post as* Kapellmeister *at Stuttgart, but in 1869 went to Berlin as first* Hofkapellmeister.

will tell you! Kindermann and Sigl are working hard at the *Meistersinger*, which is to be given as soon as possible with a cast from here. Betz will probably be conspicuous by his absence, but Kindermann is taking enormous pains. . . .

161]

Nuremberg, Rotes Ross
November 7, 1868

Your pianoforte here is charming. Have also been to Fuchs's shop, where there are delightful uprights. Hear to my delight that the public is deserting Schwechten and Biese's latest style for you. There is a very good music-teacher here, Lina Ramann, who has long been intimately connected with Blüthner. We must try, one of these days, to get her away from the old Leipzig swindler. Richard Pohl[1] accompanied me here. The last (seventh) *Meistersinger* performance last Tuesday in Munich went off well.

The mechanism of the pianoforte is somewhat key-swollen and shies at repeated notes. Have recommended rubbing with hot cloths. Will you do me a favour? See Mützelburg and ask him to send me back a French book, the biography of St. Just in two parts. It would be best if you took it yourself and forwarded it to me. (He would forget.) Hildebrandt's death was a great shock to us. In considering the possibility of a visit to Berlin, the idea of seeing this glorious artist and charming personality was definitely an attraction. Well, at least Würst is still living.

A pretty to-do after the concert! The porters have been treating your pianoforte in a nice fashion. I discovered eventually that they had placed it in the cold unheatable hall two days before — it gets frightfully hot with a thousand people in it. I fought like a Trojan to overcome the deadness of the mechanism. Finally all the hammers were warped. I had to pound away to make a Chopin nocturne sound. In the last piece everything gave out, even in *forte*. So nothing for it but to give in and tell the audience that I could not go on, as the keys refused to

---

[1] RICHARD POHL (1826–96), *writer on music, disciple of Liszt.*

sound. I am going back to Munich tonight at three a.m. with a bad cold and very depressed, and a rehearsal in front of me in the morning. Call that a pleasure, confound it!

162]

Munich
November 12, 1868

So I am your " very dear Sir," am I? I suppose you think that because I wrote in an excited, sleepless state — being obliged to travel back from Nuremberg at three in the morning — and told you of the unpleasant incident, I was being " unfriendly " towards you. Very well, then, read it in print. Fortunately Pohl stayed a half-day behind me in N. and helped the committee to edit the above statement, which is in all the Nuremberg papers. In this way every unpleasantness is provided against. . . .

I shall give an evening recital at Nuremberg on a Bechstein as soon as possible. Are you satisfied? Sophie Menter [1] is playing Liszt's E flat Concerto at the second subscription concert (November 18) on my new Bechstein.

Are you agreeable?

There! Now will you send me soon the promised cigarettes? And — quite a special favour — get your agents to send you several copies of No. 557, morning edition, of the *Nürnberger Korrespondent* and have the *feuilleton* article reprinted in the Berlin papers!

Will you?

One of *your* keys at least will never stick, no matter what the change of temperature; namely,

your sincere friend
Bülow.

[1] Sophie Menter (1846–1918), *pianist (daughter of Joseph Menter, the violoncellist), pupil of Liszt and Bülow, married Popper, the violoncellist.*

163]

Munich
November 17, 1868

THE enclosed notice shows that you are being played in Munich. Have you seen the Berlin *Neue Coulisse* and *Allgemeine Musikzeitung*)? First number, November 13. Publishers: Fränkel, Französische Strasse 52. It's *great* — you must order it, support it.

Am playing for charity on the 28th at Augsburg and again, probably on December 8, at Nuremberg (Hans Sachs). My wife has gone to her stepsister at Versailles, as she is really suffering from mental strain. You may imagine that this parting, which is essential for her, is not making me very cheerful. Thank Heaven there is plenty to work at.

164]

Munich
December 7, 1868

I FEEL I must thank you again after the event for letting me see you at Nuremberg. It was like old times — those times of my early concert tours " *avec l'accompagnement de Bechstein,*" which were the only gleams in my Berlin misery. And I know that it was not unpleasing to you either, to have a little drink with me again, especially as (unfortunately for myself) I did not play as well as I might, and you will therefore still be able to give my rivals the same preference and admiration as at present. But, secure in the watertight shelter of your friendship, I will now tell you what has happened to me since Sunday at 3.15–25. . . .

. . . Yesterday, ninth performance of the *Meistersinger*, very fine in parts. Only my vice-Betz heaved and dragged so dreadfully that I had once or twice to beat time openly on my desk for him. House full; no applause in the middle, but many recalls. . . .

Tausig is requested to send his latest photograph. Jordan and Fimäus ought to fill him with chocolate too now. You might do the necessary staging. Does Papa Aloys [1] go to see " Minna " too?

165]

Munich
March 19, 1869

CONGRATULATIONS on your splendid successes. I was delighted with the *Signale* article from Warsaw. And now have you quite forgotten your old Bülow or should you like to help in a good work?

From the 16th to the 20th of April my father-in-law is stay-ing in Regensburg, where I propose to visit him and arrange a little surprise for him; namely, to give an evening recital there on the 17th for the benefit of Peter's pence. Very well, you will say, and give your blessing. But that takes me no further. I require a fine Bechstein grand. My own, which sounded splendid here in Henselt's concerto [2] the other day, I do not wish to take with me. It would be very nice if you would send an instrument to Regensburg and of course come yourself. What about it? R.S.V.P.

166]

Munich
April 4, 1869

THERE has been delay in hearing from Regensburg. Also I was quite out of sorts for two days in consequence of something very annoying, so that I have not been able to answer your letter before.

The Regensburg concert remains fixed for April 17 (in aid of the Holy Father's fund for the restoration of the little Theatre of Marcellus in Rome). Program will please you.

[1] *Tausig's father.*
[2] ADOLF VON HENSELT (1814–89), *pianist, pupil of Hummel, composer of pianoforte music and of a pianoforte concerto in F minor.*

Keep your word this time and give me the pleasure of your presence. More than ever do I need friendly encouragement. I have been through evil days and am on the point of falling into a state of acute depression.

167]

Munich
April 11, 1869

A GREAT blow to me! Liszt is not coming to Regensburg, but goes first to his triumphs in Pest and then straight back to Rome (end of April). I had been looking forward so desperately to playing before *him*. Now everything is so arranged at Regensburg that the concert must take place, and at the appointed time: Saturday, April 17, at seven. I shall go by the first train, arrive soon after ten, and return to Munich at half-past twelve at night. Shall I hear or see anything of you?

PS. I have been rather seriously out of sorts for a week owing to a dreadful upset. Have utterly lost all desire to stay here. I am a fool to sacrifice myself like this. Nothing but the sacrifices I have already made deters me from leaving at once.

168]

Munich
May 15, 1869

. . . SINCE you left I have become daily Munich-wearier and more childishly wretched. If Hülsen chucks out Eckert he might have me in his place. Even the things nearest one's heart wither in this month of May. Tausig would rejoice to hear me thoroughly abusing myself. . . .

As owing to my wife's persistent illness she and the children cannot at present leave Lucerne, and as my mother is staying longer than she proposed with my sister at Wiesbaden and I am physically too exhausted to bear solitude without being afraid of, one not fine day, releasing myself from myself, I have taken a charming young musician [1] into the house. He is the son of

[1] Dohnginstler (Tonkünstler).

the late famous Servais of Brussels, a talented and well-brought-up young man who bears a fabulous resemblance to my brother-in-law, Daniel, and therefore, of course, to Liszt. You may have met his slightly younger brother, who is now 'cellist in the Weimar orchestra in succession to de Swert.

Best thanks for " holding off " the composer Lessmann [1] in Berlin. I get bothered quite enough. Thanks also for the message to Papa Heintz, who seems to be blissfully happy to have his child among the ranks of the married. You will see from this ghastly scrawl that I am in a very low frame of mind, morally in the condition of " the morning after." Positively it is only decency and a sense of duty that makes me write to you today. Don't let it disgust you to the extent of putting you off writing soon. Best regards to Tausig, who presumably is in no rosier state than I.

PS. In August (*Rheingold,* the 25th) you will come as promised and stay with me?

169]

Munich
June 4, 1869

FIRST a piece of news for you: I am absolutely determined to give up my post here in a short time from now; in other words, to retire for a full year from October — purely to regain my shattered health — and at the end of the year, according to whether that end has been achieved, seek a new sphere of work. No one here knows the irrevocability of this decision. Only those who have been sympathetic (that is, not really malicious) eyewitnesses of my struggles and sufferings can suspect that I must have lost all desire to go on battling in this vile place. For weeks past everything has been in utter confusion — nothing but worry, disappointment, fruitless toil. I must try to get out of it. Whether I succeed is a question; but try I must.

Where to go from here (other matters I could only explain to you orally, impossible to write about them) I have not really decided. Perhaps to Wiesbaden if there is a chance there of

[1] OTTO LESSMANN (1844–1918), *pianoforte pupil of Bülow and critic.*

earning anything as a pianoforte-teacher. Otherwise to some
non-German town, but all that is not pressing. Since I decided to
desert Munich at any price, at any sacrifice, I have begun to
feel some hope of new stirrings and refreshed nerves.

I need your help, however, to carry out my decision. For
the next year I must definitely not have to rely on my earnings,
but be in a position to wait calmly for the future. Could you let
me have back the old deposit of, originally, two thousand (it
will now have come down to fifteen hundred: you have three
times sent me a hundred, I believe, and spent other sums for me)
by the time when I shall have left Munich. Say yes or no. Then,
for years I have heard nothing from friend Perl, who has a
similar sum of mine in his hands. I don't like to write to him.
Would you, as my authorized representative, go and see him
and tell him that I have — done something stupid; for instance,
stood surety for someone else (which God knows I am capable
of doing, though not so fond of it as you); in short, that I am
in need of cash. Above all, I want to know how my balance with
Perl stands, whether it has increased or diminished.

Do not, my friend, distress me by supposing that I am in the
act of doing a foolish thing in cold blood. A few words, and I
could explain to you perfectly and obtain your agreement and
consent to my " strange " step; but in writing I cannot express
what is essential. Please preserve secrecy on this matter to
everyone, particularly towards those in the position of Tausig
and such. *It had to come as it has* and the further consequences
are perfectly logical. I am having a terrible amount of work
and anxiety over *Tristan,* which, according to the unalterable
ukase of Herr and Frau Vogl,[1] must be brought out on June 22.
There will be an outcry, but I don't care. I shall do my duty
until the last moment, although my legs will hardly support me.
As a matter of fact, it was with *Tristan* that my activity began
here four years ago and it is more significant than you can
imagine that it should come to a close also with *Tristan.* . . .

[1] HEINRICH VOGL (1845–1900), *a great Tristan after Schnorr's death; his wife
Therese (1845–1921), one of the finest Isoldes.*

170]

Munich
June 21, 1869

YESTERDAY a letter and my account from Perl, today yours from Dresden. Meanwhile the newspapers have, without any foundation, denied the truth of my resignation. I am undoubtedly entitled by medical certificate to a holiday, but shall only take it until October 1; that is, draw my salary until then, after which I shall simply send in my resignation definitely. I am glad you see no ill temper lurking behind it, but realize that I simply cannot go on here, although you cannot know *all* the motives for my departure. I shall stay until the beginning of August to carry on at the music school until the vacation. Then off I go; destination still uncertain — I may not decide until I reach the station. *At least* six months will be needed for my nerves to recover and that is why I must not be dependent on what I earn. Perhaps this lovely state of nerves will last even longer, perhaps I shall never be strong again. But I will not be such a hypochondriac as to assume the probability.

You see, don't you, that I cannot ask for anything in the nature of a pension after being only two years and a half at my post? Indeed, I wish to leave here with clean — that is, empty — hands. I am thus obliged to cut into my small savings and am in need of the sum of fifteen to eighteen hundred talers for travelling, invalid comforts, and so on.

That is the explanation of my recent bomb-shell. Herr Perl has, I see, handled my pennies in a fatherly way — I stand better than I thought. You will understand that, in such a moment of upheaval, when I am faced with a total change of position, place of abode, and conditions of life, it behoves me to know the state of my finances so that I may be quite clear about them.

Many a thing is not clear to me at present and I beg you *urgently* to explain.

Herr Perl has not taken the two thousand talers I lent you in 1866 into account at all. He has allowed my securities to mount up and it seems to me that it is not to me but to friend Perl that you owe that sum, which he advanced to you, so to say, on the security of a pledge from me. In this, if it is so (and according to Perl's account it can hardly stand otherwise), I see unpleasantness ahead for myself.

For: how can you suppose for a moment that I could have lent you that money at five — or, indeed, at any — per cent? You, from whom I have accepted with military complacency the most shameless presents: grand pianofortes, chests of cigarettes, and what not. Does it look like me? Would there then be any talk of a " favour " on my side? What would that have been but practising usury on an individual, a friend, instead of investing it at good interest in a company or an institution?

That is quite against my intention. You would today owe me (or Perl, as the case may be) two thousand exactly and no more, had not my credit been reduced by some hundreds (was it three, or two? *Two* I remember perfectly: one — it may even have been a hundred and fifty — you posted to St. Moritz, and the other last year to Wiesbaden). Therefore you owe me either 1,700 or 1,750 or 1,800, but *not*, as you wrongly suppose, 2,195 talers. Do you see?

The thing now is to clear matters up with Herr Perl. On his showing, you owe him two thousand and are to demand two or three hundred from me; for, as I said, Herr Perl has let the borrowed two thousand in securities remain at interest, as if he had this sum in his own hands, not sold them to you. Do, my dear fellow, clear this all up for me. I shall want that sum in a month or five weeks, must have it available. If I demand it from *you*, Herr Perl will naturally have to sell out securities for the amount he has of mine, just as if I were demanding them of *him*. That is surely as clear as " two and two make four " — or as clear as the impossibility of my turning out and replacing Herr Eckert under the guise of my own superiority. For Berlin is not one whit less detestable to me than Munich; on the contrary, I should choose this place, in spite of all that revolts me here, rather than the power behind Potsdam (Schleissheim). So do me this favour soon, won't you? Yesterday we began the new rehearsals for *Tristan and Isolde* with Herr and Frau Vogl. It went remarkably well. Only shows what steady application will

do. The Vogls had precisely as many months as the Schnorrs
had years in which to learn their parts. Tomorrow is the private
performance for His Majesty and an invited audience in the
stalls (at 10 a.m. tomorrow, Tuesday). On Wednesday I shall
of course be in bed again. Richter will conduct the last operatic
performance before the holidays on Sunday the 27th: the *Meistersinger*, with Betz and Mallinger. So tomorrow will be, I suppose, the last time I conduct this orchestra. With all that I have
gone through here and should have to go through again, the
thought still makes me very sad. That you will understand. But
it cannot be helped. It is not the place for me. . . .

Eighty-four bars — not more — did we cut out of *Tristan*
(ten in Act I, seventy-four in Act III). That was an achievement. And just as I began with *Tristan* here, so do I end with
it, and in this there is a certain *chic*.

What is all this correspondence business between Tausig and
Wagner? I am quite in the dark. Do warn Tausig in his own
interest against a public break with Wagner and party (what
party: Liszt in Rome, Brendel [1] in his grave?), for he would
only make himself ridiculous.

171]

Munich
July 3, 1869

[*Note-paper heading of the Bechstein firm*]

THAT is the only joke I am capable of in my present frame
of mind.

You and Perl are two charming people, and it is lucky for
me that you are both so well-disposed towards me. My best
thanks, and I beg you will continue. Very well, then, I submit.
You owe me two thousand — one hundred at four per cent —
and I hope it will not inconvenience you to repay me this sum
in the course of the coming year. For during this period there
will be nothing incoming, but only expenditure. Probably I shall
require five hundred by October 1. Shall you be in Berlin at

---

[1] KARL FRANZ BRENDEL (1811–68), *pupil of Clara Wieck, writer on music,
succeeded Schumann as editor of the* Neue Zeitschrift für Musik.

that time? Where I shall be is doubtful. Until August 6 I shall be occupied here. By then I'm afraid I shall be stony broke and shall have to find some solitary little hole in the mountains instead of staying at Wiesbaden. I will write to you about it as soon as anything is fixed; at the beginning of August, that is. My mother, who will live with me in future, would be quite willing to go to Wiesbaden, or still more to some place near, as she grew accustomed to the neighbourhood last year. If I possibly can, I shall act according to her wishes — Raff [1] and Seyfried are as good company as I could desire. I neither wish for, nor should be able to stand more in the way of society. I regard it as exceedingly kind of Tausig to propose to visit me, but he will get no pleasure from seeing me and I as little from seeing him in my weak state of nerves (I am hardly conscious of existing in the morning and only live from about four o'clock in the afternoon until evening; it is apparently the case with all nerve patients). Besides, our meeting and intercourse would give rise to all sorts of outbursts, explanations, reminiscences, and so on, and I feel I must avoid all such things at any price. Will you, therefore, gently dissuade him in such a way that he will not feel hurt.

I to join forces with Joachim and Co. in Berlin!? What are you thinking of? Absolutely impossible. I am too powerfully drawn *away* from German soil, I am too well known, too much discussed. If, as is *not* likely, I ever feel like conducting again, I might just possibly consider Hanover, hardly Dresden. You shall have my reasons orally. . . .

You have no idea how wearing it has been, this weighing the ups and downs of what I realized to be my irrevocable decision.

PS. Perl was right. It might have been unsafe to put a large sum into my hands (particularly in the event of Wiesbaden). The idea of some desperate *coup* is never far away. My thanks to Perl and to you for taking this into consideration.

---

[1] JOSEPH JOACHIM RAFF (1822–82), *the composer. Follower of Liszt. Bülow was one of the first to introduce his music to the public.*

172]

Munich
July 31, 1869

SINCE I wrote last, there has been a new and still worse turn in my affairs. Listen! I have been unavoidably forced by certain quite recent events to take a step which I would have made any humanly possible sacrifice to avoid on my Master and father-in-law F. L.'s account. Before leaving Germany I *must* try to obtain a *dissolution of my marriage.* I should like to do it as smoothly as possible and yet with all haste, but do not know how to set about it. Would you be so kind as to send me a copy of the *Prussian divorce law* by return? Can you also recommend me a reliable, *thoroughly enlightened* attorney in Berlin, personally known to you, with whom I can communicate about the preliminary steps? Delay means danger for me.

After this letter much will become clear to you; as for instance why I have handed in my resignation for the second time and why care has been taken not to have it refused in high quarters this time.

Herewith a copy of the first *decree,* which is to my credit and will, I hope, make a good impression on you as my friend.

Oh, my dear Bechstein — everything within me is crashing! And it had to be!

None of my friends will now envy me either my past life or the finale which is now beginning.

PS. The examinations at the music school end on Thursday, August 5. I then go into the mountains for a week, as a short rest is absolutely essential before I proceed to wind up my affairs here. There is no one to " support " me but my poor dear mother — and here I am without a penny. A pretty situation!

173]

Munich
August 5, 1869

Many thanks for the prompt dispatch of the judicial pamphlet, from which I regretfully gather that it will be necessary for me to come to Berlin myself, probably about the 20th, to consult a lawyer. Your letter came next day, but I appreciate silent sympathy even more than eloquence. My situation is so incredibly and uniquely horrible that any other way out than an exit from the world altogether requires superhuman pluck. . . .

In the beginning of October I am going to Florence, where I hope to get some peace. Aibl will send the pianoforte after me. I am no longer in correspondence with Rome, or with Switzerland. That you will understand. On the other hand, Herr Richard Würst wrote very politely the other day. Irony of fate! Do you think your friend Seyfried can advise and help me at Wiesbaden in this private matter, which *must take precedence of all else?* God, how solitary and friendless I am here! My existence is more dreadful than I could have imagined. If only it were all settled! The best would be for some sympathetic soul to give me the necessary dose of Prussic acid! Is there no accommodating chemist in Berlin? I would leave him my whole library and whatever else he wanted. Come, you know so many people!

I'm sorry, but I have no real confidence in Holthoff (since the Lassalle affair); all the same, he is undoubtedly the cleverest legal adviser. Will you, therefore, let me know whether he is in Berlin or is amusing himself abroad?

Tell me, why has the word you might have spoken always frozen on your tongue? It would have been real charity to be open with me. Think of the years of misery that I have endured with regard to, for instance, F. L.[1] But no more now. I am dog-tired. The heat is African.

PS. Mützelburg was here the other day, Jenssen likewise. It is terrible to have friends visiting me *now*, however discreet they may be. The fact that I shall emerge stainless — even in the

[1] Liszt.

eyes of a malicious world — is but poor consolation for the outcry there will inevitably be against the great Master. But it has come to a point when I can make no more sacrifices.

174]

Wiesbaden
September 4 [*1869*]

A COMFORTABLE night in bed after a cold one in the train has so far restored me that I am moved to devote the first stroke of my pen to you this morning and to thank you, as well as words may, for your hospitable friendship, your affectionate sympathy, and your truly brotherly care of my unfortunate self. My journey to Berlin was perhaps the most critical episode in my year of misery. Your friendship made it bearable, helped me through it, persuaded me almost that, with such a friend as you, one could not be doomed to go under altogether. Your brother has also a share in my gratitude, for his delightful manner helped me over more than one attack of despondency. . . .

175]

Wiesbaden
September 19, 1869

. . . I RECEIVED your kind letter of the 16th. Best thanks for all news. That was a curious commission that Klindworth gave your stepbrother. Sorry I cannot take any more outside (Roman) advice, but experience has unfortunately shown me that I should often have had less to regret if I had followed my own instincts. Since suspicion has fallen on my friend Hallwachs on whatever grounds, I must make an energetic protest. You have my word for it that H. is the only serious and competent official at the Munich Court Theatre.

I think your fear that the composer might go to Berlin for the *Meistersinger* performance is unfounded. He may have arrived at the idea, but from that to putting it into execution is ever a far cry with him. Perhaps the uncommonly witty and comparatively tactful leading article in *Kladderadatsch* on September 12 has misled him as to public opinion in Berlin.

In Munich, meanwhile, the moment cannot be far distant when opinion will set in the right direction. Read, for instance, R. W.'s excellent and extremely moderate *reply* to Perfall's [1] paid articles. Hans Richter also launched a defence in the south German press on Saturday which has guts in it and is convincing. They will be able to call Perfall's cowardice cleverness if he holds his tongue. How entertaining the inner struggle between that cowardice and his equally great vanity will be!

Should R. W. go to Berlin, I have no doubt he would be delighted if you called on him. So do not fail to look him up. I am anything but satisfied with this place. Shall probably leave the day after tomorrow, for I have leisure for neither work nor rest.

Raff is fairly busy. Also he bores me with his well-meaning but far from objective view of things, which I should rather be spared. You see, you are an exception among all my so-called " friends." Most of them fancy they know more from hearsay than I from my own experience, and feel it their duty to preach to me. That kind of thing exhausts one's patience even when nerves are normal, which mine no longer are; and the recapitulation of an odious past — in the attempt to prove to " friends " that anything " sensible " they may have to say has been considered and reconsidered long ago — is a task to which I am no longer equal.

Just now Raff came in. He tells me that the Seyfrieds reached home safely last night at eight. I may see them today and will remember you to them.

Do, my dear Bechstein, see that our projected American tour for next spring comes off. I have a really great idea: 1870 is the centenary of Beethoven's birth and I am very keen on exploiting America as a Beethoven-player if Tausig does not forestall me. Thank you for the " lady's letter." No need for congratulations. The person in question will be older than myself on the 15th of this month! How are all your family?

My first letter from Florence will be addressed to you. I really must not put off the journey any longer, though I don't

---

[1] KARL FREIHERR VON PERFALL (1824–1907), *Civil Servant, composer, intendant of the Königliche Hoftheater in Munich, an anti-Wagnerian.*

mind telling you that, in spite of the impossibility of staying in the Fatherland, I am finding it very hard as a German musician to tear myself away.

Could you not find out, directly or indirectly (through Kroll, to whom my kindest regards, please), from Simson as to the progress of my affair? Although, of course, I can wait until something happens.

176]

Borgo San Frediano 10
a.p. terreno

HAVE at last found nice quarters, in which I have just spent a good night. Otherwise I should not have had the strength to dip my pen. Two big, incredibly high rooms in a sort of palace, on the ground floor. View over, or into, a charming little garden and beyond that the Arno. Ah, my friend, if there is any place where I can recover, become myself again, and find the will and the power to live, it will be in this land beyond compare. Florence with its surroundings is no mere legend — it is far lovelier than what one hears of it or dreams. Everything thrills me incredibly. I pity all the friends and dear ones who cannot share my bliss. Until now I have lived in a transport of delight. Every scrap of the city and its environs is more interesting and picturesque, either grander or more graceful — sometimes both combined — and in any case worth more than everything I ever admired or enjoyed in the whole of my former life put together. I think it will not be long before I feel quite at home. . . .

Have you heard nothing from my counsel, Simson? Would you be so good as to ask him whether the case is coming on? It is really terrible that the second half of one's life should have no other object than to repair the follies of the first. Had I not come here, I should have ended with " gas out," as the French say. Here, however, the inducement to live is too powerful. I hear nothing from Munich and I see no papers, not even French; the Italian I do read, purely for the sake of the language, which I hope to speak easily and fairly confidently within a few months. Therefore I have to ask you: has my end been attained? Have

they at last stopped talking about me and my affairs? Is all the
scandal at an end? At Wiesbaden it was horrible. Every day
some new unpleasantness in the reading-room, while Herr Hans
Wachenhusen found it necessary to make copy, in the Viennese
papers, out of having met me there, and indulged in all sorts of
infamous variants on my appearance. What a pack of swine
they are!

How are you and yours? Please distribute greetings all
round.

Have you seen Kroll again? Would you ask him in my
name to commission his publisher Fürstner to send me a complete set of his edition of classical works? Madame Laussot,[1]
who put me up for a fortnight with a truly Bechsteinly hospitality, is giving pianoforte lessons to a talented girl — for her own
pleasure and with admirable results — and the Kroll editions
will ease her task considerably. In time it might possibly lead to
some such undertaking on the part of an Italian publisher, for I
am told that the feeling for German music is making slow but
visible progress. . . .

Talk of the wolf! I was interrupted just now by a visit from
Wehle,[2] who wanted to inquire about rooms here. Meanwhile
the weather has cleared up and chased me from my writing-
table. All the better for us both. Page 8 of the *Vossische* supplement is more amusing for you than the letters I inflict on my
friends in such years as these. Look upon this as a cheap form of
telegram to inform you that I have not yet plunged into the
waves of the Arno. Mind you don't forget that American scheme.
N.B. You would have to fetch me from here, and for a week I
would do the honours of this paradise for you like a model *valet
de place*. Not to have seen Florence would haunt one in one's
grave.

Write my address very plainly (name underlined, no title),
for letters are often overlooked here; some never leave, some
never arrive. In various respects the conditions are extremely
primitive here, but for a man who is fed up with Germany that
is no drawback. N.B. With the exception of Kroll and Perl,
please don't talk to anyone about me. I yearn unspeakably for
oblivion.

[1] JESSIE LAUSSOT, *Florentine musician.*

[2] KARL WEHLE (1825–83), *pianist, pupil of Moscheles and Kullak.*

177]

Borgo S. Frediano 10
Florence
November 4, 1869

QUITE forgotten your old pianoforte-slave? Or did my recent
" respected " go astray? It does happen here. As a set-off, the
post officials are much more polite and helpful, even cleverer.
Heavenly land, heavenly people. (But dear!) This outburst of
approval is the more surprising in that I have been very much in
the wars. Imagine a fortnight of premature winter accompanied
by every kind of obstacle. Snow on all the mountains, which
is not yet melted in spite of two days of gorgeous weather. But
with it all a deep-blue sky above and the loveliest green below;
flowers still in bloom in the public gardens, even a few roses.
As I am still without my winter clothes, I was frightfully cold
and had an attack of my old obstinate type of influenza. An even
worse calamity was that I got chapped hands at the pianoforte
and sprained my right in addition, so that I have had a week's
enforced idleness and, as you see, am guiding my pen as if it
were a broomstick. Quite cheery all the same — thanks to the
absence of all the German complications and the incredible art-
treasures of this unique city. How I wish you could potter about
with me here for a week or two, go driving, do the theatres,
which are very entertaining (charming ballet-dancers, etc.)! At
the Pergola, the leading opera-house, they are giving *The
Huguenots* as a novelty, and, upon my word, the performance is
no worse than elsewhere, across the Alps. Only the Sass (from
Paris), who has got herself engaged here for the season, is pretty
awful. I suppose the fashionable supporters of grand opera will
see and hear no more of that " elephant who had not swallowed
a nightingale " — which is what they used to say of Alboni.
     But let us have an end of these raptures of mine. (If it can
be managed, I shall be buried here too, though not just yet.) To
change the subject, then: did you receive my letter? And have
you no message for me from my lawyer? Pull yourself together,
honoured patron, friend, and co-knight of the Order of St.

Michael (no Russian order yet?); tear yourself away from the breakfast table between the sixth and seventh supplements of the *Vossische Zeitung*, take a walk through two rooms to your elegant " Levinson," and scribble a few lines. I correspond with three people only: my mamma, you, and young Spitzweg in Munich, whom I commend to you. He complains bitterly and implores me to put in a good word for him. Says he does everything to push your pianofortes, hoping eventually to pave the way for them in spite of Wüllner's intrigues; but that you always let him down, keep him waiting three or four months, and so on. What truth there is in it you know better than I. The grand I played on last year in Munich is at last sold. Among other news I should like to hear how you are, and your family. The whole B. family combined to make a complete conquest of me in August. You and yours are really very happy people, you almost reconcile me to German family life. . . .

Were Tausig's tours a success? What is Rubinstein doing? An ex-pupil of his, a charming Russian woman, called on me yesterday. I say, Bechstein, there's a dancer here I've fallen madly in love with. You never saw the like, nor did I. She is not merely a virtuoso, but a toe-poetess. It makes me sick to think of that living old-clothes-woman Judith David in Berlin.

. . . If only my hand were in condition again! I tell you, I mean to practise until I am able to play them all to blazes next spring. My nerves are really beginning to recover. Energy and the joy of living are beginning to rouse my sleepy limbs and banish sleep with an immense yawn.

You'll keep to that visit in spring?

Meanwhile yours ever,

GUIDO DI FIRENZE

PS. If possible, do warm up Simson. I am thirsting for my dream of liberty. N.B. They drink no liqueurs here, and indeed it would be not only a sin and a shame, but folly into the bargain.

178]

Borgo S. Frediano 10
Firenze
[*undated*]

Wнат a splendid fellow you are! Your letter quite warmed me up. I was almost in despair. No sooner had I done a few days' real practising when a kind of rheumatism of the joints set in in the right hand. The result has been a pause of several days, so that I cannot get on, just when everything was so favourable too. This is an exceptionally hard winter, though; the changes of temperature are in so far worse than elsewhere that it is impossible to establish normal conditions of clothing and diet. Well, I must not bewail myself to you. It will get better, I hope, and anyway I should be a fool and guilty of ingratitude to the leading of Providence were I to draw a parallel between the minor ills which I endure and the terrible major ones which I have shaken off and put behind me by my flight.

Many thanks for the cheering news that my divorce case is making good progress. How I long for the hour when the good tidings of the *fait accompli* shall be proclaimed! True, I already have my freedom, but mixed with it is the bad conscience of an escaped criminal.

Have made a five-day pause, a rather unwilling one. The rheumatism in my right arm was quite intolerable and made me unable even to put my overcoat on and off without help. If the weather here is a disgrace, what drenchings you must be having in Berlin! Certainly you can protect yourselves better, but then you miss the heavenly intermezzi of the chronic spring breezes which blow here almost daily about midday and in the evening. This lovely weather is nearly as perfidious, though, as German friendliness (I mean south German cordiality), and you have to serve your apprenticeship.

Thank you — no! Don't send me five hundred talers as a first instalment in December as you suggest. I have it in me to be a terrible spendthrift, and now that I am transplanted to this soil, so favourable to the development of extravagance, I want to commit no follies — not even for the most divine of dancers

(one flings diamonds about in her case) or actresses (how adorable these Italians are in comedy! I have just reached the stage
of understanding what they say — the written language I now
read as fluently as if it were Berlinese) — no, no follies, which
might cut short my stay here. Also, I have begun to give a few
lessons to English and American flappers, at fifteen francs a
time, so shall last out easily till New Year. Lead me not into
temptation, my friend. Yesterday I heard a charming new Italian
opera in the big Pagliano Theatre (six tiers and so comfortable!): *Ruy Blas* by a young Milanese composer, Marchetti.[1]
The Pergola Theatre, where the Sass has already screeched and
tremolo'd Valentine in that novelty (!) *The Huguenots* for the
twenty-sixth time, is a more exclusive and aristocratic house,
really for opera. There the stalls cost ten francs including the
entrance fee, which the boxes have to pay likewise. But to my
mind the finer, larger Pagliano is not inferior to it, although the
stalls cost only four and a half francs (six and a half in front).
In both theatres there are usually the same orchestra and the
same bad chorus. The orchestra is not to be sneezed at; these
fellows believe in what they play and there are violinists with a
warmth of tone unknown over your way, splendid three-stringed
double-basses, and excellent brass. Yesterday I heard crescendos
there of such force and fire as I have dreamed of, but, in my
waking hours, was never able to achieve with those beery court
players. There is a really admirable conductor, Usiglio, as elegant as he is energetic (whereas Eckert looks like a brier). The
prima donna is a young Hungarian, Ida Benza, with a fine car-
cass, a fine voice, tolerable vocal dexterity, and no greater
tendency to sing out of tune than our German song-cows. A mod-
erately stupid tenor and a very reliable baritone. In short, I had
a great musical treat, as the music of the young composer (who
was called out eighteen times during the evening) contained
much that was of interest. Verdi's latest operas: *Ballo in Mas-
chera* and *Don Carlos,* have set a new standard, and the old style
of plot is greatly toned down (I would not have it extinguished
for the world). Here and there were successful attempts at
dramatic characterization and samples of colourful instrumenta-

[1] FILIPPE MARCHETTI (1831–1902), *opera-composer. His* Ruy Blas *was first
produced at La Scala, Milan, in 1869.*

tion. The libretto is one of the best of recent years. I always think of you during such entertainments and should so much rather have you for a companion than Wehle — who again sends his kind regards. . . .

Will you do something to please me? Read the enclosed *canard*; then have it copied and smuggle it, if you can, into some of the most read papers. This is not just arrogance on my part. Those Munich swine deserve to be given a little fright on my behalf and they will get it when they read this extract from some Vienna or Berlin rag.

I am furious that your first letter was lost. It may have contained some more about the transatlantic scheme (when starting, how long lasting), and it would bore you, naturally, as I well understand — I should be the same — to tell me it all over again. Apropos, there is a good sculptor here, a rich American named Bol, whose wife is a sister of Chickering. Would it be diplomatic for me to get in touch with them? What do you think?

I grant you complete amnesty for communicating my recent letter to Kroll. It will not have interested him much, for I have quite ceased to be witty and am content to be soulless. But tell K., all the same, that I am fond of him, that he is the most sympathetic of all my colleagues, and that I consider him the most high-minded among them, also that I wish him and his every possible good thing. Very best wishes to the members of your own dear family and do send a flying message soon. I will be content with three pages, now that I have discovered how much better the three-stringed double-bass sounds than the four.

PS. I cannot compose anything for Mortadella's (Würst's) bazaar until I have, as Angelo says, Italianized myself more in music.

179]

Borgo San Frediano 10
Florence
December 8, 1869

You have a finer nose than I — at least for management of my own affairs. " Man proposes, woman disposes." What a fine true saying that was that old Tichatscheck [1] used to write in people's albums: " Life is beautiful, but costly "! Well, you will have guessed what I want. Be so good as to send me, if possible through our friend Perl, that first instalment. The weather is still disgusting beyond anything, though not precisely winterly. In spite of chronic influenza, my rheumatic pains have — touch wood! — departed, and I practise as if I were twenty years younger, and have even shed lustre on the meetings of the Cherubini Society (Madame Laussot's singing association) by a number of performances on your grand. A very good Italian notice on it already. Extraordinary things may happen here in time. By " extraordinary " they mean, here in Florence, " concert-like " — a conception almost unknown. Wehle cannot get over this state of things. He cannot arrange a soirée, everything is against it. They are as little the custom here as white beer in Munich. Hall unattainable, fellow-artists ditto, audience most ditto of all.

But Florence is lovely, even in the vilest rain, and Italian women are without a doubt the most seductive bipeds in the world. Germans I avoid here like the plague. (See the interesting autograph enclosure.) The good lady has built herself a house which transports one direct into the Anhalt quarter [of Berlin]. It is not far from the station either. Her society consists chiefly of redskins of all nationalities. I have paid my first ceremonial visit and she will not see me again. My old acquaintance Ada von Treskov, on the other hand, who is married to a certain Pinelli, secretary to the Ministry of Justice, is decidedly entertaining, and I go to see her sometimes just as if she were called Liliental. I speak and write the language fairly fluently now. The best way to learn it is by dialogues under the bed-clothes, but going to hear Italian comedy also helps. Never, even in Paris, have I seen such admirable acting. You cannot imagine how plastic, lively, graceful, and delicious it all is. You do not miss music here in the least. What more could I say to signify my pleasure in the place! (Not that there is any lack of musical talent in the nation.)

[1] JOSEPH ALOYS TICHATSCHEK (1807–86), *operatic tenor, created the roles of Rienzi and Tannhäuser.*

. . . Write again soon before I go mad, which is not impossible.

GIOVANNI DI (not DIO)

[*Enclosure*]

Florence
Saturday, December 4, 1869
Dear Sir,

I have been hoping in vain for a repetition of your pleasing and gratifying visit to me. How delightful it would be if you would give me the pleasure of your company next Monday evening! Do let me benefit a little too by your presence in this beautiful Florence. With kindest regards and friendly greetings,

LUDMILLA ASSING

180]

10 Borgo San Frediano
Florence
December 25, 1869

I OUGHT to have acknowledged the safe receipt of the two thousand francs long ago: but for one thing I was laid up by the bad weather (forty-five days of *incessant* rain — the whole country devastated by floods); then I was waiting for the promised letter, which no doubt you have had the good intention to write without being able to find time. Meanwhile Merry Christmas has invaded us. May you and your family have celebrated it happily. As for me — but never mind. . . . I must not let melancholy get uppermost or there will be no end to it. If only there were a little sunshine! It looks, however, as if the Holy Father had tucked away the world's water-drains into his pocket. We must feed ourselves, like eunuchs, on crumbs of hope.

Who do you think tapped me on the shoulder under my dripping umbrella in the Lung' Arno the other day, drawling " Good morning " in true Berlinese? Baron Korff, the African, just back from the opening of the Suez Canal, accompanied by Mr. Taglioni junior. The weather was so appalling that I accepted his invitation to kill the hour and five minutes until his train went (to Bologna), in the Hotel New York. He was really quite

nice and seemed most pleasantly surprised at such a chance
meeting with this ex-celebrity; all the same, I was devoutly
thankful he could not honour Florence with his Berlin canal
perfume any longer.

Did he deliver my greetings to you?

Yesterday I had a bit of printed satisfaction. On the occasion of a *Tannhäuser* performance the critic of the occasion
lamented my departure in a manner very pleasing for me, very
unpleasing for my successor. I began to recall vividly all my
Munich distractions and thanked Heaven for Italy's cat-and-dog
weather, which, take it all in all, is more refreshing to me than
the pleasantest day in Germany. Have now established a trio in
my *salon*. Two splendid colleagues (the leading players here),
Giovacchini and Sbolci, artists and gentlemen, I tell you, such as
I never came across in either Berlin or Monaco. A fortnight ago
we played three Beethoven trios, a week ago the three Schu-
manns. You would have enjoyed hearing us read them at sight.
And I seem to be congenial to them, for they stayed the other
night from half-past eleven to half-past three. At the same time
I am looking after the future generation by harnessing my pupil
Buonamici, who is coming on splendidly, to two pupils of the
above-named gentlemen. When they have practised together
awhile, I shall lend a hand with their ensemble. This kind of
undertaking is to be kept strictly private at present, publicity is
reserved for next season. The best part of it remains this non-
tendentious playing for one's own satisfaction.

Your grand at Madame Laussot's has to stand a good deal
from me just now. Also a purely private show. Between seventy
and eighty ladies and gentlemen of the choral society. They
have a queer way of printing the programs later, after the soirée
is over. You should hear me play Chopin's *Allegro de concert*
now! I am working up several new things and reviving all the
old. Am totally reformed as a pianist. The fact is, I forgot how
to play in Munich.

I have read the *Kladderadatsch Calendar* — pity it's so
putrid. . . . How is Tausig's health? As good as his reputation? I hear extraordinary tales of his successes. He has some
enthusiastic admirers here at the Austrian embassy: Count
Sailern, Prince Wrede, and others. Do remember me to our good

Kroll. Let him try to prevail upon his wretched publisher to send us a copy of his classical editions. I guarantee it will be worth that lanky young Jew's while. I propose to Germanize things musical here as thoroughly as I Italianize myself. There are all sorts of things brewing, but more of that later. I have some influence with the big pianoforte-shop of Carlo Ducci and shall see that he writes to Johannisstrasse 5 one of these days.

Well, good-bye. I have no writing fingers left, they have to be preserved for playing. May you have a much better new year than the old one has been. I wish it may be the same for your old friend, who would be so glad if he could entertain you *here*.

GIOVANNI DE BÜLOW

181]

Florence
January 11, 1870

*B*UT, my dear old Bechstein, what's the meaning of this?Not a line of congratulation on my reaching the age of discretion? [1] Are you faithless, or dead? You have spoilt me so all these years that I am doubly sensitive to this more than ordinary neglect. Or did you suppose I should not appreciate a line from you unaccompanied by a consignment of Gilka or Pulgian cigarettes? You need not fear. There are quantities of cigarettes here everywhere (Russian Dresdens) and grand benedictine too. (As a matter of fact, I have given up liqueurs, though.) But, really, I begin to be anxious about your health, so intriguing is your silence. Or is it that my last letters — I have written several times — have gone astray or that yours to me have been lost?

For my sins, who do you suppose did congratulate me instead of Karl Bechstein? Richard Würst, with the ulterior motive of obtaining a bazaar contribution, it's true. To punish you for your unkindness I send you the enclosed note, which is really a marvel of wit and good taste!

Brizzi and Nicolai have been here, asking me to inspect a capital Bechstein semi-grand at their pianoforte-shop. This I duly saw and praised. Mr. Astolfo Nicolai I liked very much, a

---

[1] Schwabenalter, *age of forty.* — TR.

very decent fellow, terribly solvent, always pays on the nail, and so on. The same cannot be said of Mr. Carlo Ducci, whom I mentioned to you the other day. I have made my own inquiries. A swindler, probably heading for bankruptcy. Accordingly I advise you to make a point of sticking to the first-named and have nothing to do with the latter, should he apply to you.

Brizzi and Nicolai have a small concert-room, seating a hundred and fifty. We shall *probably* give some trio-evenings there in March, when I shall play on a *Berlin* keyboard. Generally speaking, there will gradually — *pet à pet* — be some quite nice things to relate of the Italian Bülow in Florence, who has exchanged his Hans for Guido.

Count Zaluski has been transferred here from Berlin. Sends kindest remembrances to Tausig.

What's doing in Berlin? Are you and yours all well? If you don't write soon, I'll " thee and thou " you, confound it. (We should by rights have been on that footing long ago as knights of a common buttonhole decoration.) . . .

182]

Florence
January 19, 1870

ALWAYS the way with me! No sooner had my complaint been lodged in the letter-box on the bridge than the postman turned up with your charming letter. These lines have no other purpose than to thank you for it. It would be more sensible to wait a little, for at the end of the month there is a concert here for the benefit of the Pisa flood victims, at which I have promised the Duke of San Clemente to play the following: Trio (the big one) by Beethoven, with Giovannini and Sbolci; *Ricordanza — Venezia e Napoli,* by Liszt; *Allegro de concert,* by Chopin.

On this occasion, if it proves large enough, I propose to manipulate your baby in public and report to you afterwards.

Bülow and Bechstein in Italy: it must come. You could do good business here. People buy lots of pianofortes — there are new Erards, Pleyels, Herzes, everywhere. Which reminds me, I saw and honestly admired a Chickering at the house of Madame

Ball, sister of the manufacturer and wife of the sculptor. Really excellent. I cannot recall Steinway's very well, so I may be mistaken in giving the Bostonian preference over the New Yorker. Won't you, my dear man, inquire of Simson about my unfortunate affair, either directly or through our friend Kroll? The thing is a perpetual anxiety to me until it has reached its unavoidable solution. Have you any idea of the costs? The next instalment of five hundred would meet it, do you think? That would be charming. For the coming quarter I can live on the Florentine money from my lessons, which will by then amount to two thousand francs. What a blessing I do not need to claim the pension offered me from Munich! They would like me to come along humbly asking for the fulfilment of their voluntary offer, I know. They will not have this pleasure!

Talking of Munich, I should be immensely interested to know how Tausig is liked there and how he likes it. Do tell me all you hear of his impressions and communications. The kind offer of cigarettes I have already declined with thanks in my previous letter. You will not be angry? . . .

183]

Florence
February 1, 1870

LAST evening I was partly wishing that you were here and partly cursing you for all I was worth. If it were not so expensive, I should send you a telegram in the Tausig manner.

1. I wished you were here because of the capital concert and my immense success. I am in devilish good form now and was in the best of humours and played accordingly better than ever or anywhere before. You don't begin to have a notion of the perfection, correctness, and warmth of our Beethoven trio ensemble. Italy is where I belong, I have mistaken my vocation hitherto. How do you like the prices of admission? Mind you don't show Karlchen my program, or he will turn venomous about me too. The net takings in this small hall were between three and four thousand francs, an unheard-of sum here.

2. My curses, on the other hand, were directed against

your miserable tin kettle of an instrument. I was only able to play one piece, Liszt's *Ricordanza,* on it and the basses rattled quite *à la* Perauss. Buonamici managed to accompany the choir on it. I had to return to the big Pleyel, which, though it would not have borne comparison with a new full-sized Bechstein, was nice and full and clear and easy to play.

Your wretched " *Schwechten* " I sent to the Grand Duchess Marie of Russia a week ago for a (gratis) soirée, at which it sounded quite well. In a hall, however, it does not come up to your standard or mine and is only good enough for very mediocre requirements. All of which goes to show that you should buck up and send along a regular monster quite soon, for who knows what we may not undertake here during the winter? The beginning was so uncommonly encouraging that we must go on.

This last moment has given a nasty jar to my pleasant mood. A letter from Simson tells me it is essential that I should come to Berlin *at once* and *for several weeks* on account of all kinds of legal pettifogging. This is ghastly. First, my health is still in far too delicate a state to stand the fatigue of a journey at this season; and, for the rest, a long absence might most seriously upset my plans for establishing myself here, quite apart from my lessons. However, it will have to be, I fear. Necessity knows no law. But, I assure you, the mere thought of returning to Germany makes me feel suicidal. Comfort me a little, dear friend. . . .

184]

Florence
February 21, 1870

BEST thanks for your letter. The enclosure contained the offer from Nicolas Rubinstein of a handsome post in Moscow, which I refused by return of post. If it will not be too inconvenient for you and your wife, I will certainly accept your hospitality for the duration of my involuntary stay in Berlin. Your personal kindness and friendship will substantially lessen the pain of my absence from Florence. How home-sick I shall be! There will be the joy of my return, however. N.B. Have you a quiet little room in which I can drudge away undisturbed? I want to do a lot of work in Berlin and to see as few people as possible — least of all, musicians.

I am postponing my journey as long as I can, partly because of the time of year and health considerations, partly because of my musical plans.

On March 7 is the opening of Carlo Ducci's concert hall. After refusing for a long time, I have at last consented to conduct this concert. A small but exquisite orchestra; pieces by Cherubini (born in Florence, 1760), Spontini, Rossini, Weber, and Mendelssohn. We shall see how the experiment works. Ducci, the best pianist in the place, is to play himself by my express wish.

Then, on the 15th, there is the Cherubini Society's second concert, at which I have promised to play. I *am counting damnably* on the punctual arrival of your pianoforte, which, Astolfo Nicolai tells me, left Berlin on the 4th.

After my return from Berlin come the Beethoven trio evenings and popular concerts in the big theatre (Beethoven symphonies). How's that, eh?

More when we meet.

It is a feather in your cap to have brought T. and R.[1] together. Eberle is *half* right. The finance department of the Royal Bavarian Cabinet wrote to me quite on its own and I am to have about five hundred florins a quarter from now on. With my lessons I am earning, *this winter,* nearly seven hundred francs (180 reichstaler) a month. For the present, enough to live on. Seven hundred represents, I may say, the minimum of my expenditure. The theatre swallows a lot. But what a sordid topic! . . .

185]

Florence
March 17, 1870

At last your pianoforte has arrived, and in good condition. It is a grand instrument, and Buonamici has sold it straight away to a family from the Romagna. But it has been some time on the

[1] TAUSIG *and* ANTON RUBINSTEIN.

way. It is a very good thing that both concerts have been put forward a week. The first (orchestral) one was amazingly successful. The orchestra went frantic about me, and after every item *I* was called back twice. . . .

I start from here on Wednesday the 23rd, to go to Milan in the first place, where the Quartet Society has invited me to play in public. I may appear twice. That depends upon the news I am expecting from Berlin. I must say Herr Simson is not very assiduous; probably has precious little time for one poor single individual. I will write you from Milan as to when I propose to invade you. Seeing you is all I look forward to; the rest is horror.

For a week I have been in misery with toothache, an ulcer, and sleepless nights. At the concert I had to keep my mouth full of cognac to keep going at all. All the more intoxicating was the triumph. — After a few lovely spring days there have been violent storms, wintry cold, and snow on the mountains.

I have a great favour to ask Tausig. A charming young woman, Countess Dönhoff, *née* Princess Camporeale (a Sicilian), has been taking lessons with me this winter while staying with her mother, the wife of Count Minghetti, the minister. In a month she has to rejoin her husband in Berlin. She has a great passion — and *great* talent — for music, but after me she will have no one but Tausig as a teacher. Let him do me, and himself, the kindness of taking her on and finishing her — I have not had time — and making her a dangerous rival of Mimi Schleinitz,[1] whose " friend " she is. I have promised the Countess to give her a few lines to Tausig. Please let me know whether he will honour my recommendation or let me in for a fiasco. The lady is a marvel, dainty and pretty enough to drive one crazy, and nineteen years old.

And, by the way, will you keep this between the *three* of us, at least at present. . . .

---

[1] COUNTESS SCHLEINITZ, *a worker in the cause of the Bayreuth Festival Theatre fund. To her Wagner addressed his pamphlet* Das Bühnenfestspielhaus zu Bayreuth.

186]

Milan
March 27, 1870

Here's an end of joking — my visit draws threateningly near.
Yesterday I tinkled here with great success — Beethoven and
Bach too! — and am repeating the program at a matinée today
at two. Then a couple of days' rest and sightseeing before I start
early on Monday. . . . Would you please inform Advocate
Simson of my arrival? I will wire the exact time.

The enclosed telegram from Florence is only meant to convey to you that your grands have become the fashion. At least
they have begun to be. I am now having mine sent from Munich
to Florence, where I have now definitely set up my tent. Already I feel home-sick for the place. The people are amazingly
fond of me: at the last concert it rained flowers and dainty
gifts. I have been appointed president of the Cherubini Society, corresponding member of the Royal Conservatorium;
and Victor Emanuel has at last sent me the Italian Crown
order, a rather distinguished decoration, at the instigation of
Schleinitz. . . .

187]

Florence
April 22, 1870

Here I am again where I longed to be, renewing my glowing
impressions of last autumn in this glorious spring weather. The
one condition lacking is the essential and personal one of health.
I have to pay heavily for my rashness on Good Friday in Berlin:
a violent attack of influenza, with singing in my ears, maddening
toothache, and other charming *Vossische* supplements. Also I
committed a folly against which I beg to warn you: it does
not do to see Venice unless one is prepared to find Florence
small and unimportant after it. I had only one day (Tuesday)
for a fleeting glimpse in passing of the water-city, but how

overwhelmingly beautiful and alluring it is, how unique in its imposing splendour! . . .

This morning I received the welcome news that my Bechstein has arrived from Munich. Heaven be praised! I am so thoroughly spoilt through staying with you in Berlin that it goes against the grain to exercise my fingers on a hired Pleyel here.

There is only one Bechstein!

I enclose your bond, the old one, which it is urgent you should have back in case of life or death.

Perhaps you will be so good as to put the enclosed photograph of me in an envelope and pass it on to the " eccentric " pretty lady in my name.

I wish you would give me a brief account of the latest performance of the *Meistersinger* — it will have taken place by now — and tell me whether its future in Berlin is assured, as I very much hope. No news of Tausig? When do you suppose he will come back? I am asking on Countess Dönhoff's account. . . .

188]

10 Borgo S. Frediano
Florence
May 8, 1870

     . . . IN my intoxication over the excellent outcome of my experiment I feel I must telegraph to you: orchestra charming, public ditto. Really, with patience and a little swank, one can do all sorts of things here!

Would you be so kind as to tell Bock that I am waiting in pain and in vain for the busts of Beethoven and Cherubini? The last Cherubini Society concert comes off in a week's time and it would be a catastrophe for me if the busts did not arrive. (I am of course playing my own Bechstein there; it is heavenly.) . . . On June 8 I return, as you know, to Berlin. May I inflict myself on you on the 15th? Send me a line meanwhile or I shall put up at a rival hotel. Tausig?

189]

Florence
May 26, 1870

. . . SPITZWEG now suggests that, subject to your approval, the thousand-reichstaler Rubin-Bechstein which was left in Munich might be sent to Würzburg, as Nestmann will presumably not be able to get one of your pianofortes deposited in each of these places on three consecutive days. Send along your opinion on the matter, please. The Beethoven has duly arrived intact and is really a fine specimen. Many thanks for definitely ordering the Cherubini. A tradesman like Bock will not believe that I shall still buy my present though the price has gone up a couple of talers! . . .

One more favour: would you go to my advocate, Simson, and ask him whether the hopes he held out of a speedy settlement of my affair still hold good if I make the sacrifice of coming back to Berlin on the 16th? It is worse for me than you think. Italy — the country, the people, the climate, all combined — has become so essential a condition of my physical well-being that I dread a set-back, even in the excellent conditions of the Hotel Bechstein, and the beginning all over again here after it. It is no small thing, I assure you. I am old now and must have some peace if I am to do any good in the world — that is, in my new country, for no one cares a straw about me in my old German home. . . .

190]

Florence
June 5, 1870

YOUR letter finds me engaged in preparations for the journey. So glad you went to Weimar. You are sure to have seen my divine Sicilian pupil, Countess Dönhoff? . . .

H'm, Tausig my rival! Must decline to compete. But if he would like me to act as substitute for Ehlert at his Hochschule during my Bechstein orgies in Berlin, I am at his service for the evenings; it will keep me from hanging round the theatres. . . .

191]

Hotel Bellevue
Gmunden, Austria
August 11, 1870

My first impulse, after shaking off the abundant dust of the journey in an invigorating pine-bath, is to thank you again in writing for all your kindness to me as friend and Amphitryon during my third and last stay in Berlin. Give me the pleasure of an opportunity to thank you once more in person. (I will not say of retaliating in kind, for that is impossible.) Let us meet in Italy, and soon! I travelled day and night and am dog-tired. Gmunden in the rain does not thrill me, although it is, I am sure, charming in fine weather. In any case I am here for a week, so will you please forward to the above address any letters that have arrived or may still do so? I wired to my mother on arrival, leaving the rest to her; but I expect she will come here and help me to obtain the rest I need after the distractions of Berlin.

Gmunden seems to me rather like a larger Kösen, except that it has a very splendid lake, is surrounded by magnificent mountain chains, and has Viennese instead of Berlin Jews. Among others I met Rubinstein's Lewy [1] and his brother [2] the famous horn-player and singing-master. . . .

. . . Vienna, where I was able to potter for three hours and a half, made an unexpectedly fine impression. It has grown infinitely more beautiful and may now claim to be more important, from a material aspect, as a world-capital than our own Berlin. You would like it very much. So do go that way round when you come to Italy.

Am very anxious for news from the theatre of war. We get them a day later, of course. Anxious, but not upset or frightened.

---

[1] KARL LEWY (1823–83), *pianist.*
[2] RICHARD LEWY (1827–83), *waldhornist, later singing-teacher; taught Mallinger, Lucca, and Sembrich.*

The Austrian press is in part very abusive, for the majority of the population, much as it hates Prussia, hates France still more. No one doubts that the government will preserve the strictest neutrality. . . .

192]

10 Borgo S. Frediano
Florence
September 9, 1870

I wrote once from Gmunden, more from the desire to thank you again for all your kindness and hospitality than to put you in the position you so much dislike of having to reply. Today's epistle has no aim other than that of preventing you and my friends from quite losing touch with me. After a terribly watery stay at Gmunden — which must be a paradise under a clear sky — I took my mother for a tour in upper Italy, which appealed to her very much. We were particularly lucky in the weather during our ten days in Venice. At Verona we parted. My mother returned to the neighbourhood of Munich and I, after four days' sightseeing at Milan, to my so-called provisional establishment, where in spite of the seductive weather (would it might seduce you!) I intend to work off my long idleness.

Madame Laussot is also coming back, unexpectedly. I went into her drawing-room, but could not coax a sound out of the pianoforte; which leads me to assume that the new set of hammers which you kindly promised has not yet been sent off. Would you be so very kind as to dispatch it as soon as possible?

What says the metropolis about the peace? To *me* it seems the end of all things. No one really believes in the defence of Paris. The disgraceful behaviour of the big-mouthed nation to the Emperor makes me long for the severest treatment to be meted out to them by the victors. It is a fact that Napoleon only gave way to the war-party with the greatest reluctance. Here there is only talk of the Roman problem, which is actually to be settled within a few days. The government is very honest, but weak, and is haunted by a substantial dread of Prussia. Do you ever see Perl, I wonder. I wrote to him too from Gmunden and copied out the desired Mützelburg poem from the visitors' book at the Traunsee inn — a truly devoted deed, considering the weather. Tell him, I hope, when the war has worked itself out, to welcome him here as arranged. Greetings also to Remack and above all to your dear brother.

Have you heard of the doings at Lucerne on the King's birthday? That was quick work. . . .

Now for one heart-to-heart request. Tell me straight, please — no misguided generosity. Can I count upon your being so kind as to provide me with pianofortes for my proposed tour next year? . . . Did I tell you that the Vienna Gesellschaft der Musikfreunde had offered me the directorship of the conservatorium and the Philharmonic concerts? I sent a flat refusal — positively I could not now live anywhere but here. Do come and look me up. You would never have to regret a journey less.

PS. As regards the Beethoven festival in Milan, nothing is definitely settled. It will probably be about the end of November and the beginning of December. . . .

193]

Florence
November 22, 1870

You will see from the enclosed program that you played a brilliant part in my Beethoven soirée yesterday, which was more successful than the first. I played on a small grand of yours, which quite took the starch out of the big Erard which I used at the preceding one. It seems to me the best way — let the public make their own comparisons and judge accordingly. An American woman made the appropriate remark to Madame Laussot, who replied that the worst Bechstein was certainly far better than the best Erard. I shall play on the same instrument at the third and last recital, on Friday. On Saturday I go to Milan for a fortnight, where (on the 4th and 8th of December) two big Beethoven concerts take place, and am hoping to find a large Bechstein in Erber's shop ready for my performance of the E flat Concerto. It's an old promise, you remember? I am sorry you did not hear me yesterday; was quite pleased with myself and rejoiced in the end that I had not acted upon my friend Richard W.'s kind suggestion that I should "commit suicide" about two years ago. The trick I brought off here is something that no one has done before: I played everything without music and with the precision of a needle-gun. In the case of trios and such-like there are obvious difficulties in the way.

How are you, your charming brother, the family, the factory? All well and happy? I should be glad to know it and most grateful for a line of greeting to convey the happy information. As regards anything else that happens in Berlin — well, I confess that Germany grows more remote every day, and even Italian distress interests me more than German war splendours. I hope, by the way, I am not morally treading on your corns by expressing this my private expert opinion. . . .

. . . Ruff is about to publish a stout volume of my pianoforte pieces, which are very, very pretty and bear the title: *Carnival of Milan*. My Beethoven edition is at last complete, too. In short, I have not been exactly lazy. But, as usual, I am talking too much of myself. Excuse the uninterestingness of the material.

194]

Florence
January 28, 1871

. . . WELL, thank God, your small grand from last year is still unsold. It did brilliantly in my recitals (Schubert, Mendelssohn, and probably, the day after tomorrow, Schumann), programs of which I enclose. Yes, it really sounded beautiful, pleased everyone; and I am glad I refused Bösendorfer's recent presentation-offer and sent Ducci and his Erards to the devil. You are *hors de concours* and have no longer any rival in the world.

As far as my health is concerned, I am rather exhausted by my many lessons, rehearsals, and the incredible amount of practising I put in. Even the current program I play altogether without notes, and this, to my knowledge, no one else has done, not even myself up to date. . . .

There, I was nearly forgetting to congratulate you on your

promotion. From now on: *Imperial* German — or Prussian — court purveyor.

I don't know which exactly, for I read no papers. I have only *one* feeling left, that of horror for this barbarous slaughter of human beings. Were it not that my dear stepbrother Henry had fallen at Chateauneuf on November 18 (he was not yet eighteen), I should be the most determined pro-Frenchman, such is my state of mind. . . .

195]

10 Borgo S. Frediano
Florence
March 3, 1871

. . . I CAME back a few days ago from Milan, where I had a look at the *carnevalone*. It was well worth it. By a special privilege handed down by St. Ambrosius, it is held there from Ash Wednesday to the following Sunday. I enjoyed myself hugely — and with a good conscience after my hard labours here — but on arriving home, found a demand from the Berlin commissioner of taxes. Would you be so very kind as to inquire (Perl is, so far as I remember, on the Commission of Assessment) whether it is absolutely essential that I should be bled yet again. Could I not ignore it, or should I run the risk of distraint by the Prussian ambassador? If this cup (or collection-bag) is not to pass me by, may I beg of you to requisition forty-eight reichstalers from friend Perl and satisfy the Prussian State demands, so that I may be left in peace for another year? I don't know what I should rather not, or, rather, what I should not rather pay than these particular forty-eight talers.

Herr Karl Tausig was here during my absence, staying with the mother of his goddess (whom I prefer to the daughter), Countess Minghetti, whom he delighted with his fine playing and who took him driving everywhere with her. He is said to have looked rather ill and, as the weather was not mild enough for him, to have faded out again one fine morning. But why should I tell you this? You will already be far better informed. . . .

One more request. You remember that fine collection of dying warriors' masks (from the Schlüter arsenal) which I had photographed for Simson (Eckenrath, corner of Charlotten and Leipziger Strasse)? If they have come down in price, would you send me two complete copies, as I can use them here as presents? Would you be so kind? . . .

196]

Florence
May 5, 1871

IT is not like me to have let so much time elapse before thanking you for your welcome letter and the various parcels which, though late, arrived safely from Brizzi and Nicolai. The truth is, I have been really ill for a month past. All the old pains in the joints began again, accompanied by new horrors, as, for instance, real neuritis, for which I tried several remedies without much result. But what am I about, to worry you like this with my health bulletins! I am, however, obliged to refer to my condition, because you will presumably wish to know whether I am going to carry out the proposed American tour (from September on), and I can give you no other reply than that I do not know; for the decision will and must depend on my state of health. A hundred and fifty concerts in six to seven months is no trifle. Heaven knows I shall have to work up my paternal feelings if I am to find the courage for that plunge. The aim of leaving my daughters a decent dowry one day must hallow the means, this public tinkling. And I shall therefore take all possible pains during the next quarter to recover my health and mobilize my fingers sufficiently. Between ourselves, though, I have not much faith in my success. All this time in Italy I have been deluding myself, but I may as well admit now that those painful years in Munich and the neighbourhood have radically undermined my constitution. I blame myself, as you know, in the long run; but it is rotten to be thrown into circumstances over which one has no control. Robert Radecke [1] would perhaps have come through

[1] ROBERT RADECKE (1830–1911), *pianoforte pupil of Moscheles, violin pupil of David. Filled a number of important posts, including that of* Hofkapellmeister *in Berlin (1870) and director of the Stern Conservatoire (1888).*

the whole thing better, but on the other hand he would not have
been so good a conductor of *Tristan* as I. . . .

Yesterday I had a lively reminder of the new imperial city:
who should tap me on the shoulder at lunch but Herr Paul Meyer-
heim (whom I greatly admire as a painter). He introduced his
prosaic wife and his most horrible horror of a mamma-in-law,
Madame Lehfeldt, with her son — that is, his brother-in-law —
one of the most sneering, filthily conceited objects conceivable.
Heavens, I thought the whole Spandauer Strasse had descended
upon me.

The last announcements you sent me concerning Herr Richard Wagner's Berlin plans have put me in a state of great suspense and I implore you to go on sending them. *Little* as these
things *now concern me,* you will understand that it is my heart-
felt wish that he and his wife may have complete success in all
they undertake. May they be spared any of Berlin's dirty tricks
in no matter what form or disguise! You will do what I ask,
then, won't you? . . .

My dear Bechstein, I have been cursing you frequently
for some time past; my pianoforte, in other respects still quite
well-behaved, has had an epidemic of string-snapping which
drives me to fury because I always seem to hear the old saw:
Can't do one thing at a time, two it has to be. But why this practical joking? Is it with a view to keeping it in tune? Or does the
disadvantage balance the advantage? Honestly, have you made
Perl repay you for the expenses I put you to? Do please not
let me sink any deeper into debt, and for heaven's sake drop
all this about my services in connexion with your pianofortes.
Precious services, these, when I secure for my concerts, straight
from the maker, the best pianofortes and those which show off
the player most favourably. It is quite absurd. . . .

My ten pianoforte pieces, published as *Carnevale de Milano*
(Ruff has not yet sent me copies), are probably still unknown
to you. You'll like them, I think. Give Bial my kind regards and
ask him to play you the stuff some time. He's quite equal to
it. . . .

197]

Florence
May 21, 1871

I MUST at least send a line to thank you, best of friends. How charmingly you have met my unreasonable wishes! The account of R. W.'s appearance in Berlin and his reception gave me great pleasure. The Berliners must have behaved very decently; otherwise Gumprecht [1] would certainly not have withheld his wrath so self-denyingly or Engel so determinedly wrenched himself free from the navel cord of the *Nationalzeitung*. Even Dorn is not altogether thorny — he blossoms out here and there. His praise of W. *as conductor* reminds me of Gutzkov's eulogy of Wagner *the poet*. A characteristic spectacle of jealousy and envy playing hide-and-seek with themselves, or so it appears to the onlooker. It was a great relief to me to hear from you that Frau Wagner's state of health is so visibly good. How fortunate for this woman to be separated from her first husband, for whom she was *far* too important, and be able to wipe out the first sad half of her existence with a second (please God!) better one!

So you advise me not to go to America? But why? I shall not rest until I have fulfilled this duty towards my daughters, for whom, as you know, I am unable to do anything else. Unfortunately I am still kept waiting day after day for definite news from Mr. Strakosch, whose artfulness consists, I suppose, in taking me by surprise in the last month, when I shall be so busy as to have just time to say an unconditional yes.

Herr Tausig has done an excellent piece of work in the Beethoven quartet arrangements, which he has dedicated to Countess Dönhoff. I have not yet seen his new *Studies,* but have ordered them from Munich. Sorry as I am to hear of his bad health, I am convinced that mine is much worse. I am being gnawed away gradually by the rats of my past. . . .

So glad that you are prepared to be very nice to Frau von S. Could you find out from her, I wonder, whether she prefers the

---

[1] OTTO GUMPRECHT (1823–1900), *writer on Wagnerian subjects, director of the* Nationalzeitung, *1847.*

Rubinstein or the Tausig fingering. This is purely a piano-teacher's question.

Why did you not warn me that those testimonials to the wearing qualities of your grands were coming out? I could have given you an expression of opinion in better style and more apodictic. Anyone might think from this one that I was capable of coquetting with Schweighofer and Co. . . .

PS. If I do not go to America, I might consider doing some concerts with Steinitz. It would be very kind if you would some time let me know when he would be available, taking into consideration Herr Tausig's inscrutable plans.

198]

Florence
August 10, 1871

. . . I HAVE now planned out my winter campaign more carefully. First I go, immediately after New Year, to the most difficult but also the most important place for a pianist: Vienna. If I make a success of it, as I hope, I may also go with Steinitz (that is, Steinitz may take *me*) to north Germany if it looks profitable. I am wondering now whether Steinitz knows the ropes well enough in Vienna and the neighbourhood. The only man who could really help me in Vienna would be — Bösendorfer. Should you think it disloyal and a denial of my *Beflügler,* my dear friend, if I wrote to Bös.? You know his pianofortes are unsympathetic to me and that it will cost me a hell of a lot of trouble to get accustomed to the touch, but I am afraid that Bösendorfer is too much of a power in the land and that I shall have to bite into this sour apple. Tell me what you think and tell me also, honestly, whether you would really like me to play on your grands in Vienna or whether you are indifferent. I am indebted to you in so many ways that I wish to avoid even the appearance of — well, you understand me and we have been through thick and thin together for so many years that I should not like to negotiate in any way with Bös. without first informing and consulting you. So send me a line please, without ceremony. . . .

199]

Brescia
August 12, 1871
(*Just starting for Bassano*)

Brescia is not only one of Italy's most artistic and (from the antiquarian point of view) interesting cities, but also one of the most musical, thanks to Bazzini, whose birthplace it is. This violin virtuoso and composer, who is settled here permanently, has established a philharmonic society, at whose orchestral concert, last Sunday, I played Beethoven's E flat Concerto to an audience of about fifteen hundred people, the accompaniment being excellent. . . .

Did you read my Tausig obituary? His widow wrote me a few really touching lines and sent me a medallion with a lock of his hair. I received them just as I was leaving and have not yet been able to reply. . . .

200]

Florence
August 17, 1871

I was so touched by the real kindness of your last letter that I should have written long before this to thank you had I not had to devote my pen exclusively to an urgent piece of work — though I had to think of you every quarter of an hour while I did it. "How was that?" I'll tell you. In about a week from now the following conversation will take place in your sitting-room. My Karl is still sitting at the breakfast-table, smoking his third cigarette, which, through his absorption in the *Vossische*, goes out every moment and runs through another ha'porth of Marseille wax vestas. A step is heard; Oscar comes stamping in from the shop. "Are you there, Karl?" "Yes, what is it?" "I've brought you something new." "What?" "The *Signale*." "H'm, h'm, h'm! A long article, a jolly good article on Karl Tausig, I see." "Yes, but guess who wrote it." "Surely not — "

"Yes, it comes from Florence; at least, not from Florence itself, but some little hole of an Italian resort — suspicious sort of a name with something like 'harem' in it." "Well, hand it over, I must look at it at once." And Karl's print-weary eye brightens. Carefully folding the greyish newspaper, which unfortunately cannot be utilized later for the noblest portion of the body, he takes leave of it with a tremendous yawn by way of a polite tribute to the intellectual maxims of the *Vossische*; then picks up my article in the *Signale* and reads it with friendly interest and an occasional approving grin. Yes, my dear Bechstein, I counted heavily on pleasing you a little, if no one else, when I first chained myself to the writing-table, unwilling and rather embarrassed, to accede to Mostrich's urgent request. It is seven years now, as you know, since I wrote anything on music, and it seemed to me as if I could not write printable German any more unless it were *à la* Karlchen Miessnick. But soon I got better with it and wrote (and rewrote) for practically two days and a night. Yesterday morning I sent off the possibly too thick manuscript to meet its fate at Senff's hands. Good luck to it and to me.

A thousand thanks for the offer of Tausig's pianoforte. But I have qualms — will tell you later — and really my old and trusted companion does me very well in spite of its persistent string-snapping. Later, when I return to Italy as a small capitalist from my concert tours, I may perhaps have the money to buy myself a beautiful pianoforte and should then ask you to choose me a really exquisite one as if it were a *los amigos* cigar. I implore you, for your part, to protect me in my ignorance in practical affairs against the wily Steinitz by arranging for us to meet occasionally and enabling me to correct my ridiculous bashfulness. Thanks very much, too, for your advice, even if I can't follow it, to convert francs into talers. Would you, by the way, be so kind as to hide my address from people like the importunate Papa Steinitz and in general render me unapproachable as far as possible?

Your last letter crossed mine. Don't be offended because I did not wait for an answer, but, relying on your friendly bill of indemnity, wrote to Bösendorfer about Vienna. For go there I must; if I do not succeed (though I believe I shall) on this most difficult and ungrateful ground, all my dreams of virtuoso-dom may go to the devil, and I'll end my days somewhere as a musical village schoolmaster. . . .

201]

Florence
October 3, 1871

I AM just back from an unduly extended autumn holiday spent in magnificent Venetian villas and am feeling desperately flat in consequence. The first letter I pick out from the pile is the one with the wild men's seal, which, however, contains no greeting from you but a silent recommendation of the Becker pianofortes in Petersburg. "What's all this? " Why, that Herr Paul Peterssen, Becker's partner, requests me in a most cajoling manner to play in Petersburg and Moscow *during* my tour in Germany and Holland. Naturally I shall, quite politely, decline. By the way, did you receive a few lines in my fist from Berlin?

I have let myself in for rather an unnecessary amount of correspondence with Steinitz. He has a passion for letter-writing — I can hardly keep up with him — and frequently contradicts himself; that is, forgets or appears to forget our earliest conversations, in which I explained my inexorable principles with considerable force.

All the same, I hope to get on with him, though it may cost me something; for he is practical to a degree, and the general tone and manner of his letters to me are quite decent. And the fact that in the mean time I have been vigorously warned against him by so-called friends makes one reason the more (as, knowing me, you will not be surprised to hear) why I should stick to him. As regards the money-making side of it, I quite agree with him in the main; one thing he must realize, though: that one treatment does not suit all, and that my personality, my particular reputation, makes it necessary for me to observe certain precautions which another virtuoso might not find necessary. Well, I imagine he is up to the ears with his arrangements for the concert-party in Scandinavia, and no one can serve two masters at once satisfactorily.

If, in the course of conversation, you should have an opportunity of warning or enlightening him about me, you would be
doing me a great service; for once I embark on useless correspondence, with all the misunderstandings it entails, I am lost.
I should be capable then of throwing up the whole thing. . . .

202]

October 25, 1871
Florence

YOUR letter, just received, has both saddened and alarmed
me; saddened on account of the sad news of your friend Seyfried's sudden death, in which I feel for you sincerely, as I had
a great liking for him; alarmed because of your own state of
melancholy and your hypochondriacal thoughts of death, which
are due, of course, to a disordered state of health, of which,
however, you take too black a view. For heaven's sake, for your
friends' and relations' sakes, do not merely spare yourself, but
keep as fit as you possibly can!

I am writing at once, although I only returned this morning
from Rome, full of grandiose impressions, but also full of influenza. I went to see Master Liszt on his sixtieth birthday (after
three years' separation), and both he and Princess W[ittgen-
stein] seemed greatly pleased. It did me good to find him in
such good condition physically and most kind and invigorating
mentally.

You, my dear Bechstein, were much in the picture. The
Master was delighted to hear that your pianofortes had been
praised as they deserved by Adolf Henselt and he several times
expressed his great appreciation of your gentlemanly habit of
invariably greeting him with a beautiful grand when he visits
Germany. On November 10 Liszt is definitely leaving Rome to
settle *permanently* in Pest (except for short trips to Weimar).

But you want my answer to the Berlin proposal. *Your* particular scruple is *not* mine. Yesterday the Princess asked me if
I could " not possibly *come to a reconciliation* with W." I pro-
tested vigorously, saying: " I have never *broken* with him; what
need, therefore, for a reconciliation? "

Frau von S. would seem not to have profited much by her association with artists if she really thinks otherwise. There is, however, another drawback: I am very much afraid that it is impossible, physically as well as morally, for me to live anywhere but in Italy and among Italians. Besides, I have still to be a travelling virtuoso for another one and a half to two years — that is unalterable. . . . On *one* condition (quite between ourselves, old man) I could, and should be obliged to, bring myself to accept a post in Germany or Russia: that is, if the seventeen-year-old star of my life could be persuaded to become my permament companion. Then I should have to have a position to offer her, and if I could take this young Italian with me to Germany, I might be able to forgo my new and actual home. But there is at present nothing to prognosticate. First this father-of-a-family-as-pianist role of mine would have to cease and the seventeen-year-old star in question become two years older. Perhaps I may change my point of view with time; at present — that is, today — no other is possible. But to come to the point: the gentlemen in Berlin will certainly not agree to any such vague arrangement, and as you will presumably be required to give them a definite statement from me, simply say *no*, with my regrets and thanks. Unless, of course, you like to refer them to my visit to Berlin in the end of January, when they could treat with me direct. . . .

PS. Beethoven edition out at last, Cotta. This piece of work will make people want me!

203]

Florence
December 28, 1871

. . . WHAT do you say to this farewell concert of mine? Takes your breath away, doesn't it? A morning concert, not given, but *requested by his admirers*, as it reads, literally translated. . . .

On Monday, the 1st, I really start travelling straight through to Vienna. I want to hear Rubinstein's big concert there on the

3rd. I am playing on the 7th, 8th, 13th, and 18th. Write a line to me, just a greeting, to Hotel National. . . .

204]

Frankfurt a. M.
April 6, 1872

PROFESSOR LEBERT conjured me by all his gods, and until I was nearly deaf, to risk all the credit (such as it is) that I am unofficially supposed to possess in your estimation — in short, to put in a good word or several for a young pianoforte-shop manager in Stuttgart. The idea is that you should be prevailed upon to send him a consignment of Bechsteins. There is an immense demand, as their unrivalled superiority is acknowledged there. Sale all the more certain as so many rich foreigners winter and summer in Stuttgart. There, I have kept my promise, as you will bear witness to these gentlemen, I hope. A pity you were not at Munich on the 2nd and Mannheim on the 4th. In the one place you would have rejoiced over the audience, in the other over my baton. Actually these two free concerts are the pleasantest within my recollection. . . .

On June 1 I begin my work in Munich, which will last until July 15. Revision of *Tristan* and *Meistersinger.*

Good-bye, my dear pianoforte-pope. . . .

205]

Prague
April 17, 1872

IT was impossible to write to you before the concert yesterday, yet there was nothing I was in a greater hurry to do than to thank you again with all my heart for the hospitality and other kindnesses you heaped upon me.

What a delightful success that cosy Lucullus-like dinner of yours was! You intended it, I know, to sweeten not so much my departure from Berlin as the journey here to my last concert; and in fact I travelled most comfortably and, in spite of the proverbially vile April weather, played in the best of moods, achieving a most satisfactory material, and a quite fabulously colossal musical, success.

I could give a long series of concerts here, notwithstanding the unfavourable season, so receptive and music-thirsty are both musicians and amateurs after their long drought; but honestly I am a bit tired, though not exactly exhausted, and various motives conspire to drive me into the south-bound train. Tonight I expect my mother, whom I telegraphed to postpone her proposed night journey. It depends upon her health whether I go to Vienna, where I intend to spend a day for the sake of looking up our poor Tausig's lady and also our common friend Bösendorfer. He sent me a really — for Viennese workmanship — very respectable grand. Oh, but it was a terrible hour of temptation that I spent in Herr Miko's shop yesterday. Close to the Bö[sendorfer] stood a fascinating Be[chstein], which Kapellmeister Smetana of the Bohemian Opera-house had introduced to the public last Sunday with great effect. You approve of me, I hope, from your point of view, for resisting the temptation. When I come to think it over, Steinitz has made a lot of *faux pas* and his truffle-nose is not so keen as they make out. Austria might have been exploited in quite a different way. Graz, Pressburg, even Pest (let alone Vienna) would have yielded much more as a continuation of the tour than the rotten Rhine Falls and a very uncertain Switzerland. Still, I must not be unjust. Perhaps it merely irritates me to have to pay him his share of Prague this month, a hundred and thirty talers. But thank God for a Samson to watch my interests in the American deal. . . .

206]

Naples
May 6, 1872

How goes it? I am so-so. The reaction has set in with frightful exhaustion, rheumatic twinges, attacks of yawning, and so on. I have therefore every reason to congratulate myself on having plunged into the southernmost south after depositing my mother safely in Florence. She enjoyed the journey and was not at all tired. I even had the brilliant inspiration of arriving here precisely on the 25th, in time for the principal act in one of the most glorious and devastating special performances that H.M. Vesuvius has deigned to give in this century. You need not suppose the enclosed picture to be exaggerated. It looked exactly like that. Imagine in addition the seething motion and incessant thunder such as Wieprecht could not produce on his drum even at the monster concerts. *I*, if you please, sat in a bar of a ship on the beach, ate mussel soup and drank fiery red Capri with it, and listened to Neapolitan folk-songs. Moments like that atone for years of toil and trouble. But for five days after, when the volcanic Calvary had finished belching, it was terrible. Perpetual darkness, a thick merciless rain of ashes, black sand, and even small stones. Impossible to move in the street without an umbrella or a handkerchief to veil one's eyes. But how the gay life here would amuse you! The row is incredible — Berlin's liveliest quarter is as dead as ditch-water by comparison. Yes, I mean it. . . .

A proposito, your rival (in personal amiability — don't be alarmed! You beat him on that score too and by many a length) Bösendorfer has been plaguing me with offers of pianofortes. Have at last agreed to his sending me one to Munich for my six weeks' stay there in the Kanalstrasse. Do you regard that as disloyal? You know you never have anything in stock (may it long continue!) and have ruined yourself sufficiently already for your grateful but unable-to-pay debtor.

207]

Munich
September 5, 1872

ONE hears nothing of you these days, old friend. How are you? Sitting in your bow-window or have you gone to Switzerland? The latter I hardly think likely, for you would surely have called at my summer residence, which is Munich this year, either on the journey out or on your return. Or can you have avoided me purposely? I can hardly believe that, though, for you surely cannot bear me a grudge for my having had a bite into that sour

Viennese apple the other day. It was all to the honour of the north-German pianoforte-smiths' art, remember. You know how it happened. Or do you prefer not to know? Our common and personally so charming friend B. had sent a grand to M. for me, which I found on my arrival at the end of May. As soon as the date of the Wagner concert was fixed (it went splendidly, financially and artistically), I wrote to Vienna to express my deep regret at being unable to use the pianoforte that had so kindly been sent me (for practising) at the concert on account of its defective mechanism. At the same time I asked Spitzweg to telegraph to you. The speed with which Berlin responded to our *cri du cœur* was marvellous. But — but no less marvellous the speed with which Herr B. dispatched a mechanic to put the Imperial Royal Austrian instrument in order. What was I to do? My decision was promptly made: *I* would play the Beethoven sonata and accompany the songs on the Bö. (my reputation plays for me); Hartvigson [1] should have the Be. for the Weber *Konzertstück*.

On the program it looked very grand — concert grand by Be., Berlin: Hartvigson; concert grand by Bö., Vienna: Bülow. But in reality it was very different, I need not explain *why*. The personally so charming Viennese, who had naturally hurried over, fled from the concert-room in terror; but thanked me afterwards in the most touching way for not taking a flying leap from Vienna to Berlin in the middle of the sonata, which he would " have found quite natural " on my part. I can assure you, my dear fellow, it was as much as I could do to force my ears and fingers. You will probably have read in different papers some wild-goose stories with my name attached. Much has been half fixed up, much projected, and very much has turned to water or gone up in smoke. For the present this is all that is definite: to-night I go to Baden-Baden for two or three days, then to Wiesbaden until the end of the month. From October 1st to 20th or thereabouts I shall be pottering round Munich, officially because H.M. the King wishes me to conduct the new performances of *Tristan* and other things; but actually on account of private matters. What else is to happen from the middle of October is not

---

[1] FRITZ HARTVIGSON (1841–1919), *pupil of Gade and Bülow. Filled teaching posts in England at the Royal Academy of Music and the Royal College of Music.*

yet quite certain. I may possibly accept the pressing offer made to me to exercise a musical dictatorship of sorts over the opera and so on in Warsaw. It would suit me quite well and I could get away any time for concert excursions (minus Steinitz) to all sorts of places in Russia; but any work I did there would be so entirely without influence on the actual civilized world of music that it would seem almost like squandering my powers. . . .

208]

Baden-Baden
September 29, 1872

WHAT would I not have given to have you there last night? Was in such good form, audience ditto — great reception, hurrahs, and unusually enthusiastic recalls — and a horrible soulless, toneless, wooden-touched Erard into the bargain.

Do come to the rescue. As a result of this dazzling success I am to show off my conducting and playing at the last concert of the last gaming season here, but can only accept if you send Herr Alffermann (pianoforte-shop) a grand. It will be bought up like hot rolls, you may be sure. Will you? Heaven knows I am reluctant to bother you, but without you I am only a " fragment," as you know. I had no time to write from Wiesbaden and thank you for your welcome letter, but in order to see your Kätchen I called on Frau Seyfried. Kätchen looked very well, happy and bonny; had just had a pianoforte lesson with Music-director Freudenberg (recommended by Raff), undoubtedly a better man than that unfortunate Berliner Zech, who made such a mess of things at a concert there recently.

I am terribly sorry that you have had so much worry with your men. But, my dear sir, the strike was invented long before Lassalle, and *my* personal friendship with this learned genius (for he was that in a far higher degree than the agitators) was based not in the least on socialism, but on sociableness. I am therefore as innocent as a new-born lamb, in spite of the music to Herwegh's song.

Frau von Mouchanoff is here, dazzling as ever, lunching with me, dining with the Empress, and finding the morning entertainment the better of the two. . . .

My health is good just now (touch wood!), fingers almost in order, disposition vigorous — in short, a fairly rosy outlook.

Did not go to America because Steinweg, who called on me in Munich in June for the purpose, emphatically dissuaded me. He had given Grau, Rubinstein's impresario, a guarantee and was not, therefore, in a position to do me the same service; assured me that I should hardly make fifteen thousand dollars, whereas next year I could probably make twenty-five. In fact Steinitz has rather let me down. I dare not undertake it at my own risk and so thought better simply to wait, and for next season — that is, the one now beginning — to be content to potter about Europe again. Many a headache has it cost me. Instead of one year, I shall now have to spend two in slaving for my children before I can begin to think about myself. But enough of this. Thank you for your consent in the matter of Frau von Welz, who will write to you direct. (Well able to pay, I believe.)

My choice did lie between Mannheim and Warsaw, but the Jews' intrigues have dished the first for me and I am quite glad, after the event. Congratulations on your — fourth, is it? You will soon have outstripped me there too. . . .

PS. If you happen to have any more *small busts* of me, would you please send *two* to Herr Raff (Wiesbaden, Stiftstrasse 10) for himself and a Russian pupil?

210]

Amsterdam
January 4, 1873

. . . A MEETING with Herr Wagner at Cologne? No, no, my friend, not in *this* century. How could you suppose it? As to whether the contents of W.'s letter as quoted (it is evidently to Niemann, for Herr Wa. has *not* written to Hülsen) correspond to the facts or not, I can only say I do not care a damn. The experiences I have had in life have taught me once and for all how certain things should be dealt with! . . .

There is quite an uproar in Belgium because I am playing

your pianofortes. Really charming threatening letters from Pleyel and Wolff in Paris! It would appear that we German artists are not after all so abhorred in France as to be considered unworthy of advertising Paris manufactures. I got quite a lot of amusement out of it. . . .

A good thing you did not fall into the Bayreuth trap. I should have resented it very much. Congratulations on your sound instinct. It looks to me very much as if an attack were meditated. . . .

211]

Baden
16 Schloss Strasse
September 15, 1873

Is it really quite impossible for us to meet during this summer, my dear Crœsus-Nimrod? There is so much, important and unimportant, for us to talk about. The written way does not appeal to either of us and is in many respects so unsatisfactory! I was delighted to hear that Karlsbad suited you so well. . . .

You know that I have to allow the Rubinstein-weary transatlantic public a year in which to recover its breath. Not until the *end of August 1874* do I go to America for the " Bülow Concerts " under the direction, not nominal this time, of Ullmann. That is all very well, but the worst is that I shall be able to give myself no rest from tinkling; my fingers must not get rusty (which is apt to happen with my small hands), and in fact I must chain myself to the mast or keyboard.

N.B. On my return from America I shall accede to the Grand Duke of Baden's repeated requests and establish myself, though not for good, at Karlsruhe. I hope that my private means will then allow me to throw up the job from one day to the next, should it prove too niggling or uncomfortable. But this between ourselves. . . .

. . . Our good Bösendorfer wants to do the Russian tour with me, assuming, of course, that I play his pianofortes. Honestly they cannot seriously harm your reputation, though they may damage mine; for they do not (and yours do) provide the

playing-fields that I need for my fine shades of touch and tone.
All the same, I am attracted by the prospect of so pleasant a
companion on whom I could fall back in case of trouble. But
more important than even this consideration is my anxiety that
our relation should not be in the slightest degree tarnished by
such an arrangement. Write soon and tell me what you think,
quite straightforwardly. Bösendorfer proposes (remember we
have had no direct correspondence about it, a common friend
here is carrying on the negotiations) to engage Steinitz for himself as caravan-leader (he knows the country), which would
assist me admirably, as I should have no dealings with him
direct and B. would keep him in order. I'm sorry for you, old
man, but you see you must read all this and let me have a reply
very soon. Don't be angry. . . .

212]

Baden
September 20, 1873

THANK you very much for your frank reply. I have taken all
possible care not to misunderstand it, for to be misunderstood
is a fatality one likes to spare others as well as oneself. Unfortunately it has fallen to me to be misunderstood by you of all
people. You ought really to know me better than to feel obliged
to repeat B.'s Petersburg offer, after being told I had declined
it, by proposing to guarantee my concerts in Petersburg and
Moscow for any sum I liked!!!

But enough of that. As I said, I am so far from intending to
hurt you — surely my straightforward question was proof
enough — that I shall now either give up P. and M. altogether
or else swear allegiance to the old flag: yours. Eighteen years of
friendly relations are not to be so lightly jeopardized.

On other points, too, you have misunderstood me. " Positive " advantages I should not gain through having Bösendorfer; on the other hand, it would be an inestimable satisfaction to have the company of a kindly, cultured gentleman who
would both keep my humour (which is sadly falling off) up to
the mark and at the same time watch carefully to see that my

health does not suffer. In that respect neither Schäfer nor that greasy Jew St. would be of any use. Even at a distance the thought of that trivial idiotic coarse fellow makes me seasick, and I don't mind telling you that it takes a tremendous effort to bring myself to carry on with this virtuoso moneymaking business at all. So you see, for the sake of a moral support such as B.'s company would be, I should have been capable of dispensing with the *advantages* which *your* instruments provide for my effects. Or do you perhaps think that Bö. has " *guaranteed* " my concerts? . . .

Karlsruhe is practically off the cards. I have known it these two days past. You ought really to congratulate me, for I cannot exist in Germany. After America I go straight back to the promised (though unmusical) land of Italy. . . .

213]

Zürich
October 14, 1873

I AM extremely sorry, but there is no help for it; I cannot spare you, I must speak out, must use language! It can't be done by word of mouth — my friendship for you debars me from saying it to a third person — so it will have to go to you direct in writing. In spite of catarrh and headache I have been trying all the afternoon to bring your grand into a proper frame of mind. Passages like:

and many similar ones are simply *not* playable in strict *tempo* and with rhythmical precision. Ten times running, the second B either does not sound at all or is distressingly feeble. Yes, really, incomparable as your pianofortes are in respect of nobility, fullness, and colour of tone, not to speak of their splendid equalization and other advantages, they do leave an immense deal to be desired in their repeating mechanism. I am frightened to death to think what may not happen to me tonight — that is, what notes will refuse to sound. And you will remember that is an old lament of mine of many years' standing. But this particular defect has grown more marked of late, it seems to me.

Ask Vulkov what I suffered or professed to have suffered last season. The said Vulkov has always stood up for you vigorously, it is true, shifting the blame — when it was possible for him to deny the fault — on to the temperature, the transport, and other possible influences; but once, when it really could not be done, he had to admit, though with obvious reluctance, that I was right.

And now I am bound to fear that I shall have offended you. Every man has one spot in which he considers himself invulnerable and you will reply that this imperfection exists solely in my imagination and is an obsession of mine, perhaps even a fault in my technical equipment, and so on. Very good. You have the right to do so, but I stand by what I have said. And this my unalterable opinion is intended to lead to a practical conclusion: will you *please* send me for my Russian tour — or at least for the capitals, Petersburg and Moscow — instruments in which the fault I have described is either non-existent or less noticeable than in the last grands you were so kind as to place at my disposal. You see, one of my specialities on which I really pride myself is a superfine sense of rhythm, and to this I can hardly give effect on your grands. Otherwise, my dear Bechstein, I must renounce the idea of a Russian tour altogether, or at least as regards Petersburg and Moscow, where it will be heavy going against the two Rubinsteins. You will see from the enclosed letter from Bösendorfer (which is for your strictly private perusal) that I have cried off the journey for two, as soon as your letter came to hand, thereby respecting to the full your personal scruples and fears. . . .

214]

Cassel
October 24, 1873

Young Scheel brought me your note, which made me feel extremely sorry that I wrote the other day in so desperate a tone while still under the influence of the Zürich pianoforte's bad reputation. You misunderstand me completely when you accuse me for definitely blaming the mechanism of your pianofortes and tell me that you feel hurt — as, if that were so, you would have right to be. It is a question of one particular point, but one which is *essential* for me and my rhythm, and on this point I have always, if you will remember, expressed my dissatisfaction on every opportunity, although you invariably put it down to my imagination.

I fear it will be impossible for us to speak to each other, as you for your part deny the existence of a fault which I find more and more marked in the newer grands. You will never convince *me*, I may say, except by the practical method of showing me a pianist who can play certain passages, maintained by me to be unplayable on your instruments, with the precision, clearness, and speed which I consider appropriate. . . .

215]

27 Duke Street, Manchester Square,
London
November 11, 1873

How have you been since we parted in Düsseldorf? I have been fairly well in spite of a cold and a cough, rain and fog. Very handsome comfortable rooms here, service admirable, food much more homelike and even cheaper than on my first visit in the spring. Made my first appearance on Saturday at the Crystal Palace, where I scored a success with Beethoven's E flat Concerto. I was in a good mood, the accompaniment was excellent, orchestra all one could wish for, and the best conductor in London: a German, Manns, formally a military bandmaster.

Shall you be much surprised by the following confession? I might have made it a week ago, but wished to have time to confirm my convictions: the Broadwood action is for my style the most comfortable, lightest, and surest — practically ideal. It is no fancy of mine — I tried all sorts of things on these grands (which also register progress in colour and strength of tone), and not a note failed to sound, neither repetition nor anything else gave the least trouble. It seems to me — you'll have to admit it yourself — that that is pretty good.

On the other hand, a quite new Erard that I played on at Benedict's yesterday was wretchedly uncertain and uncomfortable, though quite beautiful in patches.

You do understand, don't you? I am speaking of the Broadwood action, and if I describe it as the most admirable that has ever come under my paws, it does not mean that I should dream of comparing it with your grands for brilliance, delicacy, and poetry of tone.

Old Br. is in the country in Scotland. If he comes back within the fortnight, I shall not fail to remember you to him. Herewith a few programs of coming concerts (two of them gratis — for the good cause).

I shall not earn very much money here, but shall live in comfort and aim at really big artistic successes. As I have so much to do this winter, I mean to take things easy and not waste my strength, which I shall want in Russia, you may be sure. . . .

216(a)]

27 Duke Street, Manchester Square
London
November 26 [1873]

SORRY I could not answer sooner, but I only had your letter and enclosures this morning on my return from Liverpool, where my evening concert lasted so long that I almost missed the night train. It is now six a.m. From nine to twelve I have the first orchestral rehearsal of Bache's concert, which I am conducting. At three comes my recital, and in the evening there is an ensemble rehearsal for the chamber concert on Saturday, tomorrow and the day after being full up. That's how we live here!

First, then, my best thanks for the friendly reception of my finger-confessions. Why did I not get them off my chest before? Because — well, because I am more modest than I am reputed to be; because, distrusting my own technique, I always suspected that my faulty touch was to blame. . . .

This is real bad news that you have taken such praiseworthy

pains to obtain for me from Moscow. There's evidently a hitch
in the essentials. On Ullmann's advice I arranged to go to Russia
in January and February, as you know; March and April are
booked for Scandinavia with Monbelli.[1] It is nearly as good as
a contract. Good advice is dear at this point. I will write to
Ullmann at once — hope I can find him — and ask him what
to do. Don't be offended if I say that I really dislike Herr
Vogt. (You need not be, for you neither made him nor invented
him.) I feel very little confidence in him and, from his writing,
take him to be one of those typical Austrian literary men who
are not really educated, but affect to be. Look at the way he
flings his foreign quotations about! If the fellow would only
tell us, who do not go by the Russian calendar, when Lent begins.
I cannot think it is before the end of February, but if so, it
would be far too late for my plans elsewhere. I'll let you know
more when I have heard from Ullmann. The Monbelli duo
may not come off either.

Newspaper articles? Yes, I know that kind of thing is indispensable. Unfortunately I have no collection of them either here
or in Munich. Do you mind writing to my body-critic Dr. Richard Pohl, who has a store of them? The only thing is, I don't
know where Pohl is for the moment. He must have left Baden,
but three weeks ago he was still hesitating between an offer
from the Baden *Landeszeitung* at Karlsruhe and Heyl's *Neue
Blatt* at Wiesbaden. Since then I have heard nothing of him.
You could easily find out from Herr Winkler (through his sister) whether he is at Wiesbaden. If not, Karlsruhe. . . .

PS. Kickman here makes pianofortes something like yours.
Tone very fine! But I must stick to Broadway.[2]

216(b)]

27 Duke Street, Manchester Square
London
December 2, 1873

Now that Monbelli is married to General Bataille — Ullmann
confirms it — my Scandinavian tour becomes very doubtful.

---

[1] MARIE MONBELLI, *singer, pupil of Mme Eugenie Garcia; a favourite at
Covent Garden.*
[2] *Presumably Kirkman and Broadwood.* — TR.

Moreover, it could be postponed until the middle of March. If I could but lay hands on a Russian calendar that would tell me the beginning of Lent! But I am sure you are better able to do that in Berlin. Do try. But I forgot to finish my first sentence, the end being that the Russian tour could easily be fitted in now as a result of the Monbelli wedding intermezzo. Moscow could be dealt with later. I am assuming that concerts are permitted in the theatre season in Petersburg. But there are always such a confounded lot of ifs and buts in my plans. Now, for instance, I hear that Anton Rubinstein is returning next year and will give concerts in Petersburg, Moscow, and the whole Russian empire. And I believe it. He needs more money than his American tour brought him in. If this news is well founded (it came from Fritz Hartvigson in Petersburg to his brother living here), I am done; that is, I shall be the loser and must stay at home.

To compete with Anton Rubinstein in Russia would be madness. We Germans are not so particularly well beloved there as it is.

So now, my dear man, do try hard to find out with all possible speed whether the said news is true and at what date the Russian Beethoven-Liszt is expected in his proud fatherland. I must know because I have to see where I stand. A simple solution would be to come back to England in January. I am gaining ground here day by day and may end by staying for good. For everything that I hear about Germany makes me very sick and tired. This between ourselves. . . .

217]

Herr Wierviorski
27 Duke Street, Manchester Square
London
December 13, 1873

HAVE run out of note-paper. Found your letter just now when I came back from rehearsal (Liszt pianoforte concerto) at the Crystal Palace. Concert tomorrow. I have to dress and go straight off to the concert (see back of this) for obvious reasons.

Steinitz receives from me, as from Tausig, twenty-five per cent net after all our common expenses have been paid. I do not consider that too high if the person in question knows his job. I only said that in this country I paid ten per cent and had a really princely Christian countenance to look at instead of a Jew's greasy face. . . .

218]

27 Duke Street, Manchester Square
London
December 8 [*1873*]

BOTH yours received. The first crossed mine. Willingly accept Grossmann's recommendations if he is not personally too Stein-itzy. It costs less here. For ten per cent you have a gentleman as agent. However, I have no objection to twenty-five for Russia if the man is worth it, and with Grossmann's experience one may assume it. The chief questions are: (1) When must or can I begin in Russia? (2) Have I Rubinstein's deadly rivalry to fear or not? As I have no time to lose, having worn myself out by playing in Germany and in any case not caring to stay in that uncomfortable country, I am only awaiting answers to the above to make a fresh engagement here for a month — January 11 to February 11. I wrote and told Ullmann that I was giving up the Scandinavian tour, as the Monbelli business makes it too precarious. You know, she has married General Bataille, and who shall guarantee us the exact length of their honeymoon? Did I tell you I was giving a concert in Dresden between the 2nd and the 8th of January? Have written Friedel about it and am expecting to hear the date any time now. I hope you will come over; it's not so far from your bow-window.

Could you not find out for me where Pohl has hidden himself? The good man has chosen the wrong time to be silent just as he sometimes does for writing. Am returning Grossmann's letter herewith. Next Friday there is a Wagner concert; unfortunately I am only part conductor. . . .

219]

27 Duke Street, Manchester Square
London
January 14, 1874

HERE I am again. Brilliant success on my reappearance the day before yesterday. Ill yesterday, but pulled round again today. Very much ashamed of myself, for after an hour's searching I cannot find the letter and name of the Polish concert agent whom Grossmann recommended. Do come to the rescue. Not a letter, but just the two lines of address, so that I can write quickly.

My bold Eisenach scheme succeeded beyond all expectation. Hall full, audience enthusiastic. All Bach, as you know, and yet no trace of monotony or weariness during the whole two hours and a half. We did the Triple Concerto with an amateur, Frau Ziegler (quite good), on three Bechsteins of different ages and generations, capitally in tune, and producing a capital effect.

But I must stop. No, I still have to thank you with shame and emotion for that heavenly upright at Königswinter. When they thanked me, I turned crimson. For these blushes you are to blame. . . .

223]

Reval
March 1/13, 1874

MANY thanks for your letter received yesterday. Am very anxious to see the grand with the Pleyel mechanism in Petersburg on Monday.

Junker has done what he could to soften the pianoforte that was sent here from Vilna. It sounded much better last night, but it's the old story with the repetition. A number of passages refuse to sound on your instruments as on those of your bad imitator Blüthner. I cannot discover the wrong principle that is at the bottom of it because I have unfortunately never had time to teach myself the laws of construction, nor did I ever find any-one to instruct me. I will gladly take the trouble, if you are agreeable, to write out a dozen or so of the principal passages in my repertoire which simply cannot be played on your grands, particularly the overstrung ones, or at least not according to the spirit of the composer. I would even go so far as to propose a prize to the pianist who succeeded in giving me the lie in this matter. Let him give a practical demonstration of what I maintain to be impossible: namely, the rendering of the said passages with delicacy of accent rather than with noisy *bravura*. You must believe me, it is no special kink or impotence in me that is re-sponsible; the fault lies with the instrument. Will you agree to this proposal? Let me know. . . .

What is the good of being a great man if you are a great ass at the same time? Grossmann, as his opera shows, is a master of instrumentation, but he has instrumentated my Russian tour pretty rottenly. As my (St.) Stanislaus is very slow in speech, lazy, absent-minded, and forgetful — did he not lose my ticket, luggage ticket, and various papers on the Riga platform? — I have sent him on to Petersburg in advance with instructions which he will only half or badly carry out. I believe he potters round for a couple of hours over the simplest business letter. Telegrams I always have to revise myself, otherwise they cost twice as much or are unintelligible (telegraphing from here is very expensive). We shall see if he improves. Owing to the cir-cumstance that people compare me with Anton-Beethoven-Liszt, and will of course want to place me far below, my first concert promises to be full, but the proceeds will probably be eaten up by the second. However it may turn out, the whole thing has been completely mismanaged and I should have done far, far better to stay in England or even to go to Scandinavia with Monbelli. That wretched Bösendorfer is to blame for it all, confound him.

224]

Vilna
March 4 (February 20), 1874

I AM quite unhappy. At this price the ease in repetition is far too dearly bought. There is nothing left under one's fingers; all the nuances of touch, colour, and shading have gone to the devil and there is a complete lack of elasticity and impetus — in fact, it's now a mechanism for consumptive flapper virtuosi. The Warsaw pianoforte was uninspiring enough, but this one reduced me to despair last night. Never have I played with so little zest or had to make so great an effort. Do not suppose that in my dejection I am making you responsible. It can only be my fault, I must have expressed myself unintelligibly; but the misunderstanding is really a fatal one. For heaven's sake do not send this unlucky No. 6,678 to Petersburg. I have such nerves about that place, where my first concert is wedged in between the two Rubin-rocks (16/4 March). . . .

The weather continues to be fine. Not at all cold, dry, clearest sky, and sunshine. Frau von Mouchanoff and Herr Grossmann vie with each other in kindness to me. His opera was given in my honour, and I was rather in a hole as regards compliments to the author except for a few quite pretty numbers in the Hungarian style. Grossmann's activities and his general complaisance are incredible, really praiseworthy.

A lot of tiresome *grands seigneurs* here. They fritter away my time and have repeatedly interrupted this heart-felt outburst, for instance. Think how our beloved Tausig would have sworn in my place! . . .

225]

Viborg
March 7/19, 1874

CONGRATULATE me, I am at last rid of the idiotic Pole with whom Grossmann's inconsiderateness saddled me. It really was a most irresponsible thing for him to do. The fellow proved himself a colossal Assinski-Dishclothski. Everyone who has had dealings with him — at Vilna, Riga, Petersburg — should blame Herr G. as he deserves. I am really unspeakably glad to be relieved of this half-baked creature, who has belied his decent appearance by the most Jew-like methods of doing business. Herr Wölfel of Petersburg has been most charming and helpful in obtaining this release; he is far more reliable than the talented and personally amiable Warsaw chief.

I was not only morally but physically so ill from the effects of the continuous irritation he caused me that I joyfully agreed to pay a biggish sum to buy him off. This I did to avoid prolonging the affair, and not to avoid a lawsuit. Figures are, as we know, most eloquent: from ten concerts, including the first Petersburg one, which was sold out, I received altogether 2,485 roubles; Herr W. received 1,493. How do you like that? I have the receipts. Wölfel knows all about it, as I could not bring myself to associate with that animal any more and did practically everything myself; whereupon Wölfel stepped into the breach and rendered as many services as Herr G. disservices. I have now engaged a nice well-educated young Russian, who has already toured with a big singer; have sent him on in advance to Moscow, Charkov, and other places. In this way I hope to make good my losses.

The concert here was not worth while in spite of a " housefull " theatre, but I find Hartvigson's society refreshing — he accompanied me here — and it was an escape from the racket of Petersburg. . . .

Number 6,717, with the Pleyel mechanism, is better to play than number 6,677, and both are beyond comparison finer than those I have had on my tour until now. These, like the Steinwegs, have been at their best in the most unfavourable localities, but as regards repetition it is the same old story. I am sorry to see you did not understand my objections (which are fully shared by Leschetizsky); it may have been my ignorance of the technical terminology of pianoforte-construction. No more need be said about it, however, as the whole problem has been brilliantly solved by Herr Wölfel's brilliant master-mechanic in H. and G.'s shop. Junker listened attentively to his very clear explanation and told me, quite openly, that he considered it to be the right one. You simply take the Wankel and Temmler patent mechanism (which is on the same principle as your own) and look for the so-called safety-catch (which yours does not possess). This raises the hammer before the key has sprung back into position — which in *allegro* is not possible. You see, my friend, Columbus can still lay eggs. When you have introduced the safety-catch no grand pianofortes will be able to compete with yours in any respect, and the perfect action will have been achieved. . . .

Please, please get me news from Hamburg. Could you not write to Gross to the effect that I was very much exhausted and unless everything was thoroughly well prepared so that I could go through my part of it in a week at most (April 28 to May 8), I should have to decline to conduct *St. Elisabeth* and the rest. Most important of all is to find out whether the Master, Liszt, has been properly invited and what has been his reply. Do please do something about it. It is much more easily done from Berlin than from between Viborg and Charkov. . . .

226]
                            [*Telegram*]
Petersburg
March 23, 1874

Protest against role commercial traveller for various agents and its imputations. Request immediate rectification of undignified position by you and Grossmann Warsaw. Bitterly regret my confidence.

                                        Bülow

To Hermann Grossmann, Warsaw

Bülow beside himself. Talks of imputations which stamp him as commercial traveller. How can this have happened? Please put it right at once. Bülow's interests must be paramount. Your interpretation in today's letter incorrect.

                                        Bechstein

                            [*Telegram*]
Petersburg
March 23, 1874

Herr Leschetizsky Wölfel employ Herr Baron as advocate in dispute.[1] Instruments sent to Moscow. Quarrel furious.

                                        Junker

[1] "Herr Leschetizky Wölfel Herrn Baron als Advokat in Streit benutzt."

227]

Moscow
March 28/April 9, 1874

Hᴀᴠᴇ heard nothing from Berlin for a long time; neither have I received any letters which you may have been so kind as to forward from London or Munich. However I am almost indifferent to everything now. I only yearn for the end of this in every respect misguided tour. Arrived here yesterday to spend the Russian Holy Week in Klindworth's consoling society and get myself into condition again physically. . . .

I may as well confess that I cannot think of your last letter without an angry rattling in my throat. You say: Wiewiorski has now come back to Warsaw and poured out all his woes. I was not aware that this lousy Pole stood nearer to you than my insignificant self.

Well, it can't be undone now. But as I still want to save what can be saved — assuming that my rheumatic pains and maladies abate — I have instructed Suamenski to arrange two concerts at Orel and Kursk for the end of next week if it is worth while. These places are on the road to Kiev. Then I am going to Warsaw for a couple of days to give your friend Grossmann a dressing. From there I shall go to Leipzig and Munich via Berlin. I expect to spend only an hour or two in Berlin. In my present frame of mind it would give none of my friends any particular pleasure to see me. You see, I can neither find satisfaction in relating my troubles nor succeed in putting them behind me or lying about the whole thing to myself and others.

Herr Junker (whose pleasant society is unfortunately the only thing for which I owe you thanks this trip) will let you know the time of our arrival in due course. By the way, I don't know whether he delivered my message the other day. It was that the No. 6,645 grand which we found at Witzmann's in Odessa (and of course used there) was to my mind by far the best of yours that I ever played on. Certainly it is far finer than 6,677 and 6,717, the two which were manufactured for me. Unfortunately that " for me " is bound up with the reminder

that it was you who were the first offender in all this Grossmann-
Leschetizsky and Nikolai business which put me in such a
rage. A pity that one only learns by experience such as mine
that " in Russia one is betrayed and sold " (Klindworth's own
words). Considering my successes all over this country, I might
have reaped great pecuniary satisfaction also if the thing had
been reasonably well organized. For instance, the Moscow concerts (of which two have now been abandoned) might have been
given one after the other had there been time to put off the
second concerts at Charkov and Odessa. The blame lies solely
with the irresponsible person (to put it no more strongly) who
through you gave me that inexperienced idiot as a companion.
(Junker will tell you some choice things about him.) He is
now actually using me to advertise himself in the *Signale*. I
have written to correct it, as it was a little more than I could
stand. . . .

228]

Berlin
April 28, 1874

I NOW feel very sorry — as always after the event — that I
gave vent to my despair over that miserable Russian tour in a
way that upset and even hurt you. Nikolai was to have assured
you of this, but you had already left when he passed through
Berlin.

A letter from Pohl at Karlsbad (it should be called Karl's
Rest for you) tells me, however, that he met you and thought
you looking well. I would send him a word in reply if I did not
feel that, having time for one letter only, I must give you precedence in order to express regret for my offending pen. But you
will admit yourself that this most unpleasant failure in Russia is bound to hit such a straggler among pianists (I was
born in 1830) harder than it would have done ten years back.
The sacrifice of health, strength, and, above all, time is very
serious for me. However, " it will pass over," as the fox
said when they pulled his fur over his ears. I will think no
more of it, if only from economy, and you must waste no more

sympathy over it either. Believe me, the finest, most genuine fellow-suffering will never counterbalance the suffering of the actual victim! . . .

. . . Once more, thank you for Junker. He had plenty of opportunities for development and was invariably handy, willing, and obliging. Herr Seiffert met me at the station here on Sunday morning. I paid a second visit to your brother today and was very glad to find him steadily improving in spite of the sudden unfavourable change in the weather; for it is snowing here, though not, I hope, in the Bohemian forests. . . .

229]

Hotel de l'Univers, No. 21–2
Florence
June 1, 1874

How did Karlsbad suit you? As well as last year, I hope. Did you have my letter there? It must, I think, have given you satisfaction. But there it is: an abusive letter will bring an answer quicker than a friendly one.

Italy did not please me much at first and by no means provided the desired recuperation. May was very April-like in Milan. After a fortnight's stay there, when I also found the musical conditions most unsatisfactory (the *Allgemeine Zeitung* printed my impressions), I had a few really fine days on Lake Como at the Villa Carlotta, whither my new royal friend George I (H. M.) of Milan graciously transported me. There I was able really to refresh myself. I then came on here, where my social commitments are legion, and am really glad to be back, if only for my former attachment to the city which once gave me back my health. . . .

230]

Salzungen
July 4, 1874

I HAVE put off, from day to day, my letter of thanks for the pianofortes, but here it is at last. A thousand thanks. If I were not able to practise a little by way of preparation for the next London season, I should have left this wretched village again, for it abounds in shady sides (morally speaking — the sun's glare leaves nothing to be desired), incessant noise, children's shrieks, the grunting and cackling of live-stock as they are driven past, and from five to eleven at night the perpetual functioning of a roundabout organ which penetrates so distinctly to all quarters that a man can neither think nor write sense. But where could I go with the certainty of being left in peace? Besides, I still have the last winter season, particularly the Eastern one, so very much in my bones that I am practically incapable of moving. It is really dreadful to be such a homeless vagabond. For two and a half years I have led this hotel existence, always packing and unpacking. Rubinstein, who is twenty times as strong, has at least some sort of home in the intervals! But once I begin a lament, there is no end to it. I shall endure things here, then, through the summer, difficult as it is, and shall see if the salt-water baths will do me good. They are fairly strong.

There was a mishap with the grands, after all. Don't be afraid, the instruments are quite undamaged and have been safely set up. But Director Müller, who took the flat for me (externally one of the handsomest in the town), had not taken the impracticable staircase into consideration. It was absolutely impossible to get your grand up to my room on the second floor. It had to be smuggled through a window into another flat on the garden side, which is nothing like so convenient for me. But it can't be helped and I have resigned myself. The second grand has been handed over to the tender mercies of my English pupil, the lady from Liverpool of whom I told you. If her enthusiasm, doubly remarkable in a Briton, were not so touching, I should wish her at the end of the earth. But she has talent and has left husband and children to follow me all the way from Liverpool to this Thuringian backwater. Not so bad, eh? I will guarantee that she does not ruin your pianoforte. In the case of this one I managed things better. Its measurements were taken into account before engaging rooms, and the passages were also tested. It stands on the ground floor. . . .

231]

Meadfoot, Torquay
November 24, 1874

I RECEIVED your much appreciated letter yesterday morning before leaving London and am answering it today from the English Nice, where I gave a decent recital this afternoon (taking sixty pounds). Tomorrow I go on to Plymouth.

Business is quite flourishing, and my health is holding out, although the perpetual changes of weather in England make it confoundedly difficult to keep free from colds.

Tell me, is it true that my old pupil Herr Fritz Hartvigson treated you so abominably that you had to administer a well-deserved snub? Klindworth told me, and Nikolai had told him. I should have to be thoroughly ashamed of him but that I am certainly not responsible for his bad manners. I did notice in Petersburg that during the twelve years since I had taught him in Berlin, he had developed little musically and for the worse as regards character.

Hallé is a gallant musician and a perfect gentleman. We are on very good terms as colleagues, though he finds me very embarrassing. His playing cannot be called interesting, but it is irreproachably correct.

So Rubinstein has broken his vow not to play any more for the fiftieth time? I wish him success with his opera, but do not suppose he will do any better with it than the composer of *Don Cesario.* . . .

Do you know of a good engraver in Berlin? I want to give somebody a Christmas present of Bismarck's head on a seal. I wonder if you would order it for me and see that it was delivered to me at the right time.

I shall pay a week's visit to Berlin at the end of April or beginning of May, if not earlier even. All sorts of things have to be put in order, a will made before my American tour, and so on. I hope Simson will again be at my disposal.

It's true, nothing definite has been arranged with Ullmann. I am very cautious and, as a Prussian, all for the free-hand policy. Don't be misled by newspaper reports, as, on principle, I now never contradict even the most preposterous rumour. It is nice of you not to be going to be angry with me any more, if I understand you aright. Those unpleasant Russian experiences had made me feel bitter and unjust towards you also. You might tell me some time in what relation you stand to the great powers Grossmann and Leschetizsky. Was anything changed by my intervention? Remember me to the good Nikolai when you have an opportunity. . . .

232]

Hull
December 7, 1874

MANY thanks for the zeal with which you have taken up the matter of my seal. Bismarck's head must be engraved on the plate. Handle not unduly faddy, but must be ivory.

What a speech that was of his, upon my word! What a colossal hero! He will tread the serpent underfoot if anyone can. The English papers are full of him these days. I am really proud to have been his admirer from the very first. You can bear me witness. . . .

233]

London
February 23, 1875

I AM very sorry to have inflicted a letter upon you recently: first, because I shortly afterwards received news which made my inquiry unnecessary; secondly, because you read meanings into my letter which were not there, and were accordingly moved to make communications which I regret to say I considered most improper.

I can only reply that I release you at this point for ever — especially as I signify nothing to your business — from the uncomfortable position of signing yourself or thinking of yourself as mine, " notwithstanding, gratefully and respectfully " ("notwithstanding" having reference, I presume, to Gross-mann and Co.). If you wish it, I am prepared to give you my solemn word of honour for this statement.

234]

London
April 12, 1875

As you have thought fit to abuse a confidential communication on my part with regard to the grand pianofortes on which I am to play in America by repeating it to another manufacturer (who named you as his source), I cannot refrain from express-ing to you my profound and just indignation.

235]

New York
June 1, 1876

I HAVE long felt the weight of a wrong I once did you in the Old World. A misunderstanding, which may be put down to a passing derangement, led me to offend and even insult you by letter and I feel the need, now that we both have our feet in the New World, to ask most sincerely for your pardon.

Had it been possible to arrange a personal meeting with the opportunity of a detailed explanation on my part, you would certainly not have opposed my oral attempts at amnesty. Un-fortunately it was not in my power to bring this about, though the desire arose instantly on hearing of your arrival. When I broke the chain of my frightful drudgery (at the hundred and thirty-ninth concert), I was physically and mentally so ex-hausted that I had to submit to (unfortunately inadequate) medical treatment in the most complete retirement. I leave New York the day after tomorrow to return in the first place to London. I have no choice, for no attempts to recover my shat-tered health would give me any prospect of success in this country. It is therefore impossible for me to look you up — apart from the conflicting information as to your present address. In view of all these difficulties may I hope that you will be willing to lend an ear to a sick man's request that this ugly episode which parted us may be forgotten, the said sick man having paid perhaps too dearly for his various errors?

It is so extremely improbable that we should ever meet again in person — my shattered nerves and exhaustion, brought on by overwork in a career for which I am not really in the least suited, leave me faced with an incurable lingering illness — that it will be all the more comprehensible to you that I long to see only the earlier brighter side of our old, close on twenty-year friendship stored in your memory, and the recent black spot blotted out or at least blurred.

I was delighted to hear from Herr Edgar Schuberth that you gave him the impression of a strong man in the bloom of health. Let me both congratulate you on this and express the hope that your dear family enjoy the same permanent good fortune.

I am quite unable to use my brain, as the result of a stroke I had in London fifteen months ago. For a time the damage was neutralized by new interests, but recently the symptoms have again become severe. I am incapable of consecutive thought, and that is why these lines give so faulty an impression of my feelings, even of so inextinguishable a one as my gratitude for all the sympathy and friendship you have shown me.

Once more I ask to be *forgiven* — in silence if you wish.

236]

Hanover
September 29, 1876

Your very kind letter, my dear *Beflügler*, has deeply touched me. The prospect of seeing my interim residence here beauti-fied by one of your grands enables me to flap my lame wings again a little. Possibly I have only fallen to these depths through *not* having a Bechstein in use. Should I in course of time regain the desire and the strength to take up my pianist's career again, I shall have only you to thank for tempting me. I do not need to tell you that I know of no more poetic and sympathetic tone than that of your instruments, for you know it; you know too that on no other grand can I show off so effectively the non-shady sides of my talent. I am now congratulating myself vigorously, therefore, on my positive refusal to allow . . . a concert grand straight from overseas to be placed in my new apartment.

The prospect of a visit from you here fills me with *great* joy. I desire most urgently that the *break* made " over there " in our temporary estrangement should be sealed by a personal reunion. So keep your word. Remember, I shall for months be unfit to make a move towards you and not even in the frame of mind to express myself in writing as I should wish. Yet I owe you so many explanations! . . .

PS. My friend here is genuinely hurt at being spoken of by you as a non-Bechsteiner. When *he* sits down to play, which does occasionally happen, it is at no other instrument than yours.

237]

Hanover
November 29, 1876

I HAVE put off thanking you for and replying to your sympathetic inquiries for so long because the oscillations of my " rebellious " nerves, as you call them — to me they seem rather invalid nerves — do not really allow me to say anything positive, and a bulletin corresponding to these oscillations would be as unedifying for the reader as the writer. In general a tendency towards improvement may perhaps be registered, although no more considerable a one than those in the contemporary Stock Exchange reports when Turkey's leanings to concessions used to be telegraphed. At least my doctor's effort to restore the broken connexion between spine, brain, and other nerve-centres by galvanism is not yet to be written down a failure. It is just a month now since this daily cure began. After tomorrow there will be a pause; then we shall see about going on again. By sending me that beautiful grand you provided me with an invaluable companion and consoler for the none too many " better " days. But the maximum of finger exercise (which is bound up with many obstacles) that I can permit myself in

a day is two hours, and that, as you know, cannot resuscitate a
ruined technique. . . .

238]

Hanover
March 28, 1877

Your amiable acceptance of my modest gift delighted me.
Knowing you as I do, I can almost imagine that you found it
difficult to accept it and all the more must *I* thank you for con-
firming my claim to be a friend of the house. How I long to
come one day as a healthy person!

The experiment I am risking tomorrow may be the first
step towards it. By the time you read this, I shall have turned
my back on Hanover. Letters from my family at Arcachon made
it morally essential that I should go there at once. The doctor
did not protest in the least; perhaps he wanted to be rid of me,
for which I cannot blame him. Anyway, I am taking the plunge.
It does happen — has happened to me indeed — that one avoids
falling ill simply by having no time to do so, being kept from
it by better and more important things. At Arcachon I can be
of some use to my family, or at least try, whereas here I am
only a useless *burden* to myself. Don't let yourself be alarmed
at my venture. I will send a sign of life from " there." My stay
at the Palazzo Bechstein has certainly done much towards arm-
ing me for the excursion. It is a positive stone off my heart to
feel that I have the courage to travel *alone*. Think if I had had
to beg for your company on the plea that you had several times
so kindly volunteered it! You would have been capable of ex-
posing yourself to fresh colds while barely recovered from the
last and I should have become the fiend instead of the friend
of the house. Don't do it again — take cold, I mean — for even
homœopathy is said to tire of working wonders sometimes —
who does not go on strike nowadays? . . .

239]

Vollhardt's Private Hotel
Kreuznach
July 25, 1877

"Touch wood three times," as the Saxons say. I have reached the point of being able to contemplate a return to playing without too despairing an outlook. If no set-back or other incident intervenes, I shall go to Baden-Baden in August for an after-cure. There I shall meet my good old Florentine friends, Professor H[illebrand] and Madame L[aussot], Pohl and others, which will give me the best opportunity of picking up threads and becoming human again, or at least of attempting it. May I for once be more prompt than you and forestall your invariable offer to provide me with a pianoforte by asking for one? I expect to be able to take the flat which I had at Baden in 1873 (Schloss Strasse, care of Gimpel, the artist), a most suitable one for undisturbed and undisturbing strumming. You must not furnish it with a concert grand of the highest quality though, for firstly the performer is not worthy of it, and secondly my state of nerves would not stand any great volume of sound. I can only begin with homœopathic doses, limiting myself for the first few weeks to one and a half hours. (If I do not obey the doctor in this, he will carry me off to Gastein, which place he threatened me with at the start.)

Since we met, much has happened in the course of my illness, but I will spare your eyes the reading, and my pen the writing, of it. There were mistakes of all sorts, unscrupulous doctors, dangerous experimental cures, and so on. The only satisfaction I had in my misery was that I had provided my mother, whom I fetched from Arcachon to that non-health resort Bex, with a more or less welcome distraction. A clever doctor at Vevey (at whose house I met the " good " Ratzenberger, who has greatly deteriorated) at last sent me here in the beginning of June. It was a good move in so far that, after the innumerable ignoramuses whom I have consulted in these fifteen months, I have at last found the right Æsculapius in the person of Professor Röhrig, a Meininger by birth, who also lectures in the winter at Freiburg University. For the sake of this excellent adviser, then, rather than for Kreuznach itself (for what I have to drink is Neuenahrer, a kind of Karlsbad spring), I have now put up with this horrible existence for seven weeks. It seems, however, as if my patience would in due time be rewarded.

You will probably have read in the papers that I have accepted an engagement for a two months' season (November to January) in Scotland. I am to be a " Bilse," [1] in fact, and conduct four or five concerts a week: some in Glasgow, where I shall stay; some in the neighbourhood of Edinburgh, Greenock, and Dundee. An orchestra of about sixty, composed of the very best London players, and no pianoforte-playing from me — unless I feel able to give them one concerto with accompaniment in each town in order to eke out my far from princely salary. I have again been too " modest " — thirty-five pounds a week is the agreed sum — but these people have put vast sums into it in former seasons and their well-meaning efforts in the interests of art deserve encouragement. This between ourselves of course.

How are you and your family? What is Oscaro doing now? Does the war in the East affect your business? Let me have real good news about it all soon.

. . . Would it be troubling you to ask you to find out if Perl is in Berlin? I shall have to get him to send me some money to Baden. Tichatschek used to write in people's albums: " Life is beautiful, but costly," and the second half of the statement is as incontestable as the first is doubtful. Well, " better times coming," as they say in Marschner's *Templer*, though it is the fool who sings it! . . .

[1] BENJAMIN BILSE (1816–1902), *conductor of the Bilse concerts in Berlin. In 1882 part of his orchestra seceded from him and formed what in time was to become the Berlin Philharmonic Orchestra.*

240]

Schloss Strasse
Baden
August 16, 1877

I HAVE now been two days here in a tolerably good frame of
mind (so far) and am delighted with your magnificent pianoforte, which furnishes my really presentable flat (perhaps the
finest in the place as regards its quiet position, view, and so on)
in the most comfortable way. For the thousand and first time,
my best thanks!

Kreuznach was dreadful. Still, the doctor there succeeded
in freeing me from a few of the worst of my physical ailments,
so that I feel sufficiently revived to tackle the rest little by little
(chronic catarrh, for instance). Your letter arrived safely, but
is unfortunately mislaid, so that I cannot rely on my rusty
memory to answer it properly today. I shall be very glad to do
" a little " propaganda for your grands in England. Unfortunately I shall only play very occasionally, if at all, next winter.

In Scotland I shall do ladies' work — a Field, Moscheles,
or Beethoven concerto — every fortnight or so. If you think it
worth while to send an instrument there, I shall be glad to display it to my visitors and endeavour to make them fall in love
with it. You know me well enough to be sure I am not afraid
of Broadwood's anger in the press. " Many enemies, much
honour," was always my watchword and always will be.

How is your brother? I wish him a speedy recovery, for one
thing because it would put you in a position to carry out your
threat of a visit here. Then you not only can but must stay with
me. I have a whole floor, with a spacious bedroom for you and
a charming drawing-room with a balcony. Madame Laussot,
Professor Hillebrand, and Buonamici [1] are expected here in
about a week. I shall stay as long as weather, the mood for
playing, and the money last. Apropos — is Perl in Berlin?

On September 8 Sarasate will be playing, amongst other
things. Doesn't that tempt you? Etelka is said to be coming too.

[1] GIUSEPPE BUONAMICI (1846–1914), *Florentine pianist, pupil of Bülow at the
Munich Conservatoire, later professor of pianoforte there, retiring to Florence in 1873.*

241]

Schloss Strasse 16
Baden
August 20, 1877

SURELY we two old friends should be beyond playing the game of misunderstanding.

It was my most ardent wish to Russianize England for you. All I meant to say was that the beginning might have to be diplomatically postponed, to my personal regret, on account of finger-weakness and possible complications arising out of " Breitholz's " hostility. Since you know you can count on me, why do you not do so? Is it humiliating for you? . . .

I am glad that you have opened my eyes about A.! The fellow was swindling me, then, with the zeal and enthusiasm that was wasted on you?

Did you know that it was Frau Clara [Schumann] who started the opposition to your grands in favour of the " wild " Harz-Steinwegs, three or four years ago? . . .

Madame Laussot and Professor Hillebrand are here, both well and, as before, very charming to me. The dog-days have been so unbearable that I perspire as much when merely writing and in shirt-sleeves as in the good old days over a Liszt rhapsody. Nevertheless I am glad to be here. It really is the most paradisical spot in the whole empire.

The Svoboda operetta company has been here — very pretty performances of *Fledermaus* and *Cagliostro*. I naturally did not go to Suppé and Offenbach. I am making gradual progress except for occasional but really very few nervous attacks; but only homœopathic doses of even the mildest activity can be risked.

I trust I need not yet give up hope of seeing you here. I shall certainly stay another month. We could chat without interruption about repetition mechanisms while moistening our lips with fine Marsala.

242]

Baden
August 29, 1877

Dᴵᴰ my concert notice give you a fright? Calm yourself, your
" old " one not only was good enough for me in the Duo for
two pianofortes, but surpassed the Mock-Steinway both in
strength and in charm of tone.

In spite of the incredible heat and an equally incredible
degree of perspiration, together with a sleepless night, I still
feel quite reasonably well. Think of wearing a white tie, patent-
leather boots, and tail coat after an interval of precisely five
hundred days! A pity you were not there. It was a positive fire-
work, that Beethoven symphony. The audience was quite de-
mented, intoxicated. So that's all right. A pity, what a pity,
that my old friends (Pohl excepted) were not present at my
resurrection concert! Frau Laussot is ill unfortunately.

I could tell you a really startling piece of news, but it is to
be a surprise for you (on February 1) as for the rest of humanity.

Now don't go and imagine extravagant things! . . .

Your pianoforte in my room pleases me more every day.
For love of all the saints, do give up that damnable *double
échappement!* [1] Who knows that your Hanover instrument is
not partly responsible for my not being able to play again!
Glasgow is a fixture. Shall play on C. B. on the few occasions
there.

[1] *An important invention in pianoforte-manufacture, by which the action was improved and quick repetition of a note made possible. P. Erard, nephew of the inventor
S. Erard, patented it in 1821. The elder Erard had taken out a patent for an earlier
state of the invention in 1808.*

243]

Sydenham
November 2, 1877

From Thursday on, care of Mr. Stillie, 30 Brandon Place, Glasgow

As soon as I received yours, I drove, in spite of a heavy cold, to 10 Rathbone Place and made certain of that essential with Stahl, who was very amiable. Allow me to rectify your errors. Hanover fulfils all my ambitions. A court theatre without a court; an intendant who is the *solitary* instance of a gentleman in that profession and my best friend. Therefore, long live Radeckert! . . .

. . . If I go to Berlin on Bilse's account (I hope he pays *high* fees — how much shall I ask?), I shall of course only stop for the rehearsal and concert, as every day brings its own worry in Hanover, though not indeed every night its pleasure. You understand me, I hope? Playing for charity is off. What are the " bearded " and the " unripe " there for? . . .

What about the pianoforte that was ordered for Frau von Knigge? Did Oscar receive my letter?

I now have Broadwood as an enemy, since I told him I should make no use of his offers in Scotland. It has caused me no sleepless nights, however. . . .

PS. How were the *horns* and *hounds* in the first finale in *Tannhäuser?* Do have a photograph taken of the hunting-scene. As for St. Elisabeth, tell her not to make the usual twenty-four-bar cut in the " Prayer."

244]

144 Holland Street
Glasgow
December 9, 1877

A LINE from you at last; late, but satisfactory. *We* shall go slowly but surely. Stahl is a decent-looking, for all I know decent-feeling blockhead, but finicking, badly orientated, and by no means sufficiently apelike. Boosey is clever and brisk.

Draw your own conclusions.

Glad you appear to have *understood* me. Not so easy, as I realize from many other cases. The first essential is to be impartial when working for anything. Bad jokes on the right only catch on in conjunction with ditto to the left. . . .

You talk of gratitude and so on. Very well, then (it is mutual by the way), do me a favour or two.

1. Have a serious talk with Perl about my money affairs, paving the way, so to speak, for a withdrawal if his interest in my financial welfare should have dried up. This Russian-English depreciation annoys me very much. For the moment no money needed, but must be prepared for any emergencies. War (victory) makes expenses. Have many a project *in petto;* please note, nothing impractical. You will devote half or a quarter of a morning to me, then, won't you?

2. Inquire of Bilse in *your* name when he thinks of giving the concert for which I am to fill the hall.

I shall be back in H[anover] on Monday, January 14, Rudolph's Hotel. Concert (subscription) on the 19th.

He must get ahead with the Berlin scheme — distribution of time important on account of repertoire, etc. Tell him too from me that I shall play Bronsart's concerto in the first part and Rubinstein's number three, op. 45, G major (Bote and Bock), not Tschaikovsky's, in the second. No solos. Finally, ask him privately and confidentially what fee he proposes to pay, giving him to understand that I am not *bad* and therefore am not in the least inclined to let myself go *cheap.*

Will you?

Best wishes to Oscar, and may he follow my example and become convalescent.

Notices of my tour just out (day after tomorrow), published in pamphlet form (the demand was enormous) by Senff. Ask for it by return and you will have it at once, earlier than Westermann (-meyer?), Duysen, Spangenberg, Noack, Biese, and the rest.

Kindest regards to you, your wife, and Herr Seiffert. (This is the place to hear Strauss played *à la Viennoise.*) Write soon to your faithful old Bechstein-thumper.

245]

Rudolph's Hotel
Hanover
January 20, 1878

So glad that you are sending a pianoforte for Thursday. Your Glasgow ones were splendid; they conquered everyone. Did Bessy send you the programs and papers? Last night, gave a very successful concert to an ice-cold audience; tonight conducted a very successful performance of *Wilhelm Tell* in front of an appreciative one. Will that do for the first week? . . .

246]

Hanover
January 25, 1878

THE concert last night was packed and every item went off magnificently; public singularly enthusiastic.

Next week I shall put in an hour at His Excellency Botho's. Where does he live? I should like to stay at a hotel convenient for both him and the station. (N.B. Let it be known that I am "honouring" Berlin.) Besides you I wish to see no one. At most, possibly Lienau (Schlesinger). : . .

247]

Hanover
February 14, 1878

VERY nice of you to write for once unasked. I am glad you liked " Fressipoff " and that *Carnival* was *da capo'd*.

N.B. Beethoven she cannot play. So all the better, eh, if she leaves him alone?

Indirectly you gave me an idea. What do you say to my giving an evening concert in Berlin shortly for the benefit of the Bayreuth fund?

I do not wish to be considered a renegade and, apart from that, should not like the feminine Rubinstein and the masculine Essigtopf (" vinegar-jar ") to have it all their own way. . . .

248]

Baden
August 7, 1878

It was a really delightful surprise to see your handwriting. Drudgery seems to suit you, as it does me, and the sound-board seems to me to be all right. How many grands in three weeks' time? I cannot say exactly. One stays in London, another will certainly be in Edinburgh and can be moved to Glasgow (eighty minutes). Two would be quite enough for the tour, as the London one can also go on its travels. Say four, then, as a *maximum*. And they need not all be *grandissime* models. A rich tone is needed for the Edinburgh hall.

The Berlin recital is of *great* importance to me. To send the proceeds to Bayreuth — not for the composer, that is, but for *Parsifal* — amounts to a moral necessity. So set my mind at rest. Berlin must have sunk very low if it cannot listen to my reading of Beethoven's complete testament: the sonata cycle of op. 101, 106, 109, 110, 111. Well, if the middle classes cannot listen (and I include Würst among them), let them walk out.

Do me the kindness, my dear fellow, not to regard me as a rival of Herr Rafael Joseffy [1] or any such Christian or Jewish bandoleer. I flatter myself that I represent a rather more ideal standpoint in the music chronicle of the last quarter of a century (*à peu près* since you first sponsored me). As for the wiseacres in trousers or petticoats, I do not feel compelled to give in — to disguise my *trend* — for the sake of seeing a few more paying individuals perspiring in the hall. . . .

PS. Bronsart has got away with it this time at Erfurt; Breitkopf and Härtel have asked for all his manuscripts! It is a success which really rejoices me.

---

[1] RAFAEL JOSEFFY (1853–1915), *pianist, pupil of Moscheles, Tausig, and Liszt; pianoforte-teacher at the National Conservatory, New York, 1891.*

249]

(Postcard in haste)

Hanover
Tuesday night
1878

I AM about to pack after conducting a second and really ideal performance of *Lucrezia Borgia*. I travel to Brussels tomorrow, reach London on Friday evening (Sydenham, that is, where I am staying a week with my brother-in-law von Bojanovski, the consul-general). I then go on to Scotland and shall live in Glasgow, where my first concert takes place on November 16. . . .

250]

16 Schloss Strasse
Baden
August 14, 1878

CAUTION!
   I am thunderstruck by this communication which has been travelling all over the world for a fortnight. Read it, please, and *advise me*. Send back the letter. Can you not raise a substantial sum in my name from Perl on the pretext of a big undertaking that I have in prospect or something of the sort? Treason and deception on all sides; have I really sweated all these years in vain? Perhaps it is not so bad as I think. You have so often reassured me when I asked for information. All the same . . . your semi-grand sounded very well last night. Can Alfermann sell it? But that is his affair.

251]

Schloss Strasse 16
Baden
August 4, 1878

THAT is a glorious mount that you sent to me here, more docile under the saddle than any I seem to remember. Many thanks. It is possible I may ride it in public on the 13th (in a small hall) to assist a very nice concert singer, Fräulein Anna Lankow. . . .

Please remember that in the middle or end of October there is to take place in the hall of the Singakademie a pianoforte recital by Herr Hofkapellmeister Dr. H. v. B. Program: the five pianoforte sonatas of L. van Beethoven. Raised prices.

Probably in aid of the Bayreuth fund. What does Karl Bechstein think on this point? Please ask Davidson too. He behaved very nicely at Erfurt. I shall be back in Hanover on August 22. Do come to the *Flying Dutchman* on the 27th (Associates' performance). On the 28th Goethe's *Tasso* with Liszt's symphonic poem as overture. . . .

253]

Hanover
August 25, 1878

Cannot tell you how pleased and grateful I am to have your assistance. You have raised me from the blackest dreams to shining reality. Sing Te Deum! You have the papers, then, praise God. The next most desirable thing would be to find their exact worth. (You mentioned a friend versed in the Stock Exchange.) Yet I want to consider a little first. My desire to be rid of anything doubtful is of course stronger than ever. A mortgage? Good, but does that not mean complications? Are not State and Imperial bonds more solid? Besides I like the certain prospect of disposability at any time.

The thing is, then, to realize, even if only gradually, as soon as any reasonable chance offers. Sell Austrian, Russian, and Italian; Americans and the Bank of Saxony might still rise; Russian premium loan to be held perhaps so that one could make on the drawings which, I believe, take place quarterly. Unfortunately I should have to collect information about all that, which means wasting as much as a week. Do go on helping me with your kind advice, my old *Beflügler* and new banker. The balance in cash you must please take for yourself as payment on account for the captain's swindle. For I do really think

I have been had in this case. Ah well, one has to sacrifice a ring to Fortuna or the gods *à la* Polycrates. . . .

254]

Frankfurt a/M.
(at Raff's)
August 27, 1878

Two words in haste: could you make a sacrifice for the good of my great cause and come to Hanover within the next few days? (Sunday, *Flying Dutchman.*) The journey is really nothing. I have rehearsals and cannot possibly go to Berlin. I enclose Perl's letter, received before leaving Baden, which gave me the sensation of being able to breathe again. As you see, he confesses to the deposits and specifies all my securities. If it is at all possible, do fulfil my request; you know I shall ever be willing to do the same for you.

255]

Hanover
September 29 [1878]

Accuse me of neglect, but not ingratitude for not yet having thanked you a thousand times for the official and non-official provision of pianofortes. There has been a great deal on these days and I have in addition a colossal *grippe.* I may very well sneeze at the wrong moment in the *Prophet* tonight. . . . On the 9th a Sisters of Mercy concert; on the 12th a subscription concert, at which I shall naturally parade under your flag and should like a really brilliant (fireworky) instrument for the occasion. Can it be done?

Bronsart sent you a touching letter of thanks the other day, or so he said. It is an immense blessing for us all, for the chorus has now received the " core," and the ballet the chest from the chorus room. So all are happy, to the last dancer.

Almost simultaneously with your last letter came an offer from Bock to do some arranging, which, as you will see from today's papers, I promptly accepted.

Perl is sulking. Smelt a rat, I suppose. Our chamber-music concerts have suddenly begun to flourish. There are a hundred and fifty more subscribers than last year. Prices are raised too, as there are eight evenings instead of six. Hanover is becoming the world's music centre! Do you know, your beautiful upright is so heavy that the floor of the room is sinking already? But, then, all beautiful things are heavy — prima donnas, for instance. . . .

256]

Brighton
Last of November 1878

I MUST seize this free moment to assure you of my delight in your last year's output. All four grands are glorious, just what I always dreamed you would produce in the end. Why did it not happen earlier, my friend? True, you can retaliate with: " Why did you not learn to tinkle earlier as well as you do now? "

It seems to me that this last short but energetic tour — eleven concerts behind me, six (including today's) still to come — will at last bring your name the recognition it deserves. Certainly you appear to be becoming dangerous to your rivals. Steinway spends no end of money on advertising in just those towns and on those days when I play " you." . . .

Symphony concert on the 14th. By the way, you must send me something very good for the court concert at Arolsen in January (King of Holland's wedding).

259]

Hanover
May 5, 1879

WELL, how are you? Hülsen has ordered *Cellini* [1] for Thursday. Why don't you come too? Schott is going to London with me (recitals June 16 and 23).

[1] BERLIOZ'S opera Benvenuto Cellini, *performed under Liszt at Weimar in 1855, and under Bülow in Hanover in 1879.*

N.B. I have promised to conduct and play at the Tonkünst-lerversammlung at Wiesbaden. Therefore. pianoforte pleas! (a) Liszt's *Faust Symphony,* Bronsart's *Frühlingsfantasie;* (b) Tschaikovsky's concerto (dedicated to me).

Robert le diable newly rehearsed. Went very well at the second performance today. . . .

261]

Hanover
October 13, 1879

SCHWERIN next Saturday after all. But to turn to something more important:

Can you give me asylum in your house for a short time? Early next week I am going to leave Hanover for good. I shall go to pieces if I expose myself to this *liver-sucker* any longer. My only salvation lies in flight. Don't worry about the cause. It is only one more of many similar experiences — briefly this: that by way of thanks for my having put *him* in the way of big things, *he* is depriving me of the small ones. True, I may have made it easy for him to carry out his long-cherished project. But I shall choke if I write any more.

262]

Hanover
November 3, 1879

. . . Do you know, the Welfenzeitung has given me a really fine " necrology " in spite of my well-known devotion to Bismarck. Read it yourself and send it if possible to Her Excellency Mimi. It is just as well that it should be realized in high circles that I have not become *locally unpopular* here, for all that my worthless opponents choose to say. Not that I expect to profit in any way by these eye-openers — it is too late for that — but it is a point of honour with me not to have it assumed that I was thrown out by general consent.

I hope I may continue to count upon your support in these

matters. I need friends and am perhaps not too undeserving of them. *Nero* [1] was a great success on the whole and I was sincerely delighted with the master's triumph. Shall you go and hear the second performance (8 p.m.)? I expect so. In that case send me a line about it.

263]

Hanover
Sunday morning, November 1879?

Forgive me what I cannot forgive myself — the letter of the day before yesterday — and forget it too, I implore you, dear magnanimous friend. I was quite unmanned in my despair — hence the cry for help; though you yourself are to blame in so far as you have given me your never-failing sympathy, of which I feel myself as unworthy as of that from any other quarter. Diseased and incurable as I am in body, my mind and heart are even more definitely ruined. Both of them have long been broken and it is only the restless life I lead, the failure to pause and take stock, that has kept me from a clear perception of the fact and the decision to which it must lead.

Heaven give me the strength — should my deep despair not suffice — to carry out that which honour demanded of me in 1869 on purely moral grounds!

Consider me fortunate when you hear that all is over, and fulfil my request — you have often told me that your time is now your own — to come over in haste and take over the painful duties which Herr v[on] Br[onsart] will assume to have devolved upon him through my unavoidable departure. I wish to spare him all the mortification and outward unpleasantness I can. . . . I can only find consolation now in semi-lies. Shield my memory as well as you can, I beg of you.

I have become so loathsome and such a burden to myself that, having long since signed my own death-warrant, I see no alternative but to save others the worry of my existence. How could you suppose that, in this condition — which appears to me dishonourable rather than pitiable — I could accept your

[1] *An opera by Anton Rubinstein, first performed in Hamburg, November 1, 1879.*

hospitality, desecrate your house with my presence? No, even I with my deranged brain am not so vile and unscrupulous as that. It was only a criminal impulse to live that caused me to forget how things really stood, the other day, and to scream for help like a drowning man.

I am horribly ashamed of my performance. You must forgive me for having selected you as the victim of this lapse into animalism.

Thank you with all my heart for the kindness which breathed from your reply. May fate reward you and yours for your generosity to me!

Good-bye. I want you to be happy and *not* to mourn for one soon to be released from the hellish torment of an existence more marred perhaps by suffering than by guilt.

264]

Sunday afternoon

Pity me — do not despise me — I cannot keep the word to which I pledged myself only this morning. (You will have read my letter by this.)

The idea of a possible way out has gained the upper hand. Immoral as I feel it to be, I now will and must accept your offered help because I am unable to take the one step incumbent on me. May your generosity not land you in misfortune. Please fetch me away from here as soon as you can, the sooner the better. Take no notice if I cry off again, for I am so near madness that I marvel at being able to write two consecutive words.

265]

Meiningen
April 19, 1881

. . . The great Master is able to rise above the tumult that rages about him everywhere by reason of his marvellous strength, elasticity, and amiability; but I, the little master, am prostrated by it or at least shorn of my power to perform.

You understand, don't you? It was only through Schwarz, who arrived yesterday in time for the last concert, that I heard of *your silver-wedding celebrations*. I have no words to express to the two honoured parties my regret at having missed the occasion. Shall I now come limping after or take care that I do not overlook the *golden* one? I shall certainly look forward to that. See that you do your part!

Immediately after the Liszt concert I am coming back here to pack, for I am going to Wiesbaden early in May to see my poor blind mother, who, I have reason to fear from the latest reports, is near her end. I may (not yet settled) conduct the Ninth again at Leipzig on May 22 for the orchestra's benefit.

By the end of May I expect to be in London to *see* the Meiningers play and *hear* Anton Rubinstein. I suppose I may send " my " grand to the theatre?

266]

Meiningen
October 20, 1881

Just a word of grateful acknowledgment on the concert grand's arrival. The old one has been sent to Mr. Hatton at his hotel. Maestro Brahms finds the new instrument quite excellent and very easy. He is going to use it when he produces his Second Concerto for the Duke's benefit. It has been fully rehearsed and is great stuff, I can tell you. He plays it exquisitely too. We are all enchanted with him and his new works. As a conductor he took the orchestra by storm, and his benevolent forbearance has inspired us to renew our efforts, which are often thankless enough, owing to the paltriness of the conditions here.

On January 4, 5, and 6 we are giving, as a start, three Beethoven concerts in the Singakademie. If the experiment is not a failure, we have of course another series in prospect.

267]

Meiningen
January 8, 1883

I WAS greatly touched that you and your brother should have thought of me today. Thank you most warmly for these signs of unchanging friendship.

I assure you I can do with such good wishes. I have been through a horrible time and am only in the first stage of a recovery, which is not proof against relapses, and will possibly never be a complete one. Still I shall take all possible pains not to give the lie to these good wishes. Perhaps — perhaps I may be able to make my first reappearance as your (formerly so happy) flier (*Beflügelter*) by playing here on the 23rd. For Berlin I shall hardly be strong enough this season. . . .

268]

Meiningen, Sachsenstrasse 16
September 19, 1883

MANY thanks for your kind greetings. I *hope* to be in a position within a few months to receive your kind congratulations on my recovery. What I cannot accept, on the other hand, is your thanks to me for playing your beautiful instruments on my proposed concert tours (these are not yet certain, owing to my frequent relapses). *You* have indeed no further need of my " protection," but the good music that I am going to play does need your pianofortes. And — forgive the inevitable begging — my unworthiness the player now finds it very necessary to make himself thoroughly at home on a Bechstein again.

If, therefore, you could lend me a grand for my study, I should be greatly obliged.

270]

Berlin
November 12, 1887

My best thanks for your kind invitation. I had, however, accepted one from another quarter shortly before. Help me to be sorry for myself.

271]
                    [*On a visiting card*]
Berlin
January 5, 1888

Hans von Bülow regrets very much that he is unable to accept the kind invitation to dinner, for which he sends his sincere thanks.
            [*Enclosure (newspaper cutting)*:]

According to a credible report from Kentucky, a professor there has taught his monkey to play the pianoforte. This docile animal has achieved such a degree of virtuosity that it not only plays fluently *à quatre mains* with its four paws, but can turn over the pages with its tail at the same time.

272]

New York
Hotel Normandie
Broadway, Thirty-eighth Street
[*Undated; April 1890*]

Let me thank you most warmly for your kind forethought, which really touched me and to which I owe the circumstance of my second American exhibition of myself being as pleasing as the first (1875–6) was uncomfortable and damaging to health. Your excellent suggestions had the result of making the Knabe so presentable that I was not ashamed to appear in his company. You will understand that it was impossible for me to conceal from the public the satisfaction this gave me. I did not, as you know, pronounce myself satisfied with Chickering. In the short but lucid testimonial that I handed out to Knabe's yesterday, I made special reference to your recommendation of the firm's pianofortes. You will not, I hope, mind our both having revelled in the rage and injured feeling which this kindled in the great Pechstein Way!

Do take care of your health, you who have provided my complete equipment since the year 1855. The end of the century promises to be quite nice and as if it might be worth while to breathe. Best greetings and wishes to you all, also from my wife, who is thoroughly enjoying herself in the New World. Next Sunday we are dining with Karl Schurtz [sic].

PS. New York: Beethoven cycle, April 1, 2, 4, 5. Mixed recitals: 8, 10, 12. Philadelphia: 24, etc.

Should you see Ehrlich,[1] please give him my kindest regards and tell him I am taking every opportunity of fulfilling to the best of my ability the wish he confided to me before I left. He will realize it in due course. Charles Wolff's company invaluable! A splendid companion and cicerone!

273]

Weimar
February 16, 1890

I HARDLY remember playing on so exquisite an instrument as the one you sent me yesterday. The ideal richness of tone and colour and the extraordinarily responsive action, which obeys the slightest whim, aroused general enthusiasm in the very large audience, beginning with myself, for I was revelling in it.

My warmest thanks, old pal (yes!) for thus restoring my youthful strength and halving my sixty years. Just as yesterday's concert by its redeeming linkage of past and present (and future?) will remain ineradicable in my mind for the rest of

[1] HEINRICH EHRLICH (1822–99), *pianist, pupil of Henselt and Thalberg, teacher at the Stern Conservatoire, critic of the* Berliner Tageblatt, *arranged excerpts from Wagner's operas for pianoforte.*

my life — or of the century — so also will my grateful recollection of your invaluable part in it. I have but one absorbing
regret: that you were not there to rejoice in our common triumph. Our friend Wolff will tell you as much more about it as
you want to hear.

PS. In trunk-packing haste:

I suppose I can have the same grand for May 3 in Berlin
and the 6th in Hamburg?

274]

Hamburg
January 6, 1892

How can you imagine that I should blame you for not having
provided the newer boudoir grand for which I expressed a wish?
As regards " forgetfulness," I can counter this with the beam
in my own eye. Have I not neglected to this day to send you my
sympathy in your family loss? Though, truly, many a so-called
free day is lost to me through pain which makes even reading
and still more writing impossible. To come to the point on which
I have enlightened you: *I am the first to consider myself as belonging to the dead-and-done-with pianists,* so that in refusing
to admit that I had been rejected by *the* pianoforte-architect
par excellence I should write myself down as idiotically sensitive.

But — and this is the extenuating circumstance in connexion
with my importunity — as long as there is breath in a man, he
does not accept his bad luck with absolute resignation. This
being so, I have rashly promised my so-called friends (" *Hono-
ratioren* ") in Hamburg to give them a recital about February
12 in aid of a charity (they say that the aim sometimes justifies
the means, you know). Whether this project will prove successful in my present miserable state of nerves is extremely doubtful. I must, however, do my best to carry it out. And to that end
I need the support of one of your newer pianofortes on which I
can practise, not only finger technique, but the fine shades of
expression in my own room. The alternative is to break in my

Baltimore Knabe, which I find rather difficult to manipulate. But lest I should offend you by so doing (I could not damage your reputation), as once in Russia when I played a Becker, I sent a message to your representative Herr Dr. Bartels the other day.

275]

Beginning of September 1858

IT was a great satisfaction to me, beloved friend, to know that
you had arrived in Venice. I heard of it first through the newspapers, and a few days later through a letter of Karl's to my
wife. You will easily believe that I am consumed with the
desire to hear from you personally as to whether life there, as
regards externals, is likely to prove tolerable if not exactly comfortable for you. Do therefore satisfy my deep desire to know.
Today I wrote the last notes of the pianoforte arrangement of
Tristan, or, rather, of as much of the score as I possess, and
am as much refreshed by the pleasure it gave me as I am
cramped in the fingers from the labour of it. I flatter myself,
however, that my arrangement will satisfy you and I want you
to get Härtel's to send you a copy as soon as it is engraved, so
that you can tell me your opinion in so far as I can profit by it
in my further efforts. I can assure you that it sounds fairly easy
to play on the pianoforte — within limits, of course — and that
the score was studied with the utmost piety. I found one or two
isolated misprints in the upper winds. Now I am looking for
something else to do. Your music — on paper! — has been my
best medicine in " exile "; for such my stay in Berlin has really
seemed — certainly it has been no asylum for me. I have a fair
amount of freedom, however, and with no lessons and only mild
intrigues to worry me I am feeling pretty well. My wife has
been extremely kind and nice again. I wish you ever saw her
in a different mood from that which she has always worn at your
house. In your presence her flow of conversation seemed to dry
up and her frank expansive nature to withdraw into itself.
There was a compliment to you behind it all, though a mis-
placed one: " awe put her under a ban." Now she is always
afraid you think her too childish and altogether unimportant to
be able to love you and understand you. Yet she is just one of
the very few who can do so. But that's enough of marital leader-
writing. In our own house it would all go better.

Tell me, is it true that you have been officially invited to a

Lohengrin performance in Vienna? Yesterday's papers had it, with a flattering supplement for His Apostolic Majesty. It would be gorgeous beyond everything, and a good omen for future developments.

Shortly before our return there was a *Tannhäuser* performance, for which the house was sold out. Unfortunately the tenor Humbser (from Hamburg) is said to have been inconceivably incompetent. The Queen of England had very much wished to be present, but was prevented by a sudden indisposition. At both the court soirées at Babelsberg, however, I had to play selections from *Lohengrin* and the Bridal March was even *da capo'd* straight away.

The Grand Duke of Baden and his wife asked after you very particularly, the Princess of Prussia too and really in a peculiarly sympathetic way, even though it reduced itself to regrets at your not yet being pardoned. The Prince began to rave about *Rienzi* to me; it is far more to his taste than *Tannhäuser*. This seems to me to point to a possible revival later. As for me, I am sorry to say that so far no fee has arrived for my court performances, so we have had to postpone indefinitely our trip to Dresden to hear *Rienzi* there. Lehmann is back, and in such a complete state of deterioration that one " fears the worst," as they say. The worst in this case would be if the opera plans should be upset (for you) by unduly extended holidays.

I have just received the enclosed note from Fräulein Frommann, my object in forwarding it being to try to induce you to write to your brother. He was here with Johanna [1] for a few days only, in connexion with the court concert, but is definitely coming back at the end of the month.

I have still to thank you for your hospitality this year. Painful as it was to see you suffering and the most sacred thing in your life in danger, I would not for the world have missed being with you at that time. Once more I found it so delightful and so refreshing to be near you that I shall be able to live on the memory of it for a long time to come. If only I could have been of some use to you! It would have been something to ward off evil, even if I could not bring you good. But, alas, it is the

[1] JOHANNA WAGNER (1828–94), *niece of Richard, opera singer, pupil of Mme Viardot-Garcia; the original Elisabeth in* Tannhäuser.

way of the world: this one has the will, that one the power. Do not despise my impotence. That reminds me of that confounded Jew, whose hecatomb did actually reach me in Berlin via Zürich and was followed, a week later, by a decidedly polite and well-meaning letter from the sender in Paris. An ass, not a knave: but it's all one. . . .

276]

Berlin
September 11, 1858

IF I have waited forty-eight hours, my dear friend, before answering your last letter, you must not take it as a sign of lukewarmness. I missed Teichmann twice the day before yesterday and found him at home yesterday, but it was only today that I got the sort of answer out of him that you would want. It was to this effect:

That you should at once send me a receipt for seventy talers for Teichmann, as representing an advance on your share of the dividends for the current (third) quarter of the year. Teichmann will then honour my demand at the box-office and I shall immediately send you Austrian money, or rather bills. This solution of the matter seemed at first to present peculiar difficulties; I really did not dare to expect today's answer after my yesterday's visit. But Teichmann proved to be obliging and amiable. He sent me to consult a lawyer, Justizrat Licht, about my power of attorney, and legal opinion has it that you should have a judicial act made out according to the forms of the country in which you are at present living; that is, obtain through an Austrian solicitor the powers necessary for me to draw the sums that are due to you. There is, it appears, no other way of doing it. And in fact it seems to me essential since, in spite of Teichmann's courtesy, there is no avoiding the delays caused by the receipts and so on, and your point is that you want it immediately. And, by the way, don't think me a cad. Had my still outstanding fee for the court concert come in, I should have sent it you straight away. Equally as a matter of course do I insist on your claiming the remuneration for the pianoforte score of *Aulis* from Härtel's. I always did regard that piece of work as a very minor service rendered to you.

Goldstein is at Dieppe. He was the only soul I could have tapped at the moment. Unfortunately I had already transferred the hundred reichstalers in question to his firm on receiving them. Nothing else possible anywhere. Stern had played me a nasty trick into the bargain. Before I had written from Zürich to say I was arriving here on August 19, he had sent off another letter to Herr Pflughaupt, a pupil of Liszt, asking him to take my place. And although this fellow only deputized for me for six hours, his travelling expenses have run up the fee to a much more dazzling figure than I was at all prepared for. For the moment, therefore, I am likewise a *Hessen-Casseleer* (penniless).

Curious the way our letters crossed! I wrote on the 8th, but don't know whether you had the letter — as all the address Richter gave me was Palazzo Giustiniani — and on the 9th your letter arrived. *Tannhäuser* has been put on only once so far. Receipts: 1,007 reichstalers.

Teichmann hopes it will be produced once more this month, though, worse luck, with Tuczek,[1] as Johanna only returns the month after.

Lohengrin will certainly not appear before the end of November. The chorus has at last undergone a satisfactory and indeed essential reorganization. No one can really replace Krause as Telramund; Salomon is too stiff and his voice too low, Radwaner too Austrian and cloying. The King, Fricke; Elsa, Fräulein Wippern (quite a good choice, voice and production magnificent, looks not too prosaic, not much experience of stage routine yet); and the Herald, Pfister, who will certainly be more suitable than Bost.

Fortunately Formes[2] has heard *Lohengrin* in Vienna, so that he has received some enlightenment as to his part — which he thought "very boring" — from Ander. What Johanna will make of Ortrud musically, Heaven only knows; you can be happy about the dramatic side.

[1] LEOPOLDINE TUCZEK (1821–83), *coloratura singer, Berlin Hofoper, daughter and grand-daughter of conductors; pupil of Josephine Frölich, one of the four sisters who were Schubert's friends.*

[2] THEODOR FORMES (1826–74), *celebrated tenor at the Berlin Hofoper.*

A thousand thanks for your dear letter, which both touched and shamed me, on the ground of my admitted helplessness the other day. More presently; it is urgent that this should go today. I will just end up by trying to make you laugh at two bad jokes. The first is a Saxon *jeu d'esprit:*

Ganz leise kräht er:

Solution: *Kanzleisekretär.*[1]

The second is a sample of culture in high circles: scene in an exhibition of paintings. The great lady, who has selected the painter Richter as her cicerone, stops in front of a picture of Lessing to remark: " Does not this shade of colouring remind you of old Duroc? " " Duroc? Really I do not know of any Duroc, Your Highness." " But, as a painter, you must surely know Duroc! I mean the one who painted Marie Antoinette, the famous picture."

Sorry if you are not in the mood for them. Well, good-bye, I must hurry. Do not be angry, and do be sure that another time I shall be better equipped to render you any small service.

PS. Remember me to Karl, please!

277]

Berlin
October 10, 1858

I STILL have to thank you, dear and honoured friend, for your last letter. I should have replied sooner but that I was ill. It lasted nearly a fortnight this time and was particularly tiresome because I really have not time for that sort of thing. Hardly had I recovered a little when I naturally found myself in for double work to make up for what was left undone. My object in writing today — when I have nothing in the least pleasant or interesting to tell you — is to avoid any long gaps in our correspondence and also because Teichmann has been bothering me to send you a

---

[1] " *Softly crows the cock.*" *The four words, pronounced with a Saxon accent and run together, sound the same as those for* "*government official.*" — TR.

document which really serves no purpose at all (by the way, it was sent to me yesterday evening, the 9th). It looks to me now as if it is almost imperative for you to give me full powers in writing (I gave you the details before), which will put an end once and for all to this unfortunate delay in getting your royalties.

As regards the musical papers you wished to see in order to keep pace with the gutter flow of German music and drama, I have commissioned Brendel, Schlesinger, and Bock to do themselves the honour of sending you their respective journals to Venice by book post. The first of these will at least inform you as to the expected royalties. There is no question of a *Tannhäuser* performance. Formes is often hoarse and seconds *Taubert's niece* only in *Macbeth,* which, thanks to Johanna, is having a great revival in company with all the Italian trash: *Romeo, Tancred, Lucrezia.* I sincerely regret the departure of the terrible Hofmann (second tenor) from our stage. *Tannhäuser* was really his principal role and he frequently acted as deputy for the lazy Formes, greatly to the advantage of your takings. Now we have absolutely no substitute at all.

You will have learned from the political papers that, yesterday evening, the regency was at last proclaimed and the most unloved minister in Westphalia, corrupt electioneer and pietist, and darling of the *Kreuzzeitung,* has been thrown out of the government. In the departments of war and culture we hope for similar happenings. Although I hold aloof from all that kind of thing, I cannot help joining in the general sigh of relief, and the change pleases me, little as it affects me. Madame Laussot was here for a few days, but I saw little of her, as she was completely absorbed by her friend Mademoiselle Alex. Mendelssohn, with whom she was staying. Tomorrow she goes to London to see her sick mother, whom she proposes to nurse during the winter. I am giving her a line to Klindworth; she may be useful to him, just as he will be agreeable for her to know. She looks well and is as clever and witty as ever. Unfortunately she has grown plumper and also deafer. But the Ritters will probably have given you news of her, as she spent some weeks with them in Dresden.

I sent a good long letter to Karl recently. If you do not wish to write yourself, let me have indirect news of you through him. It refreshes me more than anything to keep in touch with you and with him too. Remember I have not a soul here whom I care about except my dear wife. We have no notion of where Liszt is, what he is doing, or when he returns to Weimar. He and "the Highness" have been persistently angry with me ever since Zürich.

I hope time will mend matters. Do remain solitary, for heaven's sake, instead of *living for* people who are prepared to *die opposing* you! I have an unspeakable fear that you may once more profane yourself out of kindness of heart and pity. Don't do it! Forgive my childish terror. My wife sends best remembrances. Her mother was much pleased by your kind reply. The idea of the Buddhist consignment was hers — that is, Cosima's. Daniel Stern's drama *Jacques Cœur* is to be played in Paris. The author is now propagandizing for you in spite of Franz.

Good-bye for today, and keep a kind thought of me, even if you don't write. When is the second act coming along?

278]

Berlin
January 1, 1859

How could I have " anything better to do at New Year " than to write to you, dear and honoured friend, always provided it is not for the conveyance of mere trivial " good wishes "? I grudge myself the relaxation all the less for having had you on my hands in an unpleasant sense all day. In other words, I have been copying out the violin parts of the Prelude to *Lohengrin,* which I am including in my audacious concert on January 14. I have only sixteen fiddles in all and had therefore to arrange the *violini divisi* accordingly. I had to do it myself too, for the copyist would probably have made nonsense of it. What is in the head will fill the pen.

May I tell you about my concert? It opens with Liszt's *Ideale.* Then comes Cossmann in a 'cello concerto, Frau von Milde in a *Cellini* aria, then the Beethoven G major (op. 58), the finest of the pianoforte concertos, for which I have written some jolly cadenzas. The second part opens with the *Lohengrin* Prelude so that Taubert may learn how he has to conduct it on the day of the first performance, January 18. After that, Milde is to sing Elisabeth's Prayer (the whole of it, mind!). By way of introduction to it I have put in twelve bars of the Pilgrims' Chorus, orchestrated in much the same way as at the end of the Overture, for bassoon, clarinet, and horns. I shall do no more of the orchestral part after the Prayer than is really necessary. Finally Cossmann will play a solo, Milde will sing two of Liszt's songs, and we finish with Berlioz: *Francs Juges* or *The Corsair*. I am living in an alternation of excitement and exhaustion, which must of course continue until the 14th, or rather 18th, of January. Taubert is said to be really taking some trouble over his part, but singers and orchestra are very mulish. I am curious as to the result. It looks as if there would be a more furious battle for and against than in the case of *Tannhäuser*.

I am glad we now both know what my wife is there for. I am truly lucky especially in having so understanding a wife, who only opens letters addressed to me when they are urgent. She did quite right and I kissed her hand with special appreciation for her prompt action, for which she deserves the title of " better half." You will now have fifty talers left. Don't be offended if I come back to an old problem. You know I shall not dream of pocketing that seventy talers for the arrangement of *Iphigenia in Aulis*. The money is there intact as a reserve for you in case you ever find yourself in a really tight corner. I did the work for you and want no more than your thanks at the most for so small a work of love. Do me the one favour to accept it without ceremony and see that you get into that tight corner nice and soon so that I can be rid of my ill-gotten gain. Would to Jehovitsch (as Tausig says) I could do a bigger deal for you! My concert tour with Laub in Königsberg and other places was a tolerable pecuniary success and I was therefore able to begin the new year free of debts. A most agreeable sensation. You will have heard at length from Breslau, where *Rienzi* made an even greater furore than *Tannhäuser*. A bad sign for the taste of the masses, but possibly a good omen for the brilliant revival (for such it is practically certain to be) of your dramatic *Eroica*. The Prince Regent, who is personally much more amiable to me than his wife, spoke to me recently with particular enthusiasm of the sublime melodies in *Rienzi,* which of all your works pleases him most. At the next opportunity I shall play him a transcription from it and try to sound him as to whether he would not like to command a repetition of the opera in Berlin. You would have a claim to royalties in that case, I hope? At Königsberg they have been asking for chorus-singers for *Lohengrin.* The orchestra there has a thoroughly good conductor now, a really vigorous, hefty fellow called Landdien.

Did you mind my not answering that beautiful letter of yours? It seemed to me that it would be a profanation to turn your monologue into a duologue. But you must know without any doubt that when you do honour me with a glimpse into your inmost feelings, it sinks deep into my soul and reverberates there for a long time. Or do you *not* realize that one feels so puny and helpless beside you that the only thing is to listen reverently to what you have to say and to refrain from mathematizing any rotten counterpoint to it? I shall very soon be inflicting a photo of myself upon you, which I have had specially taken for the purpose. Please don't hang it beside the Winterbergers. (You see how arrogant I am.) It will follow in a day or two, before you have time to protest.

TRISTAN: *Wie könnt die liebe mit mir sterben?*
    Die ewig lebende mit mir enden?

Excuse my asking, but isn't there a misprint?

I have puzzled a good deal over it, and as many things which are crude and unpleasing on the pianoforte sound well and

smooth on the orchestra, I have ventured to make the following
popular adaptation:

Forgive me if it is too stupid!

Liszt is really a splendid fellow, and I think the first act of
Tristan, which sends him into ecstasies, has proved real balm to
him.

Kind regards to Karl, please, and keep a little affection in
the new year for me and for my wife (ὕστερον πρώτερον),
who sends her love.

PS. Cosima has just brought me the enclosed letter for you.

279]

Berlin
January 25, 1859

I HOPE that arch-swine up in the left-hand corner is looking
down on these lines and feeling sick to death over them. If his
countrymen were not so numerous in Berlin, you, my dear
Wagner, would have had an even more colossal success here with
the first performance of *Lohengrin.* But, with the exception of
Goldstein and a few young Jews known to me personally, there
was a conspiracy among the Semites (who formed a good third
of the audience) to be noisy and interrupt and not even to move
a hand to applaud the performers. As " our people " are personally almost as cowardly as the Christian Jews whom they
have infected, there was, I admit, no opposition. After each of
the three acts the main characters were wildly applauded and
forced to come forward and it was the same with the two women
after the second scene of the second act. And now that I am on
the subject, I may as well give you the pleasing information

that these first two scenes of the second act went so extremely well that I myself — they being my particular favourites — listened with almost unmitigated satisfaction. A few brief criticisms. Chorus was better than usual, although it still leaves much to be desired. The chorus-master Elsler was one of the few concerned in the performance who fulfilled his task with liking and enthusiasm. Movements and grouping of chorus very sensibly arranged by your brother, who, I may say, never once asked my advice and, together with Taubert, overlooked several of the most important scenic arrangements in the stupidest way.

Orchestra very mulish and unsatisfactory. Bad and frequent mistakes and false entries, so that the *Kapellmeister* had his work cut out; at the dress rehearsal, for instance, when my wife was present, Hülsen had often to call the gentlemen of the orchestra to order. Prelude to Act III very good, War March ditto, Bridal March shortened by about twenty-eight bars, a cut being made between the first B flat major chord and the *pianissimo* with the tremolo on the kettle-drums. The Prelude to Act I was passed over without applause (it was far too quick and restless, the conductor's fault!); yet this same piece was received at my concert by an audience of five to six hundred with such roars of applause, accompanied by cries of "*Da capo*," as I seldom remember. I wish you could have heard that performance of mine, you would have been pleased with it. However, as Taubert had to conduct at the theatre that night, he could not hear my (your) *tempo* and so we must partially exonerate him. Now as to the individual performers. Johanna was magnificent in her acting. Singing tolerable in the beginning of the second act, but later horrible. Left out last retort against Elsa (E flat minor). Finale of Act III transposed into E minor and very much worse for the alteration. F sharp minor and major passage in Act II, on the other hand, far better than I expected. Fräulein Wippern, with her sweet bell-like voice, was very effective and better, for instance, than Köhler; but her frequent recalls for popular hits (in the finale of Act I for instance) were very objectionable. Act I was much the worst in every respect, I have heard it much better done in Breslau myself. But nevertheless there was tremendous applause after the curtain fell. Krause was best in the third act, though surprisingly vigorous and fiery in certain places in the beginning of Acts I and II; in short, not at all bad. Fricke not unintelligent as the King, but was slightly indisposed and muttered into his beard a good deal. Last of all, Formes was by far the best; sings with more intelligence than one credited him with, and evidently loves the music. His Lohengrin is beyond comparison better than his Tannhäuser, suits his voice better too. He came to see me several times and sang through the whole part. I gave him a few hints, by which he profited considerably. The scene in the bridal chamber was very impressive. The grail narration quite excellent, the parting very affecting. Formes took great pains with his acting too, studied (in strict privacy) with Roetscher for the occasion, for instance. He deserves some reward from you — I wish you would write a line or two to cheer him up — with a view to the number of performances. A very decent fellow, innocent of any low theatrical tricks, though also, I admit, of any genius. In spite of his *exiguum corpus* he looked almost handsome and produced a really overwhelming effect in places, as for instance in the second finale when he suddenly turns to Elsa and sings: "*wie seh' ich sie erbeben.*" The Herald, Pfister, was appallingly out of tune and had had everything he had to sing punctuated, as it were, for a tenor, so that, in the second act, hardly a note of the original remained. It is absolutely necessary to transfer this role to someone else, even if it were Radwaner or, in the last resort, Rost. You must insist upon it. Mounting good, though not of an extraordinary splendour; best in the second act, the daybreak was quite exquisitely done. The cuts were crazy, and there will still be a lot of monkeying with it, I can see. Instead of half-past six it was a quarter to seven when the performance began, and each of the intervals between the acts lasted a good half-hour; no wonder the opera only ended at twenty minutes to eleven. Tomorrow (Wednesday) is the second performance, next Monday the third. *Tempi* mostly too quick, but on the whole less perverse than I had feared in view of Taubert's well-known lack of rhythm and tendency to race. This must do for today. I will not speak of myself. My wife is beside herself with joy and I am particularly happy that she should be, because, poor dear, she has been so upset by the storm that broke over my head last week and is still raging. But new champions are now taking up the cudgels for me and I have be-

haved like an energetic and honourable gentleman of whom his
Master need not be ashamed. " Far better dead than a coward "
and " *Santo spirito* " are my mottoes.

The *Tannhäuser* receipts for this month are eleven hundred
reichstalers; that is, a percentage of seventy-seven.

Let me hear soon from my adored friend. You had my
telegram?

Kind regards to Karl.

PS. Should you like me to send you the press notices so that
you can study the theory of probabilities?

280]

Berlin
February 5, 1859

God knows, beloved friend, it is not my fault that the arrears
of royalties were not sent to you sooner. Immediately on the arrival of your first receipt I betook myself to Teichmann, who put
me off until the following day. To my surprise, I was then refused payment, with the explanation that the figures could not
be filled in by a stranger, but must be written out in your own
hand. Meanwhile there arrived a fresh receipt from you, in which
these folk could find no blemish, and I hope that before these
lines reach you, Goldstein will have placed the somewhat de-
pleted balance in your hands. I have left your address at the
theatre box-office with instructions that the official detailed statement should in future be sent to you direct so that this kind
of diffuseness may be avoided. I must still trouble you to send
in the receipt for the third quarter of 1858 in order to stop the
rabble's grumblings. If I happen to be in Paris in the beginning
of April, I shall arrange for Goldstein to receive the money in
my place and dispatch it to Venice. One thing more, to finish
with the business: the one *Tannhäuser* performance brought in
eleven hundred reichstalers, with a percentage of seventy-seven.
After the second of *Lohengrin* there was a pause. The next
(third) is on Friday, February 4, the fourth on Monday the 7th.
You may certainly count upon working off the advance made
to you by the end of the present quarter. The tickets are said

to be all sold, up to and including the sixth performance. The house, except for the amphitheatre, was sold out for the second, which went better from the point of view of both artists and conductor. The orchestra bungled things several times, but the whole was quite tolerable, and in spite of many a musical box on the ear I had great enjoyment out of it, which I have never been able to say of any *Tannhäuser* performance here. The audience was more quiet and attentive than I have ever known Berlin opera-goers except in the case of their beloved *Fidelio*. Applause was certainly rare and attempts at it were promptly suppressed, but only in order that not a note might be missed. Vile as the criticisms were again, they at least declared *Lohengrin* to be a step forward and had to own that its success had been more definite and wide-spread than that of *Tannhäuser*. I enclose a notice from the *Börsenzeitung*, a much read and, largely on account of its Monday *feuilleton*, popular paper, chief organ of the aristocracy of finance, which forms the theatre audience *par excellence*. You will see by the opening that my *private* terrorizing has not been without its effect. I have missed seeing the Frommann several times and it must be a month now since I spoke to her. She has acted in a fairly idiotic way towards me, but, needless to say, I shall bear her no ill will. She has toned down a good deal and is insufferably polite.

You have, I hope, received my telegram, my letter, and a later one from my wife as well as a pamphlet and Kossak's article in a wrapper. The article I found very disappointing. The fellow is frivolous and timid at the same time. How we did butter him up! The magnificent dinner that I gave him with Frau von Milde and the artist Hildebrandt seems to have been rather thrown away. A horrible race, yet one has to clutch at such straws and I have therefore invited him again, but this time my wife — who has the art — is going to make a few piquant remarks *ad hominem*.

We only heard some details, after the event, of the unpleasant episode with Liszt. Thank God it has all blown over. You are quite right to be a little diplomatic with him at times. He has grown extremely suspicious. But indeed he never knows who will betray or disavow him from one day to the next. Then think of this rain of missiles from all the papers. It is piteous and shameful, and it must not go on. I shall do what I can. My recent little state prank may have borne fruit in some quarters. They see that they have determined fellows to deal with; a few drops of blood now and then would do no harm. I for my part shall not avoid any occasions for blood-letting.

Some time I must tell you a few details which are not without interest from the cultural-historical view-point. In *Lohengrin*, for instance, I made various experiments, unfortunately without success. Listen, then: you remember an article that Adolf Stahr once wrote on *Lohengrin* from Weimar? It appeared first in the *Nationalzeitung*. When I told him he ought to publish it in pamphlet form, as there would be an enormous sale for it, the swine evaded me in the most cowardly and stupid way. At last he referred me to Dr. Zabel, editor of the *Nationalzeitung*. I approached him and found him at first not disinclined. Nothing happened, however, and it was only a few days ago that I heard the solution of the mystery. Among the principal shareholders is a certain banker, Gumprecht, brother of the blind music-critic of the paper, and he absolutely refused to have Stahr's article specially printed; his brother would not accept such a smack in the face, but would immediately resign. In which case the banker-brother would likewise have resigned his post as shareholder! What mud, what filth, O Jehovitsch!

Have just received Karl's entertaining letter. That is, it came yesterday, but I was at Brandenburg, where I gave a concert to improve my finances (forty-five reichstalers). Not too bad. I will reply as soon as I have time. Meanwhile, please thank him most sincerely in my name. His letter was not only a pleasure, but just what I needed to buck me up.

February 14 is my third orchestral concert. *Appel au peuple*. It's going to be a great surprise for everyone, and no doubt will end in a battle of sorts. We may even come to blows — it doesn't take long. No good scolding me. God knows this Babel needs it. The air must be cleared. You are represented by the *Faust Overture*; I myself shall sit at the pianoforte a good deal. More soon (after the third performance).

PS. My wife has just come along to send enthusiastic greetings. She adds that you are please not to take her crazy letter amiss, she is really ashamed to have sent it.

The dear child was made so happy by *Lohengrin. She* loves you too, you know. We both wept together!

281]

Berlin
March 4, 1859

You must not resent my long silence, beloved friend, for I have not been myself at all this last fortnight. I was physically exhausted too and had time neither to nurse myself nor to get the one long sleep I needed. But all that hangs together with the fine victory we have had. February 27 (Sunday) was a memorable day. The opposition was silenced. The *Ideale,* with Liszt conducting, made an overwhelming impression and roused undivided enthusiasm. Liszt's appearance was greeted with storms of applause, and at the end of the work he was recalled several times with even greater vehemence. Not one of the opposition dared to protest. So you see we have full satisfaction out of it. A more dazzling revenge could not have been foreseen or imagined. The press is silent. Not a word from the critics about my concert. Only in the political part of the papers is there a brief mention of the concert and its success as of a historical event of the day. But we have had our revenge for the Liszt concert of 1855. The unprejudiced admit that a crying injustice has been done. The *Ideale* positively drew sparks and we have at least something to take our stand on now. No longer outside the pale, we have won for ourselves the right to live and move. I know better than to indulge in sanguine illusions about the near future, but the importance of this concert should not be underestimated. Everything possible had been done to kill us and bury us in an uproar, but the whole conspiracy gave way before the instinct of reason displayed by the mass of the audience. The program opened with my orchestral fantasia, to which, on Liszt's advice, I affixed the title: "A Symphonic Prologue to Byron's *Cain*" (which Karl must not interpret as any fundamental disloyalty to him). The audience listened attentively, the orchestra showed its mettle, friends behaved discreetly, but clapped enough to drown two or three fairly timid hissers, who did not feel justified in depriving me of the honour of their ill will. I had really expected this in a more intense form, and that is why I sent my unpopular piece into the flames, as you might say. Next came the Schubert pianoforte fantasia, orchestrated and conducted by Liszt, which was received with great enthusiasm. I played well and was called out several times, though I naturally kept them waiting a bit to escape the reproach made by the critics recently that I most readily accepted the demonstrations of approval (that is, could have no right to protest against the disapproval expressed in other quarters). After that the *Ideale*. The second part began with your *Faust Overture*, which I am also going to produce at Prague on March 12 because it has not yet taken hold there, on account of unskilful conducting. It went well and made a very decided impression. In between, Fräulein Genast of Weimar sang two Schubert songs — one *The Erl-King* — with great success. For the rest, the Capriccio for pianoforte and orchestra on motives from Beethoven's *Ruins of Athens*, Liszt's *Mignon* sung by Fräulein Genast, and Berlioz's *Roman Carnival* all held the audience, down to the very last bar. The Princess of Prussia came in at the beginning of the second part, and this circumstance was most favourably interpreted by the crasser philistines. Next season I hope to bring off three concerts, opening the new campaign with Liszt's great mass.

As you see, then, January 14 has proved a successful *coup d'état*, and those who worship success have come over into our camp. But you will have had enough of my badly written account of this personal Berlin affair. Forgive me for boring you.

I am sorry I have nothing good to report in your own affair. *Lohengrin* has only reached its third performance, though this was a far more successful one than the first two, and the house was sold out. But now all is silence again. The Duke of Brabant, or rather Elsa's father, a Bückeburger brewer, has seen fit to die and Fräulein Wippern prefers to mourn as a human being rather than to do her duty as an artist; and Hülsen is a humane creature, as you will have gleaned from *Kladderadatsch*.

Meanwhile *Tannhäuser* was put on again last Sunday, the day of my concert, and there was a full house. All the same, I am afraid the end of the quarter will not bring you in any magnificent sum. You need not worry about the seventy-five reichstalers for Goldstein, though; let him wait till the end of June. As I shall be in Paris at the beginning of April, better write to Teichmann (who is a thoroughly good and obliging fellow) and ask him to send you the money direct; or else write to Goldstein and commission him to draw for you so that you lose nothing on the exchange.

I arrive at Prague on March 8 for rehearsals. In any case I shall stay there a week, until the 15th exclusive. Then the distance between us will be somewhat diminished. We shall be in the same country — a thought which is very comforting to me. Write to me there, anyhow, but particularly if you should have any commissions for Berlin. . . .

Your Karl really is a curious fellow. Wrote me a charming letter, which I thoroughly enjoyed. I sacrifice the hours after midnight after a very tiring day and answer him with a detailed epistle eloquent of my appreciation. Since then not a word, and I hardly know whether to be angry or hurt. Did you receive my portraits, of which one was for Karl? The Prussian postal system is so careless in dispatch and delivery that letters and parcels often get lost, are in fact never delivered.

Liszt is in a tolerably good humour, thank Heaven, and feels better than when he last stayed here. But the many callers, his connexion with the court, and so on give him no chance to rest and be alone with us, which is what we had looked forward to so much. He returns to Weimar tonight, and my wife follows him in a few days, while I hurry off to Prague. From there I also go to Weimar and thence with Cosima to Paris. As I said, it will be the first of May before I see Berlin again, but I hope in spite of my wanderings to keep in constant touch with you. Though I may not be outwardly so overworked and excited as I was a short time ago, I still have a positive craving to hear from you and even to write you these tedious letters. Alwina sent me the enclosed note for you two days ago. Cosima sends kindest remembrances. Thank you for the letter to Formes; it has given him new fire. He breaks lances for you everywhere. Such a good soul he is, one of those whose intelligence is born of goodwill.

I must say good-bye for today, but I certainly hope to continue the correspondence from Prague and to receive a sign of life from you also.

I think you will find I have not done the close of *Tristan* (A major) too badly for you. I have retained almost everything. From the first G major I modulate immediately to a minor third below:

and make the echoes of the last bar gradually slower until the complete dying away (roll of drums *ppp* on E). I also gave the middle parts B sharp to resolve into C sharp in the suspension so that the harmony appears to waver between minor and major. If you scold me you must remember that it is your own fault, for it would only have cost you a stroke of the pen to have made a decent job of it. . . .

PS. As usual, please excuse this hasty scrawl.

282]

Berlin
February 5, 1859

YOU made me swear a little the other night, my dear friend, when I was startled out of my sleep by a telegram at two in the morning. True, I stopped swearing as soon as I saw that the message came from you, but for a long time could not sleep a wink. The task you set me was difficult. A few days ago I cleared off our debts to Goldstein and asked him to send you the seventy reichstalers, which will, I hope, have been received yesterday (Friday). I am still obliged to go cautiously with our as yet un-patented court-Jew. It would have been folly in view of future transactions if I had immediately asked for a fresh loan of a hundred and fifty. Fortunately I had seventy-five lying by which I did not need for the moment, so I put it to Goldstein that he might advance a similar sum, and to this he agreed when he saw that I was doing all I could in the matter myself. He

promised solemnly to wire the money at once to a banker in
Venice, and it may be assumed that you are in receipt of it at
the time of writing. All the same, will you let me know whether
you have received this hundred and fifty? It is absolutely essential to my peace of mind to know it. Otherwise I shall have more
sleepless nights, which I cannot stand just now with the strenu-
ous life I lead. I am very curious to hear your special news
just now, by the way. That is, if you will honour me with your
confidence. I have been racking my brain over the important
event.

I hope my letters about *Lohengrin* did not vex you. I thought
I confined myself to the points that you would be interested to
know. Today I have only one purely business communication to
make: that Elsa and Lohengrin have been hoarse for eleven
days and that there has been no performance since the second
last Wednesday week. And they say Fräulein Wagner wants to
get married this month,[1] so it doesn't look as if we should have
many more performances. I hope they will put in Tuczek as
Ortrud so that the loan may soon be paid off. Certain it is that
the work itself cannot be injured by this old maid-of-all-work.
Hülsen said the other day: "I never expected *Lohengrin* to
have *such an outrageous* success." Day after day he implores
people through the newspaper columns not to worry him any
more for tickets, tells them he cannot consider any further ap-
plications, as all the seats are taken for the next six performances. He is said not to know whether he is standing on his head
or his heels, and no wonder. . . . Be assured, therefore, that the
public is clamouring so for *Lohengrin* that it will have to be given,
and the oftener the better. On the day of the next performance a
pamphlet is to appear, called: *Lohengrin and the Berlin Critics*,
which will amuse all the world, yourself included. The author
is a musical assessor, inspired by me. You must certainly have
a copy. It will pour oil on the flames. Apropos, Formes has
lighted for himself a flame of enthusiasm that continues to burn
merrily. You should hear him abusing the critics. If you will
allow me to put forward the plea again, I suggest that you should
write him a line of acknowledgment on my representation. That
stupid owl Kossak (whose notice I sent you) has offended him

[1] JOHANNA WAGNER *married Landrat Jachmann in 1859.*

badly by calling him phlegmatic in his part. That he really doesn't deserve. In any case Kossak's outburst was personal.

Confound the whole pack of them!

If I now make a really impudent request don't be more angry than a silent refusal on your part demands. I have just been invited to conduct a concert " of the future " in Prague at the end of this month, not this time of Liszt's compositions, which, as is well known, are normally applauded there without opposition. The undertaking is bound up with an academic charity, just as last year when Liszt conducted. I naturally accepted at once. As I have also to organize the program, I should like to perform an unfamiliar work of yours. The Praguers deserve the distinction. Should you care to let me have the Prelude to *Tristan* for it? That is, when you have composed an ending to it, which with a little goodwill should not prove impossible. It would be a graceful act. You would be treating the Praguers and your much harassed admirers very nicely if you did. But if this surprise request strikes you as superior idiocy, ignore it and do not despise me for it.

I wrote a fairly comprehensive letter to Karl recently. Perhaps he will let you see the part which concerns me personally if it interests you. I ought really to have written to your wife about *Lohengrin*. But, by Jehovitsch, I had no time. Please excuse me to her — I might have supposed that Fräulein Frommann had done it for me.

I must go to the conservatorium now. Farewell, remember me, and write soon, soon, soon.

PS. Please send receipt for the third quarter of 1858 (seventy-one reichstalers, six silver groschens); it is urgent.

Enclosed is a letter from Alwine Frommann.

283]

Berlin
August 24, 1859

You are right, my dear friend, " we " have been rude. It is not my particular fault. Let me explain a little. I did not reply to your letter [of March 8] from Prague because I had only

time while there to send a hasty scribble to Carl Ritter, who was
then staying with you and had written at the same time. One
does not stand on ceremony with one's contemporaries, you see.
Then, in Paris, Blandine told us with a triumphant air that she
had heard from you, but when we asked whether there was any
mention of us, she replied: " No, he did not say a word about
you." As regards the negotiations with the *théâtre lyrique*,
Cosima and I have tried repeatedly to get something done, but in
vain. Ollivier (whom I have discovered to be a detestable fellow,
bursting with vanity and selfish ambition) had either a speech
or a piece of legal work to prepare or he was on a bad footing
with Carvalho [1] because he had trodden on the numerous corns
of his vanity; or he had some other excuse for proceeding to the
order of the day. I tried to find out something from Carvalho off
my own bat, but missed him every time or was turned away. As
for the Leipzig affair, I give you my word of honour that I only
lent the score and parts of the *Tristan* Prelude after Liszt's repeated and most emphatic assurance that you had given Brendel
permission to play it at his request. Ask Liszt, make him show
you the correspondence that passed between us at Weimar, Leipzig, and Berlin some day. To give you an idea of the confusion
which reigned at the Leipzig festival I may tell you that my name
was put down on two programs to play five pieces without my
having been asked or even informed of the printed notices. They
disposed of me as if I had been a lifeless machine. " You are to
play that and that," and that's all about it. I had to spend all my
spare time at Leipzig working up these pieces. I wish you would
ask Dräseke, [2] who was an eyewitness, to tell you what my
health was like at the time. Tortured with toothache, I had to
be present at that banquet of bourgeois and philistine music-
makers and had to content myself with making faces at the vul-
garity of their toasts. First B. produced a tactless and cowardly
one to " Johann, the merry state-coachman, protector of the
arts and sciences," which led me to toss my glass full of wine
under the table to the horror of these geese " of the future."
Then Hans von Bronsart, that ultra-royalist, rose in fury and
was hurrying towards the platform to show the reverse of the

[1] LÉON CARVALHO (CARVAILLE) (1825–97), *director of the Paris Théâtre Lyrique, and later of the Opéra Comique.*
[2] FELIZ DRÄSEKE (1835–1913), *composer, disciple of Liszt, friend of Bülow.*

medal when he was stopped on his way by a gesture and almost tragically imploring look from the Master, who forbade him to speak. We both calmed down gradually, for the course of the supper and its oratorical seasoning were such that we began to look upon it as an honour that your name was not mentioned. Where the dead and the still-born are being fêted, there is no room for immortal names.

Do not imagine that I suppose you care in the least about these pettinesses. I am far from doing you such injustice even in thought, but I was anxious not to leave the secondary points in your letter unanswered. That you " have had enough of us all, your friends," is of course quite in order. But remember that, first of all, you have no friends. How should friendship fall to a man like you, who have no equal, stand outside the normal lines, and belong to another world, different from this vulgar, trivial one? Friends one looks at, you one looks up to. I, for instance, who am not exactly one of the most disreputable of my craft, I should *in all seriousness* be quite willing to become your boot-black and errand-boy, but the claim to be called friend by you is one which I should not have the impudence to make. There is just one who might have been much to you, and you to him, and it would have been on a different basis from the Weimar one. But it was not to be, and you are both the poorer. It was the middlemen who prevented it, for, as everyone knows, they make contact impossible for those whom they are supposed to bring together, by placing themselves between. Then there are all the daylight ghosts who so persistently pester my honoured father-in-law. (Unfortunately he encourages them.) It is one of my greatest worries.

Thank you for your sympathy. In spite of all my misery, I feel myself to be enough of a weed to be sure of surviving. The conductor's job at Karlsruhe would not be so bad. Better than giving lessons, I assure you. As the first *Tristan* rehearsal is to take place as early as October, I shall have to keep my nose to the grindstone. Two thirds of the second act are arranged. I am at page 250. In the *allegro* movement, to which I have now come, I propose to take the liberties which you have authorized. I have in fact amused myself by making it more difficult than you suggest. The pianoforte edition is to me the playable score *in nuce*.

Those musicians who cannot afford the expensive full score have a right to demand a pianoforte edition with text. Let Härtel have the arrangements " without words " turned out by his men in the usual way. You know I refused it as the last profanation. Your *Tristan* stands in the same relation to *Lohengrin* as Beethoven's last quartets to his first. The analogy seemed to me very striking. You now have to reckon with a later Beethoven public, and the sublime night-music (in A flat major) cannot be popularized into a " Star of Eve." Compared with Klindworth's edition, though, my arrangement will always be pure Pleyel or Diabelli. This to console Breitkopf. Well, good-bye. Let Dräseke write if you cannot. I am going to Karlsruhe for *Tristan* with Cosima, who is now nursing her brother Daniel — a serious lung case — at our house. Good-bye for today.

PS. In the Shepherd's song, I suppose I need not puzzle out any accompaniment (in small notes)? I have taken the liberty of eliminating several more misprints in Act II from the corrected score.

284]

Berlin
September 20, 1860

How can you doubt it, my adored friend? Of course I will go to Karlsruhe as the man at the pianoforte and be at your service there, whether my day's average is one gulden or three. About when ought I to start, provided Devrient [1] accepts your proposal? I have still two thirds of Act III to arrange, but could of course finish the work at Karlsruhe. Have you received Act I and are you satisfied? Heaven knows, I can do with a word of acknowledgment, for I did my honest best to make a proper job of it.

By a curious coincidence I happen to have paid compliments to Karlsruhe in the last number of Brendel's paper by praising some passable pianoforte pieces by young Kalliwoda, musical director of the court theatre. He is not a bad pianist, by the way, and is instructor to the Grand Duchess. For a South German he is not too hide-bound.

[1] EDUARD DEVRIENT (1801–77), *opera singer, actor of the Karlsruhe theatre, librettist of Marschner's* Hans Heiling, *friend of Mendelssohn.*

Let me thank you warmly for your thought of me and your attempt to provide a distraction from my existence here, whether it will result in any practical improvement for me or not. I shall fill my post as accompanist with the utmost modesty and diplomacy, you may rest assured, and Edi Devrient need fear nothing. I should have thought, by the way, that the theatre personnel might feel itself honoured by having a " royal " court pianist from Berlin prescribed for it!

There, I have answered. I now beg you most urgently to keep your promise and tell me how you are keeping in Paris. How did you get hold of your flat? My wife asks *me*, which means *you*, whether you will not go and see old Madame Liszt at 19 rue de Penthièvre some time? Do you ever see the Herolds? Has Gasperini [1] looked you up? By the way, if you want to dine very decently and cheaply, try the Diner Club in rue Laffitte and Lepeletier, near the Opéra. Four francs a head *à la carte*, including good wine; a magnificent place, extremely clean and with excellent service. Let me also press you to hear the *Pardon de Ploërmel*. Meyerbeer, the composer, appears to have written it expressly in your honour; for there is no longer any talk of a discussion as to the title: " miserable music-maker." Should you like to meet Szarvady, the Hungarian journalist, husband of Wilhelmine Clauss, the pianist? Or Gounod, who is a very decent fellow and a serious musician? Can, in fact, any of my Paris acquaintances be of any use to you in any way? There are certainly many among them who would be only too willing. Excuse this hasty writing. Your letter put me in a state of great excitement. I had begun to despair of the Karlsruhe performance and of your going there. The thought of it sends me crazy with joy. To hear this masterpiece conducted by you yourself! I feel like borrowing a brace of pistols and putting a bullet through my head after the last note. I am assuming that you want it all kept quiet and we are therefore preserving complete silence.

What a pity that my stepmother should be away from Paris just at this time! At Leipzig you made such a powerful impression on her — although she is not naturally receptive — that you might have felt inclined to call on her, particularly as you are

---

[1] GUIDO GASPERINI *of Florence, music-historian, since 1924 librarian of the Naples Conservatiore.*

living quite near her house in the avenue de l'Impératrice. You would like her daughter, Countess Charnacé, however, and my wife is writing to her today to let her know you are in Paris. We cannot bring ourselves to ask you to take the letter in person. Let her take the initiative. I am sure you will not be angry with us about it, for she is an uncommonly charming and clever woman, speaks German too, and is much easier to get on with than her mother. She heard *Tannhäuser* in Berlin, and her husband heard it in Dresden. Both of them rave about you.

Nothing particular to report from Berlin except that Hülsen has had an excellent find in the way of a tenor. Woworski is the treasure's name. He is learning Tannhäuser and is to appear in it next month. Formes is ill, I am sorry to say, and has been given two months' leave for a cold-water cure. Therefore no royalties up to date. On the other hand, Woworski will probably bring about a whole string of *Tannhäuser* performances, as the public always flock to the theatre when he sings. I have not yet seen him, as he has only appeared in *Robert* and *Lucrezia* so far, but, from all I hear of his musical capacity, he should be far better qualified for Tristan than Formes, who for his part will retain Lohengrin as one of the best roles in his repertoire.

If I only knew how to make any useful propaganda for *Rienzi*! I am convinced that there is still a rich royalty harvest in store for this opera in Berlin. (In Breslau it is more popular than *Tannhäuser*.) I suppose you did not give it up for good that time in Berlin?

Forgive this long gossip and let me hear from you soon.

PS. Your letter only reached me last night.

285]

Berlin
October 15, 1860

With pleasure, with indescribable pleasure, do I take up my pen to tell you that I at last feel human again, less incapable than before of writing a sensible line to you in particular and of asking you to withhold the recognition of my right to exist no longer. On the 12th of this month at three in the morning Cosima was delivered of a "healthy girl." The circumstances were those which constitute what is called a very happy delivery — why, I cannot imagine, for honestly it was more horrible than I had imagined to be possible. Poor women, they have a positive martyrdom to go through, and the onlooker who is, relatively speaking, bound to appear unaffected by it plays an even more pitiful part. Well, it is over, and my wife is as well as is possible and at present in a normal — that is, uncritical — condition. The six weeks' imprisonment which she has to undergo is comforting to look forward to in comparison with those bad alarming days before. As for me, after my long period of oppression, I say with Don Octavio (though in a different sense): "*Respiro*"; and one of my first new breaths is naturally blown into your eyes. In the middle of next month our daughter will receive the names Daniela Senta, if you will permit her, your eldest daughter, to choose that sacred personage for her patron saint. It would be my own and my wife's greatest happiness to dedicate her one day to your service. Should she have any of the talent requisite to an Isolde, she shall be a singer. It will be the devil's own luck if she is not furiously musical.

But enough of the nursery, although I really do not know what else to write about. I live more cut off and unsociably than ever and am scrupulously careful to avoid troubling myself about what is spoken or written (I won't say "done," for only in the Jews' quarter is anything done).

After innumerable postponements, signalled by red placards, your *Lohengrin* was given again for the first time this season. As the house was overflowing, a repetition is announced for next Sunday. The two Italian companies at the Royal and Victoria theatres appear to absorb the rest of people's interest. The Berliners are mad with enthusiasm over a certain alto, Fräulein Trebelli,[1] who is being idolized in the Jenny Lind fashion. I expect we shall see two parties rise up as once in Byzantium, the green and the blue. The court is still away. It will be all the same, though, whichever cause it espouses. The poor ballet is heading towards ruin. At the opera they are preparing for a revival of Spontini's *Nurmahal*[2] and (with more dispatch) Lachner's

---

[1] ZELIA TREBELLI-BETTINI (1838–92), *opera singer, sang much in London.*

[2] GASPARO SPONTINI (1775–1851), *the composer. His* Nurmahal, or The Rose Feast of Kashmir, *based on Moore's* Lalla Rookh, *dates from 1821.*

Catherina von Cornaro. The result will be a confirmation of two death certificates, I imagine. I cannot think what the Princess of Prussia arranged with you at Baden; the woman is, I suppose, too superficial to deign to order them to put *Tristan* in hand here. Wagner, the manager, certainly robbed me of the score a month back, and, judging by his good intentions and demonstrations and his report on Taubert's enthusiasm for the work, I thought it seemed clear that if it depended on these two gentlemen they would do their utmost to combat any assumptions from on high. But the opera-house certainly cannot carry on for ever without one of your operas and I assume therefore that they will look out *Rienzi* or the *Dutchman*. If only I could warm them up a little at court about it!

Liszt has good news from Rome: he has had to wait a long time. The Princess appears to have worked the dispensation at last and announces her return at the end of the month. I do not yet feel jubilant, for I see the workings of an unfavourable star in this affair, and all the former good news proved to be premature. In the beginning of November my father-in-law is coming to us for the christening. The child will naturally be received into the bosom of the " one and only," although certain honest and sensible men have advised Judaism.

I have not been able to get going yet with my various items of work and musical plans for concerts and so on. It seems likely that I shall keep as quiet as possible this season and only think how to earn my travelling expenses — and perhaps my wife's — to Paris for the *Tannhäuser* performance.

Alexander Ritter passed through here the other day on his way to Schwerin, where he is now going to live. His wife will take up her old post at the theatre. Karl is still in Naples with Winterberger, where he seems to be squandering his capital (according to accounts Alex. has received from Petersburg) and behaving like a fanatical Bourbonist and Austrian. I suppose I must not expect to hear from you yourself, as you will be having to toil by day and night, but it would be very nice if you would depute Lindau or Flaxland to send me your news. The arrangement or disarrangement of the *Tannhäuser* Overture has aroused your displeasure, I hope. Kindest regards from us both to your wife. Do not be too angry with me.

286]

Berlin
October 20, 1860

THANK you enormously, O divine one! Your few lines have so refreshed me that I am in ecstasy. All hail to your brain-child, who puts the old foam-born lady in the shade. Daily rehearsals, you say! I could dance for joy. I was half dead with fright from depressing reports that had been spread by vagabond theatrical agency pirates. Heaven give you patience and tranquillity among it all! You will need them.

My wife, who was not at all well today, was also quite refreshed by the news from you. She sends kindest regards to you and Frau Minna and thanks you for your inquiries. Do you want a Wolfram? A week ago Hardtmuth, the court operasinger, wrote to me from Dresden asking me to send him the French translation of *Tannhäuser* at once so that he could get Wolfram into his head. Hardtmuth is a man of musical culture with a very attractive personality. He might perhaps be regarded as a reservist for possible emergencies. I have not heard him on the stage. In my Prague concert the year before last, he sang Schubert's *Wanderer* in a very sympathetic, metallic voice. The song was encored.

Liszt is spending these days in Vienna to put an end to certain royal intrigues. The conclave of cardinals in Rome decided in favour of his marriage, the dispensation is in the Princess's hands, and the main question is in order. But unexpected villainies which suddenly reared their heads in Vienna with a view to upsetting the decision sent Liszt into a flaming passion (as a woman who was there told me) and he hurried to the capital to straighten things out. The first *Tannhäuser* performance in Paris may possibly coincide with his wedding. A case for a double celebration. Popular feeling runs high just now in Weimar. All classes are uniting in preparation for a grand demonstration (torch-light procession and so on) on Liszt's birthday, the 22nd. I only hope he is back by then. It will be to some extent a demonstration *against* Dingelstedt and possibly a more exalted personage. The neighbouring towns of Thuringia — Jena, Apolda, and others — are to join in, so we shall see some fun. Bronsart is on the right path at Leipzig. He may yet cut out the Gewandhaus by his Euterpe concerts. His vigorous talent will certainly defeat Reinecke's flabby mentality in the contests of the present season. Otherwise nothing has happened in the world of music to annoy or to please me. In Germany there is only the *Tristan* performance to get excited about.

Dräseke has been at home in Coburg for some time but is now again in Dresden . . . feeling very lonely and out of spirits, as he is faced with the prospect of shortly becoming entirely deaf. I wish this evil fate might have fallen on some other of us young ones — myself for example — instead of on the most gifted among us. Tausig is going to tour Scandinavia. He seems to be fairly well off financially and is also on better terms with Weimar again. But these petty family affairs have no sort of interest for you now. Be indulgent with me for gossiping and let me thank you again a thousand times for your note.

287(a)]

Berlin
November 17, 1860

I HAVE just learned from the *Presse Giacomellina*, dear and honoured friend, that you have been ill and even in bed. Confound the impertinence of the Paris climate! I hope there is truth in the added announcement that you are nearing the last stage of convalescence and will soon be able to support the torture of rehearsals again, as there is then no need to give oneself up to fruitless anxiety.

In writing today I have no intention of troubling you for a word in your own hand, but ask you to let me know through Flaxland or his Berlin assistant, my obliging patron Herr Sulzer, how you are and also the approximate date of the *Tannhäuser* performance. I am most anxious to be there and should have to make preparations beforehand. For example, I propose to make a concert at Basel pay my travelling expenses. The folks there have given me a choice among their concert dates, which are already arranged.

My wife has not yet completely recovered and is rather weak. I was a patient myself for a week and was tied to my room. In short we have not had much enjoyment at home. Only the child is fairly well. She is to be christened tomorrow week: Daniela Senta — and my father-in-law is coming over for the occasion. Soon after, he seems to be going to change his place of abode. He has had some most painful experiences of perfidy and meanness lately and is in a more depressed mood now than I ever thought to see him. But that is between ourselves. You will probably hear more from him direct. There was much talk of his moving to Paris in order to settle there as a *pianoforte-teacher!!!* But this again is between ourselves. I could tell you things and give you explanations that would surprise you.

I am sending a cutting from *Kladderadatsch* which concerns you. All Berlin, or at least the large responsible majority, is indignant over the doings of the Academy. Two thirds of the votes are necessary for admission — the six musicians (Meyerbeer was not opposing you) naturally voted against and the painters for you. The painters were so indignant at this that they turned down all the other musicians — for instance, Halévy, proposed by Giacomo. Rietz had come up for election first, before you, otherwise he would have suffered the same fate.

Do you consider it very pushing and outrageous of me to have authorized a young man, Paul von Bojanovski, to use my name as an introduction to you? I think you will forgive me when you get to know him. As a matter of fact, when I decided to do this for him, I had in mind the possibility of your being able to employ him. One never knows when there may be an occasion. He is a young nobleman who has been ruined and is now earning an honest living in Paris by teaching languages and acting as correspondent for foreign (that is, German) papers. (Several journals employed him recently at the Warsaw conferences.) He is on the *Weserzeitung*, the *Münchner* (*Süddeutsche*), and others. He is under great obligation to my family and is a decent well-bred fellow with the greatest admiration for you — I think you may very well find him useful. In what way, I leave you to discover after seeing him.

By the way, Beckmann is a very dangerous person. Everyone here regards him as a French spy. Take care that Niemann does not open out to him too much. Perhaps you will give him a hint. Excuse this precocious advice. I really have heard very suspicious things about B. from various quarters. Cosima's kindest regards to you and Frau Minna. Good-bye, and if you must be ill again, do let me be it for you.

[*Poem enclosed*]

Inscription for the portico of an
Academy of Arts

This is the house, this is the hour, the place,
These are the sacred halls where art doth reign;
'Twas here that honorary members were elected
And here that Richard Wagner was rejected.
But 'twas well done: an artist such as he
Would find small honour in the Academy.

287(b)]

Berlin
March 30, 1861
Address from April 3:
Schönebergerstrasse 10

THE news from Paris leaves me speechless, dearest friend. First I felt like bursting into the laughter that definitely marks the beginning of lunacy. But now it seems to me rather that I must have been a lunatic to expect any other results. The rabble does not play hide-and-seek with me in Paris as it does elsewhere: it fulfilled its social mission with regard to you without masks, compulsion, or Germanic scruples. I don't know how you feel, but the serenity of your mood after the first evening seemed to me to have undergone no change. Fundamentally the motives which lead to suicide and to taking up one's life again are identical: extreme disgust and a surfeit of worldly things may lead equally to self-destruction or to the most complete self-indulgence.

Your poor wife! What must she have suffered! We have

thought much about her and would gladly have expressed our sympathy, but where could we find a comforting or soothing word?

I had to spend a week at Karlsruhe and I only heard yesterday through Countess Flemming, wife of the Prussian minister, that I had spent it to good effect.

On such placid ground the least thing takes time to prepare, and Kalliwoda is acting in a cowardly, unenterprising way like the German he is. I hoped he would have done all the small amount of spade-work necessary so that I should have some ground on which to stand in demanding a reply. But until my arrival he had not even attempted to see the people concerned, but had on the contrary avoided opportunities of doing so. Yet this fellow is a thorough-going musician, clever and well-intentioned and a favourite with the Grand Duchess.

But I will spare you the futile details. Here, briefly, is the result:

The Grand Duke agrees to the idea of a dramatic music festival (as I christened it for the sake of intelligibility) with or for *Tristan and Isolde,* under your direction of course. He will have the principal artists engaged beforehand according to your wishes. For Brangäne (if not for Isolde) Frau Boni is available: a beginner full of ambition and energy, with a wonderful organ and an unusually fine personality. I consider her capable of being trained; she is teachable. Then for Kurwenal there is Hauser, as satisfactory for the part as anyone in Germany: magnificent voice, has the freshness of youth, and is genuinely musical. Mark, don't know; Tristan, probably Schnorr, who after all seems to me the least of all evils.

I imagine your stay in Paris will in no case be long. Do please go straight to Karlsruhe next and pay your respects at court, having announced your arrival beforehand through the Baden minister in Paris. I am counting entirely on the magnetic effect of your personality on the Grand Duchess, who is your fervent friend and admirer. On three mornings I had to play *Tristan* to her for nearly an hour each time, only Fräulein von Sternberg (her lady-in-waiting and a friend of mine) being present. She listened with rapt attention, following the poem the while. If that was all a Berlin pose, I'll eat my hat! On

Friday the 22nd, her father's birthday, I delivered my great *coup,* a musical surprise which came off brilliantly. Together with Hauser, who sang Donner, Froh, and Wotan — and jolly well too — I presented her with part of the *Rheingold.* There was no time to get in other instruments, no space, either, in the tiny room of the Prussian ambassador, who had invited a crush of people. This is what we did:

From page 198 of the pianoforte score — where Donner conjures up the spirits, preceded by the Valhalla motif, transposed into B flat, on the pianoforte by way of introduction — down to page 208, " in Valhalla dwell with me " (with the storm slightly abbreviated); after which, by way of epilogue, as it were, came page 54 of the pianoforte score. Don't scold me too much for my crazy expedients; the effect exceeded all expectations. With my own hand I had written out programs with the words and a brief preliminary explanation for Their Highnesses. They were most grateful to me. Indeed I was given plainly to understand that they would like me to move to Karlsruhe as successor to Strauss, who is shortly to be pensioned. *I declined.* That put an end at once to the suspicions (very much in evidence) of my disinterestedness in view of my repeated visits to the court. Kalliwoda is now in a blissful state on his release from the nightmare of being driven from the conductor's chair by me and he and his colleagues will work for the idea which I brought forward *without in the least compromising you.* As dictated to them it was this: " The Grand Duke nominated R. W. as general music director with a yearly salary of five thousand florins. R. W. has no other obligation than to conduct a few concerts and those operas by himself or by Gluck which he desires to single out for special performance. (Kalliwoda takes Strauss's place as a working ordinary conductor.)"

This idea has at last been laid before the Grand Duke in concise form by the Flemmings. How long he will go about pregnant with it Heaven only knows. What I could do has been done. I could not go to him about it myself. It would have been necessary to stay yet another week for that. And that was impossible, as I had received most disquieting news of my dear wife's health. On my return I am glad to say I found this news to have been somewhat exaggerated. Still I am not yet out of suspense. In

June she will have to go to Reichenhall on the borders of Tirol (ten miles from Salzburg) for several months, and everything must go by the board so that I may take her there and superintend her treatment. Otherwise the cure will be useless, as she never can take her own weal and woe seriously.

I will not write more today. My private sorrows become non-existent in the face of such of life's problems as concern those most precious to me: you and my wife. Nothing of consequence has happened here. I told Fräulein Frommann about everything on the day I arrived. I expect your wife will have exchanged various letters with her since then. Hülsen's retirement is certain. His successor, Dachröden, is a classicomaniac of the first water.

I found the press here wallowing in the mud of the Paris correspondence from a Jewish pen. Where I could intervene informatively, as in the case of Kossak (who was better than the rest), I did so. But really I am too old a hand to worry, *le lendemain*, over the newspaper trash of *la veille*. After all, what does it matter? You may rely upon another letter from me soon and rely, too, upon the loyalty of your pianoforte-Hans.

Kindest regards to your wife, whom I am perhaps coming to know a little better, and to Kietz, who was so good as to write to me.

288]

Berlin,
Schönebergerstrasse 10 (" Montebello ")
May 1, 1861

THE last few weeks have been very unsettling for me, dear and honoured friend, though not unpleasant. All the concert plans which I gave up at the time of my stay in Paris have now, one after the other, materialized. The persistence of the Halberstadters, Brunswickers, and Schweriners, that I should play to them, found an ally in the persistence of wintry weather, and so vanishes the last pretence of sacrificing my own interests for the sake of Roger's friends.

I brought back a great piece of news from Brunswick yesterday. In a momentary absence of bad temper three days ago the Duke gave permission for *Tannhäuser* to be played, on condition that there should be no extra outlay in connexion with it. A new and (without exaggeration) magnificent theatre has been built and is to be opened in the beginning of October. Kapellmeister Abt [1] wishes to celebrate the occasion with *Tannhäuser* and is hoping that the public response will be so brilliant that the Duke, as a good economist, will see fit to allow others of your operas to be performed.

Then Herr von Gall, who was present with me at a very decent performance of the *Dutchman* at Frankfurt (newly rehearsed, and received with wild enthusiasm), conceived the desire to transplant this opera to Stuttgart. So that it looks as if the material outcome of your " pre-March " work was not yet complete.

I hear that you have been to Karlsruhe and I was delighted that you had decided to go. You will not, I hope, have had reason to regret it. I have confidence in the Grand Duke's conscientiousness. He is said to be difficult to bring to the point, but rigid in carrying out what he has promised. I should so much like to know a little more about your personal relations with both these amiable people. The Frankfurt papers had only very meagre reports. *One* curiosity I did strike, however: *shortly before* your arrival at Karlsruhe there appeared in the *Didaskalie* (advertising organ of the Karlsruhe intendant) a further statement as to the impossibility of producing *Tristan and Isolde*. This was not, I swear, merely inspired by Uncle Devrient, but presumably written by his own hand. Perfidious swine! Every day throughout the month of April the Frankfurt *Konversationsblatt* had an excellently written, detailed description of everything that concerned the Paris performance of *Tannhäuser*. I have been nosing round, but cannot trace the writer. Whoever it is, I am delighted that a section of the press should be exerting itself to keep up the public interest in you. If the *Tristan* performance at Karlsruhe takes place, as you intend, the box-office will have to rely mainly on the influx of south German residents in the neighbourhood (Stuttgarters, Darmstadters, Mannheimers, Frankfurters).

[1] FRANZ ABT (1819–85), *was* Kapellmeister *at Brunswick from 1852 to 1882.*

But our crowned Mæcenases appreciate an artist nowadays according to what he brings in *for them*, and not according to what *they spend for him*.

I have not yet thanked you for your divinely good and affectionate letter of April 4. It came just in the rush of concert work, now behind me, which is usually crowded into the end of the week; and for the rest of the time I had to double my teaching activities in Berlin, so that my only free time was that spent in the railway carriage, and even then I had to exercise my memory. Now I have really a little peace until the middle of June, when, as I told you, I have to take my wife to Reichenhall. When do you go to Vienna? You will be obliged to go through Salzburg, coming from Paris, so we may perhaps see you on your way there or back. Reichenhall is about ten miles from Salzburg, an hour and a half by coach. Liszt left Weimar yesterday. After a short stop at Frankfurt and a slightly longer one in Brussels he will arrive in Paris, probably by May 8 at latest. He is not staying with the Olliviers, but at the Hôtel du Helder, quite near you therefore. I hope that your meeting will have the result which I have long desired in the interests of my own most sacred feelings, though so far in vain. The hour which brings you two face to face has for me the character of a Whitsun festival. Would I could be free to join you!

I sent for Baudelaire and found him most refreshing. Beckmann mentioned a Janin *feuilleton* in his letter recently, but I have not been able to obtain it. If you see B., would you mind asking him whether he received my reply? He asked me to do something for which I at once placed myself at his service, and I am still waiting for his next step. This is all for today, just a sign of life, which I hope you will answer if it is not too great an effort.

PS. Do give Liszt a word of encouragement. He needs it so as coming *from you*. His self-confidence has given way lamentably under the caresses of German criticism on paper and otherwise.

The effect of your Leipzig *letter* penetrated *everywhere* and carried general conviction. It has raised you in the estimation of all circles, and indeed it was a masterpiece of its kind. You alone could have done it. One cannot deny the Germans a certain respect for great men, particularly when it costs them nothing to affirm it.

289]

Munich
December 5, 1867

I DO not know how you are, my dear friend, or whether a longer stay in Lucerne is essential for the completion of your cure; but if so, I beg you will regard the request to put forward your arrival in Munich as *non avenu*. All the same, if it can be done without damaging you, we should be glad to have you here. There is a good deal of argument going on in the *Süddeutsche Presse,* too, and Fröbel himself stands in need of enlightenment as to the aim of the paper entrusted to him.

A mass of other things, impossible to explain in writing, is waiting to be discussed and there are certain measures to be taken in common.

That it should be so hard to bring well-meaning individuals to the state of intelligent obedience, which is all one asks of them, even when many of the preliminary conditions have been fulfilled!

290]

Munich
December 7, 1868

I PARTICULARLY want you to read the enclosed letter, dear Master, and return it to me. I felt obliged to reply that T.'s claims and statements were justified (but for him the whole thing would have been passed over); that is, that the public is used to his absence of *legato* and *mezza di voce,* and that he will presumably be succeeded later by another Walther von Stolzing. Bronsart writes that Hülsen, who has forbidden him to proceed with rehearsals of the *Meistersinger* for the present, is going to leave it to Count Platen in Dresden to pull the chestnuts out of the fire. Quite right too, in my opinion. The ninth performance of the *Meistersinger* went very well in parts. Richter took first horn after he had played the organ. Fräulein Stehle excellent; Sigl not in such good voice, but sang the couplets without mistakes and in correct *tempo*. Kindermann dragged and went wrong a good deal (had to beat time on my desk once or twice), but, all the same, did respectably well. Hammered his last to perfection. Orchestra very intelligent. House overflowing at somewhat reduced prices (*galérie noble,* two florins thirty; parquet, two florins — here that still counts as dear). On Sunday the 13th, *Iphigenia in Aulis;* on Sunday the 20th, *Flying Dutchman* with Fräulein Gungl, thoroughly drilled by me, as Senta.

291]

Munich
December 20, 1868

I AM rather late in thanking you for your reply, dear Master, but am glad to say that before it arrived I had already written to Rietz, taking the same line as you, though I expressed myself more wildly.

I hear through Heine in Zürich that you are feeling well morally and physically. (I can almost say the same of myself, thanks to the most varied gifts of fortune.) A further proof lies in the " Recollections of Rossini " which I distribute broadcast among choirs, orchestras, music-school teachers, and so on.

All this encourages me to put you in touch with what goes on here, as if you were not yet " dead " ! And you must not mind if a few uninteresting trifles creep in among the rest.

Iphigenia, which we rehearsed most thoroughly (Hallwachs did his part splendidly too), has been several times postponed, first because Agamemnon (" Minderkann ") had been too lazy to unlearn, and secondly because of the gastrically feverish Clytemnestra (Diez). It is definitely to be given on Friday, however, and the Sunday after we have Goethe's *Tauris* (see Perfall). The *Dutchman* with Fräulein Gungl as Senta (photograph enclosed) is fixed for next Sunday, December 26.

You must not suppose from the fact that we are giving *Fidelio* (newly rehearsed) today that I am allowing a theoretical indifference to your clearly expressed views on this work to me to amount to practical opposition on my part. Not that, but simply because it was unavoidable. A week ago Perfall had to repeat Gounod's *Faust* in order to make a little money, as the Cabinet has irresponsibly cut down his spending powers. On this account, then, *Faust,* of which a short account later. *Iphigenia* being out of the question, *Fidelio* was the best possible choice, as Frau Richter (who has now definitely entered upon her teaching duties at the music school) sings the name-part and by her practical achievements at rehearsals has given us a foretaste of her professional authority. The performance was a model one throughout, and the public more spontaneously moved perhaps than under Lachner's command performance. I am now really established. The Bach suite and Mozart symphony were revised by me down to the tiniest details of light and shade.

Richter is working as vigorously as ever. He becomes more popular and respected every day. We often dine together at the "Orlando di Lasso."

Grandauer has brought out a new art-paper with Grosse: *Propyläen,* which is to appear from January 1, 1869 as supplement to a new official rag, the *Bayrische Landeszeitung.* Tone good.

Perfall is occasionally too chicken-livered; also uncertain in health, of course. But the official board still thrives by God's grace and I continue to " clothe " it and keep it in a good temper.

Liszt is passing through Augsburg in the beginning of next year, when I am to see him.

My speech (see enclosure) to the orchestra at the rehearsal on Monday (the day after *Faust,* conducted of course by Mayer) was to this effect:

" Gentlemen, we have to fight against a common foe: the indifference and listlessness of the public. If we devote all our powers to the defeat of this enemy we shall be serving at once the ideal interests of our noble art and the practical interests of ourselves as artists. It is only by perfect performances of classical works of art that we can achieve this. True, the achievement of our aim seems hardly realizable when we see that such styleless bastard productions as the opera *Faust* by the semi-Frenchman Gounod can still evoke storms of enthusiasm. These depressing experiences must not, however, mislead us or cause us to shrink from our task. It rests with us to raise the better-informed, nobler-minded minority of the public little by little to a majority. Like the Danish knight in Gluck's *Armida,* let us appear before our public armed with Gottfried's glittering shield, on which the names of our German tone-heroes are emblazoned; let us lead this public into the light and seek to free it from the shackles of the corrupt-smelling opera-Armida. Let us work, let us act with all our heart; we shall then conquer the hearts of the listeners." Before this I had explained the significance of my program and proved that it was in no sense exhausting for either performers or listeners. And I was *grandement* justified by its success.

Dräseke is still here, still somewhat unaccustomed to his deafness and correspondingly depressed. Shall be glad when he leaves. Herewith a letter from Hermann Levi (Heymann?), which shows that the *Meistersinger* is being taken seriously at Karlsruhe. Bronsart on the other hand is obliged to put on *Mignon.* As for the *Dutchman,* there is no question about its success in Berlin. I have made inquiries right and left.

Not a word from H.M.

My time is up, hence this abrupt close.

PS. One thing more: do not be offended at my having given Richter for a Christmas present the seal you gave me with your bust on it. I have had engraved on it the words: " Honour your German *Meister.*"

Seems to me I am setting a good example!

292]

Munich
December 25, 1868

THERE is more to report, but unfortunately not what you expected, dear Master. Kindermann[1] has been so thoroughly put through it by the two Hanses (we never let a single incorrectness pass now) that he has perpetual stage-fright and funks the Flying (not swimming) Dutchman and still more Agamemnon, which

[1] AUGUST KINDERMANN (1817–91), *baritone at the Munich Hofoper.*

is due at almost the same time. Renewed postponement therefore. We are now going to try Agamemnon with Fischer and hope it may do. The fellow really has a glorious voice and is more musical than the baritone hero, though his brain is always asleep.

Dutchman now fixed for January 1. I took Senta through everything that she has to sing three times over with the orchestra recently and she has now sung away all her fright. I feel quite confident about her.

The choruses have been excellently rehearsed with Richter, and Bachmann (as the Helmsman) will be a great gain to the performance.

As you will certainly be interested in Mamma Richter's début, I am sending two cuttings, of which the one (*Telegraph*—Grandauer no longer writes for it) is unjust, but the other (*Unterhaltungsblatt*) just, though severe. The good lady was very good at rehearsals, but physically and morally indisposed on the evening of the performance. Well, no harm done. I am now in a position to support and protect the singing-mistress.

Your recent telegram was issued to me here in a rather "free" interpretation. Am I to understand that I sent you the Hanslick pamphlet? Hiller took your Rossini article as a personal insult and as professional obstruction, I hear; Herr Professor Schelle, the spoilt barber's assistant, ditto. The *Presse* and the *Kölnische* give proof of it. Perhaps Countess Bassenheim will let you look at them.

In the end of January I shall take about ten days' leave to give concerts in Brussels and Hanover.

I sent a pianoforte paraphrase of the *Quintettchen* to Schott the other day. To make it playable I transposed it into G.

Ritter's *Alcibiades* I have recommended to Fräulein Ziegler (who really is enormously talented — her Medea was marvellous) and she is greatly interested, as is her master Christen (her "*maître*"); we may perhaps get it put on here.

We have the *Barber* in preparation now. I am conducting. Richter is to do the *Prophet* and the *Black Domino*. In the first I shall play the organ for the first time in my life. The orchestra played really divinely in *Fidelio* the other day.

The Mallinger [1] affair is still in the balance. Perfall is acting

[1] MATHILDE MALLINGER (1847–1920), *soprano at the Berlin Hofoper, the first Eva.*

very sensibly (His Majesty likewise). She is perpetually being left in uncertainty, but perhaps time will bring the solution. Her demand was for immediate dismissal or three months' extension of leave. The Cabinet thereupon lengthened her original leave, which expired on December 10, to the end of the year and referred her to an All-Highest decision at New Year.

The children are well. They had quantities of presents and I am teaching them the rondo motif from the Ninth Symphony. Good-bye. Most sincere season's greetings.

293]

Munich
April 8, 1869

I HAVE been suffering so severely from a nervous attack for six days past, dear Master, that I stayed in altogether to recover. Saw no one and had to cancel the Academy and music-school concert. I have employed this involuntary leisure — what I should prefer would be some months' imprisonment in a fortress, where I should at least be spared pianoforte-strumming above and below me — in working at my edition of Beethoven and have finished op. 106, at the cost of great exertion. This work of mine will, it seems to me, be really worth something. Do you know that, although it only deals with a part of Beethoven's unaccompanied pianoforte music, the volume I am now publishing contains from four hundred to four hundred and fifty engraved pages? Will you allow me to dedicate this work publicly to you (with a carefully considered preface)? It will not be an entirely unworthy contribution to your " *deutsche Vortragsstil.*"

I saw Richter yesterday morning. When he called the day before, I was too exhausted to have him admitted. As I had to write to Düfflipp in the afternoon, I put it *seriously* to him that he *must* warn Perfall to obey your orders with regard to *Rheingold* promptly, precisely, and good-naturedly, not to put up any opposition as in the case of the *Meistersinger*, and to suppress the ridiculous variants by which he attempts to affirm his non-nullity. I have Düfflipp's[1] oral consent to take over the management.

---

[1] LORENZ VON DUFFLIPP, *one of the more "possible" members of Pfordten's Cabinet (as far as Cosima and Wagner were concerned).*

Flaxland very kindly telegraphed the enormous success at the Lyrique yesterday. (Have notified Dürflipp on account of Parsifal.) I lay great importance to this striking success. The enclosed copy of *Figaro* contains a Jewish manœuvre — and no isolated one — to put a fresh spoke in your wheel. Your pamphlet has had an even more striking effect than one expected. Even here, where the " chosen " are numerically few, I have been made to suffer horribly by it. Still, I feel it an honour if not a pleasure. The Lachner affair does hang together with the pamphlet, as you rightly supposed. In spite of all the ignoble exploitations of my *noblesse*, I cannot consider the step I took as a *faux pas*. Indirectly it cleared the air just as the pamphlet did, although for the moment the atmosphere is heavy with *eau de mille chiens:* the effect of the spring sun on the town gutters.

What I demanded categorically from Perfall and finally from Dürflipp, as Perfall is a cowardly good-for-nothing swine (I will go into it more at a calmer moment), was a rescript from on high which should impress upon the members of the court theatre and orchestra their duties towards me as their chief. Only a few of them are delinquents, but these few are the more fanatical. The intrigues of a Strauss (horn), a Vogl, a Bausewein, a Kindermann, or a Stehle are becoming such a common danger objectively and professionally that I can no longer maintain my subjective, personal indifference to them if my exhausting activity is to have any meaning. P. shifts the blame on to me whenever I am the object of a dastardly attack; which is natural, as he has to put on record his independence *vis-à-vis* a member of the coterie which made him intendant. If I make a serious complaint he threatens me with his successor. For six months now he has been telling me that he has taken the preliminary steps towards his resignation. As if the *Mère*-fall and the little *Père*- and *Mère*-falls objected to the extra two thousand florins of salary! The latest, by the way, is that he is becoming sultanesque. . . . Who in the world would be Perfall's successor? Is Schmidt to rise again from the dead? No. After all, it was Merinos who rescued us from the worst of their intrigues. It is generally said, by the way, that the hitch in my case is the matter of Lachner's pension, which has again been refused him. This leads them to think there is no solid basis and they play at weathercocks so as to be safe *en tout cas.* Merinos has not of course given up Wüllner or his leaning to opera. Meanwhile he is having Rheinberger's *Seven Ravens* [1] rehearsed by way of preparation for *Tristan* (Vogl has the principal part in both), has granted Stehle and Mallinger leave at the same time, and has sent for a beginner from Linz, Fräulein Kaufmann, who is to appear in the *Huguenots* and *Trovatore.* (You may be sure I shall not conduct these for him.) All this harmonizes quite well with Richter's mission to obtain new opera-recruits at a time when the Church closes the theatres.

The whole story must seem to you almost an accusation against myself, considering that I described Perfall as possible and recommended him to you. But who else was there, when you come to think of it? Only a foreigner; and the most acceptable one, Puttlitz, was turned down in high places.

What about Moy? You know him. Could we try him, if only as a " new " interim-broom?

Karlsruhe: the charge against Levi is unfounded. The article in question has been inserted in all the papers through the medium of a Jewish " autographic correspondence " in Frankfurt. Levi looks worse than he is and has always been a Wagnerianer, as I learn from his friend Dräseke (they were conservatorists together at Leipzig). Besides he owes those ovations, most unusual tributes to his conducting, to his revival of the work. As things are, that is, considering the progress that has been made in Judaizing the German people (without intermarriage), I venture to think that the Jews who are in agreement with your pamphlet will be equal in number to the non-Jews of the same opinion. I am seeing the dark side: I no longer believe in the possibility of our being saved from general degradation — i.e., Judaization — the disease has spread too far. And since the positive forces in State and society — nobility, Army, clergy — are no longer very powerful, regeneration can only come through the masses. But they would need a bell-wether, and, there again, none but a Jew would be able to qualify for the mission. So we should have to wait for the coming of the opposite of a Messiah — namely, one who would fasten his people to the cross.

Excuse my sub-Devrient style, I am really only writing to you

[1] *Rheinberger's opera* The Seven Ravens *was produced in Munich in 1869.*

for my own distraction, and the harm it does you to read this is less than the good it does me to write it.

I fully endorse the choice of singers for *Rheingold*. Even if I did not, I should raise no opposition. I too should have suggested Stehle for Fricka, and Schlosser for Loge. Bausewein-Biedermayer as Fafner is the only thing that I am afraid of, as it means Kindermann's singing Fasolt. If only the voices could be changed over, an exchange of roles would be better. Old Frau Diez will not be able to let them swing her as Rhine-" mother " in the first scene. By the way, she does not sing six-eight and nine-eight time with the necessary rhythmic precision. Yes, yes, Master, there are triple and there are quadruple musicians and singers; Schlosser, for instance, belongs to the first, Kindermann to the last.

I have just had a visit from Kahnt, the music-dealer at Leipzig, who was present at the first performance of Liszt's *St. Elisabeth* in Vienna. A stupendous triumph for the composer, whose work is to be repeated next Sunday. I am glad — also on Ludwig II's account. As Schott has been decorated, Mr. Kahnt now desires to be similarly honoured as the publisher of *St. Elisabeth*, and to work it through me. But I soon got rid of him, which was not difficult.

Julius Lang always reminds me of La Pommerais of blessed memory, whose head you ought really to have had glued on again. Couldn't you ask for a couple of photographs from Paris (one for me)?

Cornelius, who had gone to Paris with his brother, asked for an extension of leave (and obtained it). Lucky beggar, he always comes off better than I. I hope he will write you an entertaining letter about *Rienzi*.

The Jews' telegram to Nachbaur (of Breslau) I have had put into the *Signale*. We must nurse the effect of the pamphlet carefully. And, generally speaking, we need a chronicle; that is why Pohl's engagement here is very desirable. Perfall should install him as secretary in his office; Pohl, however, would be *sworn in* by you.

This evening you will see my children. I could not bring them to the station, unfortunately, and the weather was vile too. It was hard to leave them; rarely as I see them, I have grown tremendously fond of them because they so steadily retain their native kindness of heart. Their mother will, I believe, have her pleasure in them and I rejoice for her sake that she should. My mamma is leaving me too, a few days hence, to go to Wiesbaden. Then I shall be quite solitary — that is, without friends. Without enemies would be my preference. Well, I shall try to work in spite of the noisy streets, to which I am growing increasingly sensitive, and the evening concert season about to commence at the English café opposite.

I propose to give notice to leave Barerstrasse at Michaelmas, if Cosima agrees, and for the present to move into your rooms.

My Regensburg concert tour for Peter's pence (the restauration fund for the Theatre of Marcellus) is not yet fixed, as Liszt is having himself fêted at Pest, and the rendezvous he was to have given me at Regensburg will probably fall through. I have now definitely realized that Liszt, if his life is to be prolonged, feels a pressing need of dazzling successes to compensate for the monstrous things without number that he has had to endure. Sorry as I am not to see him before he returns to Rome — he is naturally somewhat embarrassed with me too — I submit with a good grace as to all the doings of Providence.

His Majesty has deigned to promote von Hersch, the banker, to the rank of hereditary baron. Also traceable to the pamphlet perhaps? It would be just like Lipovsky, of whom I could tell many a clever and generous tale.

Some days ago I had another " iñvaluable " experience with a sixteen-year-old pianoforte-Bochert (Bochert in German means: a young Israelite in his callow years). Why, why must you be so right in everything, and wrong only when for once you do not look on the black side?

294]

Munich
July 3, 1869

You must have taken my letter, dear Master, for a feverish eccentricity of the moment. It was not that, however. I had kept it by me two days, and posted it at last because my conception of things and my condition had undergone no change whatever. It is not merely the *Tristan* rehearsals with Herr and Frau Vogl (who, I must in honesty say, are so keen as to be marvellous) and the terrible memories bound up with them that give my nerves the final touch, but also my vexations and disappointments; and the dirty tricks that have been played on me have reached such a climax that my joy in life and in work is turned to gall, in fact destroyed. I have had enough — enough of myself and enough of living in Munich, or indeed in Germany at all. The conditions are against my doing useful work for " art " either here or anywhere else. It is better therefore that I should be replaced here by a younger man, and this naturally brings me to Klindworth in connexion with the approaching performance of *Rheingold* on August 25. I enclose the letter I had from him recently. It is impossible for me to answer him. I can no longer make pretences or gloss over certain things. My head swims, and every day there are times when I feel I am on the way to madness.

My mother was so anxious about me last month that she obtained a certificate from Dr. Rubner to the effect that I was in danger of serious illness unless I had some leave, but I could not bring myself to make use of it as long as I could keep going to the school or the theatre.

I am still keeping it up: mornings at nine, conference (to fit in rehearsals and so on); at ten, orchestral rehearsal of *Tristan* (it will be impossible to do really fine work with it); three to six at the school; six to eight — or nine, for the Vogls are indefatigable — pianoforte rehearsal of *Tristan*. Some transpositions in the second act and cuts in the third — made with the utmost piety, as you will believe — have cost me much thought, but will come out all right. With *Tristan* my conducting comes to a close. There will be a fatalistic rightness about it. Richter may take over *Rheingold*. There are still the examinations in the end of July; then I am released from that post also. As for the rest, I must take what comes.

I am sending a letter I had today from Düfflipp, together with a copy of Lipovsky's letter to him about *Tristan*. I begin to think that certain earlier rumours were not quite groundless. To order a performance of *Oberon* in its original form, with the prose of the first text complete without any omissions, really smacks of Charenton!

I am most grateful to you for suggesting that we should have a talk together. Writing is frightfully difficult for me and there is so much that cannot be expressed in a letter. We shall in any case be compelled to meet before long to discuss certain situations the probable outcome of which I begin dimly to foresee. It will be all the same to you, I expect, if we put it off until after *Tristan*.

Frau Richter has caused me a good deal of trouble by her passionate self-assertion and pretensions. She is perpetually demanding special treatment for her pupils at the school, just as if they were her private ones. Dispensation from the obligatory tuition in pianoforte and theory is one such privilege, and, for another, she takes them at her house in the afternoons after their mornings at the institute, for which (naturally) they pay her, at the rate of twenty-five florins a month. We are therefore snowed under with requests for exhibitions from women who already have scholarships. Concurrently with their first voice-production studies these young ladies practise the parts of Isolde, Brangäne, Brunhilde, and Sieglinde. Their teacher assures me that they will do brilliantly in the examinations, and when I protest against her accepting so many pupils who seem to be without talent because they take away from the others, she replies that the excellence of her method of producing results out of nothing will thus be displayed at its best. So there you are. But what with one pulling this way, the other that, and quarrels and scandals without end, I see no prospect of being able to smooth things out or organize anything and I realize that I am not equal to running this institution. Among the instrumental classes one has to do so much policing on account of childish pranks, yet it is quite without effect, as the council and intendant have so often shown favour instead of inflicting punishment that the statutes are no longer respected. It may be that my colleagues will see wisdom in the next school-year, but so far as I am concerned it is too late. I am dead tired, dried up, speechless with disgust. " Only one thing do I still desire — the end." I hope to see you soon. How would Lindau do for our meeting-place?

295]

Munich
June 12, 1869

My silence with regard to your intentions about *Tristan* might easily lead to a misunderstanding, dear Master, to prevent which I am now going to explain to you briefly my personal opinion. I have had a most trying time and some really bitter moments with the Vogls. But all the same, after these last rehearsals (with orchestra) — although we shall of course need many more — I can defend the official performance of the work from a musical standpoint. I cannot see in this any profanation of it, but, on the contrary, a significant act, a proof of what goodwill and enthusiasm, goaded on by categorical orders from All-Highest quarters, can do. I could not therefore conscientiously send in my resignation on the ground you suggest — namely, that I was obliged to lay down my baton on account of the clash between a sense of duty and a sense of honour. Forgive me for opposing you. I cannot admit that my doing so implies a lack of piety towards your work.

PS. Fischer was surprisingly excellent as Kurwenal (we might give him Alberich, particularly as there is no one else anywhere). Bausewein is certainly more correct musically and less lackeyish than Zottmayr.

296]

Munich
June 21, 1869

The fifth public performance (newly rehearsed) of *Tristan and Isolde*, dear Master, really came off yesterday, Sunday, June 20, 1869. The house was sold out, but again season-ticket-holders were admitted, apparently by all-highest orders. In the first and second galleries and in part of the stalls a continuous thinning was evident, but in the crowded pit (at one florin) they stood it out to a man from five-thirty to eleven-twenty. Herr and

Frau Vogl achieved wonders from the musical side. The big dialogue in the second act was in fact far more effective as regards tone and words than four years ago, when the blissful Ludwig damped his voice to please the noble Malwina. The orchestra was quite attentive and discreet except in minor details. I for my part conducted far better and with more composure than before. This was due to my practice with the baton in between. On the dramatic side I have nothing particularly bad to relate, simply because my eye and ear were too incessantly concentrated on a precise rendering of the music. Frau Vogl displayed definite talent in the first act, although the catastrophe at the close was a complete failure (the dumb-play over the mistaken potions seemed to me absurd), but both parties had declared that they needed at least another fortnight to perfect themselves in acting and this they could not have. Herr Vogl sang the first part of Act III (the larger half) excellently and Bausewein and Fischer were infinitely better than their predecessors. (English horn and trumpet on the stage more accurate too.) Brangäne was far worse, dragged perpetually. Frau Possart (formerly Fräulein Deinet) has in fact only a minimum of voice left. I had to leave her the part because no other singer would have been able to work up the part in time. (Even Frau Diez would not have been capable of it.)

These notes are given by way of excuse after the event for my refusal to do as you wished and lay down my baton before the *Tristan* performance. I am going to do it now. My resignation had been handed in, but some months ago I had solemnly bound myself to do all that lay in my power to fulfil the King's wish. This I had to put first as my duty, and I was able to do so without failing in piety towards your work. There was no bungling, no profanation, I can assure you. The performance of *Tristan* yesterday was a better performance than any that any of your operas has ever had at any theatre. I would hardly except even the Dresden and Weimar ones of *Tannhäuser* and the Vienna *Lohengrin*.

Yesterday's event is therefore, and remains, one of great importance in the chronicles of music. It was a fresh and irrefutable confirmation of the performable quality of *Tristan* even under difficult conditions. His Majesty is alone to blame for our not being able to devote more time to it and achieve a more finished production. His two ukases were as follows:

1. On August 25, *Rheingold*, because, owing to the necessary reconstruction of stage and orchestra, that is the final date fixed for the closing of the court theatre.

2. Your works to be produced in chronological order.

Tannhäuser, Lohengrin, Tristan, Meistersinger will be given private performances; the public outcry against these ought to be suppressed instead of merely ignored.

Richter is conducting the *Meistersinger* on the 27th, with Betz and Mallinger. He put it aside for the whole of last week to make way for the *Tristan* orchestral rehearsals with pianoforte. I should still have the strength left to conduct it for the tenth time, but, for one thing, I owe it to Richter and his magnificent achievements to give him this pleasant satisfaction, and, for another, there is more point in my closing my career with *Tristan*, for so I come full circle.

Tomorrow (Tuesday) at ten there is a private full-dress performance for the King and an invited audience in the stalls. The two Vogls are neither hoarse nor exhausted nor ruined and have just consented to sing.

Most of our friends I neither would nor could see, having stayed in bed yesterday morning and today; but Alexander Seroff,[1] the Russian Wagner, was here; also the faithful Kurwenalistic Kalliwoda and the singer Hauser, who has now become an enthusiast. Kalliwoda is sure to write and tell you his impressions; he was present, as you know, at the first (real) performance here. The poor fellow has fallen a victim to " Uncle " Devrient's hatred of you, and the young Jew Levi has taken his place. He thinks of emigrating to America. I found his enthusiasm very delightful and also that of young Servais, who lives with me and has been studying the great work day and night, learning German properly at the same time so that he might understand the words better. You see I do not revel in unpleasant impressions only, but register the pleasing moments too.

I have managed therefore to keep my word to the King without militating against your work, or, at least, that is how I see it.

As I shall be kept here next month by the music school and

[1] ALEXANDER SEROFF (1820–71), *Russian composer, Wagner enthusiast.*

also do not feel well enough to come and see you (as I once suggested) ; as in addition a meeting with me would be painful and
embarrassing for you while I, in my present frame of mind,
should inevitably be dangerously upset by it; and as, finally,
Cosima has received a complete explanation in a lengthy letter,
it seems to me that a meeting between us two is superfluous. It
is better that I should bid you a last good-bye in writing when I
definitely leave Munich.

Meantime accept my sincere and whole-hearted wishes that
you may enjoy good health and creative strength.

PS. I have unfortunately mislaid Klindworth's letter, but
will send it another time. He is very unhappy in Moscow because he cannot realize his ambition of paying off his debts and
being able to get away soon. In the summer he will try to come
to Munich and Lucerne.

Hans von Bülow
to
Cosima

.

297] [1]

Munich
June 17, 1869

I AM grateful to you, dear Cosima, for having taken the initiative and shall give you no reason to regret it. I am indeed too unhappy myself — through my own fault — not to wish to avoid wounding you by any unjust reproach whatsoever. As regards this most painful separation, which you have felt to be necessary, I recognize all the wrongs on my side and shall continue to lay stress on them in the inevitable discussion on the matter with my mother and your father. I have made you a poor, a sorry return for all the great kindness you have lavished upon me in our past life. Your own existence was poisoned by me and I can only thank Providence for having offered you some compensation, however inadequate, at almost the last moment, when courage to go on shouldering your burden must have been failing you. But, alas, since you left me, I have lost my sole support in life and in my struggle. It was your mind, your heart, your patience, indulgence, sympathy, encouragement, and advice — last and most especially, your presence, your face, and your speech — which, taken all together, constituted that support. The loss of this supreme good, whose full value I recognize only after its loss, has brought about moral and artistic collapse — I am a bankrupt. Do not think that this pitiful cry implies any irony or bitterness towards you. My suffering is so great that I may permit myself to express it since I abstain from accusing anyone of being the author of it but myself.

You have preferred to devote your life and the treasures of your mind and affection to one who is my superior, and, far from blaming you, I *approve* your action from every point of view and admit you are perfectly right. I swear that the only consoling thought that has from time to time lightened the darkness of my mind and mitigated my external sufferings has been this: at all events Cosima is happy over there.

It has seemed to me necessary to preface my personal

---

[1] *All the letters in this section are written in French.* — TR.

explanations by this introductory statement, to which I attach importance as an authentication, or rather a profession, of absolute good faith.

Now I must ask your indulgence (for the last time) if the statement which follows is not perfectly lucid or correctly expressed. Pardon me if I am driven to boast, as I used to do, of my busy life (" He *has* a lot to do, that sacristan," Loulou once said to you in church).

Today and tomorrow I have orchestral rehearsals of *Tristan* from nine till two, School of Music from three to six; then correspondence, visits, and so on; and my physical weakness is such that every two or three days I am obliged to stay in bed a whole day doing nothing. It is true that I sent in my resignation a week ago. The reason I alleged was my shaken health. Everyone understands that; Rubner — I can give him further proof — gave me a certificate two months ago. Intrigue, calumny, obstruction, ill will — in fine, anxiety and " *dispiaceri* " have merely accumulated month by month. Since in your absence (I need not expatiate on my mother as a substitute) I had no compensation at all, my moral and physical force, my desire to continue a game not worth the candle (which had burned very low), diminished in inverse proportion. The few things which I have perhaps to enter on the credit side provide no serious counterweight and give me no encouragement to go on. My work for the King of Bavaria only brings in four thousand florins a year (I have never expected an increase of salary), which does not cover my expenses. I am firmly convinced that in carrying on my work and filling my place here I shall not in any way serve the good cause, the cause of art, and that, largely for that reason, my personal ruin would be complete within a year or perhaps two. Moreover my position is fundamentally false. I have come to look upon myself as a king's favourite, and the belief that I gained that favour by marital complaisance is pretty wide-spread. Klindworth, in spite of his lack of reputation and even supposing that he had only half of my ability, intelligence, and talent (which is not the case, for I consider him to be almost my equal), would have a much better chance of doing well, of making himself useful, than the present *démissionaire*. Moreover my intensive work on *Tristan,* that gigantic but devastating production, has literally finished me. The public performance is to take place on Sunday. I accept the responsibility; it will not be a profanation — I wrote to Wagner to that effect the other day — but it will be my last appearance at the head of the orchestra. My stay in Munich will end where it began. This constitutes a kind of rounding off (a fateful rather than a vicious circle), and will make it easier for me later to look back on the series of events and of my sufferings (the punishment of my faults towards you), which fall between the four years' interval between the two representations of this same work, as a nightmare.

Yes, without any reproach to its mighty creator, *Tristan* has given me the *coup de grâce*. I have not such strong nerves as you, who have been able to endure for long years distracting intimacy with a being as ill-born or as ill-bred as I and have survived that penance. Poor Eberle, Richter's pet *répétiteur*, was driven mad during the rehearsals by the opera itself (we tell the public it was excess of beer); as for me, who confess always to have lacked the necessary courage in my very numerous arrangements for taking my life, I assure you I could not have resisted the temptation if anyone had offered me a few drops of prussic acid.

The temptation did not present itself, and, cursing the while, I could not but recognize the terrible fund of vitality (*will to live*) in my nature. But how to satisfy it, except by leaving this city, which in your absence has become a *hell* for me, and by making a fresh start, I don't know where, but at all events *somewhere else?*

This separation from you — you had no other alternative; remember my introductory sentences — must be made definite. I must be separated, even in *thought* as far as is humanly possible, from all that relates to you or R. W., the two inspirations of my life hitherto (I might perhaps add your father). Don't misunderstand me; I do not suggest to you the fuss and the annoyances of a divorce. If your father thinks it better, if he prefers that your association with the life of R. W. should have this official confirmation, then I have no objection to make on my side. But since, as you know, I have no desire, inclination, or velleity to regain my freedom, I have no reason at all for proposing a divorce to obtain it. Further, I leave you our children and the responsibility of their education, as much because I believe you will give them the best they could obtain, as because I have no other to offer them, and also because I am in entire agreement with you as to the impossibility of confiding them either to my aged mother or to any other member of my family (if I can speak of a family). And if your kind heart consents to bring up our children in spite of all this *anti*pathy and the just *ran*cour which you bear their father, I see no reason why I should not leave you my name.

I should consider it petty and unworthy of the situation if I allowed myself to express a susceptibility which might be wrongly interpreted with regard to the proposals, the sacrifices, which you make to me. Permit me to reply firmly, simply, and briefly:

The allowance from your father, as well as that made you by your mother, belongs to the children. As you take charge of their education, your six thousand francs should, in justice and reason, be used for the expenses of their education. The present and future partner in your life will be willing to arrange for the investment of any savings you may happen to be able to make in this sum. As for your own fortune which you brought to our disastrous marriage, was it not the first stumbling-block, the first trouble for me, ashamed as I was of my poverty, a sentiment arising from my sense of duty and from love itself? I cannot decline the responsibility of constituting myself the financial guardian of the children with the help of your money. All that I can (for the moment) provide for them is the little legacy from Aunt Frege (five thousand crowns, invested in the firm of Frege), which, with luck, might be doubled by the time they come of age.

I beg you also to realize that I cannot but consider as your purely *personal* property the whole of our furniture. When I leave here, and that will be, I hope, on August 1, I shall take only what is indisputably mine — such as my clothes, books, and music — leaving the rest in the apartment, our tenancy of which expires on October 1. Your orders will be carried out by Maszek, either to sell or to send part to Triebschen, or to keep, and insure at the depository, such furniture as we jointly consider as belonging to the children.

On leaving Munich, or if possible Germany, my plans for the future are in no way fixed (in any case I shall not take the liberty of wearying you with them), and I attach only very secondary importance to them. The essential, the urgent matter is to get away. I am extremely anxious to take with me as little as possible of anything which might recall the past, the old life, because it is only by breaking definitely and radically with it that I can face the prospect of a new existence. There is one thing, one alone, of which I neither am able nor desire to rid myself; that is the profoundly grateful remembrance of all that you have done for my development as an artist. I shall always be [grateful] for the benefits you have lavished on me in this particular.

Permit me to set your mind at rest to some extent (so far as seems necessary) on the manner of my departure from Munich. I shall remain at the music school until the end of the scholastic year and shall inflict on myself the boredom and labour of the examinations, if my legs and my head do not refuse their part too obstinately. The opera is closed throughout July. At the beginning of August (or perhaps earlier) Richter will undertake the preliminary work for the *Rheingold*. I have also made over to him the coming representation of the *Meistersinger* on the 27th. As soon as the school closes, in August, I am going away *on leave*. Düfflipp, on behalf of the King, has asked me to think the matter over and reconsider my resignation if possible, offering me indefinite leave of absence until my health is restored. Since my health cannot be restored in the space of two months (I shall perhaps need a year), I shall give in my definite resignation on October 1, while accepting for the moment the leave which His Majesty is good enough to grant me. In this way I shall depart as quietly as possible without shouting on the house-tops. Do not insult me (R. W. will not hesitate, I fear) by thinking that I am playing a part, and that the attraction of an assured position and emoluments will induce me to change my mind and to return to the most complete travesty possible of a *Heimath*. In spite of *addresses from the pupils* of the school, polite letters from Wüllner, and some touching *proofs* of attachment on the part of certain *members of the orchestra,* I feel I have *not the strength* to begin over again here. I shall prefer a thousand times the position of teacher of the pianoforte in a small town. With a Perfall as one's chief, etc., one can only do routine work, in which one's faculties are ruined one by one. I will not enumerate all I have lost during this past year. And not a soul to sympathize! But do not fear, I have done complaining.

Do you recall the fact that I was perfectly aware of what would happen after you had left me? Do you remember that I made up my mind not to return to Munich except in your company? I vow that I do not say this by way of retrospective reproach. It was impossible for you to remain here. I understand that, I understand only too well. Therefore I only wish, in recapitulating these things, to diminish in your eyes the apparent suddenness of my resolution, which has been sorrowfully maturing day by day since your departure. The task was beyond my strength, which, morally and physically, has been steadily sapped for some time now. I have plunged into activity in order to forget; but that was impossible, especially when any illusions on the usefulness of that activity (which would have produced outward satisfaction and would thereby have induced inward peace) vanished one after the other. I am going away, then, early in August. I have asked Bechstein to return my two thousand reichstalers, on which I shall live peaceably and without anxiety for a year; if I have then recovered my health and my self-possession, I shall find a means of discovering some sort of an existence untrammelled by dependence on anything or anyone. (Nevertheless I shall certainly not forget that any new position will derive from the position which W. secured for me in Munich, but this feeling of dependence is one which I feel able in a sense to accept.)

This is a badly written letter, far from worthy of being read by the author of the one to which it professes to be a reply. It is not really a reply. It is a kind of testament from a brain and a heart that are sick, half deranged. Yet it contains nothing mad or unreasonable and I beg you to accept it as a " product of desperation." I beg also that you will associate yourself for the last time with the sentiments by which I am animated and the unchangeable resolves inspired by those sentiments, and will, by your approval and acceptance, help me to carry them out.

May God protect and bless the mother of the fortunate children to whom she continues to devote herself.

298]

Rome
October 22, 1871

Today, Madame, is the birthday of your father, my good and great Master; he has now completed his sixtieth year. Owing to the improvement, as rapid as it is unexpected, in my physical and moral health during the last three months, I was able to call and pay my respects to him after a long period of absolute separation. In the sweet, powerful emotion which filled my heart at this meeting, which it was not in my power to arrange earlier, my thoughts naturally turned towards the daughter of my benefactor and friend, formerly the very unhappy companion of a lesser man, now (I hope and have long prayed Heaven) the happy and worthy life-consort of the greatest poet and artist of our century. Thanks to the recovery of my mental and moral strength, thanks to today's great occasion, I can at last fulfil a no less imperative duty, Madame, in expressing to you my respectful and admiring gratitude for the supreme pains you are taking with my daughters' education. I have often had news of them, especially from my mother, and all that I have heard has deeply touched me; indeed my heart is full of gratitude. Since I am not able to share this responsibility, I can at least from now onwards assume the paternal obligation of providing as far as I can for their material future. It is solely for this, Madame, that I am returning on New Year's Day to my profession of virtuoso (revised and corrected). Beginning with a tour in Germany, Switzerland, and Holland, lasting until the spring, I am then (towards the end of April) going to London for the season. This is the indispensable condition for my journey to America, which is arranged for September 1. I have placed the months of July and August at the service of His Majesty the King of Bavaria, having learned that he desired another production of *Tristan* at Munich. (I keep this work jealously in my own hands.) I shall remain in America as long as is necessary to attain the minimum of the sum destined for my daughters during my lifetime: a hundred thousand francs, of which there exists at the

moment only one fifth, the legacy of my Aunt Frege. Needless
to say, if the necessity arises, you have full power to dispose of
this twenty thousand francs (5,600 talers) to provide for the
education of my daughters, and I await your instructions in this
matter.

Much as I have been touched by the graceful proofs of attachment from Daniela and Blandine, which have reached me in
the course of the last two years, proofs of which you must have
been cognizant, Madame, it has been impossible for various
reasons for me to return them. The principal motive for my
silence will be easily divined by you. Though I in no way
doubted, Madame, that the superiority of your mind and heart
would have led you to find the most suitable solution from all
points of view of the problem of explaining to the children the
separation of their parents, I did not know, and do not now
know, what should be the point of departure, the new basis for
renewing relations with my children. Since I desire, and must
avoid, the danger of the slightest contradiction or the appearance of it between the words of the mother and the father, I shall
be grateful, Madame, if you will send me the indispensable
information. Will you also do me the favour of adding to my
daughters' curriculum the study of the Italian language? This
will be henceforward the language of their father, whose further
existence is indissolubly attached to his new country. If I
had lived in Italy before knowing you, you would have been
much less unhappy with and through me, Madame. May
Heaven richly compensate you for your sad past by a cloudless
present.

299]

Florence
November 3, 1871

I HAVE just received your letter, Madame, the reply to the lines
I wrote from Rome, and I beg you to accept my deep gratitude
for all the news you were kind enough to give me. I feel I must
express without delay my entire satisfaction with what you tell
me so that you may no longer feel any uncertainty on the serious

question which you submit to me. Moreover it seems to me that the best solution of certain serious questions is not necessarily reached with the help of time, reflection, and discussion, but on the contrary they must be decided in the most energetic, the promptest way possible. Though I am personally opposed and even antipathetic to your proposal that my daughters should change their religion, Madame, I cannot but approve your motives. I should and will silence my individual sentiments, which I admit to be morbid: my hatred for everything German, my consequent hatred of Protestantism, the Germanic religion *par excellence*. But, in spite of the intensity and profundity of that hatred, I ought not to wish my children to inherit it, the less so as, in accordance with my principles, the daughters should follow the mother's religion, from which it follows that they should now, like their mother, undergo conversion. In this way a more or less evident dissonance will be removed from their future. Yes, Madame, you are right. Your decision has been determined by the wisest maternal affection. I realize too that Catholicism outside the Latin countries is at this moment much more wildly ultramontane than it is with us here, thanks to the recent extravagances of the most obstinate of all the heads of the Church of Rome.[1]

If my desire to see my daughters study the language of my adopted country seems to you inopportune at the moment — the study of English might be difficult at the same time as Italian, and it would be better to finish what has been begun — I shall of course agree to having it deferred. As I have found an excellent French-Italian grammar, a model of logic, I shall take the opportunity of sending you a copy so that you may be in a position to judge of the opportuneness of my desire. I thank you for the notice you have taken of it.

The Abbé Liszt has not yet left Rome, as you thought, Madame. He will not leave until the 10th of this month. After one day in Florence he will proceed without further delay to Pest, his permanent place of residence, where he should arrive on the 15th at the latest.

I am profoundly touched, Madame, by your gracious solicitude with regard to my forthcoming two years' tour as a virtuoso.

[1] Pius IX.

But " it must be so "; since I took the irrevocable resolve my heart has been lighter, my conscience clearer.

Moreover, to my duties as a father is joined another, that of the interpretative artist. It should be of some use to the musical world for me to show what Italy has taught me. You face far more annoyances and fatigues, Madame, than I shall do if my health permits; it is in fact the American tour that is the least terrifying; it will be much more convenient than the indispensable preludes in Germany and elsewhere. My aim once attained, I should naturally return to some corner in Italy, the only country where I can breathe and perhaps still serve my art. In one of her letters my mother said that you were thinking of sending Daniela to a boarding-school in Mannheim (I think); I shall be grateful if you will inform me of your plans from time to time, so that I may stop at that town to see her during my tour, which is despotically conducted by my agent. Thank you, and again thank you, Madame. May Heaven bless you in all things and crown your efforts with success.

300]

Florence,
Borgo San Frediano 10
November 28, 1871

I VENTURE to hope, Madame, that the delay, far longer than I wished, in my reply to your last letter will not have led you to feel anxiety about my opinions on the subject of our common interests. I am more than ever anxious to maintain complete agreement in everything concerning the education of our children, the more so that my so-called "relatives" in Leipzig and Berlin have for some time been beginning to meddle in matters which are no concern at all of theirs, and have apparently hoped to use my mother and sister as intermediaries. There is no reason to stress the details in German fashion. So long as I can avoid a brusque offensive, I shall content myself with turning a deaf ear. You understand me, Madame; that is why I think you will approve my request for a certain *reserve* to be introduced into Daniela's correspondence with " Berlin," a reserve which should not by any means exclude the continuation of the pleasant show of affection maintained there up to now.

On his way through Florence about the 13th of this month, your father read your letters, which I thought it right to show him, and expressed a satisfaction as keen as my own.

I am very glad of this, Madame, and I congratulate you sincerely as well as my great and dear Master, that his relations with his only surviving child should be renewed and may, indeed, take their natural course without fear of fresh interruption. He *needs* to have news of you *often*.

" The Abbé " Liszt approves your plans on a certain matter about which I have already replied to you, not perhaps without some regret, but indeed he grasps the force and exactitude of your reasoning.

I thank you with all my heart for all the details which you give me of the children's development. You do not, however, speak of Isolde. Otherwise nothing in these details surprised me. My philosophy, let us say my dogmas — of original sin, the immutability of character (for the developed intelligence can only soften, reduce, the excrescences of primitive organic traits), and so on — have received fresh confirmation from what you say. Blandine will perhaps one day, thanks to your care, be more worthy of her godmother's name; let us hope so. The Italian grammar that you were kind enough to ask me for has been sent to you by my bookseller. Did you receive it?

Many thanks for the other request to make a collection of my publications, programs, and the like for Daniela. I shall always bear it in mind and it will be a great joy to me to send you what there is as it comes along.

You will shortly read at Triebschen a long, perhaps rather a strange, article giving an account of my impressions a week ago at Bologna of a performance of *Lohengrin* in Italian. (I believe you get the Leipzig *Signale*.) The execution of this task was all the easier because I consider it useful from various points of view. My position in the artistic world should rest permanently on its former basis, and, as I " enjoy " a very tiresome celebrity everywhere, the fact that my profession of faith remains intact must not be ignored. Moreover, I must be able, if need arises, to come forward publicly as the champion of my daughters' mother.

I shall never be able to swallow in silence the smallest aspersion on the name of a woman who has borne my name, and whose superiority of mind and greatness of soul, inexplicable and incomprehensible to the vulgar, no one should be permitted to deny. Ah, Madame, I have endured torments of the most subtle atrocity, but in the most infernal hours of my life I have always drawn a certain consolation from my conviction that your high mission in connexion with this king among men and greatest genius of his century was inevitable and providentially ordained, and that you could not have fulfilled that mission without the driving force of a personal, earthly passion. Perhaps all the wrongs which I recognize in my conduct towards you, conduct which provoked and facilitated this passion, were in the nature of a " providential mission," indirectly serving the same aim as your own.

Let us not yet speak of the children's future when they come of age. The end sanctifies the means; what matters for me *at the moment* is to make use of the renewal of my talent, to use it so as to assure their existence for the future as far as I can. I do not know whether it will be permitted to me to return after some years of travel (in the capacity of a soloist exploiting the capital of his reputation) to the country which has healed my soul. And in this connexion, Madame, I have a request in my turn. Be so kind as *to interpolate in the children's evening prayers a name*, a name of your choice — take that of a saint, one of the purest — you will tell me what that choice is at your convenience. This name will serve to designate the person who, unconsciously, has brought about my rebirth as a man, a father, an artist, has restored to me, with peace of mind, the fine fever of life, of struggle, has in fact given me back possession of myself — an edition revised and corrected. May this quasi-confidence destroy any remains of bitterness and " posthumous " regret in your heart, Madame; the great and manifold duties which are continuously imposed on you should not suffer from it — that is to say, cause suffering to her who fulfils them so religiously. Bless the angel who unconsciously sent me to " Rome."

301]

Florence
December 21, 1871

IT is, alas, Madame, almost impossible to requite you for your last letter by replying to it as minutely as it deserves and as I should myself desire.

I have had no news from Berlin for a month; it seems to me they are annoyed with me for my reply on a certain point, which, though discreetly and gently expressed, they must have understood. As I think they will leave me in peace for the moment, I am putting off the rather extreme solution which you advise with much justice, until it becomes almost inevitable.

I venture to enclose two hundred-franc Italian notes (which, I imagine, can be changed without much loss) with the request that you will buy with them some small presents for my daughters in my name in any way you may decide.

I have unfortunately not the time to think over, to choose, suitable things and to dispatch them, the latter business being also very tiresome on account of the existing postal régime.

I repeat, Madame, that I agree with all you say about the children. I understand, respect, and admire all the noble sentiments inspired by your maternal and womanly affection. Please count, therefore, on my aid and support in any occasion where they are required. I leave Florence on January 1 and am going straight to Vienna. I hope that my German tour, which will end about the middle of April, will complete the sum intended for Daniela: ten thousand talers. The interest on this small capital will be spent on Blandine, for whom the money derived from my journey to America (I leave on September 1, 1872) will be drawn upon to the same extent. As for Soldi, the ten thousand talers which my mother will one day leave me will fall to her. All this is not a great sum, I know, but it is almost assured, if God gives me health and strength for but a year and a half.

Allow me to speak once more of myself, for it is necessary for you to be informed of my plans.

After the tour in Germany, Holland, and Switzerland I

return, if only for a week, to Florence to absorb there fresh
moral strength.

Probably I shall have to do " the season" in London in *May*
and *June* (the prelude to the American fugue); *July* and *August*
are at the disposition of H.M. the King of Bavaria. I have not yet
had a definite reply as to whether the offer for that period suits
him. (On January 22 I shall go to Berlin for a few days, and I
expect to be travelling without intermission; if there is any news
for me, care of Bechstein would find me on January 29, and again
on February 5.)

" When in doubt do nothing" — that is why I have not felt
able to take upon myself, Madame, to dictate a decision on the
point which you were good enough to submit to me — my com-
petence being so inferior to your own. The thing itself has *grieved*
me very much. The longer I live, the more I hate falsehood; a
tardy repentance is no expiation. Moreover, conscience depends
more or less on physical sensibility.

Not knowing when the journey to Mannheim will take place,
I was in ignorance of a very necessary date; in the interval between the fault and the punishment there was time for the child
to show in deed and act the intensity of her repentance. I leave
it to you, Madame. You will have done well, whatever course you
adopt. I offer you a thousand apologies; I misread the date of
the Mannheim concert and I see, on re-reading your letter, that I
owe you an apology. You wrote quite clearly: " the 17th of this
month." But I was rather unwell and extraordinarily preoccupied
when your last letter reached me. Also, these last days before I
leave here are full of very bitter sorrows for me. It is at immense
loss to myself that I am starting; so much the better, departure
will bring greater peace. You have chosen St. Elisabeth, Madame,
although there is absolutely nothing in common between that
saint and the sinner who is now writing to you. I have no right
but to ratify the choice and I adopt it accordingly.

Please accept, Madame, with my profound gratitude for the
sentiments you do me the honour to express, the expression of
perfect reciprocity on my part, together with my sincere good
wishes for the new year.

302]

Zürich
March 14, 1872

KNOWING and appreciating as I do your delicacy of feeling, Madame, your noble ardour in *doing good,* and also your prudence practised in accordance with the maxim: " When in doubt, do nothing," I have agreed beforehand with the probable result of your consideration of and reflections on the question: whether, the father being so near the children, it would not be indicated as suitable and opportune to let them visit him at some place near by during his Swiss tour. No, Madame, it would be better not. First, the emotion caused by seeing my dear daughters once more in the present state of my nerves, rather overwrought by forty-four concerts (to which eighteen more will have to be added), might be positively harmful to me; and it would be premature to see them for other reasons. Besides I am hardly ever alone and hardly have a quarter of an hour at my disposal.

Finally, for a long time I have promised myself not to see my daughters until the day when I have succeeded as far as I can in assuring their livelihood. That day is not far distant in any case.

Fortune has favoured me beyond my expectations. For Daniela there is a little capital of more than forty thousand francs with the Freges; in case anything happens to me, there is an equal amount in the hands of Mr. Louis Perl (that is to say, at the end of the tour, the middle of April), which I think it is better to settle on Isolde, seeing that Blandine, a special favourite of her grandmother, may expect the ten thousand talers which my mother has often said she wishes to leave me.

In any case I hope it will not be necessary to fall back on this for Blandine; if I succeed in America my daughters will not need to pay court to my relations, and I shall be very glad to be able to give up my share of the maternal inheritance — at the price of being for ever quit of what Comtesse de Charnacé once described in an expression as alarmingly vigorous as it was true.

To my safe return from America, then!

I expect to be travelling in Switzerland up to the second half of Holy Week; then I shall rest at Munich, where I give a " solo " concert on April 2 for the benefit of — Bayreuth. On behalf of the same cause I am playing with orchestra on April 4 at Mannheim. Then there will be a short series of concerts in northern Germany, which will end on April 15 at Dresden. After that I shall hasten to return for at least a month to the country which has given me back my physical and moral strength.

Madame Louise de B. at Bonn gave a wonderful account of the children. She would so much like to have Loulou with her for a few weeks. She seems to me to deserve this favour; I have told her that I should raise no objection on my side, while on the other hand I would not consent to leave her in Berlin. She understood. Need I tell you, Madame, that you are entirely free to act as you think best and that I approve your decision beforehand?

A thousand tender fatherly greetings to the children — all the blessings of Heaven on their mother!

303]

Zürich
March 17, 1872

BELIEVE me, Madame, I had never any intention of giving my consent to a prolonged visit by Daniela to the widow of her paternal grandfather, except on the (preliminary) condition that the grandmother requests this favour formally and directly from the child's mother. Today I at first thought I would send warning of this to Bonn, but Madame Louise is at best a sensible woman, with sufficient knowledge of the *convenances* to do the right thing, and, moreover, I cannot consider it my duty to complete or to undertake the education of my relatives. Such a step would have meant attaching too much importance to the question, and I should risk giving Madame Louise reason to suspect that her request might be interpreted as a favour on her part.

I cannot conquer my inclination to regard a certain report of the Countess K. as untrue.

If that lady's delicacy of feeling was as strong as her Germanism, she could and should, I think, have spared you that "confidence," which, though it will only have caused a shrug of the shoulders, was at least pointless. Madame de K. has become very old and very much a gossip, and it is for this reason (her falsified bits of gossip have deeply wounded one of my young Italian friends) that when we met at Dresden I avoided the usual handshaking and the rest of it. For similar reasons I shall also avoid meeting Madame de M. as far as I can without ostentation, though her chatter is at least less *monotonous* if not less absorbing. Madame de S. in Berlin has won my heart by speaking well of the children; but for that I should have treated her with the same frigidity, in accordance with my invincible (negative) sympathies.

I beg your pardon for naming all these persons; but I am anxious that the three ladies devoted to the good cause should meet with no success should they try to put false interpretation on my more than reserved attitude towards them.

I thank you, Madame, for your kind approval of my decision not to "take advantage" of happening to be in their neighbourhood to embrace my daughters. Musicians and idlers of all sorts (for example, Herr Kietz here) buzz round me in every town, so that I am obliged to use the most ingenious subterfuge to escape their amiable persecutions and to snatch even half an hour's rest. This wears me out most of all, spoils my temper and even my disposition. If I had not entered into an agreement to go on with the job, under pecuniary penalties, I should not wait a day before I recrossed the Alps. Italy is vital for me; I feel suffocated in Germany as soon as I leave the pianoforte or the conductor's desk. You know, Madame, that I am to spend Holy Week in Munich. On that occasion the date of the new performance of *Tristan* will be decided, definitely fixed. In all probability the rehearsals will begin about June 8, which will mean that I shall be again staying in Munich until mid-July. An interview might then be arranged, half-way between Munich and Bayreuth. Since my mother threatens to accompany me to Munich, which I can hardly decline, in the interest, say, of Blandine, and for other reasons also, I should not like my daughters to set foot in that infamous city.

I have full confidence in Uncle Edward at Vienna; I am

rather, and more than rather, distrustful of his silly shrew of a wife. But your father will know more about that. I venture to beg you to write to him in full confidence. As regards Vienna — *pardon*, I am overstepping my rights, if I have any.

I fear these few lines may bear to some extent the imprint of a painful impression which some news, private news, made on me this morning. But I was anxious to thank you, Madame, for your letter and for the enclosed *feuilleton* (which I return), and tomorrow there will be no opportunity of writing, as a tiring and continuous tour in southern Switzerland will then begin. Accept, Madame, my assurance that I reciprocate completely the sentiments with which you honour me.

304]

London, 27 Duke Street, Manchester Square, W.
(*until Easter*)
October 27, 1874

As your kind letter requires an immediate reply, Madame, I regret to have to write at less length than I could wish. Let me tell you in two words that by the clearness and profoundness of your views and their admirable expression you have once more completely convinced me that the best thing for me to do is merely to endorse your decisions on the education, the future, of the children. The personal impression made by the Countess von Vitzthum is far more important than the prospectus of her boarding-establishment. Similarly I attach far more importance to the conciliatory (so to speak) effect that this transference of our daughters to that establishment will have on the " state of mind " of some members of my family * than to any guarantee of the maintenance of the filial piety that Daniela and Blandine owe to you with more reason than any daughters ever did. I have touched on the only point which might have caused me some uneasiness; you know it, Madame, and I have paid heavily for my knowledge of it — society. That the life of these young people should be spared all dissonance — that is my chief de-

* *My mother has become perfectly reasonable during her later years — but not Cousin Frege, who administers our daughters' small capital. . . .*

sire, the wish for whose fulfilment I am always willing to contribute my utmost at no matter what sacrifice.

As for the arguments for and against education in common, in flocks, of girls, I feel quite incompetent to express a judicious opinion. You are an expert, Madame, and are able to judge of the necessity of forming character by these means. In any case, it will be an introduction to the school of life, salutary in many respects. Moreover, you say that contact with our friends at Bayreuth is far from being a good influence for them; a change of intellectual and social atmosphere is therefore one immense advantage. It is to be hoped that the boarding-establishment at Niederlössnitz is not attended by Saxon girls exclusively (I am thinking of the dialect for the moment, though that is a very secondary matter). The essential thing, as I have just indicated, is that your maternal authority should be, not merely safeguarded, but respected and maintained and fortified in our children's minds in the most definite way by the teachers, from the directress downwards.

As for Pietist tendencies in the Luisenstift (which I like to think won't go so far as proscription of the frequent use of the tooth-brush — I ask your pardon for this detail, fixed in my recollection by many an experience), they will not hurt Blandine, for instance; it will be an episode, a stage in the continual flux of youth . . . in any case it will be a defence against the Judaizing influence; that is, better than the principles which Madame Lina Morgenstern and Co. are likely to profess. In fact there is no need to feel any premature alarm on that point. If I add my complete approval of your intention not to separate the two sisters, it is only to show you that I have conscientiously read and re-read your letter, Madame, and that it is absolutely impossible for me not to endorse everything you say. Thus, though it is understood *eo ipso*, in accordance with my offer to you through your father, you need do no more than name the sum that I should have to contribute towards the extra expenses, justified from every point of view, that the launching and maintenance of our children will necessitate.

Once more, I regret not to be able to reply at greater length. My long illness this summer made me lose much precious time. Now that I am so far recovered, owing to hydrotherapeutic treatment, I am working to make up for this loss. I hope that my own affairs will continue to straighten themselves out " by little and little." My tour in America, postponed year after year somewhat to my disadvantage, is definitely fixed for 1875–6. Before starting I shall not fail to make my will and send you a copy, so that everything will be in order for the children. As for seeing our daughters again, it has always seemed to me that it would be better to see them once more in their mother's presence. I do not know if you will understand — I do not say "share" — this sentiment; it is based on a consideration to which I have alluded above, to the desire not to allow any dissonance to be perceived by these youthful minds. Now the day when special circumstances may permit me to express this desire to you is not so far distant as it still appeared last year — I shall explain myself more clearly another time, Madame.

Meanwhile, accept my kind regards and my very deep gratitude.

305]

London, 27 Duke Street, Manchester Square, W.
March 15, 1875

As I suppose you are now back, Madame, from the journey of which you told me in your letter of February 18, I think I may now safely write and thank you for that letter, taking advantage of one of my rare visits to the capital. I am so firmly convinced of the indisputable wisdom of the steps you are taking in regard to our daughters' education that I abstain from a repetition of my complete approbation.

To go straight to the principal and immediate subject of my letter: this sum of one hundred pounds (2,500 francs or 2,000 marks) to meet the extra costs of this year (boarding-school, equipment, etc.), a sum which I can quite afford *not to raise* on the capital of 150,000 francs deposited with the Frege firm,* I beg of you, Madame, to employ it *as suits your convenience*. I should consider it a crying injustice — in the position that I have

---

* *I propose to follow this course each year until the interest has amounted to forty-five thousand talers.*

now gained — to leave *solely* to your charge the expense neces-
sitated by the fresh *change* in your system of education, so sensible in every way.

Would you please let me know the safest way of sending
you this sum, Madame? It seems to me that the simplest would
be to deposit it at a London house in relations with a Bayreuth
banker who has your confidence.

I have the honour to forward to you herewith the letters of
the Countess Vitzthum that you were good enough to send me
some time ago.

PS. In a few hours I am starting again for the provinces, but
I shall be back on the 21st *for certain,* and on the next day,
Monday, the arrangement with the banker, whose name and
address you will be kind enough to send me, could be made.
Please excuse my haste, the necessary consequence of the kind
of life I lead here.

306]

Hall, Tirol
June 28, 1875

I ASK a thousand pardons for disturbing your leisure, Madame
— that is to say, your activities, the accomplishment of your
present duties — by a few words on a matter of secondary and
indirect interest to you, matters indeed, affecting myself, the
father of Daniela, of Blandine and Isolde. It seems to me the
more inevitable as it will perhaps be the last time you will have
any news of me. I have had plenty of bad luck this last year — a
victim of the most scandalous deceptions in England — irrepar-
able, as I have just learned from my last news from London; the
capital destined for my three daughters instead of reaching the
sum on which I had counted, that of 45,000 talers, amounts to
only 36,000 — deposited with the firm of Frege in Leipzig
and placed, I hope, favourably by my cousin Professor Walde-
mar Frege.

I have always considered money losses as reparable; therefore I have not regretted this accident excessively, and I had resolved not to inform you of it, as this small matter should not

change the situation fundamentally or superficially, but a much more serious misfortune has overtaken me. My health is so completely shattered by the toil of these last years that I have every reason to fear that I shall be incapable of starting for America this autumn (September 1), although the contract with Mr. Ullmann was settled and signed eight months ago.

I have been very ill for three weeks. The English doctors (completely ignorant) treated as gout what the medical authorities in Munich recognized to be the result of an apoplectic stroke, rather a slight one, but nevertheless somewhat incalculable in its results, certainly as to the duration of these results.

A blood-vessel broke in the brain — the healing process takes time, and meanwhile my right hand is so *" hors de service "* as to make it improbable that I can fulfil the engagements named in my contract. Nevertheless, I shall make the attempt; that is, I shall sail if it is not absolutely impossible for me to start. Until I have liquidated my debts to the past, I shall consider I have no right to take care of myself, body or soul. My first ambition is not to die " insolvent." What I recognize as my duty to my three children is certainly very little, but luck, destiny indeed, has lately taught me that this minimum is not so easy to obtain, that fortune does not shine upon me.

In fact, although I have not renounced all hope of realizing my first scheme of fifteen thousand talers for each daughter, it is uncertain whether I can succeed. At any rate I must prepare for the worst, I must face the possibility of failure.

I beg you, Madame, to place yourself for a few moments in my (involuntary) position and to help me a little with your intelligence, with your maternal love for your daughters, so that I may set about taking practical measures, to ensure a provision for the poor children.

Not long ago I offered to make an annual contribution to the extra costs of the children's education, so as to allow the capital of their dowries to accumulate without any reduction of the interest. You will believe that I am far from withdrawing this offer, but I cannot, as you will understand by what I have just told you, guarantee that my powers will substantiate my wishes.

Be so kind, then, Madame — in case anything happens, especially the worst — to tell me the amount of the annual sum which will have to be deducted from the interest on the thirty-six thousand talers to meet the boarding-school and other charges.

I do not know if this year's hundred pounds will be sufficient. Please let me know also when you propose to allow our third and youngest daughter, Isolde, to participate in this sum.

I have, now as formerly, little knowledge of business; moreover, in placing my savings at Leipzig I thought less of a high rate of interest than of the security of the capital. The thirty-six thousand talers may, it seems to me, very well produce sixteen hundred as income. Assuming, then, that one thousand a year will be enough, there will still be six hundred to add to the capital.

Be so kind, Madame, as to give these small matters some consideration and tell me your opinion, since for many years you alone have taken charge of all material arrangements and have therefore the necessary data. You will need authorization to draw on the Frege firm; perhaps Herr Feustel will be able to indicate the easiest course for us both, and his advice may enable us to dispense with a contract, which it would be pleasant for you to avoid, with the Frege firm. By the way, if you are not aware of it, I may mention that my mother is leaving our eldest daughter a small income of two hundred talers which is to come from some mines or other. You would oblige me very much, Madame, if you could find time to reply within a week or ten days on these questions of figures. I do not need to repeat that the measures proposed above, these little arrangements, are only to provide for the case, more or less regrettable, of my . . . incapacity or death.

My address at Munich is still the same: Herr Dr. von Welz, 14 von der Tannstrasse. . . .

307]

Hall
July 3, 1875

Accept all my thanks, Madame, for the prompt and kind reply which I received yesterday, my departure for Munich having had to be postponed for a few days.

Your words did me good, they calmed me to some extent, but they cannot modify in any way the personal resolves I have taken. I am bound by contract to Herr Ullmann to make the American tour, which begins this autumn and should last from eight to nine months. Moreover, I neither had nor have any other choice, and in a way there is no other course to take at the moment, as I have exhausted my resources in Europe, in my — trade. It is only my ill health that disturbs me; I do not yet absolutely despair of being able to sail, but God knows what will happen to me on the other side.

That is why I felt that I could no longer put off making my will. If I had not been robbed this winter, it would have already been done — it was a very simple matter. The sum intended for our children would have been ready; everything would have been in order. It is only because I am tormented by such grave uncertainty that I allowed myself to write to you the other day to explain the circumstances which have been seriously altered by my unexpected reverses.

I also thank you very much, Madame, for your proposal to let me see my daughters once more before venturing on the " inevitable impossibility " of the American tour; but my former resolve, fully maintained, is opposed to it and would be equally opposed were it not necessary for me to avoid with the utmost care the least cause of excitement or emotion. I have become extremely weak, even in my memory. I shall not see our children again until I have fulfilled my duties as a father towards them to the very modest limit of my ability. I beg of you, then, to consider the meeting as put off until next year after the Bayreuth festival. Moreover I have not the time; if I succeed in recovering the use of my right hand, I need six weeks' assiduous practice to prepare for my hundred and seventy concerts on the other side of the Atlantic, and I shall have to leave on September 1. I shall spend these six or seven weeks in absolute retreat in England.

Within a week at the latest this business of the will will be arranged at Munich, I hope with the assistance of Herr Gotthelf, whose name perhaps you will remember from former days. Would you be kind enough to supply me, so that this may be properly executed, with the exact dates of birth of Daniela,

Blandine, and Isolde? It is rather humiliating to have to confess the weakness of my memory even on this point, but there it is. I share your opinion that their small dowry should be handed over to them as soon as they have attained their twentieth year. That is to say, I shall try to stipulate for the inalienability of the capital, for their security as against their husbands if they marry. In case you should have any further observations to make about this, would you please, Madame, do it within the next week? It has only just occurred to me that as they will pay me six thousand francs in gold every fortnight in America (supposing that I am able to go, which I shall suppose in spite of everything until the last moment), it would be possible to realize the amount I have proposed at the end of the year. But, as I have already explained, this would only be with good luck, and I have lost the luck which smiled on me in the first years of my return to a virtuoso's career. It goes without saying that if luck is with me, all would be well, and you would be authorized, Madame, to spend for the completion of their education the interest of the capital of forty-five thousand talers, or the necessary portion of it. All these arrangements would then have been superfluous; I need not justify them afresh on the ground of the extreme uncertainty of the basis of this calculation. So much the better (I shall add with all my heart) if in a year's time I am able to redraft the will now being drawn, but, having lost all rosy prospects, I must firmly face the worst.

I think I owe you some sort of reply — for various motives, of which the first is to tell you that I appreciate to the full the considerations which led you to speak to me about it — to what you have told me about your father's desire that I should accept the post of pianoforte professor at the National Conservatorium at Pest, offered to me as a result of his kind personal intervention for an old pupil. Believe me, Madame, I never thought lightly of refusing that flattering invitation. Neither do my doubts as to the execution of this plan for a Hungarian academy of music enter into the question. Moreover, as they will hardly think of opening this institution until a year from now, acceptance would in no way have upset my American tour, which finishes in any case about the middle of June, including the return to Europe.

I have not considered overmuch my selfish interest, which makes me look upon official duties in a conservatorium as slavery of the most annihilating kind. I can speak of it as one who knows, as a victim. I would a thousand times rather give private lessons in a little town, a profession which I shall not fear to return to in my old age, if such there be. One can then, in one's leisure, recover some mental independence and become master of one's thoughts, a privilege not to be found in an official teaching position.

No, the real, the essential, the principal motive of my refusal was that I found myself morally and intellectually unable to justify the highly valued confidence of the Abbé Liszt. Time, life, and perhaps habit have modified my earlier beliefs to some extent. This has for long been a real and deep grief, but though I may hide from other eyes the change that I have in some way undergone — hide it in a positive fashion while trying my best to affirm all that my musical conscience permits me to affirm, or to help to affirm — I am not in a position to fulfil the task of an — apostolate (pardon the presumptuous expression), for which I have no longer the faith and enthusiasm, necessarily exclusivist. I have become too much of a reactionary in the domain of instrumental music, which has become my department, to be able to be the serving sacristan which your father has the perfect right to expect; others would be able to take my place so much the better in that I find myself very much worn out, more nervous than ever, more " Leopardian " than ever in human intercourse, and of this I should have so much at Pest that my small store of health would be jeopardized. I am no longer a fit candidate for the post of which your father has been kind enough to secure the offer for me. The eternal gratitude which I owe him will make me ever and everywhere alive to and eager to seize any opportunity of testifying my loyal affection, but I am much more likely to meet such opportunities elsewhere than in a very dubious temple among people who are half barbarians and half Jews or Judaized.

I fear that in trying to make myself clear I have become confused as well as diffuse. Nevertheless I venture to hope, Madame, that you will appreciate the reasons for my inability to conform to the arrangements made by your father.

I assure you that I should be much less unhappy could it be otherwise.

Since you have been so kind as to set me an example, Madame, by touching on subjects other than that of the education and future of the children, which normally absorbs our *rare* letters, I venture to follow it by concluding with a few simple suggestions which may perhaps serve to lighten the burden of your correspondence with England. Of the two prima donnas Madame Nilsson and Mademoiselle Albani, the former — leaving out of consideration her very chauvinist husband, M. Ronzeaud — cannot, in my opinion, be taken seriously on account of her very mediocre talent; you might do better with the latter, I think.

Then, for any contracts or negotiations in London, the only intelligent and conscientious man I know would be Mr. Forman, the translator of the poem of the *Nibelungen*, of which he has now completed the last portion. He is high-minded, a real man, and particularly distinguished and likable. I have had very little to do with him, but I have never met anybody more interesting and worthy of esteem; I do not know how much influence he has, but, then, there are so few people whose services one can demand. I doubt whether his like is to be found for good service and trustworthiness, in view of the confidence that would have to be placed in him. He is not a musician by profession. I might in this connexion add a few words in favour of, or rather favourably for, Mr. Ullmann; but your father, who once recommended him to me so warmly, will be able to tell you more about him. I myself have on the whole found him entirely satisfactory up till now; his politeness and sincerity certainly deserve mention. As he "adores" the Abbé Liszt, a few words from the latter would in case of necessity smooth out any difficulties that might arise.

I hope, Madame, that you will consider this incursion into what does not concern me simply as a proof that I have by no means mistaken the sense of the words " it is not my business " in your letter. . . .

308]

Munich
July 11, 1875

Your last note, Madame, which came somewhat as a surprise, affected me very painfully on the evening of my arrival. You had the best intentions, and it would be more than unjust to reproach you for it. Besides, it is my fault for having to some extent invited it by my last letter, which might, indeed would, mislead you with regard to the sad state of my nerves. Be so kind, Madame — as a special favour to me — if you should be pleased to reply in the affirmative, not to give me in that reply any news of my daughters and not to suggest to them that they should write direct to me. I congratulate them on the arrangements you have made for them.* I shall stay here until Thursday evening, when I hope to have finished the business of the will, before going to Brussels (conferences with M. U.) and from there to the seaside in England.

Although I propose, before leaving Munich, to send you an exact copy of the passages from my will affecting my daughters, I can today inform you of the arrangements I am making for them.

Dr. Gotthelf (Promenadenstrasse 10) is nominated as my executor. We shall select within the next few days the notary with whom the sealed document will be deposited.

Daniela will receive, when she reaches her majority (at the age of twenty-one) or on her marriage if she marries before that date — though I should like that to be deferred until she is nineteen — a capital sum of fifteen thousand talers (56,250 francs); each of her sisters will receive the same amount when she reaches the same age, the youngest perhaps about a thousand francs more, in which I see no unfairness. If one of the children should die before these provisions take effect, the dowry in question would be divided equally between the other two. If two of them should die, fifteen thousand talers would be otherwise disposed of. The sum provided for these three dowries, which today

The boarding-school was the only wise solution.

amounts to thirty-six thousand talers (apparently my earlier figure was badly written), will remain in the hands of the Frege firm.

I shall leave to my daughters collectively the box containing "plate and other valuables," valued at two thousand francs (it is impossible for me to verify this), which has been in store at the Bavarian Hypotheken and Wechsel Bank since September 9, 1870, under the number 8,810. The costs of storage are paid up to September 9, 1878. Dr. de Welz has the deposit receipt as well as some other possessions of some value, more recently acquired, of which an exact list will be drawn up. My daughters will also receive a part of my literary and musical library, now in the hands of Herr Eugène Spitzweg, who will receive special instructions. These include: the German and French classical authors; in music, the works of their grandfathers, including arrangements and editions, and my own small contingent; all the music which has been dedicated to me or expressly given to me by the composers. I should like to see these last small things pass into the hands of the one best qualified to value them. You will decide on this point, as on the foregoing, *a piacere*; I entrust you officially with the sharing out, the division — and that blindly, without restriction.

I have fully reflected on your observation of the other day, the result of my mention of the small legacy my mother intends to make to the eldest girl. I do not think that this consideration can be taken into account in the disposition of my personal property. Who knows? My mother is incalculable; I may yet be so unfortunate as to quarrel with her at the last moment, since I find her masked egoism more and more disturbing. By insisting on being with me in the refuge I had arranged for myself during the next two months, she is jeopardizing the execution of my American plan, in itself so uncertain, for every minute is important to me in that connexion. I am in the very unpleasant position of being compelled to take extreme defensive measures against her. I hide myself, run away, and dissimulate; also I have to leave the Continent for other reasons. Pardon this digression, which arose out of the uncertainty of the two-hundred-talers-a-year legacy which I mentioned to you in the first letter from Hall, a question which led you to ask me for compensation for our second daughter by the gift of plate, etc.

Finally, as one never knows what may happen, I leave you a free hand as regards all objects of this kind.

And now, Madame, may I confide to you a delicate, very confidential mission — a simple one, which will hardly trouble you at all? It concerns the use of a sum of five thousand francs (four thousand reichsmarks) for the purchase and dispatch to a foreign country of a small gift to a person who was prepared to love me and whom I was compelled to give up on account of my responsibilities, complicated by the double misfortune of last winter; whether this renunciation prevented fresh causes for remorse or not matters little.

There is no one in the world whom I can ask to execute this — posthumous — caprice.

If you should feel disposed, Madame, to make this small sacrifice for me (I should even wish that you would act personally — that is, write in my name), I should be infinitely obliged if you would reply by a simple "yes," so that I may insert the legacy in my will — "to Madame R. W. for a destination known to her alone."

It does not seem to me superfluous, Madame, to inform you that a week ago I had a letter from your father, for which you had prepared me beforehand. I replied to him at as great length as I could, carefully concealing from him, by giving other motives for my humble refusal, the one that I have taken the liberty of communicating to you. This relieves you, Madame, of any necessity of telling him of our correspondence on the question. . . .

PS. I almost forgot to tell you that Herr Spitzweg (for Welz) will be empowered to send you several packets of letters, carefully sealed, regarding persons still living who are nearly concerned with you. I will return to this subject later in more detail. I feel very weak for the moment.

309]

Munich
July 14, 1875

A THOUSAND thanks, Madame!
This is the name and address of the person to whom I should like to have a posthumous memento sent, to be selected by you. Mlle Sophie Alexeievna de Poltovatzki, Dobrokitovo, near Kursk, Russia.

Thanks to Herr Gotthelf's really admirable zeal, I hope to terminate my melancholy visit to this city *tomorrow*, and I shall leave immediately for England. I am much touched by your kindly remark about the seaside. But the first consideration for me should be my muscles. My nerves must take their turn next year, if there is a next year. Salt water seems to be the only means available to assist the reabsorption of the blood of the partially paralysed right side of the body and the left side of the face.

I shall not be able, as I thought, to send you from Munich a copy of my will — that is to say, of the passages relative to my bequests for the children. I ask your pardon, but it is beyond my strength. Every extra hour spent in this work represents a serious hindrance in the course of my cure, to which I ought henceforward exclusively to devote myself.

Nevertheless allow me to speak to you about some details relating to subsidiary questions:

(1) the things (more or less valuable) deposited with Dr. de Welz, and (2) my library of music and books.

It has not been possible to draw up the list of either the first or the second category. (That is south German *Gemütlichkeit!*)

1. There will be no difficulty here. The mementoes intended for various friends and acquaintances will be dispatched by the depositary. You will receive the list signed by me and the things themselves simultaneously.

2. In this matter I have to make another appeal, a posthumous one, to your kindness. (a) Books. The German and French

classics are for the children, as well as any other books you think fit to give them.

As for the works on philosophy, history (revolutions), the rare editions and old books collected by my father and myself, I want them to be sent to my friend Professor Carl Hillebrand at Florence; the French books (*belles-lettres*), which you may not think suitable for the children, together with my collection of Italian books, will be left to Madame Jessie Laussot (36 Lung' Arno Nuovo), Florence.

(b) Music.

1. Books *on* music, offering no interest to the children, such as collections of musical papers, professional pamphlets, etc., to Dr. Pohl of Baden.

2. My eldest daughter will have all the works on which the name of her grandfather or her father figures on the first page — indeed, everything that would be of practical help to her, to her technique or her intelligence, if she should study music with any success. Her sisters might share.

3. Among the scores " for orchestra or piano " (operas, symphonies, chamber-music, etc.) my friend and fellow pupil Herr Carl Klindworth will have the right to choose what may fill the gaps in and supplement his own library.

4. The remainder, which will be not inconsiderable in value, will go to the Conservatoire of Music at Pest, naturally through its president, your father.

I should be glad to think I might hope, Madame, that you would be good enough to superintend the execution of these arrangements when the time comes. I think it superfluous — in any case, there is no time — to set out all the details of my will. I have no real domicile at Munich and even less elsewhere, my only helps are decent semi-idiots which I cannot shake off because I cannot replace them — it would, moreover, necessitate the removal of my belongings, which would be difficult, almost impossible, more on account of my absolute lack of leisure than the actual cost. I can only rely on another " yes " from you.

If I return safe and sound from America about the middle of June 1876, I shall try to find some sort of place to live in, perhaps at Meiningen (with the help of your old friend and beneficiary, Baroness Ellen von Heldberg), and only spend some months of the year — to raise money — in England. I shall then be able to make some practical arrangement less Bohemian than the sheer chaos of my existence during the last six years. Of course I shall in that case ask you once more to let me make the same contribution to the education of my daughters as I have done this year.

As I approach the end of my present task, imperfect and incomplete as has been my accomplishment of it, I feel that a certain calm and a certain hopefulness have been restored to me. My condition is certainly rather serious, and, although I am not disposed to take this too tragically or pathetically, I have thought it my duty and by no means inopportune to make preparations for a fatal ending.

I thank you most heartily, Madame, for helping me by appreciating my situation as you have recently done. . . .

310]

Chicago
February 6, 1876

Please excuse, Madame, my having been obliged to defer so long the duty of acknowledging your letter of January 6, of thanking you sincerely, and of repeating my respectful admiration for all you are doing for our children, an admiration which includes full and complete approval of the points of view and the measures taken which you have kindly communicated to me.

I regret that the " roving life " which I lead (indeed without distaste for it or excessive fatigue) does not allow me to explain fully the news — still unknown to my mother and others — that I do not intend to recross the Atlantic, that I have found my real fatherland here (" *Wo ich nütze ist mein Vaterland,*" we once read in the *Wanderjahre*) ; in fact, I consider myself henceforward dead and buried as far as Europe is concerned, and I am now taking the first steps to obtain a citizen's rights in this free country. I propose to spend the last quarter of my life in my own fashion and for my own satisfaction — which I find in the prosperity of my art — and to leave the rest to the grace of God.

I venture to ask you to read the enclosed cuttings from the

press, which will tell you all you may like to know should you deign to be interested.

I am taking another and a greater liberty, Madame, but, believe me, from the finest motives. The New York *Tribune*, an enormous paper, is about to make the mistake of engaging as American correspondent at Bayreuth Mr. Franz Hüffer, a semi-musician, three parts ignorant, who writes English badly — a combination compromising for the good cause " in every respect." I have done my best to persuade them to choose a serious-minded and excellent young man (a former pupil of Mr. B. J. Lang), of Boston, who speaks (and writes) French, *German,* and American equally well and is far superior to the Englishman.

I therefore venture to ask your assistance in persuading the New York editor to accept Mr. William Apthorp. Mr. Lang will make himself responsible for carrying out your wishes generally, with the help of the Chickerings in New York.

It is my most ardent hope, as you know, that Providence will give you complete success in the greatest musical event of the century. Believe me, Madame, that the impossibility for me *of either being present or not being present* at that event has been the chief motive for my irrevocable resolve.

311]

Glasgow, 144 Holland Street
December 29, 1877

Believe me, Madame, that I sincerely regret having to trouble you for a moment.

Has due consideration been given to the consequences and to the tenor of a certain letter from Bayreuth, dated the 22nd instant and addressed to a certain Harlequin of a violinist?

I shall do my best not to allow myself to be drawn into a " war to the knife " which might ensue, but I cannot guarantee that the " struggle for life " will not force me to revolutionary " *décembriseurs* " action which may perhaps be regrettable in the interests of art.

I was flattered, Madame, that *you* were good enough to read between the lines of my *Reiserezensionen* a manifesto of musical Bonapartism, of which I am the representative, and which will before long crush the other parties; I had, besides, deputed " Polonius " [1] to explain my point of view, but he becomes more and more idiotic every day and has now come out quite on the side of the Newfoundlander, it seems.

Believe me, it is not my fault that I have failed to expatriate myself; destiny put real obstacles in the way of my leaving Europe definitively for America. So here I am in Europe, and *here I stay*. I shall continue to fight for my ideas with all the means that will serve my end, including the methods of those who neither give nor take quarter. I hope these lines will convince you that there is perhaps a conciliatory mission for you to fulfil.

312]

Hanover
January 14, 1878

MY best thanks, Madame, for the letter by which you were kind enough to reply to mine from Glasgow. I should have acknowledged its receipt at once had I had the leisure to do so. I desire at the same time to offer my regrets for the painful impression which my epistolary outburst must have caused you and for the waste of your time, but, alas, as soon as I returned to Germany I found once more the same deplorable things going on which would drive me to the same measures, if I had again to inform you of what was taking place in the press. You can quite well see that the Wagnerians of tomorrow are *forcing* me to war to the knife, and if they are able to shelter with impunity under the authority of the Master, it will be impossible for me to calculate the effect of my blows. I am the more distressed as I have just been reading on my journey the sublime poem of *Parsifal* (disfigured, alas, by a hideous " blot " at the end of the first act), which has made me so proud to be an early Wagnerite, certainly the oldest among living musicians. It is the *Missa Solennis* of the second Beethoven.

[1] *One of Bülow's nicknames for Richard Pohl. "Nohlen-Pohlens" was another.*

I think I have made arrangements at Sydenham for Daniela's visit which will satisfy all your moral demands — you know very well that they are strictly my own. I should like the visit to take place as soon as possible (my sister will write to our daughter), as my poor mother is gradually losing the use of her eyes and also, alas, though one must not exaggerate, the use of the " mind's eyes." Her grand-daughter would be beginning life with a *very kind deed* if she *brightened* her grandmother's last months by an affection which it would be so much the easier to offer her as it is merely by way of a return.

Pardon me, Madame, for writing rather too briefly on the second point and perhaps at too great length on the first. But:

> The world is mine for yet another evening,
> Then will I use this evening to the full.

313]

Hanover
January 17, 1878

I THANK you, Madame, for sending me the letters of Madame A. W. and have the honour to return them herewith. I read at the same time, since the same mail brought me No. 6 of the *Signale*, the principal item of the printed matter with which the manuscript deals. I regret not to be able to modify in any way my opinion of the very vulgar " though rich " violinist winemerchant; but I regret still more, Madame, that I forced my earlier regrets upon you. Alas, we can no longer come to a mutual understanding. Far be it from me to meddle in affairs which are no concern of mine. If it is felt that no change in the politics and especially in the personnel of Bayreuth is necessary, it is obvious that there is satisfaction with the *status quo*. If it is thought possible to carry on without the people who alone supply the subsidies, all is for the best! For the sake of Ludwig II one must put up with his " Jews."

It is I who have been ill informed. I thought that the author of *Parsifal* meant to address the nation and not only the Church, outside of which I cannot believe that anyone will be found to appreciate the bad taste of the " goose-swan " erudition on the subject of Wolfram von Eschenbach and the rest.

Nevertheless permit me to defend myself from the reproach of having divulged a matter which is a " *secret de Polichinelle.*" I have only followed the example of Heckel and Co.

Believe me, Madame, there is no one on the Continent or across the Channel who does not know how things are. Musical opinion will only be satisfied by a clean sweep, beginning in the house itself. To conclude, I flatter myself that the Russian policy which once ruined Weimar will not prevail at Bayreuth, where a Bismarckian policy is what is wanted.

PS. I intend to give some pianoforte recitals, three in all, of the last five Beethoven sonatas, next winter in the Hanover district (Berlin, Bremen, Hamburg) for the benefit of the Bayreuth fund. Do you think I shall find in the tea-kettle committee of the Wagnerverein people with the sense to organize the thing decently (sensible choice of dates, place, without offering reduced prices for the ruck of the members), or would it be better to do without them, which, frankly, I should prefer? Then, what would be the correct term to use at the top of the program? Bayreuth Fund, School of Music, National Theatre? Please send me a word when you can, Madame.

314]

Hanover
May 6, 1878

As I have not been able, Madame, to inform you before this of certain arrangements that I have made, may I now ask you to make yourself acquainted with them at second hand by reading the enclosed letter from my cousin Frege? Would you then have the kindness to return it to me and to indicate the Bayreuth house to which the four thousand reichsmarks which will be sent to you in the future in my name can be paid in, half at the end of June and half at the end of December? As this sum only represents *at most* two thirds of the interest on the children's capital, that capital will not be prevented from rising gradually to the sum of a hundred and fifty thousand reichs-marks, as has been agreed.

I ask a thousand pardons for this informal way of doing things; but I am horribly tired in body and mind, thanks to the pernicious natal air which I have breathed too long; and amongst all the wearisome tasks, for which I feel myself more and more unfit, the task of writing is the one I find hardest. In accordance with family tradition, no one has said a word to me for months on what has been decided with regard to Daniela's journey to Sydenham. I asked that her stay there should not coincide with my visit to London (first fortnight of the month of June), my life being already more complicated than it should be and this journey being indispensable for me.

I should be very much obliged, Madame, if you would tell me what is being done in the matter.

315]

Hanover
September 24, 1880

I HAVE such boundless confidence, Madame, in your wisdom that I must suppose you to be as much in the right as you have always been in sending Daniela to Bonn under the charge of Mlle de M. in spite of my prejudices against this pseudo-idealist. But my knowledge of the subject is so superficial that it would be more than rash to allow my prejudice to amount to a serious conviction. You know more than I do about it, and I leave the matter to the providence which you represent for my daughter.

In any case I think that the impressions received from the northern tour should if possible be supplemented by informa-tion, diversion, modifications, and rectifications in the south. Could Princess W. undertake a sort of indirect and tentative supervision? Are you in correspondence with her?

Daniela will travel via Florence, I suppose. Then my old friend the excellent Madame Laussot might give her advice and perhaps more than that. Please bear her in mind. She has a heart of gold. (She at last attained widowhood, by the way, two months ago.)

I need not say how ardently I approve of Daniela's return home; I was getting rather anxious over the prolongation of her visit to my family.

Allow me, Madame, to take advantage of the occasion to submit to you a letter which I received from Berlin a month ago. I shall play the last five sonatas of Beethoven at Berlin on October 23 for the benefit of the Bayreuth fund, without asking for the help either of Tappert or of Davidsohn. (I consider the Semite the less Jewish of the two.) The time is at hand when I shall be able plainly to assert and emphasize my sympathy for the good cause in my own way, as far as circumstances permit. After having newly rehearsed *Rienzi* and the *Flying Dutchman* I am going on to recondition *Tannhäuser* on October 6 (using the German original, of course), when I shall have the assistance of that excellent producer Mr. de Bronsart, with whom I am on terms of complete cordiality and understanding. Last of all, we have, we think, found the right man in the actor Alexander Liebe.

Last Sunday the fifth representation of *Rienzi* (the fifth under my direction) was such as to make me regret the absence of an ambassador at least of the composer. Schott is developing marvellously and gives a most finished performance. He has come much nearer to the ideal of the hero than any of his rivals, not excepting the old marionette at Dresden. Herr Seydel will have no choice but to reconsider his *worse than frivolous* criticism.

I hope to be able to " produce " Herr S. as an equally good Tannhäuser eventually. My system is to make an improvement at each rehearsal, to rebuild the edifice little by little, thereby departing completely from my colleagues' methods. I shall succeed if my life is spared.

By the way, I have nominated " Polonius " as editor of the *Neue Zeitschrift*, promising at the same time a quarterly subvention of a hundred crowns, to be withdrawn if I am not content with the paper. Of course he will have to abstain from carping where Bayreuth is concerned. Anti-Semitism, however much I react to it personally, is also forbidden. Forgive these slight divagations.

316]

Meiningen
December 9, 1880

First of all, Madame, I must offer a thousand apologies for having delayed so long in replying to your letter of November 13. You would certainly accept them if you had any idea how distracted I am by all sorts of people and how entirely absorbed by the task I have undertaken for the last quarter of this year. It is true that it is nearly over, and that I can only congratulate myself with the result of a piece of work almost beyond my strength, which is undermined by continuous ill health; but these last weeks will finish me, owing to outside complications.

Frankly, I am not overjoyed at the prospect of seeing your eldest daughter arrive on the 19th to compare the Ninth Symphony as executed with the resources of a small town with its performance at the great festival of May 22, 1872. Moreover I shall not be alone for a moment during these three days (December 17 to 19) and shall be quite unable to fulfil my duties as a father, morally and materially, for all the hurly-burly still revolves round the pivot of my poor self in this hole of a place. However —

As for your plan, Madame, of sending Daniela to the Countess S. at Berlin, I do not think I have any right to raise objections.

I gave you a long time ago (and never has confidence been better justified) full powers, and with them full responsibility to arrange everything for Daniela as you think best. I am profoundly convinced that you will always do what is right.

I am very sorry not to be able to write to you in a way more acceptable to you and the children. My mind is never free at all even for a quarter of an hour; every biped brings a faggot for the stake on which I am being burned.

But be assured, Madame, I am determined to acquit myself in time of all the duties that destiny has laid upon me. Unfortunately, there are so many of them! I will write to you about it as soon as I can get a little breathing-space.

317]

Berlin
April 28, 1881

Meiningen, Friday.

ONCE more, Madame, may I express to you my most devout thanks. What an adorable child! What a mind you have formed! It makes me weep to think of her, and I think of her without ceasing. This day, April 27, was a revelation to me. I thank Providence for having given me this inexpressible joy, a happiness which is such that it cannot be vitiated by any of the bitterness, regret, or remorse connected with it. Teach me, most generous and noble woman, what duties I have to fulfil as a father towards this much loved being, who has conquered my whole soul in one moment! I should like to build a shrine on the spot where your father brought her to me. I understand Père Goriot — pardon, I am wandering from the point, because what in him was madness would for Daniela be merely supremely right, a divine enthusiasm.

Thank you, thank you, thank you! I am indebted to you for a happiness without compare, painful as it may be.

PS. A thousand blessings on you, wonderful woman! Daniela's bearing admirable in all circumstances. Worthy of her mother! May I express my admiration, gratitude, and deep respect?

318]

Meiningen
October 19, 1881

As I said in my telegram this morning, Madame, Daniela's letter got lost yesterday in the hotel on my arrival. I only had time to read it as I came out of the rehearsal at eleven o'clock. I am returning herewith the letters of the Princesses Wittgenstein and Hohenlohe, which I was only able to look at a few hours ago. Hence the request in my telegram for Daniela's address in Rome; I propose to write to her as soon as my endless tribulations, complicated by a very unsatisfactory state of health, are rather fewer.

You were right, as always, Madame, in letting our daughter accompany your father on the journey to Rome. It is better for her to look after her grandfather, who is more worthy of her care and has at the moment more need of it, than to care for me. The only source of anxiety in Rome is the climate; nevertheless I think it cannot be more unhealthy than that of Meiningen, which makes me regret more every day having been reduced to choose this village as place of residence.

In taking an apartment, which has given me more trouble than expense in furnishing, I was guided to a considerable extent by the prospect of having a roof to offer to Daniela. I had hardly any choice and had every kind of ill luck in procuring what was required, so that it would have been impossible for me to invite my daughter to spend the last months of the year with me. In January and in March the orchestra is, in accordance with the desire of His Highness the Duke, to give concerts in Berlin, Hamburg, and so on. In February I intend to tour Austria on my own account in order to meet my expenses. Therefore there will be no opportunity of seeing my daughter again before April. But I should be very grateful to you, Madame, if you would be kind enough to let me know how long you have arranged for Daniela to stop with her grandfather in Rome.

I hope to be able to make arrangements for some months of the summer and winter of next year which will enable me to invite Daniela without fear of inflicting on her the duties of a nurse. Although Daniela has been sufficiently instructed by you that " life is far from presenting a plain field of ice where one has nothing to do but glide," the transition from the comfortable and well-regulated life of Bayreuth to the kind of existence I lead here would have been too sudden; my life here is problematic and irregular, harassed by cares of all kinds and imposing on me a continuous fight against innumerable little annoyances. Moreover, I should not have been able to offer her even minor social advantages. The Duke and his wife, with whom I should be very sorry to see Daniela installed (for her own sake), are away in October; the wife of the Grand Marshal von Stein is the only person whose society is available for Daniela, and she is about to leave for France; I am busy from eight in the morning till ten at night, sometimes without having half an hour in which to exercise my fingers, on which, however, I have to rely for gaining a few pence; the more I reflect, the more I am convinced it would have been madness and cruelty to drag the poor child into such a tangled existence.

I have entered into some detail about my circumstances to stifle any misunderstandings in Daniela's mind, which would be very painful to me; her letter brings an accusation of coldness. I did not see your father on his way through Meiningen, except in company with the Baroness M., and he only lent half an ear to my explanations of the impossibility of having Daniela here with me this winter. In any case, for a long time now, to my great regret, we have never understood one another on any question at all.

I shall be very much obliged to you, Madame, if you would ask Daniela on my behalf to write to me soon and every week from Rome. I hope to be able to reply as regularly.

319]

Meiningen
October 25, 1881

MANY thanks, Madame, for sending on Daniela's letter which I have the honour to return to you herewith. I can add nothing else for the moment; I have been in bed for four days, and I fear that the steady decline of my health will force me shortly to send in my definite resignation, as the burden of my work and the innumerable obstacles I have to encounter are beginning literally to crush me.

During my tour in Austria in February — if it takes place, which I doubt — I shall have to avoid Pest. Therefore a meeting with our daughter will have to be put off until better days. As for Meiningen, I have resolved not to pass another winter there. It is even more impossible than Hanover to pitch one's tent in. Allow me to wish you a pleasant journey in Sicily, Madame.

HANS VON BÜLOW

to

LUISE VON BÜLOW

*(including two to Willi and Heinz von Bülow,
his half-brothers)*

320]

Chocieszewice, near Kröben, Posen
December 25, 1854

YOUR long letter arrived shortly before I left for Berlin.
Although I am only now writing to thank you for it, I had the
best intentions of answering at once and so testifying to my
desire to get into closer touch with you. But my three weeks in
Berlin were so cut up that I had not a single whole hour free
in which to write you a decent letter, and I was not willing to
express myself to you in the fragmentary manner which I am
accustomed to use at such crowded times to my regular correspondents. Having been so long silent, then, and having much
to be silent about, a résumé of the past became necessary if I
was to be understood, and this I found very difficult and even
impossible to write. Even now I am not really in the mood for
it, yet I think the chief thing now is for me to show you that
I am not insensitive to or ungrateful for the tokens of goodwill
that you have given me. How I should like to be able to speak
my thanks! I had hoped, indeed, to be able to go to Königsberg
after my first concert in Berlin, some faint echo of which may
have reached your ear, or rather eye, through a Berlin paper
(perhaps the *Kreuzzeitung,* which treated me quite decently).
I should then have had an opportunity of repaying my mother
to some extent for the great sacrifice she made for my appearance in Berlin. But my friend Music-director Marpurg of
Königsberg dissuaded me from choosing the weeks before
Christmas for this expedition and invited me to come instead in
the middle of January or later. As soon as I have had a fortnight's rest at Chocieszewice, therefore, and have started my
lady pupils on their musical treadmill again, I shall move on,
first to Breslau, where Hieronymus Truhn (who is now rehearsing and conducting his *Cleopatra* there) will arrange my concerts for me, and afterwards without loss of time to Königsberg.
You will then no doubt allow me to call on you and see my dear
fratelli again. Please give my kind regards to your brother,
who will not, I hope, find me too unaristocratic and ent-Bülow-
ized by my professional career.

My principal news — which, after my mother, you are the first to hear — is that I propose to settle in Berlin from April 1 next year. The main inducement and guarantee are provided by Professor Marx's offer to appoint me first pianoforte-teacher at the private conservatorium conducted by himself and Music-director Stern. The engagement is provisional for one year, and I replace Dr. Kullak, who is leaving on account of differences with these two Jewish gentlemen, he being very much in the wrong. My very modest salary will be three hundred talers, but at first I shall have only a moderate amount of work and there will be certain advantages arising naturally out of it, though not of a positive order. I have already accepted the offer and signed the contract and I confess I am well satisfied with this turn of events in my immediate future.

My Berlin appointment should give my mother an excuse for leaving that uninspiring provincial city Dresden. I have nothing to expect there, and even those who wish to live in isolation can arrange their life more comfortably and better in Berlin.

Countess Dönhoff was very nice when I called on her at Charlottenburg. It was hardly necessary for me to speak to Count Redern. He will do — and leave undone — what he can. If only he had spoken to the Queen! Meyerbeer has promised both Frau von Lüttichau and myself, by the way, that I should play at court in January. Hülsen was very curt, refused point-blank to let me arrange a concert in the opera-house, and even pretended to be indignant that Fräulein Wagner was not to sing at my concert — but I did not take the hint. Not even a free ticket to the opera did he offer me. Still, when I called at his office, he was so civil as to ask me to be seated. For this one thing at least I have to thank his aunt's introduction. Herr von Lüttichau was far ruder to Frau Clara Schumann once.

Cousin Ernst is very well. His wife has recovered from her critical illness last autumn. He sends you his kindest regards and advises you to get information from a Königsberg banker as to whether it would not be wise to sell out fairly soon.

Dr. Franck I saw only for a moment. He was at my concert, but, touched as I was, I had so little time that I had to postpone my call on him until I return to Berlin. I met Countess Kalckreuth once or twice, though I could make no use of her kind invitation to look in some evening about theatre time for the reason just given. A Berlin author (apparently a second- or third-rate one) whom I met casually at table claimed to have met you frequently, dear Luise, as well as Dr. Vehse. His name is Max Ring and his writing and conversation are very boring by reason of his pretensions to cleverness and wit.

You ask me to describe my life here. But can a plant write its own biography? My life here is of a vegetable-animal nature, you see. Certainly you will never have the pleasure of freezing as I do in this place. The three or four lessons that I give every day exhaust me so mentally and physically and are such a strain on my nerves that I am no good for anything but purely mechanical exercises, pianoforte- and billiard-playing. There is no satisfaction to be had. The *Schlesische Zeitung* is not yet a patch on the *Königsberger Hartungsche*. The only things worth reading are the *Indépendance belge* and *Kladderadatsch,* but the delivery of these is very uncertain. The insipid French *Charivari* is better left unread unless one is prepared to be put out of humour.

Forgive me if I do not describe my three lady pupils, who are of the untalented, though not the most untalented, order. I have, however, brought them to the point of doing as they are told and treating me with proper respect. One of the most idiotic imaginable of French governesses makes me very nervous by her surveillance. The stepmother of the three girls is my *bête noire par éminence;* she has a sickly sweet aristocratic-Slavonic insolence and a shallow, frivolous taste in art, which, however, she expects me to satisfy. Worst of all is her pietistic Catholic bigotry, which is always treading on my corns. But I will stop, for who knows where I shall come out at this rate?

Nature is detestable here — flat, bare, sandy flats all around, not a single hill on the horizon. It is windy and often snowy. Food and service are tolerable and I have a good grand at my disposal. But those are indeed the only amenities.

This must be enough for today, but I close with a promise to write again soon if I hear that my letters are not unwelcome. . . .

321]

Berlin
May 28, 1857

I WAS so sorry to miss you! I had definitely counted upon a little trip to Bonn after the music festival at Aix-la-Chapelle, and a visit, longer by some hours than last time, to you and your brother. Now I hear from Isidore that you are arriving here the very day after I leave. Let us hope not to miss each other so completely next time.

I have not yet found time to thank you for so kindly sending me my dear father's library. On the day when it came I had to go to bed, where I stayed for nearly a week coping with the after effects of a cold caught in my attempts to see Prince Napoleon. After that I had the journey here, which was put off from day to day on account of my health.

Please excuse me therefore for not writing to thank you and tell you of the arrival of the books.

From what my sister tells me, you found it hard to part with some among them which, for you as for me, are bound up with tender memories. I am not so egotistical that I cannot realize this, and I want to ask you most earnestly to pick out for yourself anything that has a special value for you. I am sure my father never intended that those of his favourite volumes which were in a sense partly yours should come into my possession and I should feel myself quite unjustified in taking them. Do me the favour therefore of letting Isidore give you everything to which you are particularly attached. I must tell you again how sorry I am not to have been in Berlin when you passed through with Willi and Heinz. The sight of Willi always affects me strongly on account of the likeness. I have so many things to do today — the day of my journey — that I can only send this cursory greeting. All that I had to say to you about my mother, who after a complete reconciliation with the Frege family is at last able to meet her sister without feeling uncomfortable, I must leave to Isidore to tell you orally. . . .

322]

Berlin
July 24, 1857

I SHOULD like to tell you my news — which is probably no longer news to you — before the public announcement is made. Unfortunately I was not able to tell you last time you passed through Berlin.

I expect in a fortnight at latest to be married here to Fräulein Cosima Liszt, younger daughter of my beloved mentor and master. You made the acquaintance of my fiancée in the autumn of last year and it would give me great pleasure to think that she did not displease you, but made a favourable impression. In any case she is too amiable, too clever, and too beautiful for such a gallows-bird as I, don't you think? My future father-in-law, who has been spending a week with us to make the necessary preparations, will, I think, come back early next month for the great day from Aix-la-Chapelle, where he is taking the waters. We then go straight to Zürich, as we both cherished a wish to see Wagner again for a few weeks. I have, besides, other journeys in prospect for the near future. In September I propose to inflict myself as pianist on Copenhagen and Stockholm, and in October or November to play at concerts in Danzig and Königsberg with Laub. I should be immensely pleased if there were any prospect of my calling on you on this occasion and of seeing my dear little brothers, to whom I shall always remain as devoted (in spite of being a married man) as I professed myself years ago at Ötlishausen. You will not be so unkind, my dear Luise, as to put me from now on to some extent outside the circle to which we both belong? On the contrary I feel that, once I have my own hearth and home, I may perhaps be regarded in the future as better fitted to share, in so far as you will permit me, in the precious duty of preserving my father's memory.

When I tell you that I have now been acquainted with my future wife for nearly two years — a period which makes it almost impossible, I imagine, to be deceived in one another and enter upon an *over-hasty* union — I hope that you will take my communication in the right spirit and not strike me off the list of your relations. Cousin Paul and Herr von Gruner will be my witnesses, while my father-in-law is bringing in Kaulbach and — I think — Count Redern. My mother seems gradually to be growing more reconciled to my marriage.

PS. Kisses to Willi and Heinz, who will already have made friends with Cosima.

323]

[Berlin, 1860]

Dearest — I almost wrote " Mamma," for you have been so good and motherly to my ungrateful self about my latest family event. Thank you thousands and thousands of times for your welcome sympathy. My wife is really touched by your kindness. She was so immensely pleased with the gorgeous frock and all its accessories that I hardly knew which was the child of the two — she or our still nameless little one, who is to be christened Daniela Senta next month. Your note today has roused in me a feeling that I believed to be quite dead — namely, a warm affection for my kindred, which I now seriously intend to keep alive.

God knows I have had little opportunity to feed and nurse it, but although I had learned to do without it, I always felt that something essential, something really human, was missing. Now perhaps I may be able to recapture it. You know, I think, that Willi and Heinz (please embrace them for me) will always find their brother ready when there is anything he can do for them, uncle-like though his relation to them may be.

My mother or my sister will probably have told you of the *very remote* prospect of a post at Karlsruhe for me. The possibility of being near enough to see something of you and my brothers has always weighed with me in my desire to get away from Berlin. Musical life in Berlin, which is so cosmopolitan and at the same time so provincial in its varied activities, makes such exorbitant demands on my strength and my time that I can but rarely commune with myself and study the interests

I have at heart. You would have been right to accuse me of the most icy egotism, but you chose — as I realize with gratitude — to use your insight and make allowances for my apparent but unintentional indifference. The first fruits of Cosima's pen when she is allowed to walk as far as the writing-table — an impatiently awaited event — will be dedicated to you. You made a conquest of her at your first meeting and she still cherishes the memory of those early proofs of your kindness. In this she is a true German. Her liking for you has now been intensified by your renewed token of friendship, and for this let me thank you most cordially. A bright vision of Bonn is before us and we talk of you in happy vein.

You are right, my dear Luise, these confinements are no laughing matters. For a long time beforehand I shuddered at the idea of my presumably ridiculous role of onlooker, but was afterwards forced to admit the extremely pitiable side of such a role. And although my wife has what few women (you among the few) possess: a considerable amount of courage, I am glad that it passed off so well and am impatient now for the time when I can really breathe freely again.

This winter in Berlin looks like being a fairly uneventful, stay-at-home one for me. It is possible that a short trip to Paris for the first *Tannhäuser* performance may be my sole episodic excursion. (Everything is shaping admirably there.) Then of course I shall make a point of coming to Bonn for a day or two at least, when I shall bring you my greetings and thanks in person.

You may be interested to know that this business of my much harassed father-in-law's marriage is at last satisfactorily settled, the conclave in Rome having unanimously agreed to Princess W.'s request for a dispensation.

I felt I must write, but please excuse the haste and preoccupation that are inevitable on such a day. Lots of love to the *Junkers*, who are not developing any patriotic Mal-apartism, I hope.

324]

[Fragment; probably 1869]

PLEASE forgive the slight delay in sending this family communication, also the scantiness of these lines. I was rather out of sorts when I arrived here, just in time, from Basel, and I had to stay in bed yesterday.

My two eldest girls' projected visit to their grandmother and aunt in Berlin has just become somewhat problematical. A recent letter from my people there seems to indicate that the children's visit at this juncture might cause disturbances in the Bojanovski household, though they do not put it in so many words.

But what I have principally at heart is to tell you my ideas, in so far as you will allow me, for my two dear brothers' future. My firm conviction, which grows stronger day by day, is that the soldier's profession is the best for them. Even an uneducated sword-trailer is worth more than a half-educated pen-holder or jaw-wagger; and a well-instructed, clever soldier is to my mind the most refreshing of all phenomena. Destroy the Army as an institution, and the all-prevailing Jewish contamination will bring us to a state of progress to which bestial barbarism is to be preferred on purely æsthetic grounds.

Unfortunately I am quite without the Prussian complex. On the other hand I have, as you know, been a fanatical Bismarckian since before the great statesman's successes, and it would seem paradoxical for me, simply because the mob (including "Augusta") is now converted to him, to hang up my admiration for the successor to the revolutionary from above, Frederick the Great, on the nail. May I commend to you an admirable essay by Konstantin Franz in the German *Vierteljahrsschrift*, which you will certainly enjoy: "*Die deutschen Angelegenheiten auf dem preussischen Landtage*" (pp. 72–130 of the volume). . . .

325]

Florence
May 11, 1870

My dear Heinz,

It was very good of you to remember your promise and send me the good news that you were " through." Your " No, Your Excellency," pleased me greatly also. That was well and Prussianly — Bülowishly — said. Accept my thanks and congratulations.

It will not be at all bad for you to spend the summer in Thuringia. I hope your preliminary-service conditions are not too strict to allow of your covering twice the periphery of Weimar. If Colonel von Besser — but no, I remember that he is an old acquaintance of mine. I should be delighted to introduce you to any of my Weimar acquaintances if I could feel that *you* had anything to gain by knowing such people. But that is not the case. After all, Paul von Bojanovski will be better able to bring you into direct contact with anyone who repays the trouble of a visit.

Should you meet Hofkapellmeister Lassen (a Belgian by birth), please introduce yourself to him *personally* as H. von Bülow. He is an intimate friend of mine and is as charming and widely cultured a person as he is a thorough artist. The enclosed program will be of interest to him as proving that my first attempts to regenerate Italian music by an infusion of German have been successful. My head and my hands are indeed fully occupied here, but work is a pleasure when one sees where, how, and why one is going, as one does in the midst of these lovable people. Their most distinguished class is, by the way, the Army, just as in Prussia.

Best wishes to your dear mother and your brother Willi, who tells me that he is entering the university this year. If you should think of any way in which I can be useful to you, let me know at once and I will reply as promptly. We may perhaps meet before long. I arrive in Berlin on June 15 and shall certainly stop at Frankfurt and therefore at Weimar too on the way back.

326]

Milan
December 12, 1870

M Y VERY DEAR LADY,

I have been away from Florence a fortnight and only here, in the midst of preparations for a Beethoven festival, did I receive the truly terrible news of your great loss, first from my mother, then from Willi.

I cannot tell you what a really personal sorrow it is to me and how deeply it has shaken me to see your Heinz struck from the ranks of the living.[1] It will seem new and strange to you, almost improbable even, when I say that I had the tenderest affection for the boy. His picture has long had its place on my writing-table in Florence, and my glance was so often drawn to those noble and beautiful features and those compelling eyes, now closed. Believe me, I too feel the heavy blow that has befallen you and his surviving brother. Would that I could have died in his place, I for whom life has so little in store, in spite of the lamp's sporadic flickerings! He seemed to me so safe, so happy, in his young manhood. Purely on his account I took a certain joyous interest in the war — which in my heart I abhor, fully as I consider God's judgment on France to be justified — for I was glad that my brother's inherited military genius should find so glorious an outlet. I saw in this a hint, as it were, of the high things which Providence had in store, of new splendour for the name we bear, of the pride which his mother and brothers would have in him. Now all our hopes are null. To you, the illustrious daughter and mother of heroes, I need not attempt to offer consolation. Your love of the Fatherland and your idealism will soon transfigure your maternal grief into something far above earthly gratification. Poor Willi, how I wish I could be anything to him! But I am a life-sick man living solely for my sound-world. I am forgetting, though, that he has

[1] HEINZ VON BÜLOW, *half-brother of Hans, was killed in the Franco-Prussian war.*

you. May you be long spared to him. Above all, I wish he may be given physical strength to enable him to mould his future to the credit of his family, remembering that he has gained one precious thing, though one only, by this terrible blow: the conviction that " Life is not all good things the highest."

PS. I shall write to Wilhelm on my return to Florence, which I have had to postpone for a few days through illness.

327]

Florence
December 15, 1870

M Y DEAREST WILLI,

The portrait of the dead whom we mourn and yet extol is before me as I write. I now want yours, however, my fellow-mourner's, and am writing to beg you urgently to send it me. If you would enclose a copy of our hero-brother's last letter, you would satisfy a real craving of mine. I have no words to tell you of my sympathy with the loss of your life-companion and the incurable wound received by your dear mother, who has borne up so admirably under the cruel blow! But, believe me, I entirely understand your feelings and entirely share your grief. That I am able to do so you will realize if you recall that bitter day, seventeen years ago, when I received the news of our dear father's death, you being too young to grasp it.

Your letter conveying the sad news moved me deeply by the nobility of feeling it expressed. It is indeed only by rising to thoughts of the infinite, of other-worldly things, that one can find consolation in such sorrow. Love of the Fatherland and the enthusiastic response to duty, which render our mortal bodies of no account when the call comes to sacrifice them, will, I am sure, continue to work within you so that you will receive into yourself your brother's immortal spirit although his earthly form is taken from you. Your steps will in future be influenced and guided, under Heaven's blessing, by pride in your young hero and love for your heroic mother, whose sole comfort in life you now are. Be worthy of the dead, spend your life in perpetual sacrifice, for that also is honourable; although

Heinrich's death must always seem to us the most enviable gain to be drawn from life. God be with you and your noble mother.

328]

Hanover, Unions Hotel
January 28, 1879

Dear Frau Luise,

My thanks for your kind remembrance of me must necessarily be brief as I am up to the ears in professional tasks, pleasant ones, thank Heaven. I should have been very glad to take the opportunity of seeing you and Willi again, but my few odd days of leave are already filled up. It would not be worth while to play in so small a place as Cassel for the good of the Bayreuth fund, and that is now my only motive for playing at all in Germany. Cassel is as far from Hanover, however, as from here to you. Particularly do I wish to spare myself the sight of that clownish Jew who calls himself my colleague, and this would be difficult. Why not come over to us some time? Our music is practically up to metropolitan standards and well worth a railway fare!

I am glad that Willi has taken to dancing and play (*jeux innocents*, I hope?). It is the best thing he can do, provided he also contributes his mite to the entertainment of his fellow-men. . . .

My mother has been for months at Coblenz under the oculist Dr. Maurer, who a short time ago operated on her eye. It seems to have been successful, but one must wait and see. The Bojanovskis are apparently all quite well.

329]

Hanover
March 23, 1879

You have softened my heart so much that I am now willing to come to Cassel on your account and play the last five [sonatas] — Beethoven's testament — provided that the Hessen take enough interest in the Bayreuth fund (not being deaf, I hope) to contribute a reasonable sum, say a thousand reichsmarks. It cannot be immediately, however. And now will you do me a favour, as you have presumably more leisure than I and are in touch with booksellers? I have long wanted to possess the collected works of your late husband, my father. Would you be so kind as to order copies (one of each) of all his works, at my expense of course? They should be new; second-hand ones only if out of print. I could then bring them back as booty from Cassel in about three weeks' time.

330]

Hanover
April 7, 1879

I AM playing *next season* in Cassel in aid of Spohr's monument. This is already arranged with the board of directors. If I do pay you a musical visit before this winter is over, I should play, as everywhere, only in aid of Bayreuth. But the theatre is a quite unsuitable place for so serious a recital as one consisting of Beethoven's last sonatas. Frau Essipoff's " productions " and mine have nothing in common. Will you, dear lady, cultivate the habit of *withholding* from me the wishes and suggestions of Frau von C. and other acquaintances. I cannot indulge in that kind of thing.

331]

Meiningen, Sächsischer Hof
September 13, 1881

I AM really very sorry *not* to be able to fulfil your nephew's wish, not at least *in this season*. To explain the reason of my *non possumus* would be as boring for me the writer as for you the reader. I have so incredibly much to do this week — having promised my mother a short visit during the next — that I must ask you to forgive me if I answer thus telegraphically. It can't be helped, believe it or not, as you will.

HANS VON BÜLOW
to
his daughter DANIELA

332] [1]

Munich
April 6, 1868

THANK you for your charming letter, which pleased me very much. You have made good progress in French and in your writing, and I am charmed to see that you are beginning to think, and to express what you think, in a rational manner. I hope, dear child, you will continue to have these ideas and to learn to express them intelligently. Your father and your mother will continue to love you with all their heart, and as neither the one nor the other is stupid, it is right that their eldest daughter should not be stupid either.

I was very pleased to hear that you and Loldi are well, and I should enjoy seeing you gambol and play and hearing you talk (*shouting* is not talking) on the beautiful lawn by the beautiful lake where your good Uncle Richard has you to stay with him. Your poor papa has so many things to do; more than the sacristan at the church and not such pleasant ones. (Mamma will explain that to you.) But I am hoping to have less to do in a few weeks' time, when I shall be able to kiss all my four children one after the other.

Not being able to see you at present, I comfort myself with the thought that you, the eldest, are always good, that you are very fond of your little sisters and are as patient and indulgent with them as your kind mamma is with you. Never grieve your mother, child. I still remember the spot in the garden where you told such a naughty fib years ago. Your poor mother cried a great deal over it, and remember, a mother's tears are not like those of a child, which dry up with the first ray of sunlight, like flowers in the morning dew.

I am delighted that Boni has begun to do lessons and likes them. Kiss her for me. You see, dear Daniela, work is the only true enjoyment; you look back on it with joy for a long time because it feels so good to have done your task. It keeps you well too and you won't get pains in your head, your neck, or

[1] *Written in French.* — TR.

your tummy. One more thing your father asks of you: that you should be always polite and nice to the servants who do little things for you. Try to be liked by everyone. When I see you again, I want to hear you recite Uhland's fine poem *Die Einkehr* and everything you have learned by heart since. Your father has such a good memory, you know. It is because Grandpapa forced him to use it when he was young, and I am always grateful to him for doing so. I hope the peacock no longer bites the country children, and that the poor shorn Coss, who hid away like a child that has lost its shirt, has grown his hair again. Rub his neck well for him every day so that he grows pretty again. I am glad you are beginning to like music. When we meet again, I shall want to hear you sing too. Anna and Suzanne send their best love to you and your sisters, and hope that you are well and are having a real good time. Shake hands with Herminie for me and think now and then of your father, who loves you dearly whether he is present or absent, busy or not.

PS. Do you know the months of the year and the number of days in them? You must learn that soon so that you realize how precious time is.

333] [1]

Munich
April 27, 1869

I HAVE often thought of you, though I have not been able to write all this time. I have been very busy and very unwell. My rheumatic pains seized me when I came back from Ratisbon. I saw your grandfather there. He asked after his grandchildren and was sorry not to see them. When I told him how you and Blandine were growing in body and in wisdom, he was delighted. So now, little ones, do not give your papa the lie, but see that you think well, speak well, write well, and act well. It is so easy for you to grow better and wiser under your good mamma's supervision. Thank God for giving you so excellent a mother. There are such swarms of poor children in the world who have not this good fortune, and it is harder to be brought up in a

[1] *Written in French. —* Tr.

wicked world than by a kind mamma who knows such a lot and loves her daughters so dearly.

But I have not yet answered your two letters. The first, written in French, was not at all bad, although you were in rather a hurry to get away to your friend the little Bassenheim girl. I shall send it on to Grandmamma, from whom I heard this morning that she was well and also your aunt Isa and your little boy and girl cousins. Grandmamma is very anxious to know what you are doing, and as you write so conscientiously to me about your studies and amusements, I want her to read the letter for herself.

Naturally I shall ask her to return it. For I am making a collection of your letters, and it will be a pleasure to compare them presently and see what progress you have made in expressing your ideas.

I am glad you told me of the fault you committed the other day by giving Boni bad advice. From now on, you will give her the better sort, I hope. When one does wrong — one ought not to do it, but when one does — one must make up for it by being doubly obedient and industrious. The very first step towards reparation is, however, to make a frank confession and ask Papa's and Mamma's pardon. Remember, too, dear child, that, being the eldest, you enjoy many advantages over your sister. For instance, Mamma has already taken you to hear some beautiful music at the theatre and you ought, all the more, to give a good example in every way — every way, do you hear? — to your younger sisters, so that Mamma can always say to Boni and Loldi: " Imitate your sister Daniela, who is sensible and good and gives me so much pleasure."

So Eve always says " oui," does she? She is quite right: " oui " is a prettier word than " non." And Coss makes a great racket and breaks cups and devours sugar! Perhaps it is the big Russ's example which makes him so naughty. My friend Richter tells me, by the way, that Coss was ill and made himself worse by scratching all the time. Does Mademoiselle Herminie keep well now? Better than at Munich? Give her my very kindest regards. You remember my pupil Mademoiselle Heintz? Well, she is going to marry Dr. Hallwachs, who paid a visit to Uncle Richard the other day. Tell him that. Has Mamma heard from your grandmamma in Paris? I hope she is not so ill as she was. You know, she is very much like your mamma and I have her bust just above that clock of yours which is in my room. While I was away, Anna put Uncle Richard's two rooms in order for me and I can now work there more peacefully; for above and below my old room someone played the pianoforte all day so badly that Papa simply could not write.

Did you ever find your thimble again? (Do you know what it is?) And can Boni run her hoop with the new stick?

I am tired, my dear daughter, from doing so much work, and my back hurts me a good deal. I will write more another time.

PS. Speak distinctly and keep your things in order!

334]

Munich
May 11, 1869

THANK you so much for your letter, dear child, from which I see that your writing is steadily improving. Keep on in the good way. The cleverer your ideas, as time goes on, the more important will it be to be able to set them down clearly on paper so that those who wish to read them can do so without trouble.

So you have had a pianoforte lesson? Now I really am curious to know whether you will soon show any musical talent and not plague your teacher, of whichever sex, for nothing. Your papa advises you to try to sing everything that you finger out on the pianoforte. Are you still as hoarse as ever?

Loldi is, I hope, well again, so that you can all four enjoy the fine weather as you tumble about the garden. When I see you again — ask Mamma about when it will be — you must sing to me the song of the battle of Prague and a few others which Mamma will have taught you meanwhile. Yesterday there was another performance of your grandfather's *Legend of Elisabeth*. The King was there and all the students from the music school, but very few people besides because the weather was so fine. The orchestra did not play well. They have grown lazy and inattentive and are heavy with all the Bock that is drunk here in the month of May. In fact your papa, who does not drink Bock, but is very tired from all the lessons he has to give at the school in this hot weather, grew very angry and would very much like to get away from here.

It is nice of you to tell me quite frankly and honestly when your good mamma is satisfied with you and when not.

Your name is Daniela von Bülow, and Mamma will have told you the proverb which says: "All Bülows honest." So you see you must never tell a lie or hold back the truth or you will bring shame on your name.

So you liked the wild beasts? I am glad you have seen some real ones, as you will now be able to recognize them in your picture-books and always call them by their right names.

The monkey will, it is hoped, have shown you that it is not nice when a little girl makes grimaces, for she might then become so like a monkey as to be shut up in a cage by mistake one fine day. So Boni enjoyed the story of Wilhelm Tell? I am glad. Give her a kiss and tell her she must write me a nice letter too in a month from now.

Grandmamma has had very bad headaches, but is much better now. I shall write to her again tomorrow and will give her your messages. She has not said when she is coming again, because it is not yet settled when your aunt Isa goes with Uncle to Russia.

I now have a very clever and educated musician living with me. His name is Franz Servais (you must pronounce it the French way); he is twenty-one years old and looks very like your late uncle Daniel Liszt, whose portrait you know. Grandpapa recommended him very highly. He is studying music here with young Herr Bärmann and old Herr Cornelius, and I am glad to have him to talk to sometimes, as my loneliness makes me very sad.

Tell Mamma I will try to get Uncle Richard the Beethoven quartets arranged for four hands, but that there is not at present any good and complete new edition.

PS. I always think of you children when the sun shines and the birds sing, but have too little time and quiet to write what I should be able and should like to say to you if you were here.

335] [1]

Munich
May 27, 1869

YOUR letters always give me great pleasure and I am grateful to you for not forgetting your father and for letting him know what you are doing. I send your letters on to Grandmamma so that she may know too. She asked me to send you and your sisters kisses from her. So instead of giving Boni a smack on the cheek, give her a big kiss from Grandmother.

I hear that your mamma wishes to send you and Blandine for a fortnight to your aunt Madame Claire de Charnacé. She no doubt has good reasons of which I can but approve. I have indeed nothing against this visit, which will be a great pleasure to you and in some sort a reward for your good conduct, obedience, and application to lessons. Good-bye for today, my dear Daniela. I am very tired and ill, and above all have many tiresome things to do. Keep well and always love your mother and sisters.

336]

Munich
July 17, 1869

I HAVE today received your letter, in which you tell me about your stay at Seelisberg and all that has happened at Triebschen since you came back. Grandmamma, who is, I am glad to say, very well, has read it too. She sends kisses to all the four of you and hopes that you are all well and that you love each other like good little sisters and give your mother pleasure by your industriousness and obedience. You must not think, dear child, that because it is so long since I wrote, you are not in my thoughts every day. Mamma has told you that I have had a great deal of trouble and have been much taken up with pupils who are taking their examinations in a few weeks. (Let Herminie

[1] *This and the two following letters are written in French. —* TR.

explain to you what that means.) When the holidays set in I shall leave Munich, because the climate here is not good for me. It is the same with me as with your mamma, who used to be ill a great deal here, and with you, my dear children; for if you had stayed here, you would often have had to show Dr. Rubner your tongues and take nasty medicines, whereas in that lovely Switzerland you flourish like little angels. Here there is no lake to bathe in, no swing to send you up into the air when kind Monsieur Richter pushes you — indeed you may be very thankful to be at Triebschen and you should often thank your good Uncle Richard for letting you live there with Mamma. I hope you are not too noisy, for that would prevent him from working for the King of Bavaria. I should like very much to hear you sing Weber's Cradle Song and Sword Song. You know he is the musician who composed the *Freischütz*. I hope you are no longer hoarse. Later on you must sing pieces for two voices with Boni. She will take the lower part, which is more difficult than the upper. Are you still having pianoforte lessons? Boni is afraid of fish, is she? But not at dinner, when they come in cooked on a dish, I suppose. Kiss Boni and tell her that presently she is to copy out some French fables for me which she has learned by heart; not copy them from the book where they are printed, but from memory.

I am so glad you find the *Low German* fairy-tales amusing. It is a less difficult language than Russian, which little Seroff speaks. I saw his father here. He makes a great noise when he talks, and waves his hands and feet about, but he is very fond of Uncle Richard and knows a lot about his music.

I may possibly go to Italy for a little with Grandmamma, and if I do I shall send you some sweet wine for your birthday. You must give Loldi some too.

Good-bye, my dear Daniela. . . .

337]

Hanover
February 2, 1873

I HAVE done a pretty bit of travelling and have passed through many countries since I last wrote to you, or rather to your sister Blandine. (It was quite right that you in your capacity of elder sister should reply to the letters.)

You will be able to follow my route in detail from the programs of the concerts I have given since New Year, programs of which I am as usual making a collection for you. You will find them enclosed. Once, about a week ago now, I was near Bayreuth, at Bamberg; but I had not time to go and see you or to ask your mother to send you to see me. Besides, it would have been unwise to expose you to fresh colds and to take you away from your studies, which you are, I hope, pursuing as vigorously as in the past. We shall certainly see each other in the course of the summer, when the hour for resting after my exertions has struck, or in any case before my departure for America, which remains fixed for the end of August.

I hope that your health and that of your sisters leaves nothing to be desired and that your mamma is satisfied with you in all respects. You must love her a great deal and each other too and think sometimes of your father, who is always thinking of you. He is glad to think that he is coming nearer and nearer to the goal that he has set himself in your interests, a goal that he will certainly reach if Providence allows him for his work in the future the same moral and physical strength that he has had in the past.

In about a week I shall see Grandmamma in Berlin and we shall talk about you and your sisters. Perhaps I may see Aunt Isa and her children too, your cousins Victor and Vera. . . .

PS. Up to March 10 I shall be always *en route* and perhaps rather far away — as far as Russia (Riga and Dorpat) — so do not write to me just at present, but later. I will send you the address another time. In a few weeks you shall have another packet of programs. Take good care of them.

338]

Karlsruhe
April 19, 1873

I WAS reminded vividly of you on Easter Tuesday when I heard your grandfather's fine oratorio *The Legend of St. Elisabeth* performed at the court theatre here. Do you remember how your mamma took you to the theatre in Munich for the first time when this work was played and sung at King Ludwig's request? Well, it pleased the Grand Duke of Baden just as much as the King of Bavaria, and the Grand Duchess telegraphed next day to her uncle the Grand Duke of Weimar, your grandfather's friend, to say how much she enjoyed it.

Besides this concert I have done a lot more music, but this time, not to earn money, but to make good music and support good musicians. For my actual concert tours, which I undertook for the sake of you and the elder two of your sisters, came to an end on March 19. I am therefore sending the programs of these in a separate packet. Tell Mamma that I was satisfied with my concerts and more or less achieved my purpose, so that it will make no difference to you children if anything unpleasant happens to me on the way to America or in the country itself. It is now pretty certain that I shall go there in the last days of August, and before that I shall of course see you, talk to you, kiss you, and have reason, I hope, to rejoice over your develop- ment and your healthy looks. When that will be I cannot for the moment decide. In a few days — on Tuesday morning — I am going to London. One has to be known there, you see, before one is seen and heard in America. I shall stay in London until the end of May and visit your grandpapa at Weimar in the beginning of June. It is just possible that I may be in your neighbourhood. I shall probably rest during the summer months at Baden-Baden, as I am rather tired, even very tired. But all that I will write to your good mother myself at greater length and you will then hear from her how we can best manage to spend a day or two together.

I was glad to hear from your grandmamma that Blandine

liked the adventures of Herr von Münchhausen, which I sent her from Hamburg. But let her always remember that only people called Münchhausen may tell lies, not people called Bülow.

How goes it with your French? Do you like the language, and do you speak it quite fluently, better than the other girls? Very soon I am going to send you a little library of French classics for a present, from which you will be able to extract some historical knowledge also. Remember the importance of acquiring this in good time. But Mamma can attend to your education better than I and she will see that you learn everything in due course. Just do all she wishes with the best will in the world and keep on being good and kind.

339]

Florence
May 31, 1874

YOUR letter stirred me profoundly and I thank Heaven that you have retained your purity of heart under your mother's loving care. May your first serious step in life, marked by the day of your confirmation, be blessed in its consequences! It is right and good that you should seek reconciliation with your fellow-men and pardon from all whom you may have offended before being received into the Christian community. I, my darling child, have nothing to forgive you. I am proud of you and I give you my blessing today and for all time. Remember your unfortunate father in your prayers to the All-merciful and ask that he may soon be permitted to embrace you once more.

340]

Bad Liebenstein
August 19, 1874

IT is very charming of you to have thought of me and inquired after my health on hearing that I was not at all well. Unfortunately it is the fact. I took some salt baths, which only made me worse, and I therefore moved to Bad Liebenstein a week ago, where the air is better than in Salzungen and there are good hydropathics, to see what the cold-water cure can do. It is the last thing left for me to try. Nowhere in Germany can I find the quiet and seclusion that are essential for recovery. I am besieged in person and by letter by crowds of people who want to get something out of me as a " celebrity." Beware of following my example, child; do not be " celebrated " or have yourself talked about! As soon as there is sufficient improvement in my physical condition, I shall return to London, earlier than I intended, and work for the coming winter. I can do no music at present, as I am far too weak.

I was glad to hear from my friend Klindworth that you have a decided talent for music. If you are really keen on it — above all, if you are not missing any more important lessons for it (and *any other lesson* must be considered more important) — I am quite willing for you to practise the pianoforte. It would be better of course if you had a talent for singing. There are so many pianoforte-tinklers in the world, unfortunately for their long-suffering neighbours, that it is quite unnecessary for you to increase the number of these noisy people. Good and beautiful singing is rare, on the other hand, and there is more point in it, particularly as it requires a good ear, which is often absent in the said tinklers. Well, Mamma will decide. She will not expect the admirable Herr Joseph Rubinstein (to whom my kindest regards) to waste his time over you unless it is worth while. The useful needlework lessons have my whole-hearted approval. It is an excellent thing that you should be doing some foot-work too. I expect you thoroughly enjoy your skating. My parents never had me taught such useful and delightful exercises, I am sorry to say, and I congratulate you on being better off with your mamma. So you want to learn Italian with Fräulein Karthaus too? Very well. It is a splendid language, which sounds like music, and trains one to use lips and tongue correctly. In general it is a sensible thing to learn as many languages as possible while one is young. Later on, the memory is less receptive, and learning becomes more difficult. That is the case with me in English. I neglected to learn it in my youth and am now obliged to acquire it in my old age, which is a slow process. English is more essential today than Italian, however, and that is why I should like you to ask Mamma for English lessons unless you are already having them. I am also delighted to hear that a good dancing-master has been promised. He is as important a person to you girls as is the sergeant who takes boys for marching and drill. You must have noticed that the carriage and movements of men who have done military service are far superior to those of others. The head works better too when the body is nimble and supple than when there is a general appearance of indifference and slackness.

Finally I rejoice to hear that your teeth (a complete set of thirty-two white specimens, I hope) have been properly inspected by an American in Dresden. If they have suffered damage at his hands, let us hope it will prevent worse damage in the future.

All these items of news, which show that your mother is tireless in seeking your bodily and spiritual welfare, are very cheering to me and a real consolation in my present state of physical and mental pain. Give my love and kisses to your sisters, and love me at a distance. Perhaps the time will come when it is possible to do so at closer quarters. I must write to Grandmamma one day soon and will take the opportunity of sending her your cheery letters.

341]

Berlin
April 27, 1881

I WANT you to wear the Roman pearls I am sending you in remembrance of today's anniversary. If they suit your dress, wear them straight away tonight at the concert. And ask your grandfather whether he is inclined to go with you and me tomorrow morning to visit the grave of his son, your Uncle Daniel.

342]

*Meiningen
April 29, 1881*

I THINK of you without ceasing, and without ceasing do my tears overflow from happiness and sadness. April 27 was such a bright ray of hope that I feel as if my heart must have been in pitch-darkness all these twelve years. Your reappearance in my life, which none but the father of your noble mother could have brought about, has for me an Easter-like solemnity. I should like to connect it with a Passion Week preparation, so to say, of which you will find particulars in the enclosed letter from a poor woman who teaches Italian. You will like to keep it, I expect.

Will you send me your portrait to Wiesbaden soon (Sonnenbergerstrasse 10)? I arrive there on Tuesday. Tell me quickly of *one first wish* that I can gratify, whatever it may be. The only thing I would find hard would be *not* to fulfil it. God's blessings on your head!

With an overflowing heart,

Your Father —

soon, he hopes, to be worthy of the name.

343]

*Wiesbaden, Sonnenbergerstrasse 10
May 6, 1881*

THIS morning I have at last received your three nice letters, all at once, and also one from your dear mother. My best thanks for them.

I am staying here for a few weeks, in spite of the congestion of people which I so dislike, on my poor blind mother's account. She is better just now and her condition gives no cause for alarm, but the disease that is called old age is never to be trusted and one cannot be sure from one day to the next. Your presence here would not do her so much good as to compensate for the harm it might do you. I have therefore not the courage to summon you, much as I personally long to see you and to know you better. You may not have had the misfortune to inherit my nervous irritability, but all the same it requires a certain amount of self-renunciation to deal with your grandmother, and this I find difficult enough without adding to my burden by watching you suffer. For me, to share a trouble is to double it (not halve it), and of the trouble caused by sensitiveness (that is, small ones) I have a long and varied catalogue. I will explain when we meet. I expect to go to London at the end of the month for about three weeks; then — if my mother is no worse and provided my sister (at present in Switzerland) can relieve me here — on June 20 to Weimar for a similar period. There you might see me and at the same time your grandfather. You could stay at my hotel without any inconvenience. Will this plan suit you and have your mother's approval?

For today I am writing only of immediate practical matters, as I am feeling rather tired. The reaction from the fatigues of the winter season is wont to set in for me *coi fiocchi* with the warm weather. If only I had a house, a home, a shelter to offer you! But I do not trust fate; neither do I trust my Meiningen Duke, and material independence alone is the basis on which I can afford to wait for the intendantship. As you know, I only live at a hotel in M., with my trunks half-unpacked. But no more now. Let us fix our immediate attention on Weimar. Will you be returning to Villa Wahnfried in a few days' time? Send me more news soon.

The Catholic priest in M. prays for you, who are responsible through me for putting up the organ in his church. God be with you everywhere!

PS. Thank you for going to see my old friend the American lady. She was so delighted with you that she turned quite shy. The enclosed article from the *Frankfurter Zeitung*, just received, might be regarded as a caricature-reminder of the last days of April.

344]

Wiesbaden
10 Sonnenbergerstrasse, Park Villa
May 22, 1881

I HAVE put off answering your last letter far too long. There can be no greater pleasure for me than a letter in your handwriting. Yes, that is the photograph I want: no painting, in which a third party thrusts his disturbing subjective impressions on me. The reason for my silence — the chief one — is that I felt incapable of writing suitably about your well-meant gift of Dr. von Stein's Bruno twaddle; but the intense discomfort that I felt on reading it has been entirely dissipated by your clever, affectionate letter which followed shortly after.

I feel more and more each day that we must get to know each other better, and this can never be achieved by writing, even if I had the inclination or the talent to make a lively and satisfactory correspondent.

On June 1 I have to go to London for some weeks. I intend to curtail my visit as much as possible so that I may reach Weimar on the 20th. Then *on the 24th*, if your mother approves, I want you to *come to me* (and in a sense to Grandpapa). It is my name-day, which as a future Catholic I like to celebrate in preference to January 8, for which I am too Buddhistic. I shall try to find you a suitable room near my drawing-room in the Hotel Chemnitzius.

Is your mother very busy? If not, I will send her a French novel which I have just finished reading aloud to my mother. It seems to me to be in the *spirit of the age* and just right *for you* to read, so I want her to look it over and give her permission if she thinks good. It is: *Noirs et Rouges* by Cherbuliez. Even I was almost impressed by it.

My brother-in-law passed through yesterday with his eldest son, whom he is taking to Ballenstädt for the good of his body and possibly his soul, as he hopes. My mother is growing steadily better or at least is causing her relatives less anxiety. Can you read between the lines, my dear?

The rest when we meet in Weimar, subject to your dear mother's consent. You are to help your father to place your grandfather in the position of dignity that his years demand. Will you do this? Naturally I shall see that you have no contact with anything not quite nice; for instance, I should not allow any musician (not excluding myself) to smoke in your presence; do you understand? . . .

345]

London, W., 213 Piccadilly
June 10 [1881]

Your fourfold picture was like a charitable gleam of sunlight in the musical fog of this detestable city of commercial art, yesterday. Very many thanks. I shall have to swallow this fog a few days longer while I take stock of the possibilities and make my personal arrangements for a later date. I really hope that this Sabbath will be over in two years' time and that the field will then be clear for me to relieve Herr Rubinstein, as well as Herr Richter. The beery complacency with which Herr Richter conducted the *Meistersinger* — though he was far better than his German colleagues of the baton — convinced me that the choice of Herr Levi for *Parsifal* would probably be happier. It is easier to oil Jewish suppleness with ambition than some of our German geniuses, whose talent, like that of Herr R., is of the same order as *la beauté du diable* in the handsome sex. As for the Attila of the pianoforte, it is worth my while to go and hear him, artistically uninspiring as I find this form of study. Your father has the ambition to defeat his rivals in the long run in the *ears* as well as the eyes of his contemporaries.

I need not say how I long to be away from here and at Weimar, where I hope to welcome you on the 24th. I enclose your travelling expenses. Write a line to your grandfather — he will have returned from the Magdeburg Tonkünstler pandemonium — to tell him that I shall be coming on the 18th and you on the 24th. He may have some objection and then we might have to reconsider it.

Good-bye for today. Try to keep on (or to begin) loving

me, for I need it. I have been let down so often, *en gros* as *en détail*.

346]

London, W., 213 Piccadilly
June 17, 1881

I HAVE been very much out of sorts for a week and it seems to me highly improbable that I have any prospect of getting better if I stay much longer here. Therefore I have suddenly decided to go back to the Continent this very evening. I expect to be in Meiningen by Tuesday morning at latest, and a few days later — certainly before the 24th — in Weimar to prepare for you. The rest orally. I must just add many thanks for your letter the other day, which, owing to gout in my head, I kept two days unread under my pillow.

347]

Munich
Ottostrasse 12, c/o Herr Spitzweg
July 15, 1881

THANK you for your letter just received, which brings me at once the news of your indisposition and the more pleasant report of its having passed away. May the unfortunate episode of our failure to meet at Weimar have no further bad consequences for you and the harmony of your existence! As far as I am concerned, I hope to recover from them by means of hard work (hard on account of the temperature), and then in August, with a good conscience, to do something for my health after neglecting it more than was reasonable. To put it more plainly: I have a great deal of innocent music-paper to besmirch, as I must orchestrate my *Royal March* (for Ludwig II), which I propose to send to you and your sisters, if they care to see it, together with some other music shortly. This is instead of that *Innocence* which you mislaid (bad music I call it). You will assuredly not repent the purchase of the last dramatic poet of our century, but do not plunge too blindly into his poetry. Begin with the historical pieces and prose writings, reserving his classical tragedies (*Argonauts, Sappho,* and so on) for later. Meanwhile I will have sent to you tomorrow the promised works of Alfieri (autobiography and tragedies); read the second volume first (*Don Garzia* and *La Conjura de' Pazzi*). With them will be the more useful *Grammaire historique de la langue française.* I hope you will make good use of this, the *considered* study of which, a little at a time, should provide a healthier form of mental gymnastics than the stumbling over stones and fourfold roots.

Write to your grandfather some time, and should you receive a reply, direct or indirect, please let me know how he is. I must be brief today, as my already tired hand has still to promenade on music-paper for some hours. God bless you!

348]

Munich
July 19, 1881

In a pile of much travelled letters just to hand, I find four addressed to you, which I am at once forwarding.

You will have received my last letter, also the little parcel of books. A larger parcel is to follow in about a week, consisting of books which, on an overhaul of my library, I deemed to belong in a sense to you rather than to me. Some of your dear grandmother's, for instance, and others that are a legacy from Daniel, your uncle. The various pieces of music which are being sent along with these will, I expect, wander into the special possession of your sister Blandine, but I leave you to settle the distribution amicably between yourselves.

On the other hand, you will receive, the day after tomorrow, an heirloom which is a collective present to be shared by you and your sisters in the same room. This handsome gift, which was given me nearly a quarter of a century ago by your grandmother, has lost nothing of its outward or inward value all this time. You will like to have it and will find it useful. Only let the Bayreuth clock-maker regulate that tendency to lose which it possesses. In other respects the chronometer goes and strikes perfectly. I have been testing it myself for a few days.

> Employ your time, it flies away amain;
> Be orderly, for thus more time you'll gain.

I hope you are not suffering, like your father at this moment, from the heat and the need to fight against it.

349]

Munich
July 21, 1881

I AM answering your letter, which gave me unmitigated pleasure, by return, as I am on the point of starting on my travels. The heat is so comet-like that I am able neither to keep awake by day nor to sleep by night. Impossible to work with one's hands at anything that demands co-operation of the head. I am hurrying off to Switzerland and shall settle wherever I am best able to breathe. As I wish to vanish until the end of August, I cannot very well send off your letter to my mother from Munich and I am therefore returning it. Her present address is Leberberg 5, although I am not sure of it. Last time it was Villa Anna, Sonnenbergerstrasse. As my father's second widow, Frau Luise von Bülow (*née* Countess B.W.-Dennewitz), also lives in the Sonnenbergerstrasse, it would be safer to address to my mother in her full name: Frau Franziska. Really, though, I am of opinion that nothing is served by continuing to write. Especially as you have no need of extra correspondents. But that is as you please. Equally superfluous does it seem to me to send a reply to Rome. As the Sibylla of your grandfather's biography [1] telegraphs daily to Fräulein von Schorn and receives a reply, the letter to you is an attempt to get in touch which you should silently ignore. As far as I know, you do not owe the lady in the Via del Babuino one word. But enough of all that.

Carl Lindau's *Der beste Ton* (Erfurt, Bartholomäus) you will have to have transcribed, as my copy was lost at Weimar. Propaganda *for this* in your immediate (unavoidable) neighbourhood seems to me very desirable and useful.

[1] PRINCESS CAROLYNE SAYN-WITTGENSTEIN, *Liszt's famous friend. At this time she was living in Rome (Via Babuino).*

One of your sisters might study the book and then insist upon having the most important rules of conduct observed by anyone who acts clownishly. That provides a collective way of killing time, which is to be preferred to individual time-killing.

Count Gobineau's *Nouvelles asiatiques* I ordered and have just received and shall presently be sending to Frau von Ov[erbeck] in return for a transatlantic curiosity that she is going to show you by my request.

The clock-maker has again kept me waiting two days. Even the firmest north German determination can make no headway against this south German slackness. I will stir him up again this afternoon and tomorrow morning, however. Tomorrow (Friday) evening I am thinking of exchanging the heat of the Bavarian residential capital for other heat elsewhere. That music is a winter sport and unsuited to the summer seems to me to be truer than Portia's idea of it.

Fix your hopes on M[unich], where you will hear all the Beethoven symphonies, and better than elsewhere.

Let my bad scribble be a warning to you; though that is really no longer necessary. I can conscientiously congratulate you both on your talent for letter-writing and on the practical cultivation of it. Only keep your little head from being filled up with persons and personalities. I have been working for years, and not without some success, at eliminating unessentials of every kind which check intercourse and make it difficult to control my own thoughts or what gives rise to them.

350]

Meiningen, Charlottenstrasse 4,
December 9, 1881

I HAVE put off thanking you for your good letter from day to day, for I hoped to emerge from my very depressed mood as also from the nigger labour imposed on me by the conditions here. The mood has improved with the improvement in my physical state; as regards the second " drag-shoe," I can only hope to breathe next week, when the seventh subscription concert (orchestral) and the sixth and last chamber-music evening will be

over. But I fear it will be difficult for you to hold out so long —
I hope so indeed — and you might misinterpret a longer silence.
Hence these few lines, if my fellow-men — in particular the
official *seccatori,* including the *Serenissimus* — will allow me
to write them.

It was another excellent idea of your mother's to send you to
Rome. I am convinced it was the best thing and I am sure that
you share that conviction and will retain it to the end of your
life. It is a special joy to me to hear that you are nursing your
venerable grandfather. Who but you, with due respect for the
services rendered by Fräulein von S. in collaboration, would
have been able to take over this mission at just this moment?
You seem able to stand the climate too, thank Heaven, though
worse than this it certainly could not be.

Take this opportunity of shaking off your " paternal " accent in the *linqua toscana.* If you knew how unhappy I had been
all my life over my inheritance of a stammering tongue and my
clumsiness in general, and how happy I was to find, when we
met again, that these tendencies, these " original sins," had been
reduced to a minimum by the wholesome influence of education on your excellent mother's system! For this reason you will
have so little difficulty, thank God, in putting up with all the
various " Steins " who come your way: the Rubinsteins, the
Schornsteins, and so on, contact with whom always sends me
into a blind rage. To come up against something unpalatable in
a fellow creature and have to say *tat twam asi* — dreadful!
That is really why I find it so difficult and so depressing to live
in Germany. Self-love has ever been the least of my faults,
but in such cases one feels like smashing all the mirrors. But
to return to things that matter. I am hoping for the support of
your grandfather's sympathy when he hears that I have not yet
sent in my resignation and may possibly not be forced to do so.
The Duke appears to be more and more aware of the fact that
I must now be a *freier Herr* in more senses than one if he wishes
to keep me partially and employ me occasionally. He is sensible
enough to see that he can offer me no equivalent for the sacrifices
I have made in health, time, comfort, money (yes, money!),
and must therefore ease things for me in other ways. The engagement of a serviceable conductor for next season would be of

paramount importance to me. I have already found one who would do, in the person of young Mannstädt, who is probably known and appreciated at Bayreuth, where he coached Betz, Niemann, and others in their parts for the festival performances.

Up to January 3 I shall have all I can do to polish my players, now that I have brought them out of the rough, for we have twenty orchestral concerts ahead of us in Berlin, Hamburg, and Breslau. On the 4th, 5th, and 6th of January there is a cycle of Beethoven concerts in the Singakademie, on the 7th a Mendelssohn evening, and on the 8th and 9th two Brahms concerts with the composer, who is playing one of his concertos, with me as conductor, and conducting the other, which I am to play.

This is a crushing blow for Joachim and his Crusca, my child: something he never dreamed of, something from which he will *not* recover.

You will not be able to see the implications of all this and it is impossible for me to explain it to you. What a pity you cannot be in Berlin for this *epoch!* It would be an unspeakable joy to me because it would provide the best opportunity of our drawing nearer to each other. Well, I must close.

Thank you for all the *minuti dettagli* of your dear *nonno*, to whom I send *miei più ammiratiosi rispetti.*

Write again soon.

PS. Please remember me to Sgambati, the last of Italy's musicians.

351]

Meiningen
December 19, p.m. (1881)

Many thanks for your letter and also to your grandfather for his. I cannot write to him *alla buona*, as I do to you.

My nerves are again in a turmoil. Last night I read the *lettres intimes* by Adler (who is occasionally a Geyer),[1] with a preface by Monsieur Gounod. The great Master is sure to have them. Borrow them of him. They are extraordinary and terribly true to life. The sleepless night and today's rehearsals with the orches-

---

[1] *An "eagle" who is occasionally a "vulture." — Tr.*

tra, also my experiments with my Bösendorfer (I am tired of
Bechsteins for the time being), on which I have been thunder-
ing out the Spanish, Italian, and Hungarian rhapsodies of your
nonno in preparation for my February tour, have combined to
make me very weary. All the same, I am sending a reply by
return, as who knows what the next few days may bring forth?

I wish this next month were over. I am not nervous about
the Berlin expedition, but it gives me a lot to do if I am not to
be nervous about it in the end. It is a frightful risk, and for me
to bring it off successfully you would have to be just celebrating
your second birthday; that is, your father needs to be two decades
younger. However, nothing venture, nothing have. After all, I
have the cleanest musical conscience with regard to Beethoven.
If only none of my forty-eight-year-old fingers comes to grief on
the journey; if only, if only! I might go through an endless list
of, I trust, groundless fears, but to enumerate them might be
fatal.

Peccato once more that you cannot come and hear us this day
week. The not very piquant menu will be served with such supreme elegance that even the Master would find it *anti-papa-
verico*. So do come to Budapest for January 10. Why do you hesitate? Because of the journey for him? Believe me, locomotion
is necessary to him, it is medicine, it belongs to his diet. Or is it
that you have grown so deeply attached to the Eternal City? Oh
— don't forget — buy and read *Transformation* [*The Marble
Faun*], in two volumes, by Hawthorne, *at once*. It is in the Tauch-
nitz edition and is far more delightful to read than *The Scarlet
Letter*. A wonderful reproduction of the physiognomy of your
former residence, a triple extract of its atmosphere! If, as an
" obedient " daughter, you find yourself shortly in a bookseller's
shop, would you inquire for me whether Achille Torelli's dramatic works have appeared in print? I knew the author, a charming fellow, and found great enjoyment in his pieces, which impressed me by their elegance of expression and unpopular lack
of dénouement, so, to come to the point, get them for me. I shall
ask you for them in Pest, where I shall spend *a few* days in
February, if only in passing. (It seems to me unbecoming for
your grandfather to be asked to listen to ordinary pianoforte
recitals, for which his faithful followers are indirectly invited

to take tickets, yet I am *forced* to give concerts on my own account. It is the old story of meeting the costs of furnishing my flat and so on.)

I think of taking this opportunity (April 15) to start on a pianist's tour of Scandinavia: Copenhagen, Stockholm, and other places, where I am still unknown. For both mind and soul freeze for lack of *braise*. My use of this slangy term, which will not be unfamiliar to you, is pretty well a proof of it.

Baroness von Overbeck was here for the Brahms concert, asked after you in the warmest manner, and of course charged me with the usual " *milles choses*." Her trip did her a lot of harm and she has been seriously ill in Berlin for some weeks. Professor " Leiden " would seem not to be the right homœopath.

Please give Count G[obineau] my *sympathies respectueusement admiratives*. His fellow-townsman *au cœur* (?) — *léger* does not exist for me, but that need not concern you. Little Kap[ellmeister] M[annstädt] turns out to be a Jew. I chose him because he was a good musician and was available, *and* because of his attachment to the Crown Prince, whose washing he irons! In order that the orchestra and its traditional style, which I have sought to establish with such exemplary zeal, should have any prospect of a permanent basis, it was necessary that the future duke of M. should be interested. But think in how many different places I have toiled *pour le roi de Prusse,* only for my Jewish successors to root up all I have done. It is the curse of my life. But in this case I had no choice. Klindworth is too well off in Moscow and would be badly off here. Kapellmeister M., with a salary of four thousand marks — one thousand less than mine — does not take up his work here until September 1, 1882.

Have you got to know Frau Minghetti yet? A really interesting woman, even though she is, as the *Berliner* says, a very " late " Froufrou!

Best wishes and a " happy Christmas," my beloved child. . . .

352]

Hamburg
January 10, 1882

You did keep me waiting a little, but all the more did I enjoy your splendid letter, which Friend Bechstein handed to me at the station last night by way of provision for the journey.

My very best thanks! All that you write is so charming and sensible and refreshing to read, and it gives me such intense pleasure to be able to give an unqualified approval to many of your views and the resolutions which arise from them! *Mille grazie!*

Certainly I chose the first suitable visiting-hour to go and see your excellent friend, if only in remembrance of the 27th and 28th of April last year. On the following day I was having a cosy lunch with her, when Anton Rubinstein arrived, and made himself so unpleasant to me that our long-threatened break became a fact. Thank God it has come to that at last! An accomplished fact can be as refreshing as a Seidlitz powder. The original cause of our quarrel was his behaviour to my excellent old fellow-pupil and friend Klindworth, who to my great delight was present at our six orchestral concerts in Berlin.

It is war in that quarter, then, but with Countess Mimi all is idyllic, peaceful, and extremely comfortable. Your doing! She is going to write to you and tell you of my doings, which have been most surprisingly successful. Then she is going to invite you over in March — when there will presumably be a second Meininger campaign, in which you could share. All the same, it is a pity you were not here this time. It was *very good*. I was more content with myself and the world than I have been for years. Can you not obtain the notices in the *Kreuzzeitung* (or the *Börsenkurier*) in Rome by diplomatic means — that is, from a diplomatic source?

I have sent all my cuttings to the Duke and have therefore nothing by me to enclose. Only the menus for today and tomorrow. Those you shall have, and — while I remember — the itinerary, so that you know where to write.

12th, 13th, Kiel; 14th, Bremen; 15th, Hamburg; 16th, 17th, 18th, Berlin; 19th, 20th, 21st, Leipzig, Cöthen, Halberstadt. On the 22nd, back to Meiningen, after which, on the 26th or 27th, I propose to start on my pianist's tour of the black-and-yellow portion of central Europe *pour varier mes plaisirs et les ennuis d'autrui*, or the other way round.

So glad that *Transformation* came in useful as a practical Baedeker for Rome. Delighted to hear of the gratifying improvement in your good grandfather's health. Sincerely sympathize in any other event that calls for congratulation or condolence.

Do write again at once, as I shall then receive the letter to-morrow week (Wednesday) in Berlin. I am staying at the Park Hotel, near the Skating Rink (selected as a concert hall this time because of the popular character of the program). Last week I chose the Hotel de Rome, as the six concerts took place in the Singakademie. With the exception of the fourth, a Mendelssohn evening, all of these were sold out so early that there was no box-office open at night.

" The Duke shall praise his servant." The Crown Prince was there five times, and last night the Kaiser came too. What a triumph over Hanover! Whether deserved or undeserved, I can honestly say that it was *essential* to me. My " undergoings " (Stahr invented the word) on the banks of the Seine were still weighing on my — liver, more heavily perhaps than I dared to admit; for a confession of sensitiveness to irritation is too dangerous a weapon to put into the hands of one's fellow-men. Only the thick-skinned escape, and that because it hardly pays to wound them.

In between I have had a visit from the future director Stägemann, one of the most charming fellows in the theatrical world. He tells me that Hans Richter and Franck are here and will come to the concert tonight. What a conflux! Brahms has also arrived here from Berlin for no other reason but to come and hear us! So he has a heart, you see; not so big as his head, but far bigger than that of most great men, your unique grandfather excepted.

Well, dear Daniela, when are you going to leave Rome? You know that I am going to arrange for a room at Meiningen for you in the summer, and also that my next pianoforte tour is to be devoted to that home which is not yet paid for.

Good-bye now, and many thanks for your good wishes, which arrived this time so opportunely.

Never since I can remember have I spent so full and honourable a January 8 as this.

353]

Hamburg
April 14, 1882

BRAVISSIMO and *mille grazie*, my dear, dear daughter. I am quite proud to have such convincing proof in your letter of the 7th (that of the 5th had crossed mine) that your heart is in the right place. You have now made it possible for me to reply to Count Gravina. I am sending you the letter, not only that you may see to its safe dispatch, but so that you should know what is in it and also inform Blandine.

From your latest communication I gather that you are now in Venice, and am sending this registered to that address. I will write to Blandine as soon as I have time, which will be at Copenhagen (Hotel d'Angleterre), where I arrive on Sunday the 16th; or I may write from Christiania, where I have concerts on the 25th, 27th, 29th (Upsala on the 26th). Whether I visit Stockholm on the way there or back is not yet certain. I hope you are able to put yourself in my place to the extent of realizing how painful it is to me to be unable to cope with the obligations that crowd in upon me. Here particularly I have very little time because I must use the opportunity to take the Roman baths (which I invariably do in Hamburg). That means two hours each time and you have no idea how overrun I am with engagements. In addition it is no light matter to keep my brain and fingers in condition for their daily task.

There is much, very much, that I want to say, to confide, to you. Heaven grant that all my plans may succeed. It would then be possible for me to come to Bayreuth in August for Blandine's wedding. But enough for today.

For the present, then, it is settled that you spend the first fortnight of June at Wiesbaden with me at my mother's. Perhaps you could be with me for the Aachen festival (May 25–30).

I am not playing myself until the 30th, but am under the (monthly) obligation to listen to all the rest, and have besides to rehearse my pianoforte solos with the orchestra.

Is Blandine in Venice with " you " (singular or plural)? Let me have a few more details. I should like them almost mathematically, pedantically precise. Answer at once, please, addressing in the first place to Copenhagen, Hotel d'Angleterre, and to plain Dr. Hans von Bülow. The Ducal Saxon Hopkapell-intendant, Freiherr, and the rest of it, are not touring the northern hemisphere just now, but only the *suonatore di cembalo*.

Pray for me as I pray for you. Yes indeed! With God's help we may yet have a harmonious dissolution of the chief dissonances in our life's destinies. Perhaps! That is, if we act and, above all, think *viribus unitis*. For this I count primarily and indeed solely on you, my beloved Daniela.

354]

Copenhagen
April 23, 1882

THANK you for your delightful letter of the 18th, which I found here yesterday on returning from certain private towns which had been better left unconcerted: Odense on Fünen, Aarhus in Jutland. Last night I gave my third concert here, the last for the present. All three have been very satisfactory and tomorrow morning I go on to Stockholm (Hotel Royal). It is two hours by steamer to Malmö, then eighteen hours by train. There I am playing on the 25th, 27th, 29th (Upsala on the 26th), and hope to have time to write to Blandine. Perhaps you will let me have a brief note by return to say how you all are. On the 2nd and 3rd of May I play in Christiania (also Hotel Royal).

After this very business-like itinerary — which was necessary to prevent our letters from crossing or going astray, with all the attendant *malintesi* and *imbrogli* — I will now get on with the news, beginning with the least important. I am threatened with several interruptions; still I hope to achieve a few connected sentences. . . . There, a knock, and enter Mr. Niels Gade! *A tout seigneur tout honneur.* He is one of the most charm-

ing of musicians, after " Grandpapa." First, then, please thank
Frau Pinelli — call her Madame de Chavigny, she will tell you
why — . . . for her kind remembrance. She is a white black-
bird, containing in her person the contradictory qualities of a
charming blue-stocking and a graceful Berlinoise.

Secondly, do you ever see the *Allgemeine Deutsche Musikzeitung,* edited by my former pupil Lessmann, who escorted you
on that journey of evil memory from Weimar to Jena? Since
April I have been a regular contributor, and am also sending him
short articles from Scandinavia every week. I should like it if
you would read it even though it cannot obviously meet with your
unqualified approval.

Thirdly, ask your dear mother *how* she wishes me to hand
over to her Blandine's dowry of fifty thousand reichsmarks (now
in bills at Frege's, together with similar sums representing your
bit of capital and Isolde's), also when. I have naturally to give
notice of withdrawal to Cousin Woldemar.

Fourthly, I have to spend a few days at Meiningen, for the
purpose of repacking and so on, before I go to Aachen on May
25. Where could we best meet? Perhaps in M. itself. Could you
find an escort for the journey?

Fifthly, you will for the first time read a false report about
your father in the papers, which in fact is no such thing. It is
closely connected with my plans for being present at Blandine's
wedding and also for hearing *Parsifal,* to which all my sympathy
goes out, whereas the firm of Wotan & Co. is a Sansara for me.
I hope you have none of these fiendish mosquitoes (*zanzare*) in
Venice yet.

Sixthly, it was a great, great joy to me to hear that my letter
to Comte Gravina met the case. I was strangely embarrassed; it
is so devilish hard to write to a complete stranger on intimate
matters, particularly when one has received so little encouragement to do so as was expressed in the note of which I told you. I
hope to God that it will have the desired effect. I used to have no
art in writing and used often to think myself a part of that force
which wills to do good and produces evil, in fact a macadamist of
hell. I look to you to provide pleasant surprises for me in this
respect. Let it be soon, my dearest Daniela.

355]

Christiania
May 6, 1882

YOUR dear letter of April 27 was forwarded to me from Stockholm last night. I was immensely pleased to find that you had remembered me on this particular day as I you.

On the 28th I wrote to Blandine from Upsala, where I had a little leisure, but unfortunately I addressed it to the Grand Hotel, Venice. I hope it will be sent on to her at Bayreuth.

Thank you for your reassuring and favourable account of your Sicilian brother-in-law.

I return to Stockholm tomorrow morning (since my movements are an indispensable preface to any written communication) and shall be in Copenhagen on the 12th. Please send me, by return if possible, a line to tell me of your safe arrival. (Hotel d'Angleterre.) On May 17 I shall be in Berlin at the Tiergarten Hotel, and on the 23rd I expect to see you at Meiningen, or, if you prefer it, at Eisenach, to save you the roundabout way. We could then go straight on to Aachen. Wait, though, there is no such hurry; let us say the 25th. Wait once more! You must of course pass through Meiningen, coming from Bayreuth; would it not be *better to meet at Würzburg on the 25th?* Frau Ritter could fetch you. She is now, and for good reason, devoted to me. Never mind why, dear child. We can finally talk over things in Berlin (May 17–22).

Cousin Frege will carry out your dear mother's wishes with regard to Blandine's dowry. It will probably be advisable to make a trip from Berlin to Leipzig in connexion with it, however.

Your grandfather will, I fear, wear himself out again, although movement is essential to his well-being, and the sleep in which he indulges during the performance of his works is a steady aid to recuperation. But I wish your friend Adelheid could sprinkle an adequate quantity of insect-powder on the court gardens of Weimar.

All that concerns me, dear daughter, I will save up for our

reunion, which will certainly be more successful this time. We shall be together at Aachen, Wiesbaden, and — I am going to ask to have you until June 22 and will then bring you back as far as Nuremberg.

356]

Copenhagen
May 12, 1882

As I know no lady in Aachen who is a " real old maid " or an " elderly married woman " — how should I? — the only thing for you to do is to stay at the hotel with me. However, as I have invariably given your mother " full powers," it is possible that she may still exercise them and refuse to let you go.

You seem not to know the program. I am playing on the 30th only and am only on duty besides that for the rehearsals of my Brahms concert. Perhaps you will be forbidden to attend anything so heretical? Otherwise you might be tempted to go to it with me?

How did you come to write to me at Meiningen? A matter of politics, I suppose. What is the meaning of: " as regards your proposal to come to B. for the wedding, which seems to present some difficulties to Mamma "? The bewildering conjectures aroused by the many riddles contained in your few lines I am dismissing from my mind for the time being, as both today and tomorrow night I have to serve up some solid portions of music.

I therefore *must urgently* request you to write to Berlin, Askanischer Hof (where I arrive on Tuesday evening, May 16) and let me have the wording full and clear (*" alle Bülow'n ehrlich"*) — of these insinuated ukases, in so far as they concern me in my relation (or non-relation) to you and Blandine. It is after all by no means necessary for me to be among the listeners to *Parsifal:* the fifty thousand francs which I contributed have of course no value, as they come from an independent non-echo. Please tell me the simple truth, but quickly.

357]

Hotel Fürstenhof, Berlin
May 19, p.m. [1882]

ONLY a line or two today as I do not feel at all well. The inevitable reaction has set in. I hope I may shake it off sooner than usual.

About your letter from Meiningen: it was a slip. All right. Let Blandine's wedding go forward without change of place. My projects are not yet absolutely fixed, but I expect to go to Hamburg early in August, where I am to rehearse Glinka's *Life for the Tsar* at the Opera in September. I *must* be in Aachen by the 25th. Will you therefore arrange for our meeting at Würzburg a day earlier? I hope Frau Professor Wüllner will be able to chaperon you on the 30th if I am playing. In addition you will find my friend Bösendorfer of Vienna the most charming cavalier possible.

Perhaps you will write to my mother and ask her to reserve you a decent room near hers at the Villa Anna on June 1, for you could not stay at the hotel with me. Naturally I called on your friend Countess S. I have to thank *you* for her being so thoroughly kind to Marie also. I hope you will find out from *her* all that it may interest you to know, for *I* am too shy to tell you myself.

I have a ghastly headache and am going straight to bed (at eight-thirty), where I shall try to do a little work on the second act of *Parsifal*, the pianoforte score of which I bought yesterday. I intend to go to one of the August performances at Bayreuth incognito, except to you. But more of this when we meet. . . .

358]

Meiningen
May 22, 1882

AM just back from Berlin and wish to confirm my telegram of yesterday. A letter from Wüllner was delayed and I was therefore uncertain of the date on which I had to arrive at A.

It is well that you should know how I stand with W. Read his letter and give it me back when I see you.

The journey has tired me so much that I shall never risk day-travelling again. I am therefore leaving here by the evening train on Thursday, reaching Würzburg at eleven-five. We shall go on to Mainz and Cologne, therefore, at a quarter to two in the morning.

I hope you are hardened to night journeys.

PS. It will be Nuellens Hotel at Aachen.

359]

Meiningen
June 22 [1882]

ALTHOUGH not in writing vein tonight, as I am in the clutches of a formidable cold, which will not be easy to shake off, I must send you a line of greeting, even though it takes the form of a covering note for the photographs for which you asked me. Perhaps the American views which I found awaiting me may move you to pleasure or pain or whatever you like to call it. Should *one* of them — I do not need to say which — seem to you better suited to another writing-table than yours at Wahnfried, *lei sta padrona.*

Your excellent companion promised me so faithfully to see you safely home that I have no need to ask how you fared. Neither do I doubt that you feel happier in your own surroundings than when you were travelling with me, and, knowing this, I need not reproach myself for having withdrawn you too long from those who have an unchallenged right to your company and to whom you give your almost undivided sympathy. Perhaps your reappearance at just this point may help to tide them over the first practical disappointments or drawbacks. It may be that in giving you various samples of my capacity for taking things humorously I have supplied a recipe of which you may make use.

Before I take the hasty leave of you which is imposed on me today, I want to thank you most warmly for the dainty paper-knife, of which I should hardly have been aware when packing, had not Marie drawn my attention to it; also for the two

Gobineaus, which I look forward keenly to reading. I am going to bed early and *Renaissance* shall be the Sister of Mercy who sends me to sleep tonight. . . .

360]

Meiningen
June 24 [1882]

THE ducal coffer which I am presenting to your future brother-in-law as a honeymoon present was dusted yesterday and dispatched today to Bayreuth. Have a look at it with your sister to see if it looks good enough and let me know the verdict.

Shall you be writing to Würzburg? To Elsa Ritter or her mother? That would be nice, for you would be helping me to put the mannequin's head on properly. I am quite exhausted by my own attempt.

I have just had a very sensible letter from Herr Gross which tells me all I want to know. I shall have to put off answering him until tomorrow, so if you should see him meanwhile, please give him my best thanks.

I put inside the coffer a humorous book which may amuse your sister, and, for yourself, a report of the Rhenish music festival which we endured in company. It comes from the pen of Monsieur Jules Ghymers, whose attitude seemed to us both to be very correct. There's a man who might make a better *Parsifal* guest than many a German colleague! . . .

361] [1]

Meiningen
June 26 [1882], evening

THANK you for your letter, dear child, to which I cannot now reply. I am obliged, in spite of my neuralgia, to go to Frankfurt, for my friend Raff *has just died*. It was he who supported me in my worst hours when everyone else had failed me, and the least I can do is to honour his memory by appearing at the funeral. Poor widow, poor daughter!

[1] *This and the following letter are written in French. — Tr.*

If your mother claims the silver as her property, so that she may give it to your sister, I shall honour her claim without protest. The only thing is, there is nothing like all of it left. But that is not my doing. It was my mother who took charge of it at Munich in 1869 when I was forced to beat a retreat. I hope you will thoroughly enjoy making preparations for the festival.

362]

Meiningen
July 1, 1882

*T*ORQUEMADA[1] was dispatched to you immediately on my return from Frankfurt. Naturally I saw no one but the family there, and if I was rather too much with them, that was hardly to be avoided. The book provided a most welcome distraction during my journey, which in itself was bad enough to keep me from ever leaving or returning to my atrocious village again. This work of our great Victor's is by no means senile; indeed, I consider it very powerful and full of vigour. I believe you will like it. As for criticizing its faults, or rather its oddities, one may safely leave that to people of limited intelligence, mediocre minds. I hope you will do as I do and adopt as soon as possible the wise habit of not asking for perfume from a tulip.

I am deeply grateful to you for thinking so often of poor me in the midst of the sublime hubbub in which you are living. You can, I hope, still breathe and enjoy yourself, though there must be moments when you are suffocating. Could one indeed enjoy the sensation of being able to breathe without an experience of suffocation for contrast? You are too sensible to ask to be initiated into all my woes, for to describe them would be to renew them and delay the arrival of that benefactor who is called Oblivion. I have not yet even finished swallowing all the bitter pills in my mouth, and it will still take me several days to digest them. Meanwhile I have two precious consolers: my Bösendorfer, which is undergoing a strictly classical régime of Bach, Beethoven, Brahms — and Count Gobineau, whose acquaintance I owe to you. That was a great idea of yours to send me his

[1] *Victor Hugo's.*

books. I even think I shall re-read *Renaissance,* a thing I rarely do. At first I admired the writer in him, then the wise but not pedantic thinker, then the historian and poet, and finally the great artist that he is. What marvellous unity he produces by keeping the two great figures of Machiavelli and Michelangelo in play through all the vicissitudes of his tragedy, making them, as it were, into a Greek chorus by combining their roles of actor and spectator! What interested me even more intensely was the *Pleiads,* a truly model novel, modern in the highest (and proportionately misued) sense of the word. As regards *form* it is, as far as I can judge from reading two thirds of it, certainly equal in merit to His Excellency W. von Goethe's *Elective Affinities,* and a thousand times more remarkable for keenness of observation, analytical depth, and fundamentally aristocratic quality. I am not going to devour *Aphroëssa* straight away — perhaps you can tell me what the title means — but am saving it for a titbit when I have covered a few pages of music-paper.

In short, this Gobineau is a number one, a first-rate thinker and writer, a glory to the minority of Frenchmen today who are neither blackguards nor idiots. What a scandal that he is not in the Academy! However, we need not despair: he will have his recognition, even though it may come long after his death.

I shall return the volumes to you, although the " present " remains, for I intend to give myself the pleasure one day of buying a complete set, handsomely bound. Rarely have I felt myself to be in such complete sympathy with an author. There is not an idea, not a phrase nor an expression, which has shocked me or left me anything to wish for, unless it be a continuation of *La Renaissance,* of which I should like five volumes instead of five chapters.

You must not think from this that I regret not having made the acquaintance of the man himself the other day at N. On the contrary I am delighted, for my esteem and admiration might have suffered from the effect of the pity which his age and his sufferings would have produced. Esteem and pity do not go together. Besides, the Count's attachment to the creature to whom he is so weak as to dedicate his creation causes me a certain repulsion, though I try to neutralize it by remembering that the portrait he draws of her in Countess Hanska in one of the

Pleiads is not very flattering. Talking of vermin, let us not rejoice too soon on your grandfather's account over the destruction
of the Hofgärtnerei. I am of opinion that even in the insect world
only those who can replace themselves are destroyed. You may
be sure that . . . the Abbé's studio will continue to be as much
of a stable as ever. Madame de M. (*née* Princess G.) [1] will be
morally forced to emigrate after the scandal she has caused.
The problem: "*Ou vais-je passer mes soirées?*" seems to me to
render any extension of W.'s visit more than doubtful. If Bayreuth is impossible, the most desirable arrangement would be to
make Pest a permanent residence. Hungary to the Hungarians!
I am returning Fräulein Adelheid's letter with many thanks to
you for letting me see it. It is, I must say, more decently expressed than I expected.

I am delighted that "*il baule*" should have met with your
sister Blandine's entire approval. But do have the lettering
changed (at my expense) for something as Count-esque as possible; that is, if your engraver at B. is on the level of Chr.Senfft.
What about the music list for Madame la Comtesse de Gravina?

Our first violin and leader, Fleischhauer, and "Mr. 'Cello"
have started for B. today. I told them to look up Herr Humperdinck, with whom they may be able to play a little and benefit
accordingly. I hope they will do credit to my educational system. Make use of them if they seem to you to be any good.
Fl[eischhauer] is not without a certain style. . . .

363]

Klampenborg, near Copenhagen
August 21, 1882

You have now had another proof of my unfortunate "talent"
for bringing trouble upon others as well as myself. I am more
sorry than I can say that you should have met with so many
obstacles in the role of translator or transmitter that you have
undertaken. It is at least a good thing that I was prevented by
indisposition from leaving this place (which has done me no

---

[1] *Probably Madame de Meyendorff, née Princess Gortschakoff, wife of the Russian
minister to the court of Weimar, one of the Liszt circle.*

good) yesterday as I intended, or I should again have missed
your letter. In two hours I am due to start for Meiningen — to
go home and be ill in fact — so that I can only write very briefly.
It is better so in any case, so that agitation may be avoided. To
come to the point: your assumptions, dearest Daniela, are correct. I have not the smallest claim, formal or other, to send out
the announcement of Blandine's wedding. Blandine's home is
with her stepfather because that is her mother's house. I am also
obliged to postpone the meeting with her and her husband until
better times, always supposing there are such in store for me.

If after my somewhat awkward journey, which will be doubly
depressing in this bad weather, I arrive at M. in no worse condition, I will write to you from there in the course of the week.
I hope you will let me have a line about the young couple's
travelling plans. My heart-felt blessings go with them.

I am hoping to be able to annul my Hamburg project, both
on account of my lack of the greatest of all good things (since
live one must), good health, and because of unforeseen obstacles
in M.; for instance, a number of my most reliable players have
thrown me over for better jobs elsewhere. It is now my pleasing
duty to find substitutes, paste, and patch up as best I can. I spare
you the details. You can imagine from this, if you did not
already know, what a bed of thorns mine is.

Marie thanks you most warmly for your message. Her good,
devoted heart has enabled her to live herself into the heavy role
of sick-nurse with more alacrity than one thought possible.

364]

Meiningen
October 12, 1883

I LEARNED to my great joy, from Elsa Ritter — I don't know
whether I am to call her your friend — that our desire to spend
a quiet time together was mutual. The outward and inward conditions are so favourable just now as far as I am concerned that
it would seem a pity not to make use of them. My present flat
is admirably designed for you as a visitor. You will be well taken
care of and waited upon. I propose that you should come for a

fortnight: from Monday, October 29, to Monday, November 12. On the 28th of this month I shall return from my indispensable concert tour to Hamburg and Lübeck; on November 14 I play at Nuremberg and could take you as far as Schnabelwaid on your way home next day, as I have to go to Leipzig.

Will that suit you and does your dear mother agree? In writing to you from here I am very conscious of that lovely morning spent here with you seventeen months ago. The same interval separates my last public appearance and that of today. What a terrible time, now, thank God, buried in the past!

Of course you will go to court and see the dear Duke (who is so charming that one can put up with his wife) and the equally kind and clever Princess, who is greatly attached to me.

But this contact does not mean *the least* fuss about clothes. The castle has the same character as the Residence, which is really nothing but a stopping-place for goods trains, although also, as it happens, an excellent place for rehearsing music. You will hear much good music well played *every day*, if you like. In short, your papa will do you the honours of his orchestra.

We have, I imagine, such an endless amount to talk about that any attempt to write it may as well be abandoned.

Let me know soon at Meiningen (where I arrive on Sunday; tomorrow I go to my mother in Coblenz) whether my plan suits you, and please let me have news of Countess Gravina. . . .

365]

Meiningen
October 15, 1883

On returning home last night I was greeted by your letter and at the same time one from Palermo. This I am sending to you. Please let me have it back with Blandine's proper title. It is a great pleasure to find that the suggestion for our meeting in a fortnight's time looks so practicable. Let us keep to it, then.

I have just been interrupted by an unavoidable caller who is passing through. May I suggest that you had better keep this person at a little distance? She is thoroughly plebeian, trivial, and a gossip — therefore dangerous.

My health, on which you congratulate me, is not really brilliant. The journey gave me a fresh cold, and unfortunately I have had domestic worries today into the bargain. After a four-hour rehearsal this was doubly trying. Still, I hope that our horizon will be as cloudless as possible when you come. If you have any special wish, musically, please air it soon. It would be a great and novel pleasure to have something played for my daughter for once. So order something! . . .

366]

Naumburg
Saturday afternoon, November 17, 1883

IT was a great joy to receive your telegraphic message. I fancied I could hear your silvery voice in it, the voice which has grown so familiar that I now miss it painfully. The wire came just at the right time and place — namely, at the concert hall, ten minutes before we began. Although my playing was up to the mark, I was glad you were not there, for you would have been furious with the icy audience, whose motto appeared to be: "Listen, but do not clap." I am said to have pleased them enormously though. Oberpräsident von Diest, a most interesting man, and various members of the council, with whom I supped overlong, assured me of it.

The people *here* are frantically boring. As the concert is at six, I shall go straight on to Leipzig at nine and shall sleep there. I am playing the Nuremberg program and shall enjoy playing the rhapsodies in particular, as you liked them. Today's batch of forwarded letters has brought me nothing from Palermo. If you do not reply to Carolina Corvina's letter, which was left behind, you may find the enclosed cutting useful as an extra supplement. Have you received any delicate attention yet from Meiningen? And has Hamburg laid its offering at your feet? Write soon about all these matters and various others which I wish to know, but am too little inquisitive to ask for expressly.

Naumburg is besieged by barrel-organs on Saturdays. They are driving me quite crazy. It is worse than in London and prevents me from either writing or reading. Weather lovely: cold and windless, with a speckless blue horizon. Wherever one goes, though, there is this intolerable grinding, groaning, screeching at one's heels. I feel rather like a hurdy-gurdy myself today, for here I am turning out the same phrases as on Wednesday. How goes it with the early rising? Back in the old rut again? It's a pity. I still smile when I think of that wail: " It gets earlier every day! " Have you tried over Bazzini's *Lear* as a duet? And begun to read *Alexis*?

I should so like another chat with you, but a dialogue which consists in monologues succeeding each other at forty-eight-hour intervals is about as much of a dialogue as Mosz- is a Nosz-Kowski.

PS. Send me a picture of Fritz B. for paternal inspection. I have just had a look at the theatre where I am to play. It is an annex to the Hotel zur Reichskrone, built by a Countess von Hoffmannsegg. Above the curtain, on the left, a monster medallion of Richard Wagner; on the right, one of Friedrich von Schiller, both painted three times life-size and not at all badly. Only those two, no third.

367]

Dresden
Day of Repentance, November 23, 1883

YESTERDAY I received a very long and charming letter from your Sicilian sister, forwarded from Meiningen, and this morning your own, which really alarmed me. But, after all, as it is dated Sunday, I may suppose that cold you took in your open-work stockings at the Grieg quartet has now been cured by staying in bed. Please write soon to confirm my hopes. I return to M. tomorrow.

You were vividly present in my thoughts at the Chemnitz concert two nights ago. You would have enjoyed it more than you did Nuremberg. Everything went dazzlingly well and I was in the best of moods. As an after effect I became so torpid, however, that I not only fell asleep during *Götz von Berlichingen*, but snored! I beat your grandfather, you see, and in his own city. Certainly the performance was wretched, far worse than the *Electra* of Sophocles on Monday, which I found exquisitely moving. Wilbrandt's arrangement, in which the choruses are " individualized," pleased me enormously. But what an audience! Six people besides Marie and myself in the whole upper circle, and only four rows of stalls thinly peopled. Farewell to all our hopes for *Tristan.* Remember, it was the second performance only of the tragedy in a city of two hundred and thirty thousand inhabitants. Chemnitz, by the way, has over a hundred thousand, so don't go and think that I " lowered " myself by playing there.

Tomorrow, when I am gone, my wife is playing Hermione. Perhaps Fidi will send you her criticism of the performance. . . .

Your grandfather is coming to Meiningen on December 2, so His Eminence informed Friedhold Fleischhauer the other day. As I go to Weimar on the 3rd to conduct and also play at a Raff concert in aid of the music school, I assume we shall travel together. Best thanks for Germanic-Israelite-Slav triple portrait. I liked F.B. very much, very much indeed. The *folie des nez crochus* was not needed to place his really distinguished physiognomy (more distinguished than that of " Sascha's " brother) in a favourable light.

When the chest will arrive I cannot prophesy. You sent it off yourself, remember.

" The willing are led by fate, the unwilling dragged " — so says an old Latin proverb. *Volentem ducunt fata, nolentem trahunt.*

Take this to heart, my precious Daniela, and may the fate of antiquity prove to be a Christian providence! Let me hear soon that you are better.

368]

Meiningen
November 25, 1883

I WAS met at the station this morning by the two Fleischhauers, the genuine and the false (the latter quite as if nothing had happened, so set your mind at rest), who escorted me to my flat, where the sight of your two letters compensated me for the absence of the writer in whose company I had set out on my journey.

It gives me great pleasure to hear of your pleasure over the Shakspere set and I shall retaliate by giving a warm welcome to the diamond pen and the coffee-cups. *Tante grazie!*

" Charenton, Charenton, Charentaine! " Even your dear mother will laugh at the special supplement. We must stir up your grandfather now and get an end put to this republican government. Write to him *molto patetico.* For my part I am going to anathematize Tloup in the presence of His rascally Eminence when he comes here on December 2. *Lo faccia presto, presto — non procrastinarlo!* We must beat our iron (brother, father!) while it is hot.

Excuse my lack of paternal dignity. I have been travelling all night with three hours to wait at Erfurt and four at Eisenach! I am still agitated and have a pile of letters waiting to attack me. All the same, and just because of it, I am writing to you first of all.

Order for yourself (or your mother) a heavenly book: Lord Byron's autobiography, compiled by Eduard Engel from his diaries and letters (third edition, Bruns, Minden, Westphalia, 1884). . . .

Bouquet-ière brought me as a surprise a beautiful " period " lamp on a tall plinth, a truly royal gift. Your pen is bound to clash with it, I fear. Will explain another time if necessary.

While in Dresden I just managed to see *Götz* at the court theatre. It was the abomination of desolation. Write and tell me whether Siegfried saw *The Winter's Tale* yesterday, also whether and how much he liked or disliked Hermione. The truth and nothing but the truth, please. Good-bye, dear child, and write soon. . . .

PS. Munich is silent so far about my Nuremberg " no joke "!

Hofrat Schuch is *tottering* in Dresden. Perhaps I may still fill the place where We, Wa, and Wü have stood. Personally I should like it, for I still cherish a childish attachment to my native city.

369]¹

Meiningen
November 30, 1883

Y̲OUR grandfather is to arrive tomorrow evening and will come
to the final rehearsal. On Sunday morning we are going to give
him a little punch for his morning slumbers.

Lear, Ideale, Meistersinger
B ü L o W

On Monday morning we return to Weimar with Achilles, I
presume.

I have just dug out some grand cognac: *fece due bicchieroni.*
I shall bring up the Tloup affair and we shall see what happens.

Meantime do me the kindness not to collapse, my child. As
soon as you receive the usual reply: " *non posso,*" which means
non voglio, have two lines sent to Rome demanding with studied
politeness the return of manuscript and letters. On the receipt of
the second refusal it should be up to your brother to send a
more or less respectful ultimatum. In between we shall have to
consider what serious steps to take. We must circulate insinua-
tions through the press. Wolff will be able to help me. The
papers will take it up in default of any other fatality and she
will then be mercilessly bombarded with printed matter.

Let us organize for victory therefore (on the wrong side of
Emilaccio) and stand firm.

Madame Pierre was so anxious for your portrait that I took
pity on her and sacrificed one of mine (the Berlin one by Loe-
scher and Paetzsch). I suppose the enclosed note-book is
yours? . . .

PS. Will you do me a small favour?

Try to find words that would fit an old song of mine which
does not strike me as having turned rancid. I wrote it fifteen years
ago for Herr Vogl, who would have sung it had not Herr von
Perfall objected. The fragment from the *Musketeers* opera was
too French for the farmer of Tutzing, so I conceived the naïve
notion of replacing it.

¹ *Written in French.* — TR.

370]

Meiningen
Tuesday evening

QUITE right, dear child. Return to the charge until the smoke
has died away. You must worry her to extinction, incessantly,
coldly, until she is beside herself. This is unfortunately the only
means of bringing people to a sense of decency in some cases.
(" Cattle, that's what they are," your great-grandmother used to
say.)

The Cardinal, who was at my rehearsal with the Duke for
three hours yesterday, has gone to Weimar today and will return
tomorrow, probably with your grandpapa, whose *Ideale* I have
been working at all day. It is very shallow and sadly dated.

My coffee tastes delicious out of your cup. The pen will not
be initiated until I begin to soil some music-paper.

Do at least glance at my corrections on the epistle to Gitana
in Rome before you send it off.

Levi wired to me today for the parts for Brahms's piano
concerto, but I refused; not from rudeness, but from disgust at
the vile stinginess of all these orchestra officials. Did I not suffer
from it myself?

These few lines have taken me barely fifteen minutes, so I
need not reproach myself.

PS. Naturally I shall attack your grandfather about the
manuscript. It has meant separate rehearsals of the symphonic
water-poem for the orchestra this afternoon.

Ré-adieu.

371]

Sunday, December 2,
one of my favourite dates
(*Napoleon III's* coup d'état)

THANK you most warmly, beloved daughter, for your Cordelia-
like deed. But you took me by storm, so to say; I wanted you to

put the proceeds into a money-box as pin-money for the mother of my grandchild.

Your grandfather arrived at five-thirty yesterday. The weather was dreadful and he seemed at first to be quite worn out, complained a good deal of his eyes too. But after some refreshment at the castle (Hofmarschall von Röpert came to fetch him in a ducal equipage) he went gallantly to the theatre, where he was received with a flourish of trumpets ("of course," I hear you say). He then listened with unusual interest, without once falling asleep, and was fifty per cent fresher at the end than at the beginning.

Then until eleven he sat and chatted with the ducal family in His Eminence's *salons*, feeling himself very much at home.

N.B. I have made a conquest of the Cardinal as a father worthy of Daniela. He likes me — no possible doubt about it — and will do his utmost to aid all my attempts to force Monsieur Tloup to disgorge his foreign property. Your grandfather, on the contrary, with whom I spoke most earnestly and pressingly on the matter, regretted very much that he could not help me (not being in correspondence with . . .) and was very pessimistic about the success of my further efforts. We must not let this discourage *us* from doing what we can, dear child. *Each* of your sisters must take her turn and write to your dictation. Let the thought of the recipient's fury inspire you in your labours. Please God she may yet choke in her own gall!

You have no idea how the Cardinal detests her. He says frankly that it would be a most meritorious deed to poison her. He can keep up an endless flow of anecdotes to make her look ridiculous too. Why not ask Biagino to send her a love-letter too? . . .

PS. Tomorrow morning your grandfather and I go to Weimar.

The music-luncheon today seemed to suit his palate. The program was: (1) Liszt: March, *Von Fels zum Meer*; (2) Berlioz: *King Lear Overture*; (3) Liszt: *Die Ideale*, symphonic poem; (4) Wagner: *Meistersinger* prelude; (5) (to order) Brahms: *Variations* on the Haydn choral.

372]

Meiningen
December 13/1, 1883

I DULY return with thanks the priceless latest manifesto. . . .

As your mother is for closing down, I will not interfere again, unless for a change I ask Blandine to continue to exert herself.

Do not be upset by the business of those marks. The money was quite welcome. When a man has so super-intelligent a wife as mine, all sorts of extra expenses creep into the housekeeping and emerge with startling effect; and as it is not practicable to change the system of a sudden, one simply makes the best of it.

Thank you for the information about Palermo. It is fully borne out by my last letter from there. Perhaps you may like to read it (pages 2 and 3) and send it me back at your convenience. I mean to answer it as soon as the Grand Duke Constantine, who arrives today, has taken his departure. Tomorrow there is a semi-Asiatic matinée in his honour. In the evening I am to tinkle to him and at midday, alas, eat with him.

Possibly this morning's greeting from His Highness may interest you too; it will show you my joys and sorrows as intendant.

Certainly your interest, and even your dear mother's, will be roused by the humble and melancholy reply which Count Arco has condescended to make to my " lover's greeting " from Nuremberg. I have had a copy expressly made for you, as I read to you the most elegant passages in my own letter. . . .

373]

Meiningen
December 14, 1883

MANY thanks for your letter, which is so beautifully written that I cannot understand how you did it in bed. I hope you will not be there much longer, though with this weather anything is possible.

I am eagerly looking forward to the *Weaver of Segovia*.[1] Please give it me for Christmas to read with my wife when she comes home. I am glad to say I shall be able to send you a small gift again through Feustel, without prejudice to certain future arrangements, which I explained to you, though you may have forgotten. Your wish that Palermo shall *not* be put in communication with Rome shall be *scrupulously* observed.

The Grand Duke Constantine was very grateful for our music. Whether he is the one you know I cannot quite make out. Your description of his figure and so on fits, but I have not yet seen traces of the Tartar (*grattez le russe . . .*) in his face. Perhaps you are wrong. I will try to establish the identity. Tomorrow I expect your *nonno,* and the day after, Raff's widow and daughter and Wolff from Berlin. Marie comes on Monday. *Excusez du peu!* You ask why the Meiningen ducal comedians do not stage any Spaniards? First, because they would not draw; secondly, because enthusiasm for them is non-existent; thirdly, because the Iberian parts afford no scope for the display of picturesque, plastic effects such as grouping, movements, and tableaux vivants; fourthly, fifthly, sixthly — I can no more. If it depended on me, now! If everything, in fact, did not depend on money! But Iago and Mephisto are quite right there. . . .

PS. May St. George (new to me) protect you from all water-spurting and other dragons! . . .

374]

Meiningen
December 17, 1883

How very depressing it is to see the idol of one's youth turn gradually to dust! Thank God, Frau and Fräulein Raff were able to restore my moral equilibrium by their presence at the truly Dionysian-Apollinian Beethoven festival yesterday.

Your request for a picture of Countess Terzka I am delighted to fulfil and in the shape of a gift rather than a loan if you will allow me. Is not the original coming home from Dresden tomorrow?

[1] *A play by Alarcón*, El Texedor de Segovia.

Herr von W[olzogen] (I keep confusing him with Hermann, my no-raven; I have no use for any but white ones) is quite right: one can only compose bad poems properly. Sascha is successfully proving the contrary. Find me a really commonplace bit of rhymed prose, then, with as few consonants as possible so that my melody may sound really sweet. I am sure you can find one.

Yesterday when I was taking leave of the Grand Duke at the station (and taking cold at the same time), I asked him if he had met you in Palermo. Very much so, it seems. Whether it was his May mood — those two love each other as if it were a *mésalliance* — or whatever it was, I could detect nothing inhuman about him, but on the contrary found him more and more sympathetic. But perhaps my vanity is blinding me. See the enclosed letter from the Baroness, which please return.

375]

Meiningen
January 1, 1884

I FIND it hard, dearest child, not to remember you on this particularly beautiful New Year's Day — or, rather, what I mean is of course not to give a sign of that remembrance.

I am particularly indebted to you also for your Christmas gift of the Spanish dramatists. As they are as yet unknown to me, I shall wait to thank you properly until I have read and enjoyed them. Last night, on the bridge over the two years, I made peace with Marie. We were deeply affected and uplifted by the first part of the *Weber* [1] and by the third act and introduction of Calderón's martyr's tragedy. Afterwards we made ourselves first ill, then well, with laughing over the Cervantes and Lopez intermezzi. The books are now reposing at the castle, where they will, I hope, make their own propaganda.

I appear to have sent a telegram the other day which, though inspired by the purest, I might say the *noblest* intentions, led to a misunderstanding or imbroglio. For that I am very sorry — for the effect, not for my telegram. All the same. . .

---

[1] *Alarcón's* El Texedor de Segovia.

Let us talk of Salzwedel instead, the El Dorado of my favourite cake, which I hope you and your brother and sisters enjoyed as much or even half as much as we did. Just imagine, I had been hunting round for the right address for five years until, at Naumburg the other day, our "concert-father" Oberlandesgerichtsdirektor Lehmann put me on to the track through a providential turn in the conversation.

In digging among some old papers I have also stumbled on some written documents from the year 1850 which supply irrefutable proof that the oldest Wagnerianer is not that " toothless dawdler " at Baden-Baden, but your father. Perhaps the cutting may have a certain value for Siegfried or will have later. . . .

PS. Should you feel like writing to me some time, I for my part shall see that I have time to read your letters and also to reply. So listen, this is where you will find me: January 6, Eisenach; 7th and 8th, Frankfurt; 9th, Darmstadt; 10th, Würzburg; 11th and 12th, Nuremberg; 13th, Erlangen; 14th and 15th, Stuttgart; 16th, Karlsruhe; 17th, Mannheim; 18th, Darmstadt? Mainz; 19th, Worms; 20th, Neustadt; 21st, Frankfurt; 22nd, Wiesbaden; 23rd, Giessen; 24th, Cassel; 26th, Meiningen.

I am involved in all sorts of interesting things just now. Unfortunately, much of it is controversial, as for instance the lodging of an action for libel against Professor Emil Naumann of Dresden. But I fear you are too overloaded with other interests to have any sympathy with my affairs, or at least the cordial sympathy that I *require*.

376]

Meiningen
January 4, 1884

MANY thanks for the reassurance. I was afraid you must be very ill. In return be assured that you have done nothing foolish and that so trivial an omission as that of the conventional greeting would have been quite agreeable to me had it not been for your very long silence.

That would be *really splendid* if you appeared at the Adler today week and at the Town Hall concert in the evening! But as to what is being played, I have forgotten. Let Friend Gr. tell you. He is sure to have a Nuremberg paper. I enclose a program of Würzburg. Also an incredible letter from Lina (without Caro-) for which you are, indirectly, responsible. Naturally I did not mind her absolute irresponsibility in the least. She must be incurably naïve to imagine that I, at fifty-four, could think of devoting my talents to anything but eternal things or play the musical clown, the solemn and worst kind. H'm, h'm! Salzwedel is *not* mentioned in the otherwise all-embracing musicians' calendar. In 1872 its inhabitants numbered about nine thousand, including the confectioners' apprentices; it lies between Stendal and Bremen in the Prussian province of Magdeburg. Has a railway station. Noted solely for its *Baumkuchen*. This cake has received recognition from emperor and king, however. Ask Mimi whether, every Christmas in the royal castle, there is not. . . . Well, that's enough.

Aha! I have found a *still* earlier notice about myself: Berlin, November 1849 . . . when I began with the *Tannhäuser* overture and finished with *Rienzi*. I note also that it was lucky for the great Mottl that he ran no danger of being corrupted by my *tempi*, as he was conducting at the theatre the same evening. And so on.

You see I am in vein because I have such a load of responsibility. How I wish I could lift a few hereditary burdens on to you in my lifetime!

377]

January 1884

YOUR note was a real joy to me, a refreshing token of the bond between us. If in my reply I am rather pedantically business-like — from an excess of lack of time — you must read between the lines, as you can when you choose.

1. To give is more blessed than to receive. So let me keep the Alfieri now as remembrance from you. Many thanks.

2. Kl.'s letter pleased me very much. He treats my Daniela as she should be treated, and does not address her as " my dear

young lady " in the manner of the mis-conductor of *Rheingold*. This, by the way, is my favourite opera after the *Meistersinger* — yes, really! — because it *is* pure gold, free from dross. How I wish I could rehearse it (separately though) and conduct it in my own special way! . . .

3. Agree with you entirely about the French and Anglo-Saxons. The enclosed *feuilleton* may arouse your curiosity. Order the book.

4. F.B. is at Darmstadt. I shall see his uncle at Cassel to-morrow. Am still clinging to the idea that you yourself put into my head.

5. Be sure you write to me at Palermo.

6. On February 12 I shall write to Providence Gross. Perhaps he will disclose the contents of my letter on the 13th.

7. My mother has for the first time acted *very sensibly*, bless her. I shall see her again in the month of June, when I have to be in Frankfurt. So that you may understand the situation, I enclose the letter from her " converter."

8. The night of February 2 finds me at Meiningen.

On the 17th our orchestral tour opens at Göttingen. 18th, 19th, Hamburg; 20th, Kiel; 21st, Lübeck; 22nd, 23rd, Bremen; 24th, Hamburg (matinée at the theatre); 25th to 29th, Berlin.

I shall stay on into March in Berlin, then give concerts on my own account in Dresden, Leipzig, and Berlin, followed by a series in Holland. Back end of March. Double performance of the Ninth on April 2. Second half of April and part of May, London; as short a stay as possible, as I wish to take in, not hand out, money.

There, now you know almost more about me than I do myself.

Marie sends best wishes. She grows prettier and more sensible every day. We too are reading Hildebrandt's *Voyage round the World* in our free evenings.

I enclose something for your brother.

PS. No news of " Friederike "?

378]

Meiningen
January 28, 1884

THE authorities have blessed my twenty-day concert tour in the most gracious way imaginable. Never in my life have I undertaken anything in such " ideal " (a hard word, but appropriate) conditions.

A proposito, Felix Mottl has made the most complete conquest of me. A splendid fellow, a giant compared with L. S. and others.

Flabby creatures, both the straight-legged and the hook-nosed.

So you want to come to Berlin? Better not come on March 3, when I play the Raff concerto, but on the 28th or 29th of February. Listen:

German Style
People's Concert by H. M. Court Orchestra
Three overtures by Spohr: *Berggeist, Faust, Jessonda.*
"   "   " Weber: *Euryanthe, Freischütz, Oberon.*
"   "   " Wagner: *Rienzi, Meistersinger, Tann-
häuser.*

Not strictly chronological for acoustical reasons.

Does this project soften your opinion of your father? If so, do him a special favour, which it is really outrageous of him to ask. Give me back the little Alfieri which I sent you from Munich with the clock and other items. You are not particularly fond of it, but I am.

(" You forget, Sir, that other people are fond of asparagus too."

" But not so fond as I am! ")

Shall you be writing to Palermo? Please do, and ask your sister to excuse my long silence. It has been and still is humanly impossible.

PS. 1. Has Frege sent any money?

2. Tomorrow your grandmamma is to enter the Roman

Catholic Church at Coblenz, which means that I have to send five hundred marks to the poor of St. John's parish.

There's news for you.

379]

Meiningen
February 8, 1884

THIS time only a few words — without songs. One small, very easy request: if you should be writing to Countess S. or anyone else in Berlin, please *say nothing, absolutely nothing*, about *my* project for the 29th. It is a *coup d'état* that is being prepared with the utmost secrecy. The program is being privately printed, and, in short, we are acting like nitroglycerinihilists. I hope you do yourself and me the pleasure of being present at the crowning of the edifice, which is being built up with Machiavellian deliberation bit by bit.

380]

Eisenach
February 16, 1884

MY big trunk is on the way to Göttingen and I have only official note-paper to hand, a most unsuitable medium for what I wish and ought to say in reply to your recent letter.

But why waste words?

Let me kiss your pure brow in spirit and gaze with fatherly love into that one of your eyes which is less lovely than the other and therefore belongs to me. I shall be more than content to see you on the last day of the month. My wife is coming to Berlin on purpose too.

Yesterday, in turning out old letters, I found three which belong to Villa Wahnfried, and these I am promptly handing over to you. . . .

PS. Did Herr Gr. receive my letter?

381]

Berlin
Tiergarten Hotel (*until March 5, exclusive*)
February 27, 1884

My precious Daniela, my dearly beloved child, Glory be to Jesus Christ, amen!

My heart is very full and my head so overflowing with music that I can only say: life's unmixed joy fall to your lot! My own joy over *our* happiness is considerably mitigated by the shattering of my hope of seeing you tomorrow.

You know, Carina, we shall not have another leap-year's day until 1888, and perhaps I shall not see another at all. Shall you not be sorry then that you did not spend this one with your father?

But away with this detestable " me." Your *fiancé* has just sent me a very nice letter. Thank him, give him my kind regards. How shall I announce your approaching union — title, place, date — and *when* does your mother wish it to be?

I have made your excuses to the Bojanovskis. On the other hand, your *eccellentissime* friend, with whom I spent two very pleasant hours yesterday, thinks you should address a few lines to Princess Marie here and to the Duke's wife at Meiningen. *I am of the same opinion.* A thousand kisses and blessings.

382]

Berlin
Leap-day, 1884

Hardly was my letter to you posted when I received the enclosed note of congratulation from the Princess. Write the most charming letter of thanks you are capable of. You will find it easy after reading *hers.* The Duke has also sent me — and you — his congratulations by wire, but unfortunately the telegram has been used as a pipe-lighter.

This is such a serious evening that I must begin the day

scherzando tomorrow in the interests of the European balance of power.

Perhaps my latest joke may call forth your dear silvery laugh. I wish I could hear it on the telephone. Best greetings to " our Fritz."

PS. Make your announcement to the Freges brief and informal. I shall see them on Wednesday at Leipzig.

383]

In the train to Greiz
Friday, March 7

IT is glorious (I say it too this time, with sonorous conviction) that I am to see you in Dresden. I arrive on Sunday morning at ten from Zwickau and shall stay at the Victoria. At eleven I am going to hear Palestrina's marvellous *Missa Papœ Marcelli* in the Catholic church, conducted by " Wü," the " octagon." On Monday evening I am playing at the Hotel de Saxe. You will stay for that? I shall bribe your dentist. In Leipzig the day before yesterday I " fished " when Forzel congratulated me on your engagement. I'll tell you all about it.

PS. Marie had to travel back to Meiningen the same night after yesterday's concert.

384]

Rotterdam
March 12, 1884

I AM devoting the first hour after my arrival to this sign of remembrance to you. I hope that you arrived refreshed to the refreshment of your family and found good news awaiting you from Paris.

Sincere, *very* sincere thanks for the happiness you gave me by your presence in my native city. Thanks also to her who permitted it.

Where do you think I woke up this morning? At Bentheim. And the morning light enabled me to follow in the original the stroll which we took through the Hobbema and Ruysdael rooms yesterday. But "the coloured reflection was lovelier than the reality" (Faust's monologue in the beginning of Part II) and I recalled that anti-realistic saying of Cervantes: "*Los buenos pontores jamás vomitaban la naturaleza, la imitaban solmente.*"

Darling, if you should have a spare quarter of an hour, do please write a line or two to my — our — dear friend Baroness Romaine von Overbeck in Berlin (Bellevuestrasse 18 A) and tell her of your engagement. She deserves the little attention.

Well, and how was the *cognata dell' avvenire iersera?* Her plumage I quite liked in the chiaroscuro lighting. But what about her warbling? That's what matters. I cannot sufficiently insist upon it that the instrumentation of *Hans Heiling* is beastly, and although I made many a good effect with the opera in Hamburg, I always conducted it with much gnashing of teeth. Warning to the listener from the reader!

What did Siegfried say to the hermeneutical refraction of his mentor? Now I have made you really ashamed of me! I forgot to reveal to you the deep-rooted necessity to play with words which is felt by the tone-player, but you have read Beethoven's letters and have seen how much better he was at composing than at witticisms, particularly when polyphonically-minded. The endless range of attraction between the different intervals, these for- back- and side-wards mathematics, arithmetic or architecture, must tend to inflict the same trials on the rest of the world.

Did you take note of where I should be shaving my ears in the coming week? I will not repeat the itinerary, as it would look too much like fishing for your ink. Your pen belongs to your husband-elect. Even the best-behaved papa cannot compete with him.

PS. (Hiebendahl, Royal Saxon chamber-musician and master at the Royal Conservatoire.

Franz Ries, artist and Royal Saxon music-publisher.

Dr. Koppel-Fellfeld, Sidonienstrasse 19.

Frau Dr. Luise von Welz, Stephenienstrasse 23.)

385]

Rotterdam
March 13, 1884

HERE I am again, for it seems to me that in spite of Fritz's formal entry into the family circle (give him a warm welcome from me) my news will still have considerable interest for you. I therefore have no hesitation in sending you the enclosed letter from my wife. Make your own comments on it at leisure. As a matter of fact, you will learn to know Marie so well from this document that you should be on perfectly normal terms again by the end of the month, don't you think?

386]

Würzburg
March 27, 1884

IF you feel like it, come to us, to me, *at once*. We return at ten o'clock to M., where the non-prince (*Un-Fürst*) was to arrive yesterday evening. All sorts of things are going to happen, you'll see; incredible things.

So come and see the fun, will you?

In all possible outward hurry, combined with perfect peace of mind. It was glorious yesterday. Kliebert arranged the score of the Ninth according to my parts and it was most impressive as a whole. As for me, I played more Beethovenly than ever.

387]

Meiningen
April 6, 1884

MARIE thinks that the new developments in my " cabinet crisis " will interest you. See how her imagination soars! In the interests of maintaining the orchestra, I am preserving a very reserved attitude from now on, a strictly business-like, intendantish attitude, until there are signs that they are beginning to be ashamed and are prepared to divest me of my prince's role. Up to date there is said to have been no cessation of this fruitless grumbling: *mortadella.*

Fritz is by now, I suppose, on the banks of the Isar. I am still enjoying him in retrospect like a piece of good music. A capital fellow in every way. In short, you both made me feel thoroughly happy and confident. Let me thank you, and let me also hear good news of you. I am too lazy to write myself just now, having exhausted all I have to say.

388]

Dublin
May 1, 1884

I suppose you would rather have a hasty greeting than a thorough-going and lasting silence?

I hope you are having it more May-like than we in Ireland. Here it rains, storms, and freezes me to the marrow in these badly ventilated hotel rooms.

Last night I had one concert here and this afternoon I have a second. Tomorrow morning I go to Liverpool and on Sunday shall be back in London (21 Holles Street, Cavendish Square, W.). I found my mother very, very well at Coblenz. She went to my concerts in the Jesuit church, the proceeds of which reached the astounding sum of two thousand marks net. Before this trip — that is, before Stuttgart and Karlsruhe, I can hardly remember where else I have been — I had the great pleasure of seeing our Fritz. He will no doubt have reported to you. On Sunday, April 20, I had a really splendid, thoroughly nice letter from him by way of Meiningen and I at once telegraphed to ask him to call in the afternoon. This he very kindly did, and I had renewed and ample opportunity of registering my " enthusiastic approval " of him. . . .

How are you? And Blandine? You will easily believe that I have as little time for writing as I have abundant leisure for reading pretty letters addressed to me.

389]

Meiningen
May 27, 1884

Your nice long letter must, I feel, be answered in a nice though necessarily brief fashion and I can think of no more graceful way than to send you a picture of a favourite of mine, one of the most distinguished of our non-two-legged contemporaries. Can you read the life-maxim of this thoroughbred Scottish collie in his good sensible eyes? " Do not turn the gnat into an elephant."

Why not? Because we can crush the gnat, but the elephant can — do you see?

Yesterday I had news from Sicily. Had written a day or two before to ask for some, and of course the letters crossed, as is so often the case with me. So your sister writes — but of course you will have heard direct — that Monford's birthday is to be celebrated at Bayreuth, I suppose simultaneously with the first orchestral rehearsal. As you will see her before I do — she may object to the long way round by Frankfurt (where I shall be for the whole of June) in coming from Munich — I must ask you to invite her and your brother-in-law to my house in the early days of July. While my wife is away at Basel (June 15 to July 15), they can have their *letto* and *risotto* there all complete. So arrange that, won't you? Bravo, bravissimo, for using your discretion (impossible to have too much of it) in the matter of sending that newspaper to your brother. (" One heart, but *two* tooth-brushes " is my motto, the very opposite to that of the Redwitz song, so beautifully composed by your grandfather, but I hope quite in accordance with Fritz's theory and practice.) He will show it to you, and you will of course understand. . . .

Write to me at Frankfurt some time, care of Hofmusikhandlung Steyl and Thomas. The Hawthorne was for you to keep. Was there no grandfatherly breviary with it?

If the administration does not object, I hope to go and hear

Parsifal with my wife and the Sicilians. Thank heaven, Levi will be invisible.

I am beginning to gossip from sheer hurry. Is it a symptom of old age?

390]

Frankfurt, Hotel de Russie
June 5, 1884

Fɪʀsᴛ my best thanks for your letter. You are right not to go to Berlin. Why I think so it would take too long to explain. Today, after preaching Beethoven from eight to eleven in the Raff Conservatorium (tomorrow it is Bach's turn), I visited the Städel Institute, where I found so much to enjoy that I should like to go again as soon as possible. Your Moretto Madonna is not the one with the four Fathers of the Church, is it, but the one opposite, with St. Anthony on the right and St. Sebastian on the left, with an angel playing on the altar step? The former is the more famous and the only one which has been photographed. The photograph is so vague, however, that I have had to indulge my fancy of giving you one in another way: you will already have received the substitute, Barnabus da Modena. It is more than a century and a half later. I like it very much, particularly in comparison with the contemporary German horrors. May you have " no objection of any importance to make," as the Berlin critic says, when he happens to be suffering from a fit of benevolence.

A great mass of stuff has just come from Meiningen by post. Whereupon I lost both temper and courage. To think it all has to be dealt with! Even to decline invitations (" unavoidably ") takes time, but you are the last person to whom I should say that. I often think with pride and admiration of my daughter's achievements with pen and writing-paper and how she comes through the worst press of correspondence without turning a hair.

PS. Have been in Baden-Baden with R. P., his handsomer half, and mine. Survived remarkably well. Only shows how well one can get on with people if the intimacy is carefully moderated.

391]

Meiningen
July 2, 1884, evening

Your kind letter, which reached me just as I was leaving Frankfurt, did me so much good that I am writing to thank you immediately on my return to the harmonious seclusion, etc., etc., of my hearth and home.

Everything is ready for the reception of our guests here. I told Blandine not to come before the 6th, but if it suits you all better, it will suit me *very* well too, provided that the Gravinas will make allowances for my tiredness. At present my appearance is neither *maestosa* nor *scherzosa*, but a couple of days' sleep may do wonders.

Will you therefore tell Their Sicilian Magnificences in the most super-genteel style that they will be equally welcome on Saturday. I was at the zoo in Frankfurt yesterday from half-past three to eight. Nothing reconciles me more to my own kind than to be in the company of the noble beasts without words. It hurt me more to part from a camel with whom I had made friends by victualling him than from my professorial colleagues at the Raff Conservatorium, and the death of a female seal has depressed me more for the whole of last week — I mean it — than the news of an outbreak of Asiatic cholera among my blood-relations in Berlin would have done. (Not all blood is of a special vintage.) The older I grow, the better I understand the sentimentality of the Terrorists of 1794. I shall rejoice if we meet again some time in some other zoological garden. Good heavens, what else was the so-called paradise? To shake hands with a tiger, for instance, would mean such a glimpse into eternity as would enable me to bear all temporal tortures without repining. I should think it almost ideal, could I find a town in which I could live opposite to such a paradise. Every free moment should I spend there, making myself useful to the keepers and trying to equip myself to replace one of them. And that reminds me, I have discovered a glorious book — French of course — of the last century. Blandine must bring it along for you. Never have I seen such a jewel of grace, refinement, delicacy, and in the best sense anti-German *Gemütlichkeit*. One could shout for joy over every *alinea*. You are curious? So much the better. The author belongs to those whom posterity has neglected. For there are such. But there is indeed much that is new and beautiful for you to see.

But now tell me quickly how I can make things really comfortable for the Gravinas. Give me some hints on larder and cellar supplies, tea, coffee, cakes, tools of all sorts. Will they want to see chamberlains and such? Shall I invite the monkey family from the Feodorenstrasse? Do be my obedient daughter, my dear child, and help me.

392]

Meiningen
July 8, 1884

My thanks for the prompt fulfilment of my request enables me to reply at once in spite of the chronic eighty degrees in my room.

Blandine is worthy of her sister: need I say more in her praise? I hope that she too has felt some of the happiness she caused me to feel. Not that her appearance really surprised me; I was so well prepared by your loving description. I leave it to her to give you a description of our day together.

Your brother-in-law also came up to all that I had been led to expect. He is *arcigentilissimo*, as aristocratic as he is intelligent. What more can one want? If in our forty-eight hours I did not become thoroughly intimate with him, it is purely my own fault. The temperature has an unwholesome effect on my brain power; also I speak Italian now much more haltingly than I write it or could stammer it at a different season of the year.

I must thank you for having taken as they were meant — that is, seriously — my advice to your *fiancé* and the good wishes, arising logically out of that advice, for your union with him, which is not, I hope, indefinitely postponed. I consider the knowledge of human nature which I have acquired in my fifty-four years to be of more importance than any of my other possessions, you see.

It is not yet certain when my wife will be able to return, but she will hardly keep me waiting more than another week. Is there anything that I can send you by Konzertmeister Fleisch-hauer, who is making the pilgrimage to B[ayreuth] on Sunday? . . .

PS. We play whist every night. It is the only way in which I can act the grandfather. But, but, but . . . did you not once receive a treatise or grammar of this international language from me? If so, please send it on loan to Blandine at once.

393]

Düsseldorf
November 9, 1884

A LITTLE more objectivity, altruism, on your part and you would not blame me for not making my fingers unserviceable by letter-writing, seeing that they are indispensable for the tinkling by which I earn my bread. As a matter of fact, I should not find time even for the urgent correspondence of the day did not my good wife take half the postal miseries off my hands.

Today is the seventh monster concert. The first was on Tuesday the 3rd. Tomorrow I start at six in the morning for Rotterdam, where I have a concert at night.

Your dear mother does me great honour by applying to me in the matter of *Lohengrin* and I appreciate it to the full.

The great Seidel is of course in America, but Heckel, Porges, and, above all, the demigods Levi, Fischer, Paur, Richter, Mottl are all in Europe and even in Germany.

Nevertheless I feel myself incompetent to give judgment. If Telramund is overpowered by his task, let him suit himself; but if he rises superior to it, then of course no cuts. For the later works the same principles must not be applied; otherwise there would be an abyss of contradictions and incongruities. My unworthiness managed to produce the second act of *Lohengrin* without a single cut in Hanover. Nollet was willing and I did the drilling! But when you have a "*durch Dich*" twice over, to the torture of singers and hearers, it is, of course, liable to destroy the good effect. The only proper way — though the wretched stage conditions prevent the smooth working of it — would be to begin with the cuts and dispense with one regularly at each performance, so that by the sixth (or twelfth, as the case may be) the work would appear complete in its integrity. Everyone would then be able to digest it, thanks to the step-by-step preparation (*la musique est la fête de mémoire*). The late Master [1] once expressed himself very clearly to this effect once in Munich.

That is what comes of tachygraphy, you see, when one has fever day in, day out. I am not speaking figuratively, for I should not be able to get through all I have before me until the 15th without quinine and hydrochloric acid to relieve my cough and stomach pains. On the 26th I go to Berlin, and from there (after the concert) on the 27th to Petersburg for an orchestral rehearsal on the 30th: a pretty stiff nerve-test for my sixty-five-year-old bones! But I have grumbled enough. My love to Henry. I have a wish, tinged perhaps with selfishness, that you may spend a honeymoon in Arno-Dresden; it is a place, as you know, to which I owe my "renaissance." Could I but conjure up guardian angels *en masse*, I would do so for you.

394]

Petersburg
January 9, 1886/December 28, 1885

YOUR good wishes for yesterday are the last that I shall reciprocate and acknowledge from here. Today is the fifth and last concert of the first series (Imperial Music Society) at which I have to play, and tomorrow, or at latest the day after, I return home by Berlin. For various reasons I have cancelled the big Austrian tour. It is better at my age not to put too heavy and frequent a strain on one's power of resistance, and the last five weeks on the Neva have tried it fairly high. I am delighted to see from your mood that the sun is smiling for you. "If it could

[1] WAGNER *had died in 1883.*

but last for ever! " I thought when accompanying the song last night and applying the words to you.

On Wednesday I arrive in Berlin, with forty-eight hours to spare. I hope to see your excellent *fiancé* and to talk over with him the matter of furnishing which you mention. Perhaps you for your part will ask Herr Gross to get in touch with Leipzig with reference to the enclosed letter from my cousin.

My wife is at Cracow with her mamma and will meet me in Berlin so that we may go home to Werra together. She was so delighted with her Balzac that I feel I must thank you for remembering to order it for me. . . .

395]

M.
February 5, 1886

I OUGHT really to write a line to your *fiancé*, but I prefer to write two to you, since it will presumably serve the same purpose. It is a question of apologizing to Henry for not being able to keep my promise to meet your future parents-in-law in Dresden (Hotel Bellevue) this month. A professional tour to replace the Austrian one (planned for January), which fell through, will take me southward within the next few days to Switzerland and Baden. On March 5 is the last concert at Wiesbaden, on the 7th I pack my trunk for a second sharp- flat- natural-train to Petersburg.

I am most anxious to see and talk to Henry on my way through Berlin on March 11. (I must land on the Neva by the 13th.)

How is my darling child? I have heard nothing of either you or your sister for so long. A week ago I was strongly tempted to invite you to the last concert here; but I thought: who knows what engagements you may have made, and what an awkward position of having to excuse yourself I should create for you, so that, going back on my impulse, I let it alone. . . .

Curious worlds, both the musical and the extra-musical. To make existence tolerable among these bloated infusoria and their activities one must amuse oneself by shaking the glass container every now and then and taking a microscope — this is essential of course — to watch the sudden revolutions in the realm of the infinitely little. And what, by the way, is infinitely great? I mean, what single thing?

I supposed I had done F. M[ottl] quite a good turn the other day (you perhaps did not know about it, as you read no papers, and for that reason I enclose the cutting in question), and now my wife writes from Baden that he says he is afraid this will make the Viennese musical authorities hate him like poison! As a matter of fact I shall be seeing him next Thursday and have asked him to conduct a nice little opera for me at Karlsruhe.

After a normal quasi-gala entertainment (of seventy minutes, all in) the court here showed itself supremely indifferent to its *ex*tendant. Only the little Princess has honoured me with her fingering problems and I am having the gallantry to solve them for her twice a week. " *Quelle maison, mon Dieu, quelle maison!* " as they said in a French farce which ducally amused me in Petersburg.

Well, does not my loquacity inspire you to canary-like counter-twitterings? I hope so. There is still time before I leave on Tuesday.

My wife sends her love, and thanks you two or three times daily for the beautiful Balzac. (She grows cleverer and prettier every day.)

396]

Frankfurt am Main, Hotel zum Schwan
May 22, 1886

. . . I was surprised to hear that you had had to win through so many battles in the civil war of the past few months. For all my sympathy with you, the most highly tried because the most passive participant, I cannot go so far as to condole; far from it. I can only congratulate you that Henry has had abundant and lasting opportunities to prove to himself and his dear ones his remarkable firmness of character. It seems to me to augur most consolingly for the future of his chosen life-companion. *Le bonheur se nourrit d'obstacles.* On the occasions of my regular meetings with my son-in-law on the way to and from Berlin, I have gone thoroughly into the matter of your future residence, and found to my great satisfaction that he was in full agreement with my desire that you should begin your married life, not in sterile and sterilizing Berlin, but in some university town that is not only smaller, but more favoured in its natural situation. This desire has actually been gratified: Henry writes with great satisfaction of his — prospects of Bonn. As Countess Welkenstein is moving to Petersburg, you will not miss her so much, and it is not far to the zoo in Cologne. (Joking apart, I should never survive in Frankfurt but for the four-footers.) Wüllner will undoubtedly provide you with better choral music in the winter than would the Berlin Singakademie, which so disgusted me with a scandalous performance of the *Matthew Passion* recently that I shall not get over it before my last decade or decade and a half runs out. . . .

Now for an indiscreet, very paternally-minded question: Can I, and when — perhaps in September? — see you in Bonn? Not as your guest — you know I only feel comfortable in a hotel or in such comfort as a railway carriage provides — but as a several days' visitor. Since I have shaken off the chains of my horrible slavery as intendant, my so-called official post, there is a notable improvement in my humour, my purse, my health and activity. I am master of my time and therefore in a position to satisfy my need of a talk with you oftener than before. But enough for today. Let me hear from you soon, with lots and lots of details, please.

397]

Lausanne, Hotel Riche-Mont
June 8, 1886

My very best thanks for your long and full letter of June 1, which was only forwarded to me from Frankfurt yesterday; otherwise I should have replied at once. Now I have reason to fear that these lines may miss you, if you should start on your journey to Berlin for the wedding of your very admirable friend somewhat earlier. I left the scene of my final " activity " on the

2nd. This was later than I intended, but I was prevented from travelling by a most painful attack of neuralgia (which still persists) and had to make a halt in Baden and again in Berlin for tea and bed. I have been here since Saturday evening and, temperature permitting, hope to recover my strength in pianoforte-free, worry-free Switzerland; that is, if I succeed in disposing of all obstacles. If you have not yet stopped short at or fallen asleep over this long personal preface, you shall now have the conclusion. My future plans are uncertain; therefore I am making the most of the present. I am anxious that my meeting with Frau Dr. Thode should not be too indefinitely postponed, so, as I can only be present in spirit at the ceremony on July 4, I am putting off my return to Meiningen and will meet you and your husband at any convenient place you or he may suggest. *Je ne ferai ni l'important ni l'importun.* Perhaps I may some time write a practical prose manual as pendant to Victor Hugo's *Grandpère* with the title: " The Art of being a Father-in-Law." I should dedicate it to your grandfather, whose abbé's robe I shall envy with a mixture of selfishness and self-reproach on your wedding-day.

Hearty congratulations to you both, first of all on having found a roof for yourselves. Your welcome plan was sent without that small excerpt from the Bonn house-agents' list. For this autumn, in any case, I hope you will answer my languishing: " Where? " before I have to put the question to the porter of my Bonn hotel. (This in case I might be able to pay you a visit, after the festival of course, but before my winter campaign.) And now that I am about it, I congratulate you on the choice of Felix Mottl, you in so far as you are identified with Bayreuth, and Bayreuth itself with all its summer visitors. My heart (which lies in my ears) is so intensely, morbidly wrapped up in *Tristan* ('65 — '69 — '72), as also in Sachs, that I should have felt it oppressively as a profanation had Richter or, even more, that . . . Seidl been going to conduct them. Last Sunday week I went to Karlsruhe to clasp my old unfading first love, *Cellini*,[1] to my ears and heart again. It was one of the most refreshing experiences I have had for many years. I could not cease rejoicing, so correct and so inspired (the two are no

[1] *Berlioz's* Benvenuto Cellini.

longer contradictory terms for me) was my dear Felix's handling of the unfortunate Hector. But too much excitement is not
good for one at seventy-five.

Well, good-bye, dearest child, soon to be no longer bound
to me even in name.

398]

Geneva, Hotel National
June 23, 1886

M<small>Y DEAR</small> S<small>ON-IN-LAW</small>,
Thank you very much for writing so fully. . . .

May I reply to your suggestions for a meeting on Swiss
territory in the beginning of July by a counter-suggestion? In
consideration of my shattered health and the failure so far to
restore it, owing to the unfavourable weather, I feel obliged to
extend my stay here — as the least of many evils — as much
as possible.

Will you therefore come and see me here with Daniela, as
soon as you can? You will have no reason to regret it. My hotel
is excellent and has unlimited accommodation. It lies ten minutes away from the town and I hope that kinder weather conditions will enable me to do the honours of the charming and yet
grandiose scenery for the three of us. My wife has been in
Vienna for ten days with her father, who is rather seriously ill,
and is going from there straight to Meiningen for July. I shall
follow in the middle of the month. May all your projects meet
with unqualified success! My dearest love to your — bride.

I long for your dual assent to my proposal for a visit to
Geneva.

399]

Geneva
July 15, 1886

M<small>Y</small> best thanks for the gleam of sunshine that your dear letter
brought me and not less for fulfilling my painful request. By so

doing you have, I hope, rendered it possible for me to look forward calmly to my return home, which is necessary on several grounds.

God bless Henry! That in eloquent brevity is my answer to your information about yourself. As for me, my head aches incessantly from the atmospheric pressure, and an outwardly invisible wound, received when I stumbled the other day, has put sleep, the best remedy for neuralgia, out of question. Still, by the end of the week I must and shall be all right, for I am desperately anxious not to miss meeting you in three weeks' time. When exactly — day, hour — do you expect to arrive there?

It is dear and sweet of you to cherish a friendly recollection of the country inn on the canal. As for me, well you can imagine how I feel and can keep me from falling into the depths of melancholy. I am delighted that you are both enjoying Drumont so much. The brilliant success of this book has given a new lease of life to another far better-written book of forty years ago by Toussenel: *Les Juifs, rois de l'Époque*, a story of feudal finance. I will show it to Henry at Augsburg. Famous fellows the French really are. Even in anti-Semitism they are our forerunners, pointing the way.

I must call a halt to my pen. It is not difficult, for, as you see, it is not working easily any more than in my heavy head. For another thing, I must hurry so that I may give you an opportunity to write me a postcard about Augsburg.

400]

Meiningen
September 9, 1886

You really deserve to be congratulated on your ability to produce letters as charming and intelligent as usual when the heat is so stifling. It promises well too for your power to provision your new home and win through to a lasting peace. Bravo! May you keep that wonderful elasticity of outlook of which you gave so many proofs at Bayreuth. Only a few days ago our Princess referred admiringly to your social success there; you will now, I hope, lead a less cramped and complicated existence. My wife only presented herself in order to put an end to some misunderstanding or other. She was in doubt whether to do so or not, knowing the extent of your obligations, but, on my advice, she decided to act against the proverb: " When in doubt, do nothing." She was very pleased to be able to see you and sends you herewith her thanks once more and her best wishes for your new housekeeping.

Do you really want to know anything about me? My complacent assumption that you do puts me in rather an embarrassing position. For six weeks now I have led a mollusc existence, thinking and enjoying myself hardly at all, and being not free from pain. The so-called lovely season of the year is for me the most dangerous. My doctor has a great deal to do with me, or rather I with him, and for this reason my domicile here is still the most suitable in which to pass the dog-days. How well I could have worked if the temperature and its paralysing effect on all my joints had allowed me! As it is, I could do no more than prepare a small scheme for the winter which the enclosure will make clear to you. Perhaps it will enable me to supply an antidote for the Rubinstein hammering of last year. It seems probable that I shall have to write off Russia for next season. The doctor is very definitely opposed to my spending twelve weeks in Petersburg. A pity, because it would have made an admirable supplement to the Meiningen post: half-work and double pay. But enough of that. One of the most fatal forms of brooding — and one which it is almost impossible to avoid as one grows older — is the weighing of the pros and cons of any undertaking, the fear of miscalculating and therefore of damaging oneself. After state officials, it is you women who are exempt from this particular worry.

Whether I shall be able during this month to keep my promise to you, as I should like, depends too much on the internal and external Réaumur for me to be able to say definitely. If I do not go to Russia, there will of course be plenty of opportunities in other months of the late autumn and winter. Perhaps it is better to wait until you two have thoroughly settled down and I shall be able to hear one of your husband's lectures at the same time. Let me know some time what he proposes to read and on what days. Give him my warmest greetings. I received Drumont safely.

I should like to unburden my mind to you about your grandfather. It was really, I quite agree with you, a divine dispensation that he should have faded out painlessly at Bayreuth. All the same, in the interest of his posthumous fame I should certainly like to see his mortal remains removed to Hungary. St. Elisabeth was also very déclassée in Thuringia, you know. To write of such things is laborious, however.

401]

Meiningen
October 8, 1886

I MAY as well admit that I should be glad to hear better news of you as, when Henry wrote, you were said to have overtired yourself. Just a line, please, and send everything to this address now. My wife will then forward anything to me in Prague or Leipzig, where I am spending twelve days from today. At Prague I am bound by an old promise to the Bohemians, who (with all deference to German Jews) are the chief representatives of serious culture, in music at least. These German Jews have made things rather difficult for me in connexion with the rather costly sacrifice that I am making (as a good patriot I play twice straight away *pour le roi de Prusse*). I only hope that their libellous articles have not come your way or that they have done so only together with the emendation demanded at the point of the sword. For instance, there will be one in the *Kölnische*, my more than a quarter-of-a-century-old insultress, one of these days.

At Leipzig I am making the first experiment with my four-evening Beethoven cycle, on which I am relying entirely for my bread and butter this season. I hope it will be a success. I suppose I do not need to remind your excellent cousin again about the affair of your dowry. In his last letter, more than three weeks ago, he was promising to send it to Henry direct.

Have you any news from Palermo? Has the second family event passed off in as normal a way as one could wish?

Do not think it odd if I ask you to read the enclosed letter. It is from a really splendid woman, now no longer young, who first became intimate with your dear mother during a long stay at Löwenberg in Silesia, Prince von Hohenzollern-Hechingen's castle. She is not a Frenchwoman, by the way, but the daughter of an Austrian general. As she takes such an interest in you, it would be to the advantage of you both if you come to know each other. I therefore propose that you should buy (with the enclosed note) a copy of your Henry's *Franz von Assisi* and send it to her with a nice note. She deserves to have it because she will be able to appreciate it and I mentioned the book when providing a few necessary biographical details about you. Should you think well to make inquiries at Bayreuth first, please do so. Is it not comic, really, to see what fabulous stories are told of us even out of print?

There are a hundred and one questions I want to ask about you and your new life, but I will leave them unasked because I do not wish to begin to play the inconvenient role of a paternal octopus in my old age. If, however, you will write about your life and household in some detail, I shall be most grateful.

402]

Breslau
November 20, 1886
(Galiset Hotel until the 30th)

I owe you a letter of thanks, beloved daughter. By your happy choice of parents-in-law you procured for me a most refreshing cordial in one of the most stormy and yet undeserved crises in all my abundant experience. They are splendid people, so naturally intelligent and good. What more could any idealist want? Have been thinking much about you and our precious hours together some years ago in your " *père terrible's* " native place. Am longing for your pen to confirm the joyous news which I gleaned from the mouth of Heinz's father on our journey to Görlitz together.

Thanks yet again for sending *St. F. of A.* to your dear mother's wonderful friend. It gave me pleasure also. Frau von

Brodorotti received the book by the same post as the September number of the *Revue des deux mondes,* in which there is a brilliant notice of it. If the author has not seen this, Frau von B. will send on the review to Bonn.

Finis. I must hold my head higher than ever, drill my fingers, get my nerves in order. My revenge on Dresden I can safely leave to Prague, though I fear the attack will be unduly bloody. But you will see: there will be light! . . .

403]

Meiningen
December 29, 1886

YOUR refreshing letter has made the close of the year so happy for me that I am risking my fingers — writing-desk and keyboard are, as you know, hostile terrains — to send you a thanks-greeting together with the warmest New Year wishes for you both.

Te Deum laudamus that the conditions of your house and home so completely satisfy the demands I made of fate on your behalf. Best thanks for all details, clearly though briefly described. I was particularly pleased to hear that you intended to found a *Penaten-Lararium* (let my learned son-in-law correct me) and you will, I know, allow me to take a practical part by handing over to you little by little anything suitable that may be worth preserving and might get torn up in the course of my nomad existence. How often in my life have there been moments of desperation, of definite preparations for the end, when many valuables were destroyed to keep them from falling into profane hands; for instance, the greater portion of your grandfather's letters to me, and much besides! . . .

Who is this " unique " one among the professors? As far as musicians are concerned, beware of a certain humbug, Schrattenholz. Keep him at arm's length should he try to ingratiate himself with you by using my name, as he may very likely do, seeing that I only shake off his importunities indirectly (via Karlsbad in Berlin). Brombach is a neglected genius and has only the first two letters of his name in common with Brahms;

he hates him all the more deeply, too, because public opinion will not allow him to do so on the surface. Under the circumstances it seems as if you would be thrown back on " bony Casuar " with his octagonal arm-movements.

One query: do you play duets? Then get Dvořák's new *Slavonic Dances* and Robert Fuchs's Viennese waltzes. Not difficult and — delicious! And one more. But this one is as crazy as it is characteristic of your nevertheless loving father.

PS. On which *quantième* is your birthday?

Immediate Plans

January 1, go to Bremen with my wife; 4th, conduct an official subscription concert there; 5th, to Hamburg, rehearsals; 11th, third orchestral concert; 12th and 13th, conduct *Carmen* at the opera; 14th, chamber-music evening; 15th or 16th, *Carmen*; 17th, fourth orchestral concert; 18th, depart for Vienna (alone), Beethoven cycle 21st and 24th. February 1st to 7th, concerts at Pest, Graz, Lemberg, Cracow; 16th and 24th, fifth and sixth (last) orchestral concerts in Hamburg.

THE ANTI-SEMITE AHASUERUS

404]

Hamburg
January 15, 1887

Please give the bearer of these lines a kind reception. She made the journey here to revise the Raff pianoforte concerto with me before playing it at Gürzenich on Tuesday. You can hear all about us from her if it interests you. She is a thoroughly nice person, somewhat over-Teutonic, but at least not tactless. It would not be bad for you to play with her. The other day she sat next you at a concert, but was too modest to have herself introduced to you, as she would so much have liked.

Have you both begun the new year well? I wanted to send you a gift, but did not know what to choose. Perhaps you will accept the enclosed envelope instead. Apropos — or, rather, malapropos — I am writing in a fever, am terribly worn out, and have a bad cold. Fräulein H. must use her return ticket this evening before it expires, so I cannot wait for a more favourable moment.

405]

Vienna, Hotel Imperial
January 22, 1887

How I should have enjoyed your letter but for the depressing news of your bad health! Get better, and let me hear soon that you have done so.

Influenza and a pain in my right arm (from conducting) did not prevent me from doing my duty last night. On the 24th and again on the 1st and 7th of February I am playing here; 25th, Pest; 28th, Cracow; 30th, Lemberg; February 2, Graz; 4th, Pest (Grand Hotel); 10th to 25th, Hamburg (Waterloo); then presumably my Beethoven cycle in Florence-on-the-Spree and Elbathen, two days running.

Such is life, such is life!

Delighted to hear that the trouble I took over the Cologne skeleton was not wasted. Thank Heinz with my kind regards. What you wrote about Blandine made me answer her at once (that is, this morning). Shall you mind going a little short today on her account?

PS. Casuar is really a decent well-bred fellow. He stands for all the German virtues, which, as we know, do not figure in any Bayreuth show-cases. All respect to his octagonism!

Play Robert Fuchs's waltzes (duets) and Dvořák's new *Slavonic Dances* (Simrock, Berlin). Cohen will get them for you. Remember me to him. He is a nice well-educated dealer and — unbelievable, but true — not a Jew!

Heinz! Will you be generous and kind and send your *Franz* to Dr. Johannes Brahms — Vienna IV Karlsgasse 4 — and write a dedication with it? He will read it and appreciate it. My word on it!

406]

Hamburg
February 27, 1887

I FELT very sad yesterday evening when a demon on the stage, whom I did not at first recognize as Herr Wiegand, pressed me to tell him how you are. So that I may be able to give him a cheerier report, I have decided to take the night train to Bonn immediately after the concert I am conducting at Bremen on March 15, arriving early on the 16th to spend the day with you both — that is, if it will not put you out. (I have to be at Wiesbaden by the afternoon of the 17th.) Send me a line to Berlin, where I shall be camping at the Askanischer Hof from tomorrow to the 11th.

407]

Hamburg, Waterloo Hotel
March 29, 1887

I WAS just going to write a hurried reply to your letter when there came one from Heinz. So where shall I begin? And, having begun, how continue?

The enclosed cuttings will illustrate for you the impossibility of my sending such an acknowledgment of your extravagantly grateful lines as will encourage more frequent communications on your part. . . .

" Seville " has been my most recent habitation, though I had to seek it in Bremen (*Fidelio*) on the 25th and in Hamburg (*Carmen*) on the 26th.

I have Beethoven recitals on the 2nd and 4th of April in Munich, am at Berlin on the 6th, Meiningen on the 10th, and Munich again on the 12th and 14th. After that a fortnight in Venice.

Please write to me at Hotel Bavière, Munich, and tell me if Hotel Europe is not the best-recommended inn in the lagoon city. Perhaps Henry can give me information about Verona (Porta Nuova or Vescovo?) and Padua too.

In June, if it suits you both, we will hold a debate over Henrik if you have by then a more complete knowledge of his works. You are quite right to feel as you do, but Ibsen is ditto with such provocation.

I mean the beginning of June and, *D. V.*, the end also. For I intend to do the Cologne Music Festival from Bonn (Hotel Royal). It will be heavenly to escape from all the beer-drinking musicians by using a return ticket. . . .

PS. Would Henry care to give some lectures here next season?

408]

Wiesbaden, Hotel du Nord
June 17, 1887

L'homme propose . . . ! My plans have undergone a change. I hope that what is practical for me may not be the reverse for you. I should like the first ten or fifteen days of July with you at Bonn and, until the Cologne festival, to have my nerves soothed by my kind patroness here, of whom you had a fleeting glimpse at Düsseldorf recently. Something snapped in me the other day at Marburg, as a matter of fact, and I actually had to " strike." On Saturday week, the 25th, I shall travel with Frau Mutzen-becher, her companion (Fräulein Voigt), and her daughter by steamer to Bonn, arriving three-fifteen. These three ladies, all highly trained musicians, wish to attend the Cologne concerts or as many of them as our nerves will stand. It would be very nice, very natural — I almost feel inclined to use your hard-sounding word " *herrlich* " — if we all six could sit in the same row. To this end I hereby request your husband to buy six subscription tickets and hope that you will both consent to come as my guests. If possible, seats where we shall not be too visible and in such a position that any one of our number may vanish discreetly should his tympanum give in. I feel sure the octagonal Casuar will be delighted to arrange this for our " families." My personal enthusiasm for him and even more for the committee is unfortunately of so dubious a nature that I must ask Henry to undertake the arrangements. Mamma must, of course, sit farther forward. . . .

409]

Wiesbaden
Thursday, June 23 [1887]

Cento mille grazie, beloved daughter.

The three ladies are delighted with your kind invitation and accept it with enthusiasm. The mother you have just seen in D., where you took her by storm; daughter Tilda is an extremely well-brought-up flapper, as intelligent as she is naïve, a pupil of Frau Clara Schumann, but so well trained that one has no fears for her subsequent development on more independent and less one-sided lines. Frau Cecilia raves about *Tristan*, the *Ring*, and so on. The companion and governess, Fräulein Voigt (a Hamburger, daughter of a former thoroughly sound director and singing-master), is one of the least intolerable old maids I have ever met.

I thought I had better give you this brief orientation with regard to the visitors I am bringing you. I could take my oath that you will like them very much indeed. They have taken such good care of me (that is, of my poor stomach, the victim of long months of hotel cooking) that I hope to get better far sooner than I thought.

The chief thing for me at the festival is Berlioz. I shall go to the final rehearsal too on Wednesday, so make your arrangements to go with me if possible to avoid having too faulty an impression at the performance. But we can settle all this the day after tomorrow. Above all, keep well. I shall, by the way, send you a pianoforte score of the Veronese pair [1] from Frankfurt, not to play (that is impossible), but to read beforehand and follow with at the time. With all its eccentricity and general anti-German feeling (though certain parts have the highest artistic finish), the work remains a masterpiece of

---

[1] *Berlioz's* Romeo et Juliette.

thought and individual grandeur. I am longing to " see " you hear it.

At Marburg the one-time rector Franz von Liszt told me that the professors of M. and of Bonn are to hold a conference at Capellen on the 26th (Sunday). Should your husband (to whom my kindest regards) hesitate to take part on your account or mine, your father would be pleased to take charge of his wife for him.

410]

Hamburg, Alsterglacis 10
August 17, 1887

It was high time for me to try to settle down in a new place as a so-called master of the house after my five weeks at Bonn. The process of acclimatization is not yet complete, was in fact considerably hindered by such obstinate ailments as neuralgia and rheumatism, for which there are no doctors except time and patience. Every summer is, as you know, a season of discomfort for me, during which I pay for the winter's fatigues. *Jean qui agit* gives way to *Jean qui pâtit* — this time a particularly painful chronic exhaustion and acute hypochondria have kept me from answering your kind note. Apart from the fact that I had absolutely nothing of interest to impart to you, these epochs of physical and other suffering are times of silence for me. You know the comical Viennese saying: " Compared with my silence, the grave is the purest tea-party." You do not mention Blandine. Did her visit to Worms do her good? Is she thinking of coming to my ear-cure here in November? *Con* or *senza* spouse?

How the music season will shape here under my direction is not yet certain. There will be a festival performance of *Don Giovanni* on October 29 to celebrate the first performance of a hundred years ago. Following in chronological order come the whole cycle, seven evenings of opera, all within a fortnight. Besides these there is the first subscription concert on November 2. Even if I am not able to guarantee the " how " of the performances, as at Meiningen (in the " what " I was also less restricted there), this period of October 29 to November 12 should suit Blandine's plans in preparation for the Sicilian fasts.

For my début as a conductor I have chosen Spohr's *Jessonda* (probably September), as I should not like to hurt the feelings of Kapellmeister Sucher [1] — a strikingly good and temperamental conductor, particularly of Wagner — by taking over *Fidelio.*

In about a week I shall begin to rehearse the Mozart operas (at the pianoforte for the present), which, in the absence of lyrical singers, presents many a ticklish problem to a man who takes his job seriously. It is indeed not without considerable qualms that I am renewing my contract with the theatrical crowd, and it is not absolutely improbable that I shall be tempted to break away again after a brief spell. *Vedrèmo.*

The brighter side of our Hamburg existence, a handsome, relatively quiet house, with a view, I must leave Marie to describe, unless, as we should prefer, you come and have a look at it personally. It would be easier to do so from Bonn than from Bayreuth.

411]

Hamburg
September 15, 1887

I WAS greatly touched by your letter, which arrived this morning after I had spent a sleepless night (not the result of dissipation), and I may perhaps thank you best of all by telling you that I feel morally much better today than two days ago; and, as you know, the physical has usually to be taken in tow in my case. The performance of *Jessonda* last night really went off very decently (you would say " *herrlich* "), far better than the scanty and bad rehearsal led me to expect, and I am now better able to believe that my activities here need not be wasted. Do you know the piece? It has a dignity which, judging by the fairly appreciative audience, is not yet out of date.

Tomorrow will be the second performance of *Tristan* this year, with Frau Klafsky as Isolde. Her superb dramatic and

---

[1] JOSEPH SUCHER (1843–1908), *conductor at Hamburg and Berlin.*

musical interpretation of Fidelio leads me to expect far more of her than of Frau Sucher,[1] whose voice is declining (she never practises, which is all to the good as far as I, who live below her, am concerned), so that she often helps herself out with an unedifying stamp of the foot. Wiegand as King Mark was admirable; so was the new Brangäne, Fräulein Götze. Stritt does his best, in appearance at least; if only he had a little more " tenor " !

On the 19th and 25th we do the *Dutchman*, with Frau Klafsky as Senta. I am looking forward to hearing Lissmann, a true artist. Just the one for Hans Sachs. N.B. Sucher conducts. *I could not bring myself to make the cuts, which are nevertheless essential*, for the audience as well as for singer and orchestra. Opera every day: five days a week in Hamburg and two at Altona.

Your stories of little Manfred interested me very much. I must get Marie (who again sends her love) to read Victor Hugo's *Art of being a Grandfather* to me. Very, very kind of you to remember my recent request about November 4.

Yes, yes, send the bust to Frau Cecilia (Wiesbaden, Blumenstrasse 2) so that it arrives on the day. Many thanks in advance.

What about Blandine? Is she coming in November?

October 29, *Don Giovanni* (gala performance); 31st, *Idomeneo;* November 2, first subscription concert; 3rd, *Il Seraglio;* 4th, *Figaro;* 5th, *Don Giovanni;* 7th, *Cosi fan tutte;* 9th, *Magic Flute;* 11th, *Titus.*

On the 14th I am conducting a concert in Berlin, another here on the 24th, with one between at Breslau.

This is for Blandine's orientation. The best thing about her coming here would be that she could regain her strength through the good food. I guarantee that she will have an appetite, and the rest (the fattening process) will follow. To speak of less material things: I have still to thank you for that magnificent essay of your husband's on Melozzo. It really did me good to read it. It is delightful to find such eloquence combined with scientific enthusiasm. Would he could give our writers on music the recipe! But enough, I have already overrun my leisure.

---

[1] ROSA HASSELBECK-SUCHER, *Wagner singer, Isolde at Bayreuth in 1886.*

I could not rest without thanking you and sending my best wishes to accompany you to the Bavarian Tirol.

412]

Hamburg
November 26, 1887

Your request is granted before it has been expressed. I wrote two lines at once in answer to the letter. Many thanks for your charitable deed towards the rogue (owl, Grand Duke, and what not), who at writing-distance is certainly more tolerable and undoubtedly deserves respect as a political *character*. Though I can well believe that this respect cannot — on account of his rooted one-sidedness — be transformed into sympathy on your part. All the more creditable was your " practical " sympathy. I am sending his letter, which may come in useful if he repeats his visit and is not desired.

Your dear, lovable, and to my great joy more musical (than I supposed) sister leaves us the day after tomorrow, much sooner than we expected. She has absorbed a good share of good music here, though the performances were not always good, and has also, I think, digested it. Today we have still to hear Gluck's *Alceste;* tomorrow morning I am conducting Beethoven's Fifth and in the evening Mozart's *Figaro* for her. Can one be more classically fed? I could have wished you might hear some of it, particularly the two last *Don Giovanni* performances, which were really quite tolerable.

On December 5 I do the Seventh in Berlin; on the 9th, the Ninth at Bremen, and on the 12th, the *Eroica* at Hamburg.

A pity they are so far out of your reach. . . .

If you wish me to send you a line fairly often, you will have to be satisfied with this for today.

Keep nice and well and do not allow your Bach fugues to interfere with your duties towards the master of your lord and master — namely, his stomach.

413]

[Undated]

FROM Berlin I sent you, my eldest daughter, a small sign of life which will, I hope, arrive as whole as the gift you sent to Wiesbaden. Then, on arriving here, I found a letter from your younger sister, who appears to be physically and psychologically extremely fit, ordering me to write to you. Fathers must, as you know, practise obedience just as much as husbands (ask yours!) — so, tired as are my hand and brain, I am at once sending you my love and the assurance — can it be needed? — of my constant and fervent interest in your happiness and your health. I myself am baited on all sides, but chiefly from the Isar quarter. Your sister Blandine may have told you the unnecessary about it. Herewith what I owe you, with many thanks. There is still one reichsmark to come, as I had not enough *francobolli* in my drawer. But I hope I have not yet lost credit with my daughter, even in non-musical matters.

Your tenderness for the grand-ducal Bavarian artist-conductor is very touching. I too laud him as a conductor through the whole gamut, but *my* respect for his character is not at a sufficiently high level to make me feel anger with him and subsequently the need for reconciliation. All the same, I wrote him the friendliest possible letter this summer, which he can display in the corner of his mirror. I have not, however, the leisure to furnish any more of his mirrors. This I am afraid is all the *consolation* your devoted father can give you.

PS. D'Albert played *delightfully* in Berlin the day before yesterday. It was an *ideal*, an *intrinsically finished* performance. His *Esther* overture is a really good thing too, which I shall make a point of promoting in the Hanse towns. I tell you, he's no end of a fellow. I may still be able to learn something from him, since I still feel vigorous enough to admire him. His instinct has providentially set him early on the right road.

414]

Hamburg
December 25, 1887

I AM glad to know that the " song without words " from Salzwedel was well received, and made a sensation. The hearty but hasty Christmas and New Year greetings which are all I can force myself to write with my invalided right arm do not at all correspond to my intentions. But my poor wife has writer's cramp from all the bulletins she has written in the last few days; also she has other things to do. Let me first warn you to distrust profoundly, on *this* as on all *future* occasions, any newspaper notices of your papa, who is suffering chiefly from being a celebrity. According to the Berlin papers (this in the interests of Wolff's concert arrangements), I am completely re- stored; from Dresden I learn that I have a stroke, paralysis, and so on. The truth, which as usual lies in the middle street, is: in- flammation of a ligament of the right shoulder-joint, aggravated by rheumatism, which is due to overwork. For a week now I have had massage, in which I have great faith. I shall go on with it as long as possible. On January 3 I hope to be able to conduct a re- hearsal again. It has been a dreary time for me. However, I have been used to unhappy Christmases now for twenty years. Most unpleasant of all was a deficit of some thousands of marks on which I had counted this last month of the year. The Ninth (at Bremen this time) is again to blame.

When I am ill myself, I become very selfish and uninterested in other people's sufferings. It does not, however, prevent my responding to accounts of my dear ones' well-being. And as I think I may read a good one into your lines, I send you my earnest wishes for a continuation of such an idyllic state of health; idyllic in the sense of Bach's preludes and fugues in E flat and A major in the second part of the *Forty-eight*. Only today I was trying to play these old favourites again, and I thought of you and felt I must commend them specially to you. There is much soothing stuff in them: " *pax* "; also to a certain

extent: " prayer "; that is, if by prayer one does not mean
simply the roots of begging.

My hand is tired now; besides I am haunted by the fear of
your making Blandine jealous, in which case I should be forced
for the sake of " *pax* " to scribble a few words which would be
as little edifying for the sender as for the receiver.

415]

Hamburg
February 12, 1888

In for a penny, in for a pound! Having sent off a reply to
Palermo yesterday on my return from a concert (which was
interesting in so far as it showed me that I could still rely upon
my fore-paws), I cannot now leave you behind. Best thanks for
your note and the details of your present and future plans. May
everything turn out to the satisfaction of you both! I think it is
very sensible, if it can be managed, for Henry to strike this
summer and try the dry Arno instead of the wet Rhine. That
Botticelli's madonnas are more melodious than the Bonn professors I think we all agree. The *musica pegli occhi* should compare favourably with the octagonal Apollo of Gürzenich. By
the way, I want to give Marie the " Maiden of Lille " for her
thirty-first birthday. Would your husband very kindly let me
know where I can obtain the best reproduction?

Am very active again as a " fortist " (see enclosure). My
operas are: 15th, *Carmen;* 22nd, *Figaro;* 27th and 29th, *Was-
serträger* (with *Lorelei* finale, excellent effect on the stage).
Then for concerts: 24th, Berlin; 28th, here, and Bremen. It
takes my whole time to prepare for these, but the results are —
touch wood! — in the main satisfactory. My arm is no longer
mutinous, thank God, and thank the massage which I frequently
fall back on. Director Pollini told me last night that he had
heard Van Dyk at Karlsruhe and was quite delighted with him.
At the same time he asked if it were true — as everyone there
maintained — that Hofkapellmeister Mottl was engaged to one
of your sisters. . . .

I hope you will find as much pleasure in listening to D'Albert as I invariably do. A strange nature, curiously mature for such tender years. His overture to *Esther* is a most refreshing piece of music, almost too irreproachable in its manufacture. I did it here with great success. His string quartet also impressed me when I read it. . . .

416]

Hamburg
March 2, 1888

I HOPE you will benefit also by your stay at Meran. Let me know how you are some time.

I am off to Berlin tomorrow, where I conduct on the 5th and play on the 8th. On the 9th I go to Königsberg, thence to Bremen, returning here on the 14th; 15th, Lübeck; 16th, Berlin. Here from March 20 to the end of the month. So now you know where to write to me. . . .

It is possible that I shall take up opera again next year, in which case I should do the *Meistersinger,* provided my conditions are accepted: two evenings, one for Acts I and II, one for Act III. Perhaps the singers' feast that we offer will then entice you to come over, which would be very nice.

In the end of April I go to Copenhagen. In May I shall *have* to take a cure at Wiesbaden for arthritis and in June shall probably concertize in London. Perhaps we shall meet somewhere in the autumn. It depends chiefly on your and your husband's arrangements.

I am still a little tired from my Chopin recital last night. Monday and Wednesday were opera nights here, and in between — Tuesday — I played at Bremen. You see, I can't get away from public applause. The juice must be squeezed from the lemon of life's eventide. . . .

417]

Hamburg
March 25, 1888

YOUR silence was beginning to make me anxious and I was just about to send an inquiry to your husband at Bonn to ask how you were. But on my return from Lübeck I was reassured by your letter. At this moment you will be once more in possession of your long-absent professor without any of the university impedimenta, on which you are to be congratulated, which I do with the more zeal in that I am quite unable to condole with anyone.

A visit from you at 50 Lung' Arno Nuovo would certainly give us great, great joy and could only provide refreshing impressions for you. I therefore strongly advise you to come, prone as I am in most cases to ward you off.

I send my thanks in advance for the promised *Dürer*. He belongs to the *great ones* about whom I like to read something sensible, though I get little inspiration from their own creations. How often have I envied you your intelligent receptivity! Still, it is a sign of the world's progress that children should be better educated than their parents. For me Dürer is the comparative of *dur* (to swallow).

Have you good news from Sicily? The quantity of things I should like to ask you is only equalled by the lack of things I have to tell. Besides: " in youth one is monotonous, in age we only repeat ourselves."

We are all more or less like squirrels in a cage, the size of which makes no essential difference.

My brother-in-law Bojanovski has been promoted from his well-paid sinecure of a post as consul-general at Budapest to the presidency of the Imperial Patent Office in Berlin, a new appointment, which is not a sinecure. He has accordingly moved there with kith and kin. I am so thankful that he will be there to watch over my poor mother's last days. Her intellect seems now to have withered completely, while her body still functions normally and painlessly. What a sad disease is old age!

PS. Here until April 25; then Wiesbaden until the end of May — then London.

418]

Wiesbaden, Hotel Schwarzer Bär
May 13, 1888
(His Excellency Goethe deigned to live here
in 1814 and 1815.)

YESTERDAY I had your husband's parcel and today your letter. I should have time enough just now to read this edition *de luxe*, but it would be too exhausting for me to do so in my present condition. (What a pity that so readable and yet informing a book should not be available in one of the cheaper educational series . . . !) This particular cure is more tiring than I had dreamed, internally and externally, but anyway I am bound to try it for the sake of making my fore-paws sufficiently supple again to risk the London concerts (June 1st to 28th), by which I hope to make money.

I shall therefore be briefer than you, but, on the other hand, am writing by return. Honestly, your rather casual reference to my poor worthy old Jessie rankles a little. Perhaps you got mixed between all your correspondents and thought you were writing to your husband. I shall take my Christian revenge by telling you very little more about my " feeder " (at lunch and dinner) than that your greetings shall reach her ear and heart this very day. Congratulations on your nature-worship. That is right. Poly-, not pan-theism is my motto. It protects one against the plague of fetishism and its attendant plague, fanaticism. Please go *quickly* and call on your opposite neighbour — I mean the husband of Freifrau von Heldburg. That is, if you feel like it.

If you are writing to Palermo, send my love and thanks for the recent answer to my Königsberg letter, will you?

So you want something " printed "? Very well, here is the laudatory notice of my last recital this season. It suits me occasionally to go one better than the latest Liszt pupils, for a change. Immediately after paying this homage to your illustrious " *nonno*," I came here to get the inflammation out of my shoulder-ligaments. Are you gondoling too? I hope you share your husband's industrious labours in that respect. You see, I can be as stupid as anyone else.

419]

Hamburg
August 29, 1888

For today you must be content with a word of thanks, also to your husband for his attempt to justify me.

I have had another real bad period of loss of balance, and the so-called explanations which you appear to desire are anathema to me just now, martyred as I am by every kind of ugly agitation. Apart from that, though, we should not understand each other. You are too young and I too old to do so. In fact: " In letters one does not explain oneself, one makes statements, develops one's own ideas, and in consequence exaggerates." Who wrote this truism I don't know, but it's terribly true.

Whether your return to exile at Bonn calls for congratulations I do not yet know. Every *pied-à-terre* is a *pis aller*, as I see from my own case, where my sole pleasure lies in not being at Meiningen. Berlin is closed to me, on account of " *l'infamille*," as your Aunt Claire used to say.

It goes far towards reconciling me to many things that you should wish to see me again and I should hail an opportunity with delight. The most suitable place seems to me Berlin, for your husband, I imagine, must sometimes " have to go " there in connexion with his profession. It would be a good thing if you could choose a time when I have to interfere with Messrs. Mottl, Richter, Sucher's little game. I am giving you the dates so that you may see I do not treat the possibility of our meeting lightly. Each of the dates mentioned includes for me two or three days spent in rehearsing beforehand.

420]

Breslau
October 22, 1888

THE enclosure will show you that I have again the whole pack at my heels. I am worn out and have a bad cold into the bargain. *A la guerre comme à la — campagne!*

That you should be able and willing to come and see me in Berlin on November 9 (still Askanischer Hof, Königgrätzer-strasse, three minutes from the concert hall) would give me great joy *if* the program could be arranged more to your liking, but that cannot be. I am in fact doing the Fourth Symphony of Br. . . not -uckner. Neither would Herr Grünfeld, with a thumping Rubinstein pianoforte concerto, really tempt you. What about the double performance of the Ninth on December 17?

My wife came as far as here with me, but went straight on to Cracow, where her mother is very ill. She returns your greetings cordially. I must now thaw my frozen fingers and hurry to rehearsal, where I do not expect things to go particularly smoothly. Maestro Bruch, who is such a favourite on the Rhine as a choral composer, is said to be a very mediocre conductor. *A la campagne comme à la guerre!*

I am sending these meaningless lines without any additions, as I fear the pack of musicians who will swarm about me this afternoon will make such additions impossible for me. I was delighted to hear from many quarters that you were looking exceedingly well and bright at the Bayreuth festival performance. *Continuez*, dear child. As soon as the programs are at all settled, I will propose one or the other of the Berlin concerts to you. On December 17 there is, as I said, the Ninth. There is also the fifth concert a week earlier, but it is doubtful whether I shall be able to put in a Beethoven symphony there. This season I must produce the less emotional ones, the even-numbered, Second, Fourth, Sixth, Eighth, as I had the more thrilling uneven ones last time.

421]

Hamburg
December 23, 1888

YOUR letter of mourning, written on the 8th, was brought to me just as I was rehearsing the *Sinfonia tragica*, of my old comrade Felix (the name has not justified itself for him as it has for the Bavarian Hofoperndirektor) in Berlin. It was as unfortunate a moment as that in which Macbeth, while preparing for battle, receives the evil tidings of his wife. My problem was an important one: is my popularity worth anything as a means to a noble end, or is it a paltry thing to have as a possession, for which one would feel obliged to offer up one's better self, so to say? You will see from the *Nationalzeitung* (which my wife sent you) that I have come out of this ticklish affair whole, though not without all sorts of manœuvring. I came back here excited and worn, but had to conduct again on the 20th at Bremen and must go there again on the 28th. In short, I have only today found time, as you see, to reply to your letter, so dear in spite of passionate moments.

First let me say this one thing: had I undertaken to conduct the Ninth (which has repeatedly thrown me) on that December 17, I should at this moment certainly be lying on my nose with all the arrangements for the second half of the season irreparably destroyed. *C'est comme cela et même ainsi.* Perhaps this assurance may drive out your recent sorrow, which is, I hope, acute rather than chronic in its nature (for " time is a gentleman," you know), or at least the egoistical portion of it which remains. Perhaps this has already been done by Herr Kommerzrat Gross, with whom I made a point of having things out in Berlin. Do not, my darling Daniela, curse patience, which is more than a cardinal virtue (read Herder's *Prometheus* some time), for it lends a value to that which is not the highest good. If it is coupled with the love of justice, the said " not highest " good becomes not only ennobled, but holy and divine. Here, then, you have my confession of faith; unfortunately I am just as often obliged to warn myself to have a little more patience as

I am to thunder to my neighbour to act with more justice. Beware of judging your father prematurely. Do not lend your ear to every idiot and knave, to E. O. L. and Co. Here — take it — you have an interesting document, which please keep. I do not need it, as I do not collect letters which minister to my vanity. Alas, there will still be many misunderstandings. "In all the jumble of the gods, Loge's the only gentleman."

By renouncing my right to an ego I have purchased my priesthood of justice. *Nil inultum remanebit.* But only an impersonal judge can avenge. He alone can weigh right and wrong. And punishment comes only when the culprit has been given his chance — *suum (bonum) cuique.* Just now, for instance, I shall inflict minor sentences on people who least expect it; I like if possible to have the applause of ununderstanding spectators. *Quando si parta, si sparla,* even in the case of the written word, as I see to my horror. But do not split your head over anything that may puzzle you in this. Really, so many sorts of things pass through my head at once, and the importunities which are the cost of my " celebrity " are more numerous than the newspapers. If even a giant intellect like that of your grandfather fell a victim to the world — yes, yes, yes, to the world (*monde immonde*) — how much more must a second-hand talent like mine beware of letting itself be irrevocably consumed, particularly when it cannot resist the native weakness for coupling the adjective *benefico* with the noun *burbero* now and then.

Fräulein Anna Haasters, the " van Eyck Madonna," told me last night after my pianoforte class that she would make a point of looking after you in the holidays, and I did not deter her, in my own interest. Before that she was telling me of the brilliant success of your husband's lecture at Cologne on the old Cologne school of painting. This gives me the opportunity of sending congratulations, which I should like to see multiplied as far as possible.

You know that I always try to ignore so-called festivals as if I were blind and dumb. We two, Marie and I, do not now even give the maids Christmas presents, but make them in the form of frosty metal or bits of paper. This saves many a heart-burning. The really free man must have rid himself of all such obligations and have as little as possible to do individually with the general festivities. These are my views (distorted of course). But to the deformed nothing looks straight.

PS. Should Casuar octagonize the *Tragica* in the course of the winter, try to go and hear it. How gladly would I suggest a meeting at Wiesbaden, which is relatively near you, for January 24–6! But I am playing stuff for the Aachen festival, so patience, please! (You see, I am not swearing.)

422]

SS. Saale
March 14, 1889

MANY thanks for your good wishes for my journey. Your promise to meet me at Wiesbaden — you are " adored " in Blumenstrasse, which is better than being importuned — is a very refreshing one. It will strengthen my resolve to return home only one eighth an invalid. In the early days of May (1st or 4th) I leave New York again (address: Metropolitan Opera House), make a short stay in Hamburg, and arrive on the 16th or 20th at the Schwarze Bär, Langgasse. Now for a little surprise: I have engagements for two months in Boston, Chicago, and Philadelphia. Let us hope it will not be a case of:

> Today a hunter came to sing
> Whose beak had grown askew;
> Even the Masters shrank away
> For fear of what Hans Sachs would say.

But I had better stop. My jokes are still too continental. . . .

423]

Tremont House, Boston
April 16, 1889
on an unimaginably lovely spring
day such as I wish you may have in
the Old World too.

LIKE an obedient father I called on Mrs. G. Schinner, Blandine's friend, for the second time today, having missed her yesterday; and now, in my foolish anxiety to be just, I feel I owe you compensation, a little of my time (though I can hardly call it my own), a brief but cordial transatlantic greeting.

The "old man" is really on the way to rejuvenation. This country is a veritable Canaan, with St. Liberty as the mother of all good and beautiful things. This will not prevent me from returning home in great need of massage. Well, Metzger is at Wiesbaden, and my mind dwells on the short distance which separates that place from Bonn. Your husband permitting, therefore, I hope to give you the opportunity of asking all the questions that rise to your lips, when I shall answer so long as there is breath in me.

I have the greater part of my business behind me now: ten public appearances. Unfortunately I did not do myself justice here yesterday. Must regain my self-respect. On the 22nd I play at Baltimore; 24th, Philadelphia; 25th, New York; 27th, Brooklyn. Then, on May 2, I conduct a farewell concert, with the *Meistersinger* overture at the close. On the 4th we sail for home, the three of us (my wife and our splendid companion Marie Ritter) by the North-German Lloyd. I say "home," but, as old Goethe used to say: "Where I am of use, there is my fatherland." . . .

424]

Wiesbaden
May 19, 1889

Here I am, beloved daughter, at the Hotel zum Schwarzen Bär, No. 12, ground floor. When are you coming and will it be for a few days? Every place is overflowing, as always in May, but I want you to be in the same hotel if possible. You had my telegram on arrival? Best wishes meanwhile to you both. Everybody is talking of your husband's new appointment and congratulating *Frankfurt* on it.

425]

Hamburg
July 2, 1889

IT was such a pleasure to find such satisfactory news from you when I got up this morning after a three days' feverish head-cold, although your immediate object in writing was anything but delightful. I do beg of you, dear child, never again to give me this kind of a commission, which in this case it was not even in my power to carry out. I am engaged by the manager Hermann Wolff to conduct these concerts here and in Berlin. He is not allowed to interfere with the programs, but I, on the other hand, take no part in engaging the artists (a thing I always dislike doing), which is his domain. Your Hebrew "Freischütz" should know that, he and all his colleagues. Now I shall be obliged, for your sake (yes! have I not, purely for your sake, spent many, many hours in suffering and even cajoling the quite incredibly thick-skinned Engelbert!) to devote my tired pen to explaining all this to your pseudo-Hungarian Rapsbauer.

It appears that I have a double. Fräulein Haasters — whom I drove to the zoo in Cologne with another friend of your pretty sister-in-law on the afternoon of June 26, as I was not leaving until the night train — assures me that she saw me a few days before in the distance. But at the time when Casuar was misconducting the Ninth at Gürzenich, I was staying with poor Romaine von O. at Baden-Baden. Appearances are deceptive, you see. On the other hand I was once greeted in W. by friends (?) of yours, a professorial couple who bemoaned having lost you, or made as if they did. Name indistinct, not too provincial-looking, almost well-bred. Had I known that you were returning to Bonn, I would have stopped there at the (old) risk of being in your way. Now what is the meaning of this monstrous bug that you are pleased to put in my ear? I hope some time this winter to succeed in forcing the gates of this Hamburg that is so primly closed to me. There are two very obvious reasons why *we* have not invited you (not to invite is not synonymous with to repel, remember). First, my wife cannot offer you hospitality in our humble abode. N.B. This refers *equally* to Blandine.

Secondly, as I am engaged on *my own* music (I am surely justified in these last years of my life, after all the fighting, in peacefully following my own inclination in this domain) and as such music is not approved in the Upper-Franconian Lourdes,[1] but is regarded as heresy, I had, as a " disobedient " parent, to protect myself against you and so on and so on — and *not* so on.

Let us have no more politics.

Next century, long after my incineration in Gotha, then, perhaps — well, one must not expect every kind of satisfaction in one's lifetime. All the same, it is a pity, a great pity, that I cannot invite you (as I can Blandine, though unfortunately that is nothing for her to be proud of) to the so-called musical festival in the Trade Exhibitions Hall here (a bare-looking place, by the way) on the 9th, 11th, and 13th of September. I myself get more out of what I do *not* conduct than what I do. In general, music is not a summer sport and I should have refused outright had I not been under an obligation to the citizens of Hammonia for a good turn they did me.

By the way, what sort of a monstrous philistine humbug is that Beethoven house-committee in your ex-residence?

Do you know what they've done? After various futile musical papers had made an outcry about the conspicuous absence of my name from the list of honorary members, I received a long and fervent letter offering me honorary membership, naturally with the insinuation that I should help to rake in subscriptions. I *declined:* " do not wish to see my name on the same list with Count Hochberg's (and Verdi's)." That was the least offensive excuse I could make. Of course I enclosed five pounds by way of politeness. Had the president, " Ebbinghaus " (tailor or glover?) had a pennyworth of honourable feeling, he would have returned the money. But —

Another specimen of a real German mayor's parlour society. As far as I am aware, no one has yet discovered the actual room in which the mother of Ludwig van was confined. That's what I want to know. . . .

[1] *Bayreuth.*

426]

Meiningen
July 14, 1889

Yᴏᴜʀ Bayreuth bookbinder-artist has just sent me eight volumes of Arthur, one of Gracian, one of Goethe quotations, and
unfortunately a new Wildenbruch too — as if that sort of thing
. . . ! — for all of which my heart-felt thanks to you.

I hope they will be speedily followed by a line from you
unless writing to the Countess takes all your spare time.

On the urgent representations of my doctor I have given up
my intended pilgrimage to Weimar tomorrow, which would
probably have produced the material for an aggravation of my
physical and moral state. This state is not disagreeably obvious
to others, I may say, so I shall be pleased to see Sir Henry at
any time should he be so courteously disposed as to call.

Should you be inclined to read a really clever — that is,
enlightening — book, which even your dear mother might like
to have read aloud to her, I shall be glad to send you the *Dis-
cours sur l'histoire de France* by Comte Charles de Mouy. It is
quite new.

427]

Berlin
October 26, 1889

Iᴛ is indeed a rare treat to receive so delightful a budget of
news from you. I can only send you a sheaf of congratulations in
reply. I do not think one need distrust first impressions to the
extent of " first movements," for instance. Rather do they form
a foundation for happy attachments and future development.
May your new home keep its promise and become permanent.

As you see, I am full of activity, and I hope that the approaching spectre of old age will not yet signify decrepitude,
although it is true that I feel less and less desire to go on conducting today, tinkling tomorrow (30th, Magdeburg; 31st,

Hanover; November 1, Göttingen; 2nd, Hildesheim), and wind-
ing up the winter season again with America. But I hope to be
able to say: "This is my last deception " — self-deception, that
is. Necessity protects one from giving way to moral boredom
and physical exhaustion.

It is charming of you to be thinking of another meeting. In
forwarding your letter my wife announces her determination to
save the suggestion for your husband to lecture in Hamburg
from being dropped again. It should of course take place at a
time when I am not expecting to be called away on this or that
errand. Then you might be very kind and not give us too short a
measure of your time there. I shall be in your neighbourhood
three weeks from now, for I am playing at Wiesbaden on the
15th (as I told you in the spring) and on the 16th at Mainz. In
both places they have asked for Beethoven's E flat Concerto. I
propose that, unless you insist on showing yourself to the Meiningen Princess as she wishes, you might come to Mainz. I shall
have to leave there early on the 17th and hurry home, as I have
a morning rehearsal next day. Still, one would have half a dozen
hours for a chat in the afternoon. Or perhaps Wiesbaden would
suit you better. It is for you to choose.

I congratulate you, and also (if a stranger may) your stepbrother, on his coming to live with you, and I hope he will be
able to carry out his intentions to the full.

What else can I find to tell you? Oh, I was present at a performance of *Siegfried* in Hamburg recently. It was thoroughly
and surprisingly good. Very moderate costs, orchestra not over-
loud, a very steady conducting by Professor Schröder,[1] a far
better musician than Sucher, whose wife makes an admirable
Brünhild, however. But most of all I was fascinated by Max
Alvary, who has a tenor of incredible nobility and vigour. There
was artistic ripeness in every note, every gesture. He is to some
extent caviar to the public, but there is a goodly number of
sensible pairs of ears in Hamburg. You would have enjoyed
the performance, and the defects on the "production" side
would probably have worried you as little as they did me.

---

[1] KARL SCHRÖDER, *violoncellist and conductor, succeeded Sucher at Hamburg.*

428]

Berlin
November 23, 1889

Y OU are my devoted child, are you not? My devotion to you
must have shone out at you in those hours of our happy reunion
just a week ago.

Well, your wretched father is again with shipwreck, the last
surely of the many in his life.

. . . It all hangs together with my telegram of the day
before yesterday. Thank you so much for your reply, and excuse
this bad writing from frozen fingers.

To come to the point, I want you to make a small sacrifice
for me and undertake a journey to Wiesbaden. I have given *my
sacred word* not to go there again and not to write, and this word
I must keep until my poor over-driven brain can think of a
manœuvre by which I can obtain release from it.

Do me the kindness to spare my feelings as much as possible
when you report to me. I know I can trust your good feeling
and tact.

The rest later, from Hamburg. One thing more. My wife
will be sending you one day soon the books I picked out for you.
(Do exactly what you like with them.) Will you write to her a
very nice note when they arrive? It will be to the interest of
a darling daughter and her miserable but loving and devoted
father.

429]

Berlin
Sunday, November 24, 1889

S INCEREST thanks for your telegram. How well you understand my misery! First of all, let me warn you that letters to
Hamburg are not safe. So write to me, if you wish to, here by
way of Wiesbaden, where I arrive on December 6 (Askanischer
Hof).

Jealousy reaches out towards everything that is dear to me and precious; hatred pursues all who are devoted to me and (which I count higher) are kindred souls. I live in such a terrible rush that in these two days here I have not had a quarter of an hour free for my own thoughts except at night, when I fall asleep from exhaustion; it is not so much the number of heads of music notes as the crowd of human heads about me which makes my own swim. Hence this jerky style, which I hope will not make you hold your father too deeply in contempt. I must make every sacrifice to keep my wife from — running away from me, not only on practical grounds, but because our *common sorrows* have bound me so closely to her that, at my age, I could not survive the parting. That is the fact.

A calm explanation is out of the question.

Your husband must forgive me for pulling you into my troubles. It will not be for long. How I should welcome a nervous fever! But the flesh is all too strong, it seems. I have no friend, no confidant, not a soul about me who is on my side.

How I long to see you in Hamburg! They shall not take you from me. But that is just why I must — do all the other musts.

May God continue to bless you as He has done heretofore.

430]

Berlin
November 25, 1889

LET me embrace you with many thanks for the sacrifice you have made for me. I am not the only one who owes you them.

Have you inherited a theoretical thirst for justice from me? (In practice it is apt to have a very amateurish look.) Possibly. In that case — and because it is a pleasant though not easy duty to put you *au fait* — you shall hear both sides. First, here is a letter from the chief poison-mixer (a woman) in Hamburg, which speaks for itself. Secondly, here is a letter from Wiesbaden (*the last!*) which I received here. This one will explain to you my *angoscie letali* at the stage when I turned to your filial love for refuge. Perhaps you might read it later, it is slightly overwrought. I have not the heart to destroy it: look upon it as a deposit. The Hamburg letter must of course no more be read in Wiesbaden than the latter may be even named in Hamburg. But to caution you thus is almost an insult to your heart's insight. How much poison there is in the world! God preserve us from making even a non-deliberate contribution to this tool of Satan!

To bring about your coming to Hamburg without appearing to do so is my immediate heart's desire. *A proposito*, as I cannot now play the " last five " at Wiesbaden, I will do so in Frankfurt, and in aid of the Schopenhauer memorial. Ask our friend Steyl about it some time. Or is one of the Metzler firm also a member of the memorial committee?

Your telegram has just come. You are a jewel of the *first* water. I feel I cannot destroy this telegram either. I shall deposit it in the envelope with the other documents, as I may not show it.

Well, I must go to the concert. Two composers have made the rehearsals difficult for me. However, I shall be able to sweep them out of the way with the *Huldigungsmarsch* (the eighteen-year-old fairy king with the gazelle eyes aglow with pure fire — as you have never seen him — sitting high upon his horse), which is to have its first decent performance today. You and your ears will be there in my imagination.

Many thanks for Coallo, which I had already read in a Hamburg café, to which I resorted for that purpose only.

431]

Hamburg
November 27, 1889

THE K.s, your ambassadors, who honoured me with a call in the artists' room on Monday evening, will perhaps tell you that Ludwig II's *manes* had no cause to complain of *lèse-majesté*. Neither do I regret the white night which followed my ecstatic outburst and hindered by twenty-four hours my return here, where I was welcomed by your dear letter.

My wife is greatly touched and ashamed that you should value her packing of your little book (yes, yours, originally your grandfather's, and therefore inherited *anticipando*) so

highly. My pleasure in giving is, however, tinged with specula-
tion. You must pay for it as follows:

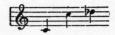

Henry will explain. See that you both are free for the beginning
of the year.

Begin by coming to the concert here on January 8, 1890,
when you will get the *Eroica;* then travel (both of you) to Berlin,
where for the last time I am playing " the five," on the 10th.
On the 13th there is the philharmonic concert in Berlin, at which
you will hear *my* orchestra *par excellence*. Never will you have
as good an opportunity of helping your father over the ominous
date.

My particular anxiety is (Fräulein T. P. *must* arrange it)
to get your husband invited to hold his lecture here between
January 4th and 8th. Should this assumption of the creator's
right to turn evil into good bring success, then your father will
gain new life and no longer be ashamed and angry at reaching
his sixties.

PS. Waterloo Hotel — four minutes from us, opposite the
theatre — would give you very respectable and cheap bedrooms.

432]

Hamburg
December 2, 1889
(*A favourite day of old with my*
family, occasionally a lucky one
too.)

. . . WOLFF wrote the notice in your honour. Much
lives that is wonderful, but nothing is more wonderful than the
human being, says Sophocles; and his fellow-Greek Felix M. has
composed a hopping " Sicilienne " in six-eight to it (N.B. the
Antigone contains really beautiful things besides). However, in
reply to your inquiry after my health, I must refer you to the

Jewess of Toledo, last act. I too am the owner of — several castles in Spain, although no Alfonso.

Did Humperdinck show you my letter? I thought vividly of you on the day when, to please you, I mustered courage to write to No. 33 Via Butera.

433]

Monday, December 9, 1889

Do, my precious child, for all the saints, be extremely cautious in your letters to me. All that is left of my life's harmony is at stake. Explanations when we meet, if you need them. But no, you will not. Are you not my very ownest child? *Sapristi, comme nous nous rencontrons!* Well, tomorrow I am rehearsing *Harold.* And *Damnation!* I feel in my soul the very vibrations produced by your reading of *Faust.* Then — *Salvation!* I pick up Brahms, and at the *Adagio* my eyes fill with moisture. Impossible that you should not weep over it too. Such a new kind of emotion as it is!

I came in feeling a little depressed, but your letter, my angel, relieved me of my burden. Thank you. *A bientôt* — speaking epistolarily.

First, though, you must absolutely come to us before the first (the 4th if possible). If only you give us time, we can probably secure the furnished rooms above us for you, which would be very nice, eh? Do me the pleasure to promise and to keep that promise. Arch-naturally, Henry must be of the party. (Four are better than three.)

434]

Kamberglin
December 11, 1889

With fear and trembling does my pen seize me to answer a question of yours, a goodly portion of *courage civil* being needed in view of the danger of seeing my harmony disturbed. Raphael's pupil Benvenuto Tisio (according to Thode) will reveal to you my favourite flower: York-colour leads, and with it Lancaster. Now I wonder what you will reply to that!

I am quite willing to adopt your flower, you know, which will certainly be neither the violet nor the Victoria regia. If one had to choose by perfume, I confess that mignonette would be my favourite, but optically one would be poorly served by it. *Basta.*

You have now a favourable opportunity of sending me a syllable about your arrival in January. At the very latest you should be here by the 7th, so as to have slept off your tiredness before the second preliminary rehearsal. Last night I was reading a very enjoyable French book: Paul Bourget's *Essais de psychologie contemporaine,* fifth edition, 1887.

I was particularly attracted by the essay on one of my favourite literary carnations, Stendhal. You will perhaps not know him, though Blandine may, and for that reason I shall recommend the book to her instead of you. By the way, your sister's last letter was quite charming. I am glad I recommended her to use the language of the hereditary enemy. It suits her well, very well.

Fräulein Haasters achieved a most gratifying success in Berlin the day before yesterday with Duseke's pianoforte concerto, a work of almost unsurmountable difficulty. You women can, when you like, be far better reproductionists than any of us of the so-called strong sex. It is just the same in plays, though not so much in opera.

Addio, cara figliuola — ti darò nuove della " nonna " a Berlino, dove mi recherò posdoman colla mia moglie, stavolta scendendo al Westendhotel per motivi da te indovinabili.

PS. No Sgambati. *Iddio sia lodato. Figuriti: giammai non risponde a Wolff: ora — bisogna far senza la di lui sbadigliacciante solemnità!*

435]

Berlin, Westendhotel
December 15, 1889

No, I am not such a greedy seeking-to-plunder-my-neighbour egoist as not to be content with what you are so good as to give me.

On the morning of the 7th you will be in Hamburg, then, at the Waterloo Hotel. The rehearsal is at ten-thirty. We shall call for you and afterwards take you home with us. On the 9th we all dine together at five minutes past twelve, Askanischer Hof.

On the 13th, after the evening concert, you will both see me off at the station to Königsberg. . . .

Tomorrow is my Christmas: the birthday of the Messiah of acoustics. We are going to celebrate it properly. The rehearsals are going well. (The final one is due in an hour's time.) I am sending you the program in advance so that you can listen in imagination.

Thank you sincerely for your imperialist impressions. Please God you are not deceiving yourself.

Marie sends very best wishes.

436]

Hamburg
December 19, 1889, evening

Tante grazie. Splendid how everything fits. On the 7th Henry reads, on the 8th Hans beats time, on the 9th we depart: you, Marie, and I, to the Askanischer Hof, Berlin, where rooms are engaged, two bedrooms with sitting-room between. Hail, Correggio! (N.B. I can see nothing in him, *colpa mia!*) The repetition of the Ninth yesterday was more ecstatically received if possible than on the 16th, and two hundred and twenty-four ladies wore white carnations in my honour. What is your favourite flower, after all? Surely I might be told by now. . . .

437]

Hamburg
December 21, 1889

. . . AM sending you a communication from a most interesting Asiatic acquaintance of recent date. Please return it.

This pathetically charming Japanese has constructed " a transposing and modulating harmonium which is theoretically most ingenious and practically of great importance for the future, a beacon light in the wild social-democratic, chaotic sea of sound of today." He realized instinctively that I — and so on and so on.

My last epistle will have crossed yours. For today I will do no more than assure you that all my favourite beasts at the zoo are looking forward to making your acquaintance almost as much as the old man to seeing you again. These distant cousins of mine are: a hyena, two young pumas, two bears, one bittern, and various Mexican *scioattotti* and musk-rats.

PS. What about Stendhal? Many thanks in anticipation anyway. Salzwedel will send you my greeting.

438]

Hamburg
January 4, 1890

IN my ignorance I telegraphed to you, reply paid, this morning. Now, in the evening paper (7.30), I read the sad news that your husband has a bronchial attack as the after effect of the " new-fashioned cold." Of course *your place is by his side.* Therefore spare yourself the trouble of any excuses or what not.

Sour apples are meant to bite into, not to serve as a demonstration of sourness. A good beginning for my sixtieth year, but there may be better things in store.

439]

Hamburg
January 20, 1890

I HAVE now been a long time without a bulletin from you and am hungry for " good news " which are not " no news." So — please! I came back from Königsberg yesterday laden with pleasant impressions and equally with influenza (which, however, I hope to work off by vigorous conducting here for the orchestral concert on Wednesday). I am of course quite at home in that particular city, which is, amongst other things, the home of the purest marzipan.

But now as to preparations for the morrow. My Beethoven evening in Berlin (*le cinque ultimo*) takes place on the 29th of this month. On the 31st is the seventh subscription concert, the program of which you will have seen in the program-book of the sixth, which I sent you from Berlin a week ago. Does it tempt you? And can you succumb to the temptation?

On February 5 is the eighth orchestral concert here, for which I return from Berlin on the 1st. Would it not be splendid if your husband could give his lecture here on the 2nd, 3rd, or 4th?

All this could still be arranged to suit your wishes and convenience, remember, if you let me know without delay.

Dunque, dunque . . .

440]

Hamburg
January 26, 1890

I T is really " *herrlich*," as you always say, to have missed you again. Well, one should take nothing tragically, said Otto the Great, and we must put a good face on it and fatten on hope like capons. N.B. On March 12 I am crossing the big pond again in the *Saale* from Bremen.

You have much to write and many correspondents; but, all

the same, you will, I hope, send a tele-bulletin to inform me of the definite departure of the lady Influenza.

I ought, I suppose, to hold my tongue with respect to the two gentlemen whom you praised to me the other day. But to avoid future misunderstandings I think it better to tell you that Herr Felix W. and Herr Max Schw. have both behaved in a disgraceful and ungrateful way to me, though they probably deny it now for shame of themselves. *Non raggionam' più di loro,* you say so prettily. Ah, how I long to hear your dear silvery voice again!

441]

Parker House, Boston
March 27, 1890

WITH only nine and a half hours to spend in the transatlantic Athens, I can write neither an interesting nor a nice letter, but at most a hurriedly correct one. The correctness consists in respecting the law of primogeniture, which I do by sending you my first greeting; Palermo will come in for the next.

The crossing was very rough and not without its dangers. We were a day and a half late, with the result that my Boston dates had to be altered. On Sunday morning at ten we arrived at our hotel (I between the two Maries), and at twelve I was rehearsing with Damrosch and his orchestra. So, as you see, I was in high spirits. In general we all felt as much at home here as if everything European from May 1889 to March 1890 had been a wild exiles' dream. I am now most anxious to hear how you are feeling, bodily and mentally.

If you would send a line to New York, care of Edward Schuberth, music-publisher, Union Square, it would probably reach me somewhere on the journey, as he has a plan of my tour. We leave New York on April 5 and do not return there until May 1. So it may be the middle of May before we embark for home. . . .

442]

Hamburg
May 27, 1890

Y OUR loving message of welcome, which greeted us on our somewhat belated arrival, touched me deeply and I thank you warmly for the thought. Unfortunately I cannot write very cheerfully. My nervous condition is complicated and unsatisfactory. During this ten weeks' absence I have suffered almost continuously beyond what I could bear in many different ways. I am repenting — visibly at present — in a physical sense. . . . In a month's time, let us say, I may be able to take up my pen to ask how you are with more pleasure. I only hope you are continuing to feel as well as your letter " over there " gave me to understand.

PS. My nerves are in such a feeble state that I am unable to take an interest in any of the things that are worth while in life and still less in politics, in which connexion I feel I can never master my detestation of — you know whom!

Would you be so kind as to tell Steyl, with my kind regards, when you are passing, that my bad health puts all correspondence out of the question for me for some weeks?

443]

[Hamburg]
July 6, 1890

A s I can write nothing that will cheer you, I must be content to thank you warmly for your dear letter and your telegram the other day and to send you my earnest wishes for your recovery. Actually writing, and even reading, are forbidden me by my doctor. I am in much the same state as fifteen years ago, when I returned from overseas with neuralgia and neurasthenia. My physicians sent me a fortnight ago to an official country retreat kindly lent by the Petersen family. But the bad weather prevented my gaining anything by it, and they now want to send me to Heidelberg to see if the famous Professor Erb will give me galvanic treatment. This will probably be my next move, but at present I am too weak to travel. In any case you shall soon hear more, and I hope better, news of me, if not from my own hand, then from that of my wife, who is nursing me with the utmost devotion and self-sacrifice.

444]

Schlangenbad
September 15, 1890

YESTERDAY Marie was made to promise to let you know the hour when we passed through your town. But I am preventing her because it worries me to have you worried or to think that you are being worried. I am so uncertain, too, that I do not yet know whether the proposal to arrive at five, moving on at seven-twenty, will be practicable.

And really, my darling Daniela, it will be better for us only to meet again — if God wills that we ever do so — when I am ·in a mood which will not bring back the painful impression I made on you yesterday, but may possibly efface it.

PS. As you see, I find writing difficult, and the effort is not worth making from the reader's point of view. Also one whim succeeds another in my wild unhappy brain. Is this not one point in a cat's favour (you do not like them, I know), that when they are ill they are nowhere to be found? All the same, if I am not too ill, I may knock on your door at five-thirty, always supposing that the doctor pronounces me free from any suspicion of influenza. Do not, I implore you, come to the station in any case. I hope you got home safely last night. I could never forgive myself if your husband had reason to regret your act of devotion.

445]

Hamburg
November 4, evening [*1890*]

I HAD intended to send you my belated thanks for your letters as soon as the two concerts here were over (they went off well and I should therefore have been glad to have you there to hear the symphony), but my very " ill-tempered " head did not allow of it. I was suffering so violently from my incurable gout in the head that I could not even read. My wife will have told you how heavily I have to pay for every fresh effort to be active. Every morning rehearsal means the remainder of the day wasted, every evening concert the whole of the following day. Even a fortnight's constant use of arsenic (the last remedy) has done nothing for me. The doctor preaches confidence, however, and ascribes the failure to the return of influenza symptoms. My sole confidence consists in thinking the whole thing must come to an end some time.

Mais — passons outre.

I should like to postpone the meeting you so kindly arranged with your brother, purely on account of my wretched condition, which makes me so uncertain. Should I be able to give him some pleasure by a worthy performance of the *Faust Overture* on November 23 at the fourth concert, that would seem to be the occasion when a greeting would be least forced. Any witnesses of our meeting — if unavoidable — would not disturb one at all.

This time I shall shorten my stay in Berlin (the first rehearsal being over). Let me give you a brief description of my " visiting role."

Arrive Friday evening. Saturday morning, preparations, with various interruptions, for rehearsal from ten to one. Change and dine. Then I have to rest, even without sleeping. Who will then be let loose on me I cannot say beforehand. The Jew whose slave I am keeps me more or less on a string too. But if I were not his slave I should be doing no music at all this winter; as you know, I can hardly touch the pianoforte — every attempt pulls me down. For the uniqueness of the thing, I should not in the least mind a fracas.

Sunday at half-past eleven is the public rehearsal, so that the best time to see me would be the hours between nine and ten or ten and eleven (there may always be some imbroglio in the orchestra to cut across these). On Sunday afternoon I " must," among other things, go and see the Bojanovskis — health and weather permitting.

Monday morning, rehearsal, ten to one, for the next concert if possible. Concert in the evening. Train back on the following day.

Oh, this Capernaum, Berlin! You have no idea how everybody pesters me, by letter or in person. If only my health would improve, I should still be equal to the burden, even if it increased in proportion as my strength decreased.

How stupid all this is! It would be far simpler to leave my Askanian cavern and wander to Mittelstrasse 16–17. That's what I'll do, and the rest may take care of itself.

You will have noticed that I called myself the slave of a Jew. Not that I do not appreciate him very highly in other respects; he seems also to be devoted to me in a friendly way, as far as it is not to his disadvantage. But this Jew is in his turn the slave of the paying public, and as such he forces me to make a number of concessions in the programs and so on which are torture to me and of which I am thoroughly ashamed. You understand, don't you? You must see that the whole business has become beyond measure repellent and disgusting to me. I have grown so weary of fighting, for my nervous system is completely shaken, as every Æsculapius assures me, unasked. And to write letters in such a mood as this, even to the dearest people in the world —

You too, poor child, have your own pains and anxieties; but on the other hand there is so much that is splendid in yourself and in your husband that you may still carry the burden of existence almost light-heartedly. God give you both the most important gift of all: health!

446]

Berlin
All Souls' Day, November 23, 1890

I HAD your dear message yesterday from Frau Hugo Becker (he played *con somma maestria*) and today your even dearer letter, for which my best thanks. The public rehearsal this morning tried me very highly. Your brother did not put in an appearance. I hope he enjoyed the *Faust Overture*, which I conducted today from my very soul, according to the motto. I may have to take advantage of Herr Kommerzienrat Ad. von Gross's kind offer, though not in my own interest. It would be nice if he could come to Berlin, say in a fortnight's time, somewhere about the 6th and 8th of December, for the last concert of the year here (see the program-book I sent you). Then the whole affair with your unmarried sister could be settled personally.

I had to try to get rid of my maddening neuralgia with antipyrin. It took a long time, but I am now out of the wood again.

Should you not like to hear the two most interesting of the Berlioz monster operas at Karlsruhe (public rehearsal) with your husband?

Were I not the slave of my diseased body and my Jewish employer (more Christian, all the same, than Thuringian dukes), " it is there I fain would be." There is nothing, absolutely nothing, which would act as such a spur to my imagination. But in these last years of my life, *Renunciation* is my stock piece.

447]

Hamburg
December 2, 1890

THIS small pause in my *lendemain* neuralgia must not be wasted, and I will use it to send you the thanks I owe for your last two notes.

I am glad you have persuaded Herr Kommerzienrat Ad.

von Gross to meet me in Berlin. I hope my brother-in-law Bojanovski will have done as I asked and so arranged the affair for
the unpractical invalid that I am by birth and education as to
make my leisure hours coincide with those of Herr Kommerzienrat. (Mine, as I explained to you the other day, are en-
croached upon from all sides.) Perhaps — this would simplify
things — he could stay at the Askanischer too. I arrive Friday
evening and have a rehearsal on Saturday morning, which will
be very exhausting. From three o'clock on I am at his disposal,
however. . . .

448]

Hamburg
Tuesday, December 9, 1890

I THOUGHT of you a great deal and missed you very much
yesterday evening, especially as your delightfully sympathetic
husband authorized me to do so. Mendels[sohn's] *Scottish Symphony* would have pleased you better too this time. G. R. von
Gross was very friendly also. The whole meeting was very
successful, largely owing to you. The " old man " was very much
ashamed of having forgotten to return Felix's card to you. He is
not given to such lapses.

Yes, this neuralgia of mine has much to answer for. I am
feeling it very much after a sleepless night and the journey.
Ecco la sudetta carta! The writer telegraphed to me last Sunday
(your brother happened to be there) that the taking of Troy [1]
had been a success. . . .

449]

Hamburg
December 18, 1890

I MUST not wait to thank you for your dear letter, and your
husband for his valuable present, until I am less " down " than

[1] *Felix Mottl conducted the first performance of Berlioz's* Les Troyens *at Karlsruhe in 1890.*

now, on account of a bad cold. May you have a truly happy Christmas, unmarred by such sick-room complications as those of 1889. May you hear everything in B major and see and smell everything around you in the colour and perfume of your favourite flower. These good wishes extend naturally to all whose weal or woe concerns you. I nearly paid you a flying visit in Frankfurt before you left, having promised myself by way of New Year's gift a trip to Troy and Carthage — I have, so to say, a holiday from my Jew master just now, you see — but *la pauvre bête* forbids it. So I shall now be able to " set up " your kind and unique present for my wife, and I myself, instead of listening to Berlioz's cold music, shall try to enjoy the warm *painting* of my son-in-law's book. I hope the work may impress the seven or seventy-seven wise men of the suburb of Sachsenhausen half as much as it does me on a glance at its contents.

PS. In talking to your brother the other day I touched upon the Musäus traditional fairy-tales of which I am so fond, and found that he did not know them. All the better, for now I can pass them on to him through you and at the same time my *Tann-häuser* score, which is a rarity as being the very first copy. Please see that he accepts them without any fuss.

450]

Hamburg
January 7–8, 1891

In the expectation that you will so far respect my peculiarity as to refrain from sending congratulations on what is for me an unhappy anniversary, I am thanking you in anticipation tonight. Tomorrow I have to leave here to conduct an unnecessary concert and the necessary rehearsals for it, so should have no time to write.

At the same time I am sending you my well-worn and treasured score of *Tannhäuser,* so that you may decide for yourself whether, in its soiled condition after forty-three years of wear and tear (a considerable span!), it is fit to offer to the son of the Master or it had better be sent to the Wagner Museum in

Vienna. Deal with it as your tact and good taste (not an inheritance from me) dictate. . . .

451]

Hamburg
January 20, 1891

ACCEPT my best thanks for this gift, which may perhaps assist
me in my efforts to improve my handwriting. . . . I have just
received so extravagant a letter of thanks from your brother
Siegfried that I am all blushes and do not know how to counter-
thank him for his kind acceptance of the *T.* score. Will you do
it in my name and tell him that his sensible way of taking it
was a great joy to me?

How happy I should be if my darling daughter Daniela
were capable of comprehending (objectively — and women and
objectivity are proverbially in complete opposition) the complicated problem of planning my next Berlin program! You
have not, in any case, the necessary knowledge of my personal
dissonances, and there remains the question of which virtue is
the easier to practise: patience or justice, the answer being possibly that the latter can, by the aid of a sort of ascetic intoxica-
tion, be achieved with less trouble. However, no matter. Tell
me, do you really know the latest poet, Grillparzer, in his entirety? I confess I have to thank him for many an hour of solace
in these last weeks, in spite of the unequal quality of my enjoyment. His prose writings — autobiographical, aphorisms, political and æsthetic essays — are extremely stimulating and
edifying. In spite of certain Austrian provincialisms and idio-
cies, too, he writes a fine " warm " German, and in this respect
one must admit even the Viennese newspapers to be far superior to the Berlin press. But, anyway, this amateurish government under the sceptre of the " rich heir " by the grace of
Bismarck makes me hate my Fatherland far more than the
Russian cold. I am definitely abdicating next season in Berlin.

May your father make you a present of Grillparzer?

452]

Hamburg
February 17, 1891

YOU may have suspected that I was doing considerable wire-pulling behind the scenes in the matter of the Frankfurt conductorship. Your suspicions were correct. My candidate — who is neither Jew, neglected composer, nor partisan — has been elected. I can perhaps best commend him to you, your husband, and your circle of friends and acquaintances generally by sending you the enclosed letter of thanks to me, which, after circulating, you might return to me in about a week, accompanied by good news of yourself.

Herr Kogel's appointment will enable me, health permitting, to accept an invitation to play at the Museum concerts next season and to visit you (from a hotel). Apropos of health, I have drawn fresh hope from my present treatment by electricity, a new method applied under chloroform. Though I still frequently have violent pains, I have reason to call the famous Bolognese my saviour after a fortnight's " sittings."

Last night I was reminded vividly of my favourite Frankfurter 'cellist, Hugo Becker. Popper, the Viennese Jew, was whining and playing the charlatan with such appalling bad taste that I fell into the state to which you are reduced when you hear of certain lady penitents' bouquets. If you see Becker, give him my kindest regards and tell him I am looking forward very, very much to playing the last Beethoven 'cello sonata with him at Bremen on April 7, and will he please play his part by heart too? Perhaps we might repeat the performance in your town some time in aid of the Arthur memorial and to spite that poisonous mummy Wilhelm Jordan, who really deserves nothing better than to be hymned by B. Scholz. Dr. Lichtwark, whom I happened to meet, poured out a stream of enthusiasm over your Henry and asked me to give him his respectful greetings. Which I hereby do. I shall soon be at the end of my conducting for this winter. Next Monday is the last concert but one in Berlin, and March 2 the last here. Then comes a short pause. On March

16 is the tenth and last Berlin concert, with the Beethoven C minor by way of a finish. No news from Palermo. Your sister is surely not snowed up?

453]

Hamburg
March 5, 1891

I CONGRATULATE you on your admirable conscientiousness. I had not given Kogel's letter of self-recommendation another thought. Now I have to thank him for bringing me a fresh message from you, which contains, I regret to see, no good news of your health.

The concerts here are now at an end. But on my return on Monday evening my wife greeted me with the news of her mother's sudden death from a stroke. She therefore went to Cracow on Tuesday to meet her assembled brothers and sisters there and she will not be with me again until March 16 for the last Berlin concert.

I am not fond of using the soft pedal, but in order to provide against disappointment after such high expectations I should warn you that K[ogel] is a Saxon Trumpetheus rather than a Greek Prometheus, but as such he is nevertheless much to be preferred to the Jew Dessoff, the Bœotian Scholz, or the whole lot of Frankfurt's ravens. As he has more talent than character, he will develop in the direction indicated by his powerful environment. The three years' condition attached to his appointment is my most creditable achievement, next to that of having eliminated the less edifying candidates. But enough of politics.

Whether we shall meet again? *Chi lo sa!* I believe and hope that we may do so as soon as we like. Above all, it depends upon your duties and commitments, and for the present, I take it, upon your health. As regards my own, I avoid all unnecessary and unpleasant brooding. I only know that I am again strong-willed enough to refuse to let the doctors experiment on me by packing me off to one place after another. For the present I must continue with the regular electric treatment. In spite of frequent relapses into unbearable though somehow borne *endo-lorissements* (there is no German expression for it), this method is the only one in which I have not lost confidence.

You still feel no interest in Grillparzer? It's a pity. Have you read Immermann's *Epigonen*? I find it most refreshing and soothing. Even that which is old-fashioned in it is to be preferred to that "new" which is already showing signs of old age. But I am forgetting that you have material enough and to spare, thanks to your husband, for the killing of that evil bacillus "time."

454]

Hamburg
March 7, 1891

On the assumption that it will amuse your husband, I am sending you Helene Raff's naïvely enthusiastic letter on his second symphony. The child has made substantial progress lately and has had some success in selling her pictures. She thought of moving to Paris with her mother, as I had strongly advised her to do, and is only afraid that the All-Highest — the all-highest Tactlessnesses — may bring the scheme to nought. This is to explain her letter. She knows little about music, so that neither you nor I need be surprised at her totally wrong judgment of D'Albert, who played more perfectly than ever here the other day. . . .

455]

Hamburg
April 24, 1891

I should so much like to hear from you again, something consoling, that is. The latest news alarmed and even saddened me, but I thought it best not to react to it. It is better that those at a distance should refrain from judging personal, local situations; otherwise both sides become uneasy.

The Lisbon scheme for me has come to nothing. My doctor

recommended the journey on account of the climate, but all the side-issues (very primitive conditions and extraordinary exertions) seemed the more risky because my neuralgia has shown a tendency to return and is particularly active today. Influenza-like elements are mixed with it. *Suffit.* An excellent portrait-painter and engraver, Herr Ludwig Michalek, has come over from Vienna to paint my portrait. He has composed and etched the finest pictures of Beethoven and Mozart that are to be seen anywhere. I had thought of sending you the former, but the news that you are breaking up your Frankfurt home restrained me. To come to the point: Herr Michalek has finished a portrait of the great Bayreuth Master and would like to have your opinion on it. At my suggestion he will be sending it you shortly from Berlin, where he goes, on leaving here, to finish a portrait of Mendelssohn, amongst others.

Hamburg has now secured a really excellent opera-conductor in Herr Gustav Mahler (a serious, energetic Jew from Budapest), who in my opinion equals the very best: Mottl, Richter, and so on. I heard him do *Siegfried* recently with Alvary (who again struck me as ideal in the title-role). I was filled with honest admiration for him, for he made — no, forced — the orchestra to pipe to his measure, without having had a rehearsal. In spite of various drawbacks and my nervous condition I was able to hold out until the last note. It lasted over four hours, although the scene with S. and Wotan (a bad interpreter) was reduced to a minimum. With all the mercantile spirit that prevails in the theatre management here, we are, I believe, better off than in the capital of the empire. Speaking of Berlin, I have been able to give a fair proof there that my head and hand are not yet out of action. (My reappearance at Bremen before that was somewhat of a failure.) But I have, I think, had to suffer for it since. Still, the net profit of fifteen thousand marks, including the fee for a general rehearsal in aid of founding a pensions fund for the Philharmonic Orchestra, is to some extent consoling.

456]

Hamburg
ultimo *October 1891*

THE sight of your really exquisite writing, beloved daughter, always does me good, and the contents of your letters have a way of being as good as the penmanship. I have never dabbled in the art of reading character from handwriting, but it does seem to me that in yours there is mirrored an inner harmony, eloquent of a victorious quelling of the disturbing situations of the past few months and having the effect of a guarantee that your future will be freer from discordant notes or more fertile in the happy solutions of such.

Thank you very much for your kind words, which refreshed me in a very dark hour. Of late I have had none but dark ones, indeed. But your letter even induced a hope, perhaps vain, of looking in on you in Florence in the spring.

It would be an unpardonable transgression should I forsake the principle that I have always followed to the best of my ability and begin to regale you with the dissonances in my own life — always supposing that you take a more than superficial interest in my fate (my own work). I therefore impose silence upon myself, although I am tempted a myriad of times to speak out to you about myself.

" O friends, not these sounds, but . . ." let me congratulate you, first on the really idyllic episode with your father- and mother-in-law, to whom please remember me; then on the choice of your winter residence. I still have the pleasantest recollections of a " cure " I underwent there (probably quite unnecessarily). Florence is for me the most Italian of all cities. I even liked being frozen there. And when the winter is a raw one, one is indeed incredibly cold. Shall you be able to protect yourself? To write a short note I should have had first to tinkle scales for an hour and to stuff my pockets with hot chestnuts when I went out if my hands were not to be useless. But then how one hails the sun when it appears and the unsuspected warmth which it radiates! Then the lovely " *musica pegli occhi*," and the population, which is as unworthy of respect as it is lovable. My old friend Frau Hillebrand used to insist that even the rogues and the hopeless philistines in Tuscany were " pearls." Shall you not go and see her, by the way? Her deafness, which must have grown worse of late, will make it difficult for her to get about. Without in the least trying to make you go, is it not possible that her experience might be helpful to you in settling in? She would be so delighted to feel she could be useful.

You have, I know, a very extensive correspondence. Is it too much to ask for a line from you once a month? (I do not think it will run to the full dozen, but sh!)

Thucydides! " *I miei rispetti.*" I can no more imitate you in that than in your handwriting. I enjoy being able to read Manzoni's *Promessi Sposi* with my wife in the evenings. (She is grateful to you for thinking of us and returns your greetings with sincerest good wishes.) Forty years ago this book bored me as much as it now delights me. I consider it the most finished product in the domain of novels that European literature has produced. *Hors de concours.* And the author of the classical (save the mark!) *Elective Affinities* was of much the same opinion, which is thus stamped as orthodox.

Ah, my dear Daniela, it must be your fault (a charitable and meritorious fault) that I no longer play in public. I had been preparing for Frankfurt next spring, when I intended to play both Beethoven concertos to you and your husband. Also I had practised every imaginable thing by Chopin and Liszt " in B major " for " *privatissime.*" This plan has now been given up, and — but I am approaching a boundary which I am bound not to overstep with regard to you. As for one's work, you are right to call it salvation. But when the brain gives way — Or when it is Penelope-work, with extremely mortal, indifferent, bored, bloodless, beer-soaked musicians — here in Hamburg, for instance, I have only raw semi-human beings to drill — then you have no idea how much energy I waste in overcoming my disgust. There is the commercial Jewish current, too, against which I cannot swim. But enough of this. As I have, however, given you a faint hint of the situation, I must supplement it by telling you that I am a complete wreck on the three days out of the seven on which I have no concerts or rehearsals, and that the insignificant contribution that I make towards the so-called edification of a few receptive pairs of ears costs me very dear. For the pains are often enough to drive one mad. Then all these attempts to ameliorate them by anæsthetics . . . and the like: in a word, can you wonder that I am very, very wretched? Do not pity me too much, though; refresh me rather by sending good news. Of Venice first (Sascha Ritter's brother died there recently). . . . I should advise one of the less good hotels on the square of St. Mark's, with only Italian *zanzare passate.*

457]

[Undated]

MANY thanks for the affectionate way in which you took my recent letter. You should read Doctor Ox: it seems to me your sense of humour wants reviving. Scottish novels, Haydn (quartets and symphonies as much as you like, but) pianoforte sonatas and Mozart *divertimenti* with two horns — that is a little too ascetic. In fact if the good God had created no Frenchmen I should long ago have sent him and myself to Ahriman. In this respect I agree with Mottl, though without going as far as Chabrier.

I am in a good mood for once, induced by D'Albert, who has just been playing in a way that transcends the imagination. A phenomenal fellow! Thank God, he has definitely cured me of any velleity to tinkle in public. There is indeed no one worth listening to besides himself and occasionally Joachim.

A proposito, your newest note-paper (Theissinger, Frankfurt), with the non-transparent envelopes, pleases me very, very much. Would you kindly ask Steyl to have some sent to me? I think I still have some credit with him. Best *post festum* congratulations on having spent and survived the turn of the year so happily. What a glorious contrast to last year's influenza budget! *Continuez d'être nègre,* I cry encouragingly with MacMahon; as encouragingly as only radically courageless people can do. . . .

458]

Hamburg
January 13, 1892

I ARRIVED home from Berlin last night, having had a particularly fatiguing time, to find your kind letter of condolence,
for which I am at once writing as well as I can to thank you. You
will, I am sure, spare me the usual trivialities of congratulating
you on your moral and physical composure under the north
German temperature which prevails in Venice. My refusal to
accede to the request expressed in the third (not belletristic)
part of your letter will not be taken in such good part, I fear.
Of all the P. family (whose acquaintance I made solely — that
is, originally — through your Sicilian sister [in 1887]), the
only one who interests me personally is the splendid old " young
greybeard," to please whom I am prepared to put up with
" the eternal feminine " . But to return:

I was really delighted to hear, first indirectly through Fräulein
Marie Ritter (niece of the great Munich master) and now directly in your own handwriting (which grows if possible more
beautiful every day), how much more artistically you are housed
and established generally on the Adriatic than formerly on the
Main. Even the Venetian patriarch, although he is dead, strikes
me as being five milliards more interesting than the most living
head rabbi or chief superintendent within the radius of the Zeil.

I know the *Messe de l'athée* and, with regard to Honoré, am
always happy to find that there is *at least one* point in the domain
of the intellect in which we are *d'accordissimo*.

Although it is idle, not to say fatal, for us to recommend
books to each other — since the recommendation usually has
the opposite effect or ends in censorship difficulties — I should
nevertheless like to mention my latest travelling-literature: Paul
Bourget's *Sensations d'Italie* to your husband and in second
place perhaps to his wife. It deals purely with Michelangelo
Buonarotti and Co. and is in no sense opposed to Michel Angelo
Neumann, or, rather, his higgling schemes.

Quando si scrive — si " stuone " Venice — *la brutta* — I really like the city best in the Meiningen representation of *Marino Falieri* or in the first act of my favourite opera after *Carmen:* Donizetti's *Lucrezia Borgia.* (I admit one has to hear it sung by singers, not screaming dolls, and only in Italy.) In the autumn and in spring it is apt to be too full of gigantic mosquitoes, and in winter — well, you now know better than I, or best. By the way, have you ever seen any Venetian dialect-players? Do not, for instance, miss Goldoni's *Baruffe di Chioggia* (or *Chiozza,* I believe, in dialect). My pen refuses to write sense today in spite of a momentary strike on the part of my neuralgia. To make up for it I have influenza, the result of my exertions when rehearsing d'A.'s symphony. (We had to work at it like niggers at the pianoforte — four hands — reorches-trating, and cutting, oh, cutting! All the same this little chap has a lot in him.)

As you will, I know, agree with me, I will fill up the envelope with some small scientific " supplements," the most amusing being the English cutting. May the God in whom you believe bless you! I have too many godheads. Why, there is a shop close by, a large draper's, with the name: " Messiah & Son " ! May you soon feel inclined to write again quite naturally to your poor father.

In a hurry as ever.

Jettatura, jettatore, jettatrice, or *gettatura?*

459]

Hamburg
January 19, 1892

My dear Son-in-law,

For some days now I have been in possession of your kind present, but the heavy labour imposed on me by the gods (that of bringing out a young Thoma symphony in the teeth of unbelieving Thomases) left me no time to reply or even to take stock superficially of the object of my gratitude. Now that I have at last been able to glance at it (between the rehearsal and concert yesterday), I am able to send my belated congratulations to the quietly industrious Frankfurt Hans and to express my joy that the fount of your warm eloquence has not run dry and that my daughter is so fortunate as to have the poet as art-historian or vice versa for her husband.

May I lend your new opus to Herr Director Dr. Lichtwark to look at?

Daniela's letters lead me to hope for a not unwelcome extension of Venetian hours of leisure for her and of business for you. The delightful transition to more typical weather, suitable for *passeggiate* in common, will have done you both good. It has brought me a marvellous increase of strength — touch wood three times! — and I may add that a young doctor, new to me, has just arrived in the neighbourhood, the very sight of whom gave me more electrical nourishment in one evening than all the galvanic, Faradayish, and other conductors in six months. (*Des rapports du physique au moral* or the other way round, by Cabanis.) The enclosed cutting tells you his name. I have had the great good luck not to misplease him — did he not kiss my left cheek? — and still less his talented son Herbert, with whom I may presumably become more intimate. But stop, I must not be too unreservedly intimate with — you!

May all the sun-gods remain, from now on, the faithful attendants of you and your wife.

460]

Hotel Washington, Florence
Easter Sunday

Aᴍ I going to see you, beloved daughter? For the present I propose to stay here for ten to twelve days. Then direct to Naples (perhaps even to Trinacria, should Blandine be tied to that place) and back via Rome to Venice — if you are there — then by way of Pola (where my wife's brother is, in the Austrian Navy) and Trieste back to Vienna. These plans can be modified *secondo il tuo piacere.* Marie sends kindest regards. *Tanti saluti al Enrico. Ottima Pasqua.*

461]

Palermo
Wednesday, May 18 [1892]

MY PRECIOUS CORDELIA,

Regan and Goneril are amusing me so well — partly because they are so charming and talk so much about you — that I fear this letter will be incoherent unless I employ a telegraphic style.

Let me explain briefly how things stand. Tomorrow afternoon we go by water and land direct to Florence, Hotel Washington. There we stay until the 27th. On the 30th I must sit for Lenbach at Munich. On June 6 I conduct the *Eroica* and other things at Augsburg, and on the 10th shall be back in Hamburg.

Why these various musts? To explain would be tedious for reader and writer. . . .

We lingered unduly in Naples, also — less than duly if you like, ask the casa Gravina — here. Which means that Rome, Siena, and the rest will have to be left out of this year's program, and, *par la forza del destino*, Venice too, which could only attract me through you (you both). But then you always insisted on wandering to my beloved twenty-two-year-old Pulciniselli and must now be sick to death of Frari and Co. . . . Why not, then, come to us at the Washington as our guest for those few days, provided of course that your husband's health permits it and that he does not particularly need you just at that time. If he did, I should have to say: " *Cedo minori* " (meaning: to the younger). It looks to me as if you had suggested Bologna for our *appuntamento* only because it is a few hours nearer to Salò. Is that so?

PS. A short telegram, then, on Saturday morning, please, to Florence, Hotel Washington.

462]

Hamburg
June 16, 1892

I HAVE now been home three days and should, properly speaking, be well-disposed to write (or to tinkle) in this cool, favourable weather. But I have been waiting all the time for an inspiration before sending you a paternal sign of life.

Such an inspiration I have just received. Yet why should I transcribe or paraphrase the original? Far better give you the text as it stands. For are you not the point of all this and must I not record my progress in obedient paternity? Here, then, you have the theatre notice used by the two of us two hours after our arrival. Piece full of exotic beauty, scenery exquisite, performance still very amateurish.

But to return to "Fayence." My former pupil seems to be the best-qualified person to produce an Italian translation of Henry's *Fr. v. A.* You agree? Very well, then. Let the grand inquisitress follow the example of Philip II, who thought he had done all that could be expected of him. At Igls you will have time to negotiate. You can write in German, you know. Sylvia knows about it, and will be enormously pleased to know the daughter of a one-time "*Schwarm.*"

Give me this pleasure, and yet another, if you will, by copying out the *valse oubliée* for me. My wife was, and is, deeply touched by your kindness to her. "*Tante grazie da parte mia.*" A reply, containing good news of you both, will find me at the end of the month on the banks of the Alster. Apollo, Helios, and the rest be with you both!

Love from your tender, proud, and faithful father.

PS. Arrived safely at Augsburg with Mottl.

INDEX